The Epistles of Paul The Apostle
to the

GALATIANS, EPHESIANS, PHILIPPIANS AND COLOSSIANS

CALVIN'S COMMENTARIES

CALVIN'S COMMENTARIES

The Epistles of Paul The Apostle

to the

GALATIANS, EPHESIANS, PHILIPPIANS AND COLOSSIANS

Translator
T. H. L. PARKER

Editors
DAVID W. TORRANCE
and
THOMAS F. TORRANCE

WILLIAM B. EERDMANS PUBLISHING COMPANY
GRAND RAPIDS, MICHIGAN

THE PATERNOSTER PRESS
CARLISLE

First published 1965
Translation © 1965 Oliver and Boyd Ltd.

Published jointly in the United States
by Wm. B. Eerdmans Publishing Co.
255 Jefferson Ave. S.E., Grand Rapids, Michigan 49503
and in the U.K. by The Paternoster Press
P.O. Box 300, Carlisle, Cumbria CA3 0QS

First paperback edition published 1996

Printed in the United States of America

00 99 98 97 96   7 6 5 4 3 2 1

The Epistles of Paul The Apostle to the Galatians,
Ephesians, Philippians and Colossians

Eerdmans ISBN 0-8028-0811-5

British Library Cataloguing in Publication Data

A Catalogue record for this book is available from the British Library

Paternoster ISBN 0-85364-746-1

INTRODUCTION

WORKING steadily through the Pauline epistles, Calvin came, probably more slowly than he would have liked, to Galatians, Ephesians, Philippians and Colossians (which he treated as a group). He was at work on them by October 1546, as we learn from a letter to Farel: 'I have now set myself in earnest to the Epistle to the Galatians.'[1] He explained that he had, in gratitude for past kindnesses, promised all his Pauline commentaries to the Strasbourg printer, Wendelinus Rihelius. When he was recalled to Geneva, he kept to his promise, but obviously began to regret that he had made it. The disadvantages of having one's printer at a great distance were very serious in the sixteenth century. Nor does Rihelius himself seem to have been over-enthusiastic, for Calvin tells another friend, M. de Falais, that 'Corinthians is lying at rest in Wendelin's desk' and therefore he is not going to hurry with Galatians.[2] What happened after this we do not know, but the Galatians group was finished by February 1548, the date of the preface, and published, not by Rihelius, but by Jean Girard in Geneva:

> *Ioannis Calvini commentarii in quatuor Pauli Epistolas: ad Galatas, ad Ephesios, ad Philippenses, ad Colossenses. Genevae, per Ioannem Girardum.* 1548.

They were slightly revised for the collected edition of the Pauline Epistles in 1551, and then thoroughly revised for the edition of 1556.

It is not known whether he had expounded this group in lectures or sermons before 1546. The letter quoted above certainly suggests that he was writing the commentary quite independently of other considerations. He preached on Galatians in 1557 and 1558 and on Ephesians in 1558 and 1559. He seems not to have preached on the other two at all. He returned to Galatians in 1562, when he expounded it in the Friday lectures, the *Congrégations*. Only the first two lectures are extant, and they, after lying hidden for four hundred years, have been edited by Dr Rodolphe Peter of Strasbourg:

> *Jean Calvin: Deux Congrégations et Exposition du Catéchisme. Première réimpression de l'édition de 1563 avec une introduction et des notes par Rodolphe Peter.* Presses Universitaires de France. 1964.

[1] *Letters*, ed. Jules Bonnet (E.T.), vol. 2, p. 58.   [2] Ibid., p. 70.

INTRODUCTION

The Galatians group of commentaries was first translated into English in 1581:

A Commentarie of M. I. Calvine upon the Epistle to the Galathians: And translated into English by R. V. Thomas Purfoote. London. 1581.

In the Calvin Translation Society it was translated by John Pringle (Edinburgh, 1854). The present edition is a drastic revision of this work.

Oakington   T. H. L. PARKER
    1964

THE DEDICATORY EPISTLE

TO THE MOST ILLUSTRIOUS PRINCE AND RULER
LORD CHRISTOPHER,
DUKE OF WIRTEMBERG, COUNT OF MONTBELIARD, &C.,
JOHN CALVIN SENDS GREETINGS

THOUGH unknown to you, most illustrious Prince, I have no fear in dedicating this work to you. Some will perhaps censure such boldness as rash and needing an explanation. But that is so easy that I can be brief. The reasons which lead me to address you are chiefly two. Although you have pursued the right course willingly and energetically, I thought it might not be a waste of time to appeal to you directly to study a work by which you will be not a little confirmed. For God has given you one advantage which most princes of our day lack: you had from a boy a liberal education in the knowledge of Latin and so can employ your leisure in reading useful and religious books. If ever there was a time when it was necessary to draw consolation from godly doctrine, it is now, when the present distress of the Church and the greater and heavier troubles which seem to be imminent leave no other comfort even to the most heroic minds. Therefore, whoever wants to stand .... to the end, should rely entirely on this support. Whoever wants a sure protection, should learn to flee to this sanctuary, so to say. Moreover, in these four epistles, my expositions on which I now present to you, noble Prince, you will find many matters of consolation very apt for these times; but I will not mention them now, as they will come up properly, and indeed better, in their own places.

I come to the second reason for dedicating this work to you. In the present confusion some are shaken, others entirely overthrown. But you have preserved an astonishing composure and moderation, accompanied by a remarkable steadfastness amidst all the storms. I consider therefore, that it will be very profitable to the whole Church, to show in you as in a clear mirror, an example for all to imitate. The Son of God bids all His followers without exception to choose to fight under the banner of His cross rather than to triumph with the world. But there are very few who are prepared to wage that kind of warfare. So it is the more necessary that all should be stimulated and taught by such uncommon examples as your own to correct their softness.

Of my commentaries I shall only say that perhaps they contain

I

more than it would be modest in me to acknowledge. But on this point I prefer you to read and judge for yourself. Farewell, most illustrious Prince! May the Lord Jesus long preserve you for Himself and His Church and guide you by His Spirit!

GENEVA, 1st February 1548

The Epistle to
THE GALATIANS

THE THEME OF THE EPISTLE
TO THE GALATIANS

IT is well known in what parts of Asia the Galatians lived and what
were the boundaries of their country; but historians are not agreed
as to the place of their origin. It is generally agreed that they were
Gauls, from which came their name of Gallo-Grecians; but from
what part of Gaul they came is less clear. Strabo thought that the
Tectosages came from Gallia Narbonensis and that the others were
Celts; and nearly all have followed this. But, as Pliny numbers the
Ambiani among the Tectosagi and it is agreed that they were allied to
the Tolistobogi, who lived by the Rhine, I think it more probable
they were Belgae from the upper reaches of the Rhine to the English
Channel. The Tolistobogi inhabited the part that is now called
Cleves and Brabant. The mistake originated, I think, from this: a
band of Tectosagi who had made an invasion into Gallia Narbonensis,
kept their own name and gave it to the country they had occupied.
This is suggested by Ausonius, who says: 'Even to the Teutosagi,
whose original name was Belgae.' For he calls them Belgae and says
that they were first called Teutosagi and afterwards Tectosagi. When
Caesar places the Tectosagi in the Hercynian Forest I take it as a result
of their migration and this, in fact, appears from the context.

But more than enough has now been said for our present purpose
on the origin of this people. Pliny tells us that the Galatians, who inhabited the part of Asia named after them, were divided into three
principal nations, Tectosagi, Tolistobogi and Trocmi, and accordingly
occupied three chief cities. They once enjoyed so much power
over their unwarlike neighbours that a large part of Asia Minor
became tributary to them. At last their inherited courage decayed
and they gave themselves up to pleasure and luxury. And so they
were defeated in war and subjugated quite easily by Cnaeus Manlius,
a Roman consul.

In Paul's day they were under Roman domination. He had faithfully instructed them in the pure Gospel, but false apostles had entered

in his absence and corrupted the true seed by false and corrupt dogmas. For they taught that the observance of ceremonies was still necessary. This might seem trivial; but Paul fights for it as a fundamental article of the Christian faith. And rightly so, for it is no light evil to quench the brightness of the Gospel, lay a snare for consciences and remove the distinction between the old and new covenants. He saw that these errors were also related to an ungodly and destructive opinion on the deserving of righteousness. And this is why he fights so earnestly. When we have grasped how weighty and serious this dispute is, we must study it with even greater attention.

If anyone evaluates the subject as it is represented in the commentaries of Origen and Jerome, he will wonder why Paul should make a fuss about some external rites. But whoever looks to the fountainhead itself will acknowledge that there was cause for such sharp reproof. The Galatians had let themselves be diverted from a straight course by their excessive credulity, or rather, their light-mindedness and folly. This is why he censures them so severely. For I do not agree with those who think he treated them more harshly because of their slowness of understanding. The Ephesians and the Colossians had also been tempted. If they had yielded to deceit as easily, do we think that Paul would have dealt with them any more gently? It was not the nature of these people that made him so free to rebuke them, but rather the shamefulness of the whole affair.

Now that we have learned the reason why he wrote the epistle, let us come to its arrangement. In the first two chapters he contends for the authority of his apostolate, though towards the end of the second chapter he touches incidentally on his main point, the justification of man, the direct and full discussion of which, however, he begins only in the third chapter. In these two chapters he seems to treat of many subjects, but in fact his only object is to prove that he is equal to the highest apostles and that there is no reason why he should not be considered in the same noble rank as they.

It is important to know why he labours so hard for his own reputation. For so long as Christ reigns and the purity of doctrine remains unadulterated, what does it matter whether he is above or below Peter or whether they are all equals? If all must decrease that Christ alone may increase, dispute about men's relative dignity is worthless. Again, it may be asked why he compares himself with the other apostles. What quarrel had he with Peter and James and John? What good did it do to set in opposition those who were one in mind and close allies?

I reply: the false apostles, who had deceived the Galatians to advance their own claims, pretended that they had received a commission from the apostles. Their method of infiltration was to get it believed that they represented the apostles and delivered a message from them. But they took away from Paul the name and authority of apostle. They objected that he had not been chosen by our Lord as one of the twelve, that he had never been acknowledged an apostle by the college, that he had not received his doctrine from Christ or even from the apostles. The aim of all this was not only to diminish Paul's authority, but to place him, as an ordinary member of the flock, far below even the false apostles themselves.

Had this been merely a personal matter, Paul would not have minded being regarded as an ordinary disciple. But when he saw that his doctrine was beginning to lose its weight and authority, he could not be silent but had to contradict them frankly. It is a trick of Satan's, when he dare not openly attack doctrine, to undermine its majesty indirectly. So let us remember that in attacking Paul they were really attacking the truth of the Gospel. If he had allowed himself to be stripped of the honours of apostleship, it would have followed that he had been claiming what did not belong to him, and such a false boasting would have made him suspect in other matters. On this also would have depended the assessment of his teaching; for they would soon have regarded it as coming, not from an apostle of Christ, but from an ordinary disciple.

On the other hand he was thrown into the shade by the brilliance of great names. Those who claimed the patronage of Peter and James and John claimed also apostolic authority. Had Paul not vigorously resisted this boasting, it would have been a surrender to falsehood and letting the truth be overcome in his person. He therefore contends earnestly on both accounts: that he was an apostle appointed by the Lord; and that he was in no wise inferior to the rest, but their equal in right and dignity, just as he shared their title of apostle. He could, indeed, have denied that these men were either sent or commissioned by Peter and his colleagues. But he takes up a far more serious defence, that he does not yield even to the apostles themselves. For if he had deviated, it would have been supposed that he distrusted his cause.

Jerusalem was then the mother of all the Churches. For the Gospel had flowed from there over the whole world, and it might be called the principal seat (*primaria sedes*) of the Kingdom of Christ. Anyone who came to other Churches from there was received with due respect. But many were puffed up with a foolish pride in having been familiar with the apostles, or at least in having been taught in their school. Therefore nothing pleased them but what they had seen in Jerusalem. They not only rejected, but brazenly condemned, every rite that had not been in use there. Such hypercriticalness is the worst of plagues, when we want the practice of one Church made into a universal law. We are sometimes so fond of a teacher or a place that we quite uncritically want to force the opinion of that one man or the customs of that one place on all men and all places, as if they were universal. And this arises from an ill-conceived zeal, though there is always ambition in it too; indeed, an excessive hypercriticalness is always ambitious.

To return to these false apostles. If they had only, through their perverted rivalry, attempted to establish the use of those ceremonies everywhere which they had seen observed at Jerusalem, they would already have been sinning grievously, for it is unjust to make a custom directly into a rule. But a worse evil was their ungodly and dangerous teaching. They wanted to imprison men's consciences by religion; for they placed righteousness in observances. Now we know why Paul defended his apostleship so spiritedly and why he contrasted himself with the rest of the apostles.

He pursues this subject to the end of the second chapter, where he switches over to arguing his main case, that we are justified in the sight of God freely and not by the works of the law. He takes his stand on this argument: if ceremonies have no power to justify, then the observance of them is unnecessary. Yet he does not treat only of ceremonies, but disputes of works in general; otherwise the whole argument would be weak.

If this seems far-fetched to anyone, let him consider two things. First, the question could not be settled without assuming the general principle that we are justified only by the grace of God; and this excludes not only ceremonies, but other works also. Secondly, Paul was less worried about ceremonies than about the ungodly notion that we obtain salvation by works. Let us observe, therefore, that he very properly begins right at the beginning.[1] It was necessary to indicate the fountain, so that his readers should know that the controversy was not concerned with some insignificant trifle but with the most important matter of all, the way we obtain salvation.

They are mistaken therefore who suppose that the apostle confined himself wholly to the special question of ceremonies, for this could not be settled on its own. We have a similar example in Acts 15.1ff. Dispute and contention had arisen over whether the observance of ceremonies was necessary. In the discussion, the apostles speak of the insupportable burden of the law and of the free forgiveness of sins. What was their object in this? It seems an absurd digression; but in fact not so, for a particular error cannot be refuted satisfactorily unless a universal principle is assumed. For example, if I have to debate on the forbidden eating of flesh, I shall not only talk about food, but shall

[1] Latin: *ab ovo* (*quod aiunt*) *ordiri*—starts from the egg, as they say.

6

also furnish myself with the general doctrine: what authority have the traditions of men in binding the conscience? I shall quote the verse, that there is one Lawgiver who has power to save and to destroy. In short, Paul here argues negatively from the general to the particular, which is the ordinary and most natural method in disputation. By what evidences and arguments he proves the statement that we are justified by the grace of Christ alone, we shall see in its place. This he pursues until the end of the third chapter.

At the beginning of the fourth chapter he treats of the right use of ceremonies and why they were appointed, showing, at the same time, that they are now abolished. To meet the absurdity that might occur to some minds as to what was the point of ceremonies, and were they useless, and were the fathers wasting their time in observing them, he makes two assertions: in their own time they were not superfluous; and they have now been abolished by the coming of Christ, for He is their Truth and End. Thus he shows that we must remain in Him. He also briefly mentions the difference between the condition of ourselves and of the fathers. It follows that the teaching of the false apostles is wicked and dangerous because it darkens the clearness of the Gospel with ancient shadows. With this teaching he mingles some exhortations to move their feelings. Towards the end of the chapter he adorns his argument with a beautiful allegory.

In the fifth chapter he exhorts them to hold fast the liberty obtained by the blood of Christ and not to let their consciences be ensnared by the opinions of men. But he reminds them at the same time, what is the legitimate limit of liberty. He then takes occasion to point out the true occupation of Christians, that they may not waste their time on ceremonies and neglect matters of real importance.

CHAPTER ONE

Paul, an apostle, (not from men, neither through men, but by Jesus Christ, and God the Father, who raised him from the dead) and all the brethren which are with me, unto the churches of Galatia: Grace to you and peace, from God the Father, and our Lord Jesus Christ, who gave himself for our sins, that he might deliver us out of this present evil world, according to the will of our God and Father: to whom be the glory for ever and ever. Amen. (1-5)

1. *Paul, an apostle.* In his greetings, Paul was accustomed to claim the title of apostle, in order, as we have said elsewhere,[1] to strengthen his teaching with the authority of his office. This authority depends, not on the judgment or opinion of men, but exclusively on the calling of God. He therefore demands a hearing just because he is an apostle. Let us always remember that in the Church we must listen to God alone and to Jesus Christ, whom He has appointed to be our Teacher. Therefore, whoever wants to be a teacher, must speak in the name of God or Christ. But since the Galatians disputed Paul's calling more than others did, he here asserts it more strongly than in other epistles. For he does not simply affirm that he was called by God, but states expressly that it was *neither from men nor through men.* We must note that he is not speaking of the ordinary pastoral office (*de communi pastorum officio*) but of the apostolate. His detractors did not dare to deprive him completely of the dignity of the Christian ministry. They only took from him the name and right of an apostle. We are now speaking of the apostolate in the proper sense, for the word is used in two ways. Sometimes it denotes preachers of the Gospel of various sorts, but here it refers specially to the highest order in the Church (*primarium in Ecclesia ordinem*). So that Paul is equal to Peter and the rest of the twelve.

The first fact, that he was not called from men, he had in common with all true ministers of Christ. As no man should take this honour to himself, so neither is it in the power of men to bestow on whom they wish. It belongs to God alone to govern His Church. Therefore the calling cannot be lawful unless it proceeds from Him. So far as the Church is concerned, a man who has been led to the ministry, not by a good conscience, but by some improper aim, may be regularly called. But Paul is here speaking of the supreme proof of his calling,

[1] In his commentary on I Cor. 1.1.

8

so that nothing is lacking in it. It will be objected: is not the same claim often made by false apostles? I admit that this is so; and indeed, they may be more arrogant and proud in this than the servants of the Lord would dare be. But they lack the reality which Paul was entitled to claim.

The second clause, that he was not called through man, belonged peculiarly to the apostles; for in a pastor this would not then have been wrong. Paul himself in company with Barnabas ordained presbyters in various towns by vote, and he tells Titus and Timothy to do the same (Acts 14.23; Titus 1.5). Such is the ordinary method of choosing pastors. For we have no right to wait until God shall reveal from heaven the names of those whom He has chosen. Why then did Paul reject in his own instance what was not only not bad but in fact laudable? I have already said that it was not enough for him to prove that he was a pastor or some sort of minister of the Gospel; for the point at issue was his apostleship. It was necessary that the apostles should be chosen in a different way from other pastors, that is, immediately, as they say, by the Lord Himself. Thus Christ called the Twelve (Matt. 10.1), and when a successor was to be supplied in Judas' stead, the Church did not dare choose one by voting, but had recourse to casting lots (Acts 1.26). It is certain that pastors were not chosen by casting lots. Why then in the appointment of Matthias? That he might be divinely appointed. For the apostolate had to be distinguished from the other ministries. And so Paul, to except himself from the common order of ministers (*a vulgari ordine ministrorum*), contends that his calling was immediately from God.

But why does he affirm that he was not called by men when Luke records that Paul and Barnabas were called by the Church at Antioch (Acts 13.2-3)? Some reply that he had previously discharged the duties of an apostle and that consequently his apostleship was not based on that ordination. But on the other hand it can be objected that this was his first identification as the apostle of the Gentiles (among whom were the Galatians). The more correct and straightforward reply is that he did not here mean to exclude entirely the calling of that Church but merely to show that his apostleship rested on a greater and previous choice. This is true, for even those who laid their hands on Paul at Antioch did so, not of their own judgment, but in obedience to the revelation (*oraculo*). As, therefore, he was called by divine revelation and then marked out and declared by the Holy Spirit to be the apostle of the Gentiles, it follows that he was not put forward by men, though the solemn rite of ordination was afterwards added.

If anyone wants to see here a hinted contrast between Paul and the false apostles, I have no objection. For they used to boast of their

human authority. Thus, it is as if he said: 'Whoever they may claim
to be their sender, I shall be above them, for I hold my commission
from God and Christ.'

Through Jesus Christ and God the Father. He says that God the Father
and Christ were the Authors of his apostolate. Christ is named first,
because it is for Him to send, and we are ambassadors for Him. But
to make the statement more complete, the Father is also mentioned;
as if he said: 'If there be anyone for whom the majesty of Christ is
insufficient, let him know that I have also received my office from
God the Father.'

Who raised him. His mention of the resurrection is pertinent to this
context, for this is the beginning of Christ's Kingdom. They re-
proached Paul that he had had no dealings with Christ while He was
on earth. But he argues to the contrary that, just as Christ was glorified
by His resurrection, so He has also exercised His power in governing
the Church. Paul's calling has therefore even more honour than if
Christ, while still a mortal, had ordained him. And this fact deserves
attention. For Paul suggests that his detractors were really attacking
maliciously the wonderful power of God which was shown in the
resurrection of Christ. For the same heavenly Father who raised
Christ from the dead appointed Paul a herald of this His mighty work.

2. *And all the brethren which are with me.* He seems to have written
communally in the name of many others, judging that, if they should
attach less weight to a single individual, they might at any rate listen
to a number and would not despise a whole congregation. He usually
inserted the salutations from brethren near the end instead of introducing them at the beginning as joint authors with himself of the
epistle. He never mentions more than two names and those well
known. But here he includes them all together. And I do not think
he did so without a reason. The consensus of so many godly men
must have had some weight in making the Galatians more teachable
and tractable.

Unto the churches. It was an extensive country and therefore contained many scattered Churches. But is it not surprising that the title
of Church should have been allowed to the Galatians who had almost
deserted Christ? For where there is a Church there is unity of faith.
I reply: where they professed Christianity, worshipped one God, used
the Sacraments and had some kind of ministry, there remained the
marks of the Church (*Ecclesiae insignia*). We do not always find in
Churches such purity as were to be desired. Even the purest have
their blemishes; and some not only have a few spots here and there
but are almost completely deformed. We must not be so put off by
the teaching and living of any society that, if we are not satisfied with

everything that goes on, we at once deny it to be a Church. Paul here teaches us a charitableness which is very far from that. Yet when we acknowledge as Churches of Christ any societies which are laden with faults, we must at the same time condemn what is wrong in them. For it is not as if the perfection of everything to be desired in a Church is present wherever there is some kind of a Church.

I say this because the Papists seize on a single word and want whatever they choose to force upon us to be regarded as definitive. But the condition and form of the Church of Rome are very different from what existed in Galatia. If Paul were alive today he would see the miserable and dreadfully shattered ruins of a Church, but no edifice. In short, it is often called Church by synecdoche, a part for the whole, where there is a portion of a Church, even though everything may not harmonize as a whole.

3. *Grace to you and peace.* This greetings formula occurs in other epistles. I am still of the opinion that Paul desires for the Galatians friendship with God, and therewith all good things. For every kind of prosperity flows to us from the favour of God. He presents his prayers to Christ as well as to the Father, because outside Christ there is neither grace nor any good success.

4. *Who gave himself.* He begins by commending the grace of Christ, in order to recall the Galatians to Him and to keep them in Him. For if they had really appreciated this blessing of redemption they would never have fallen away to alien observances. He who knows Christ aright holds Him fast, embraces Him with both arms, is completely taken up with Him and desires nothing beyond Him. The best remedy for purifying our minds from any kind of error or superstition is to keep in remembrance what Christ is to us and what He has brought us.

These words, 'who gave himself for our sins', are very important. He wanted to tell the Galatians straight out that atonement for sins and perfect righteousness are not to be sought anywhere but in Christ. For He offered Himself to the Father as a sacrifice. And He was such an offering as we must not try to match with any other satisfactions. So glorious is this redemption that it should ravish us with wonder. Moreover, what Paul here ascribes to Christ is referred elsewhere in Scripture to God the Father. And it is proper to both; for, on the one hand, the Father by His eternal purpose decreed this atonement and in it gave this proof of His love for us that He spared not His only-begotten Son but delivered Him up for us all. And Christ, on the other hand, offered Himself a sacrifice to reconcile us to God. From this it follows that His death is the satisfaction for sins.

That he might deliver us. He also declares the purpose of our redemption to be that Christ might by His death purchase us to be His own property. This takes place when we are separated from the world. For so long as we are of the world we do not belong to Christ. The word *age* is here put for the corruption which is in the world; just as in the first epistle of John (among many other places) it is said that 'the whole world lieth in the evil one' (I John 5.19), and in His Gospel Christ says: 'I pray not that thou shouldest take them from the world, but that thou shouldest keep them from the evil one' (John 17.15). There it signifies the present life.

What then is the world in this passage? Men separated from the Kingdom of God and the grace of Christ. For so long as a man lives to himself he is altogether condemned. The world is therefore contrasted to regeneration, as nature to grace or the flesh to the Spirit. Those who are born of the world have nothing but sin and wickedness, yet not by creation but by corruption. Christ therefore died for our sins to redeem or separate us from the world.

Evil. By adding this adjective he shows that he was speaking of the corruption or depravity that comes from sin and not of God's creatures or of the bodily life. And yet by this one word, as by a thunderbolt, he lays low all human pride. For he declares that, apart from the renewal brought about by the grace of Christ, there is nothing in us but unmixed wickedness. We are of the world, and until Christ rescues us from it, the world reigns in us and we live unto it. However much men may flatter themselves, they are, for all their excellence, worthless and depraved. Of course, they do not think so; but it is enough for us that the Lord declares it is so by the mouth of Paul.

According to the will. He indicates the first source of grace: the purpose of God. For God so loved the world that He gave His only-begotten Son. But we must notice that Paul usually opposes God's purpose to all men's earnings or merits. And so 'will' here means what is commonly called good pleasure. The meaning is that Christ suffered for us, not because we were worthy or because we can produce anything that will evoke His reaction, but because it was the purpose of God.

Of God and our Father is equivalent to his saying: 'Of God who is our Father.'

5. *To whom be glory.* He breaks out into this sudden thanksgiving to stimulate them to consider this inestimable benefit of God and therefore become more teachable in future. But it is also a general exhortation. So that every remembrance of God's mercy should at once stir us up to glorify Him.

I marvel that ye are so quickly removing from Christ, who called you

in grace, unto a different gospel; which is not another: only there are
some that trouble you, and would overthrow the gospel of Christ. But
though we, or an angel from heaven, should preach unto you any gospel
other than that which we preached unto you, let him be anathema. As
we have said before, so say I now again, If any man preacheth unto you
any gospel other than that which ye received, let him be anathema. (6–9)

6. *I wonder.* He begins with a rebuke, though a somewhat gentler
one than they deserved. He prefers to direct his anger against the
false apostles, as we shall see. He charges the Galatians with defection,
not only from his own teaching, but from Christ. For they could
only keep to Christ by acknowledging that it is by His benefit that
we are set free from the bondage of the law. But the necessity for
ceremonies which the false apostles set up is flatly contrary to this.
Thus they were removed from Christ, not in that they entirely
rejected Christianity but because in such a corruption only a fictitious
Christ was left to them. So today the Papists choose to have a half
Christ and a mangled Christ and so none at all and are therefore
removed from Christ. They are full of superstitions which are directly
opposed to the nature of Christ. Let it be carefully observed that we
are *removed from Christ* when we accept what is inconsistent with His
mediatorial office; for light cannot be mixed with darkness.

For the same reason he calls it *another gospel*, that is, another gospel
than the true one. And yet the false apostles claimed to preach the
Gospel of Christ; but by mingling with it their own inventions, they
destroyed the main force of the Gospel and so held a false, corrupt
and spurious gospel. He uses the present tense of the verb, as if so far
they were only in process of falling, as people say. It is as if he had
said, 'I do not yet say that you have been removed. If you had, it
would have been more difficult to return to the path. But now, while
you are still on your way, turn back, do not go a step further.'

Some read, 'from him who called you by the grace of Christ',
understanding it of the Father. But the reading which we have
followed is simpler. When he says that they were called by Christ
through grace, it is as if he reproved their ingratitude. To desert the
Son of God is in itself dishonourable and disgraceful; but to desert
Him when He has called us freely to salvation is far more terrible, for
His goodness to us increases the seriousness of the sin when we are
ungrateful.

So quickly. He emphasizes the wickedness of their inconstancy. No
time is right for deserting Christ; but the Galatians were the more
blameworthy in that they were led astray the moment Paul left them.
Therefore, just as their ingratitude had been shown up by his earlier

comparison of it with the grace of calling, so now he magnifies their fickleness by mentioning the time involved.

7. *Which is not another.* Some explain it thus: 'Although there is not another Gospel', as if it were a check against anyone thinking that other Gospels existed. So far as the explanation of the words is concerned, I take it more simply, that he speaks contemptuously of the teaching of the false apostles as being the cause only of confusion and destruction. To paraphrase: 'What do they put forward? On what grounds do they attack the doctrine I have delivered? They merely trouble you and destroy the Gospel. That is all they do.' But it comes to the same thing, for I admit that this expression corrects what he had said about another gospel. He declares that it is not the Gospel but a mere disturbance. All I meant to say was that in my opinion 'another' means 'another thing'. As we often say, 'This means nothing but that you want to deceive.'

And wish to destroy. He charges them with the second crime of doing an injury to Christ by wanting to destroy His Gospel. And this is a very dreadful crime; for destruction is worse than corruption. And with good reason does he accuse them. When the glory of justifying man is transferred to another and a snare is set for consciences, the Saviour no longer stands firm and the teaching of the Gospel is ruined. For we must always take care of the main articles of the Gospel. He who attacks them is a destroyer of the Gospel.

When he adds the words *of Christ*, it can be explained in two ways: either that it has come from Christ as its Author, or that it purely exhibits Christ. But there is no doubt that he meant by this term to describe the true and genuine Gospel, which alone should be regarded as Gospel.

8. *But though we.* Here he rises with great boldness to vindicate the authority of his teaching. First, he declares that the doctrine he had preached is the only Gospel and that it is wicked to overthrow it. Otherwise the false apostles might object, 'We also wish to maintain the Gospel unimpaired, nor do we feel less reverence for it than you.' Just as today the Papists proclaim how holy the Gospel is for them and kiss the very name with the deepest reverence. But when it comes to the proof, they fiercely persecute the pure and simple doctrine of the Gospel. Therefore Paul is not satisfied with this general declaration, but defines what the Gospel is and what it contains and pronounces that his teaching is the true Gospel, lest this should be sought elsewhere.

What use was it to profess the Gospel and not know what it meant? With Papists, who are dominated by implicit faith, that might be sufficient. But with Christians there is no faith where there is no knowledge. Lest the Galatians, who were otherwise ready to obey the Gospel, might wander here and there and find no firm ground to stand on, Paul enjoins them to stand in his teaching. He demands such sure belief in his preaching that he pronounces a curse on all who should dare to contradict it. It was also necessary for him to begin with himself. In this way he anticipates a slander from his ill-wishers: 'You want to have everything that comes from you received without hesitation because it is your own.' To show that there is no foundation for this, he is the first to surrender the right to advance anything against this teaching. By doing so, he does not subject himself to others, but, as is fair, puts them all along with himself into one rank, that they should be subject to the Word of God.

To cast down the false apostles more violently, he rises up even to the angels. Nor does he simply say that they should not be heard if they brought forward something different, but declares that they ought to be held accursed. Some might think that it was all wrong to involve angels in a controversy about his teaching; but anyone who considers it properly will see that he had to do this. It is certainly impossible for angels from heaven to teach anything other than the sure truth of God. But when there was controversy over faith in the doctrine which God had revealed concerning the salvation of men, he did not reckon it enough to refuse the judgment of men without also claiming the higher judgment of the angels.

And thus when he pronounces a judgment of anathema on angels if they should teach anything else, though he argues from an impossibility, it is not superfluous. For this exaggeration helped to increase the authority of Paul's preaching. He saw that he and his teaching were attacked by the use of famous names. He replies that not even angels have the weight to overwhelm it. This is no insult to the angels. They were created to illuminate God's glory by every possible means. Therefore, if anyone, for this same godly purpose, disparages them, he detracts nothing from their dignity. But from this we not only grasp the great majesty of the Word of God, but also our faith receives a remarkable strengthening when, in reliance on the Word of God, we can triumph over and speak ill of angels.

When he says, *let him be accursed*, 'by you' must be understood. We spoke of the word 'anathema' on I Cor. 12.3. Here it denotes cursing and corresponds to the Hebrew word חֵרֶם.

9. *As we said before.* He now omits all mention of himself or angels and repeats in general that it is unlawful for any mortal to deliver anything other than what he had learned. Observe the words *ye have received*. For he always insists that they must not regard the Gospel as unknown, hanging uncertainly in their imaginations, as if in air, but must have a firm persuasion and be sincerely convinced that what

was delivered to them and they embraced was the true Gospel of Christ. For nothing can be less consistent with faith than opinion. What then if a man is at a loss because he does not know what or of what sort the Gospel is? Therefore he tells them to regard as devils those who dare to bring forward a gospel different from his, meaning by another gospel one to which ideas foreign to the Gospel have been added. For the teaching of the false apostles was not entirely contrary to or even different from that of Paul, but was corrupted by false additions.

The subterfuges of the Papists are childish when they evade Paul's words by saying, first, that the whole of his teaching is no longer extant, and that we cannot know what it contained unless the Galatians who heard it are raised from the dead as witnesses; and then, that not every kind of addition is forbidden but only that other gospels are condemned. Paul's doctrine may be learned quite clearly from his writings, so far as we need to know it. Of this Gospel it is plain that the whole Papacy is a dreadful subversion. Finally, it is clear from the nature of the case that any doctrine different from Paul's proclamation is spurious. So quibbles will avail them nothing.

For am I now persuading according to men, or to God? or am I seeking to please men? if I were still pleasing men, I should not be a servant of Christ. For I make known to you, brethren, as touching the gospel which was preached by me, that it is not after man. For neither did I receive it from man, nor was I taught it, but it came to me through revelation of Jesus Christ. For ye have heard of my manner of life in time past in the Jews' religion, how that beyond measure I persecuted the church of God, and made havock of it: and I advanced in the Jews' religion beyond many of mine own age among my countrymen, being more exceedingly zealous for the traditions of my fathers. (10-14)

After praising his own preaching so confidently, he now shows that this was of good right and no empty boast. And he uses two arguments to prove it. The first is from his motives, that he did not accommodate himself to men from ambition or for the sake of flattery. The second is far stronger, that he himself was not the author of his Gospel, but he handed on faithfully what he had received from God.

10. *For do I now persuade according to men or according to God?* Owing to the ambiguity of the Greek construction, this passage is expounded diversely. Some render it, 'Do I now persuade men or God?' Others take 'God' and 'men' as 'divine and human standards'. This sense would agree very well were it not too remote from the words. And so I have preferred to follow a more natural meaning; for it is common in Greek to supply the preposition κατά. Paul is speaking, not about

the subject of his preaching, but about the purpose of his own mind, which concerns God rather than men. The teaching also, it is true, corresponds to the disposition of the teacher. For, as corruption of doctrine is bred of ambition, avarice or other depraved desires, so an upright conscience causes the pure truth to be kept. And so he contends that his doctrine is sound because it is not accommodated to men.

Or do I seek to please men? This second clause differs from the former, not much, and yet a little. For the desire of obtaining favour is one reason why we speak according to men. When there reigns in our hearts such ambition that we want to frame our speech so as to please men, we cannot teach sincerely. Paul therefore declares that he is clear and free from this fault. And he puts it as a question so as to clear himself from calumny the more boldly. For questions carry greater weight in that we give our opponents a chance to reply and they have nothing to say. For it is a sign of the great boldness that Paul derived from the testimony of a good conscience, in that he knew that he had discharged his duty in such a way as not to be liable to any reproach like that.

If I yet pleased men. A remarkable statement; that ambitious men (that is, those who court men's favour) cannot serve Christ. He speaks for himself in particular when he says that he had freely renounced the favour of men in order to stand on the side of Christ; and he compares the past state of his life with the present. He had been held in the highest esteem, everywhere had received great applause. And therefore, if he had wished to please men, he would not have needed to change his state. But we may draw from it the general doctrine that I have stated, that those who determine to serve Christ faithfully must boldly despise the favour of men.

The word *men* here has a limited sense. For the ministers of Christ ought not to set out deliberately to displease men. But there are different sorts of men. Those to whom Christ is pleasing are men whom we should endeavour to please in Christ. Whereas those who want true doctrine to give place to their own purposes are on no account to be gratified. And godly upright pastors will always have to sustain this struggle of disregarding the offences of those who want to have their own way in everything. For the Church will always contain hypocrites and wicked men, who prefer their own lusts to the Word of God. And even good men, either through ignorance or some weakness are sometimes tempted by the devil to get angry with the faithful warnings of their pastor. It is our duty, therefore, not to be alarmed at any kind of offences, so long, of course, as we do not drive weak minds away from Christ.

Many interpret this passage differently, as if it were a concession;

17

and they think the meaning is this: 'If I pleased men, I should not be the servant of Christ. I admit this; but who shall accuse me? Who does not see that I do not court the favour of men?' But I prefer the former sense, that Paul is relating how much human esteem he had renounced to devote himself to Christ.

11. *Now I make known to you.* This is the most powerful argument, the main hinge, as it were, on which the question turns: that his Gospel is not something that he has received from men but has been revealed to him by God. And because this might be denied, he proffers an exegetical proof, that is, one founded on an account of the events. To give his declaration the greater weight, he first says that he is speaking, not of something obscure but of what he is ready to guarantee. This opening befits such a serious matter. He affirms that it is not according to man, in that it savours of nothing human, or that it was not of human making. And in proof of this he goes on to add that he had not been taught by any earthly teacher.

12. *For I neither received it from man.* What then? If anyone is taught by the ministry of a man and then becomes a teacher himself, is his authority lessened on that account? We must always consider the weapons with which the false apostles attacked him—that his Gospel was defective and spurious, that he had obtained it from an inferior, or at least an unknown teacher, and that now he was rashly handing on something he had himself misunderstood. They boasted, on the other hand, that they had been the disciples of the highest apostles, with all of whose more secret thoughts they were well acquainted. It was therefore necessary for Paul to set his teaching against the whole world and to take his stand on its having been divinely revealed to him and not given him in any human school. Otherwise he would never have been free from the slanders of the false apostles.

The objection that Ananias was his teacher may be easily answered. There was no reason why God should not have both taught him by Himself in oracles and also, to equip him for his ministry, have used human agency in teaching him. As we have said above, that he was called immediately by God through an oracle and yet he was ordained by the votes and solemn approbation of men. These statements are not at all inconsistent with each other.

13. *For ye have heard of my conversation.* The whole of this narrative was put in as an argument. He relates that in all his life he had such an abhorrence of the Gospel that he was its mortal enemy and a destroyer of the name of Christianity. From this we infer that his conversion was divine. And indeed, he summons them as witnesses of a matter not at all doubtful, so as to place beyond controversy what he is going to say.

He calls his contemporaries *his equals*, for a comparison with older people would have been unsuitable. By *the traditions of the fathers* he means, not the additions that had corrupted the law of God, but that law of God itself which he had been educated in from his childhood and had received through the hands of his parents' and ancestors. He had been strongly attached to the customs of his fathers and it would have been no easy thing to tear him from them, had not the Lord drawn him by a miracle.

But when it was the good pleasure of God, who separated me, even from my mother's womb, and called me through his grace, to reveal his Son to me, that I might preach him among the Gentiles; immediately I conferred not with flesh and blood: neither went I up to Jerusalem to them which were apostles before me: but I went away into Arabia; and again I returned unto Damascus. Then after three years I went up to Jerusalem to visit Cephas, and tarried with him fifteen days. But other of the apostles saw I none, save James the Lord's brother. Now touching the things which I write unto you, behold, before God, I lie not. Then I came into the regions of Syria and Cilicia. And I was still unknown by face unto the churches of Judaea which were in Christ: but they only heard say, He that once persecuted us now preacheth the faith of which he once made havock; and they glorified God in me. (15-24)

15. *But after that it pleased God.* This is the second part of the story of his miraculous conversion. It should be interpreted in this way: he had been called by the grace of God to preach Christ among the Gentiles, and as soon as he was called, without consulting the apostles he proceeded without any irresolution and certain of God's will to the performance of His work. In the construction of the words Erasmus differs from the Vulgate and connects them thus: 'When it pleased God that I should preach Christ among the Gentiles, who called me for this purpose that he might reveal him through me.' But the old translation fits better, to my mind, for first had come the revelation of Christ and then the command to preach. Even were we to follow Erasmus and render ἐν ἐμοὶ as 'through me', we should still have to say that the phrase *that I might preach* is put in to describe the mode of revelation.

At first sight Paul's reasoning does not seem very strong. Although when he had been converted to Christianity he at once, without consulting the apostles, took up the office of preaching the Gospel, it does not follow that he had been appointed to that office by the revelation of Christ. But he relies on various lines of thought, and when you gather them all together they make up a strong argument. He argues, first, that he had been called by the grace of God; next that his apostleship had been acknowledged by the other apostles; and then the other arguments follow. Let the reader, then, remember to take the narrative as a whole and draw the inference, not from isolated parts but from the whole.

Who had separated me. This separation was God's purpose, by which Paul was appointed to the apostolic office before he was aware of his own existence.[1] The calling followed at the proper time, when the Lord made known His will concerning him and commanded him to proceed to the work. God had no doubt decreed before the foundation of the world what He would do with every one of us and had assigned to everyone by His secret counsel his part in life. But Scripture often speaks of these three steps: the eternal predestination of God; the destination from the womb; and the calling which is the effect and fulfilment of both. The Lord spoke in the first chapter of Jeremiah a little differently from Paul so far as the words go, but in the same sense: 'Before I formed thee in the belly, I knew thee; and before thou camest forth from the womb I sanctified thee; I gave thee to be a prophet to the nations' (1.5). For when he was not yet even begotten, God had sanctified Paul to the office of apostle, just as also Jeremiah to the office of prophet. But He is said to separate us from the womb because we are sent into the world for this purpose, that He may accomplish in us what He has decreed. The calling is delayed till its proper time, when God has adapted us for the task which He commands us to undertake. Paul's words may therefore be resolved thus: 'When it pleased God to reveal his Son by me, who called me as he had already separated me.' He wanted to show that his calling depended on the secret election of God, and that he was ordained an apostle, not because he had fitted himself for undertaking such an office by his own industry or because God had discerned that he was worthy of having it bestowed upon him, but because, before he was born, he had been set apart by the secret purpose of God.

Thus he is accustomed to refer the cause of his calling to the free good pleasure of God. This must be carefully noted. For it shows us that we owe it to the grace of God, not only that we have been elected and adopted to eternal life, but also that He condescends to use our services, when otherwise we should have been altogether useless, and that He assigns to us a lawful calling in which we may exercise ourselves. What, before he was born, had Paul that deserved so high an honour? In the same way we ought to believe that it is

[1] Latin: *antequam se hominem.* French: *avant que luy-mesme se sceust estre nay au monde.*

entirely the gift of God and not the fruit of our own efforts that we
have been called to govern His Church.

Some have reasoned too subtly (and therefore erroneously and
inappropriately) on the word 'separated'. God is said to separate us,
not in that He infuses in us any *habitus* to distinguish us from others
but by choosing us in His own purpose. Although he had quite clearly
attributed his calling to the grace of God when he put its beginning
in that voluntary separation from the womb, yet he expressly says
so again, partly that by his commendation of divine grace he may
take away all grounds of boasting and partly that he may testify his
own gratitude to God. This he is continually doing, even when he
has no controversy with the false apostles.

16. *To reveal his Son.* If we read it 'To reveal by me', we shall
have the purpose of the apostolate, to make Christ known. How?
By preaching Him among the Gentiles, which the false apostles treated
as a crime. But I think the Greek phrase ἐν ἐμοὶ is a Hebrew term for
'to me', for the Hebrew is often redundant, as all who know that
language are well aware. The meaning will therefore be that Christ
was revealed to Paul, not that he alone might enjoy and silently keep
in his own heart the knowledge of Him, but that he might preach
among the Gentiles Him whom he himself knew.

Immediately I conferred not. To *confer with flesh and blood* is to take
counsel with flesh and blood. So far as the meaning of the words is
concerned, he simply wanted to exclude all human counsels. This
comprehends all mankind in general, together with their common-
sense and wisdom, as will presently appear from the context. He
expressly mentions the apostles, to throw God's calling into the
stronger relief. Therefore he relied only on the authority of God and
asked nothing more, but took up the office of preaching.

17. *Neither did I return to Jerusalem.* He explains and amplifies his
former statement; as if he had said, 'I did not desire the warrant of
any man, not even of the apostles themselves.' Therefore they are
mistaken who deny that the apostles are included under flesh and
blood because they are now mentioned separately. He adds nothing
new or different here but only explains more clearly what he had
already said obscurely. Nor is there any insult to the apostles in this
expression. It was to show that the motive behind his work was not
human that he was forced to set the apostles in contrast to God,
because of the false claims of those scoundrels. When a creature is
contrasted to God and given any mean and lowly descriptions, it is
no insult to him.

But I went into Arabia. In the Acts of the Apostles Luke has omitted
these three years, just as elsewhere he does not mention everything.

Hence the slander of those who look for inconsistency here is weak. Let godly readers consider the severe trial that overtook Paul at the very start of his course. He who but yesterday had had the honour of being sent to Damascus with a splendid escort is now compelled to wander as an exile in a foreign land. But he does not lose heart.

18. *Then after three years.* It was not until three years after he had taken up the apostolic office that he went up to Jerusalem. Thus his apostleship was not inaugurated by the calling of men. But lest he should seem to have separate interests from theirs and to be avoiding their company, he tells us that he went up expressly to see Peter. Although he had not waited for their authority before undertaking the office, it was not against their will but with their consent and approbation that he held the rank of apostle. His meaning is that he was never an alien from the other apostles and that in fact he agreed with them very well. He mentions the short time he stayed there to show that he went, not to learn, but only for mutual fellowship. For the same reason he adds *that he saw no one else*, for he had only one object in his journey and attended to nothing else.

19. *Except James.* We must ask who this James was. Almost all the old writers agree that he was one of the disciples whose surname was Oblias and the Just and that he presided over the Church at Jerusalem. Others think that he was the son of Joseph by another wife and others (which is more probable) that he was Christ's cousin on His mother's side. But as he is here mentioned among the apostles, I do not accept that opinion. For Jerome's plea has no weight, that the name of apostle is sometimes given to others besides the twelve. Here Paul is concerned with the highest dignity; and a little after we shall see that James was regarded as one of the chief pillars. It seems far more probable to me, therefore, that he is speaking of the son of Alphaeus.

It is probable that the rest of the apostles were scattered through various countries; for they did not idly remain in one place. Luke relates that Barnabas brought Paul to the apostles; but this must be understood, not of the twelve, but of those two who alone were in Jerusalem then.

20. *Now the things which I write unto you.* This affirmation extends to the whole narrative. Paul shows how earnest he is in this cause by resorting to an oath, something that must be used only in serious and important cases. Nor is it strange that he insists so strongly on this point, for we have already seen how the impostors intrigued to rob him of the name and honours of apostle. Now we should notice the forms of swearing that the saints used, and learn in swearing only to refer the truth and faithfulness of our words and actions to God's

judgment. The awe and fear of God must govern this pleading.

22. *I was unknown by face.* This seems to me to have been added to emphasize the wickedness and malice of his slanderers. If the Churches of Judaea who had only heard of him were led to give glory to God that He had worked so wonderfully in Paul, how disgraceful it was that those to whom His power had been shown just as wonderfully in its effect, should have failed to do the same. If the mere report was enough for the former, why were not the others satisfied with the living facts?

It is said that *faith was destroyed*, not because it is destructible in itself, but because he destroyed it in weak men. Besides, it is the attempt rather than the effect that is here expressed.

24. *And they glorified God in me.* This was an evident token that his ministry was approved by all the Churches of Judaea; and approved in such a way that they acknowledged with praise and admiration the wonderful power of God. Thus he indirectly reproves their malice, in that their spite and slanders could only hide God's glory, which the apostles admitted and openly acknowledged to shine brightly in Paul's apostleship. And this lays down for us, incidentally, a rule on how we should regard the saints of the Lord. When we see men adorned with the gifts of God, we are so depraved or ungrateful or prone to superstition as to worship them as gods, forgetting that they are, in fact, His gifts. And so this place tells us to raise our eyes to their author and ascribe to Him what is His own. And at the same time we are taught that it was something to praise God for that Paul was changed from an enemy to a servant.

CHAPTER TWO

Then, fourteen years after, I went up again to Jerusalem with Barnabas, taking Titus also with me. And I went up by revelation; and I laid before them the gospel which I preach among the Gentiles, but privately before them who were of repute, lest by any means I should run, or had run, in vain. But not even Titus, who was with me, being a Greek, was compelled to be circumcised: and that because of the false brethren privily brought in, who came in privily to spy out our liberty which we have in Christ Jesus, that they might bring us into bondage: to whom we gave place in the way of subjection, no, not for an hour, that the truth of the gospel might continue with you. (1-5)

1. *Fourteen years after.* This can hardly be regarded definitely as the journey mentioned by Luke in Acts 15.2. The course of the history leads us to the contrary conclusion. We find there that Paul went to Jerusalem four times. Of the first we have already spoken. The second was when, in company with Barnabas, he brought the alms collected in the Greek and Asiatic Churches, as narrated at the end of chapter twelve. My belief that this was what the present passage refers to depends on several reasons. Thus, otherwise we should have to say that one or the other of them was mistaken. Then, the more probable conjecture is that he rebuked Peter at Antioch while he himself was still living there. But that was before he was sent to Jerusalem by the Churches to settle the dispute which had arisen about ceremonies. It is unreasonable to think that Peter would have practised such dissimulation if the controversy had been settled and the decree of the apostles published. But Paul here writes that he came to Jerusalem and only afterwards adds that he had rebuked Peter's dissimulation, a fault that Peter certainly would not have committed except in a doubtful matter.

Besides, he would never have alluded to that journey, undertaken with the consent of all the believers, without mentioning its occasion and its memorable outcome. It is not really certain when the epistle was written. The Greeks conjecture that it was sent from Rome, and the Latins from Ephesus. For myself, I think it was written, not only before Paul had seen Rome, but before that council had been held and the apostles had made their pronouncement on ceremonial observances. While his opponents were falsely claiming the support

24

of the apostles and doing their utmost to harass Paul, how careless he would have been to pass over the decree circulated among them all which undermined their position. Undoubtedly, one word would have shut their mouth: 'You bring the apostles against me, but who does not know their decision? Therefore I have convicted you of shameless lying. In their name you lay on the Gentiles the necessity of observing the law; but now their verdict exists which sets men's consciences free.'

Moreover, in the beginning he had reproved the Galatians for having so soon deserted the Gospel delivered to them. But we may readily conclude that after they had been brought to the Gospel some time would have elapsed before the dispute over the ceremonial law arose. Further, I take it that the fourteen years are to be reckoned, not as between one journey and another, but from Paul's conversion. The space of time between the two journeys was eleven years.

2. *And I went up according to revelation.* He now confirms his apostleship and his doctrine, not only by works but also by the divine oracle. In that God had directed the journey, the reason for which was the confirmation of his teaching, that teaching was confirmed, not by the agreement of men only but also by the authority of God. This should have been more than enough to overcome the obstinacy of those who worried and attacked Paul with the names of the apostles. For although there had hitherto been some room for debate, the decision of God had put an end to all argument.

I communicated to them. The word *communicated* must be noticed first; for they do not tell him what he ought to teach but when he has reported the substance of his teaching, they subscribe and agree to it. But since his opponents might raise the slander that he had won the apostles' favour by cunning dissimulation on many points, he expressly states that he had communicated to them the Gospel which he preached among the Gentiles, and so removes all suspicion of deceit or imposture. We shall see what followed. The apostles did not take it amiss that he had made a start on his own initiative, but without dispute or protest they approved what he had done; and this was by the direction of the same Spirit by whose guidance Paul had come to them. Thus he was not made an apostle by them. He was acknowledged to be an apostle. But more of this hereafter.

Lest by any means. What! Will God's truth fall unless it is supported by the testimony of men? Though the whole world were unbelieving, God's truth remains firm and untouched. And they who teach the Gospel at God's command are not wasting their time, even when their labour produces no fruit. But this is not Paul's meaning. Because the ministry of the Word is useless in doubtful and hesitating consciences, *to run in vain* is taken, so far as men are concerned, for working uselessly, when the proper edification does not follow.

It was moreover, a formidable battering-ram for shaking weak consciences when the doctrine which Paul preached was falsely declared by the impostors to be contrary to the doctrine of the apostles. Therefore many fell away. The certainty of faith, indeed, does not depend on the agreement of men; but, on the contrary, it is our duty to rest on the naked truth of God so that neither men nor all the angels together may dislodge us. Yet it is an almost unendurable trial for the ignorant and for those who have hardly any taste of sound doctrine and have not yet got it into their bones and marrow, when they hear eminent teachers disagreeing among themselves. Satan sometimes upsets even strong believers by showing them the strifes and divisions of those who ought to be one in mind and voice. It would be hard to say how many have been put off the Gospel, how many have had their faith shaken, by the disastrous free fight about the Body of Christ, because, on a most important question men of the highest authority were seen to contend against one another.

On the other hand, the agreement of all teachers is a powerful aid in the confirmation of faith. Since, therefore, Satan was trying so cunningly to hinder the progress of the Gospel, Paul resolved to encounter him. For after he had shown clearly that he was in agreement with all the apostles, every hindrance was at once removed. Weak disciples were no longer perplexed by doubt as to whom they should follow. Therefore this is what he is saying: 'In order that my former labours might not be thrown away and that I might not run in vain, I have set at rest the doubt that was distressing many, whether I or Peter should be believed. For we were in full accord in everything I had ever taught.' If many today were as heartily desirous to edify the Church as Paul was, they would take more care to be agreed among themselves.

3. *But neither Titus.* He proves by another argument that the apostles believed what he did. He had brought to them a man who had not been circumcised; yet they did not hesitate to acknowledge him as a brother. The reason is given why he had not been circumcised: that circumcision, being an indifferent thing, could be omitted or practised as edification required. For the rule that must always be observed is that, although all things are lawful for us, we ought to ask what is expedient. He circumcises Timothy lest his uncircumcision should create offence in weak minds; for he was then dealing with the weak, whom he had to spare. And he would gladly have followed the same course with Titus, for he was unwearied in supporting the weak. But the case was different. Here false brethren were watching

26

for an opportunity to slander his doctrine and they would immediately have spread the rumour, 'Look how this valiant champion of liberty lays aside, in the presence of the apostles, the bold and fierce aspect he wears among the ignorant!' Now, as we ought to bear with the weak, so we must stoutly resist the malicious, who deliberately plot against our liberty. The duties of love should not harm faith. Therefore, in matters indifferent, love will be our best guide, so long as faith always receives our first attention.

4. *And that because of false brethren.* The sense may be twofold. Either that the false brethren made a wicked attack because he was not circumcised and wanted to compel him, or that Paul purposely did not circumcise him, because he saw that they would at once make it an occasion of slander. They had insinuated themselves into Paul's company with the hope of gaining one of two objects. If he openly despised the ceremonies, they would rouse the Jews against him; but if he refrained altogether from using his liberty, they would triumph over him among the Gentiles as one who was covered with shame and had retracted his doctrine. I prefer the second interpretation: that Paul was aware of the trap and determined not to circumcise Titus. And he says that he was not compelled, so that his readers may understand that circumcision is not condemned in itself as if it were bad, but that the obligation to observe it was disputed. As if he had said: 'I would have been prepared to circumcise him if higher matters had not been involved.' For they wanted to lay down a law, and to such compulsion he would not yield.

5. *To whom we gave place.* This steadfastness set the seal on Paul's doctrine. For when the false brethren, who wished only to accuse him, attacked him and he stood firm, there could no longer be any room for doubt. For he could not now be charged with deceiving the apostles. He therefore asserts that he did not for a moment give place to them by subjection, that is in the way of subjection, so that his action would have proved that his liberty was overcome. Apart from this he was ready, right to the end of his life, to show mildness and forbearance to all men.

That the truth of the Gospel. There was no danger that Paul would lose his liberty even if he yielded to them. But his example would have hurt others. Therefore he wisely considered what was expedient. Thus we see to what extent offences should be avoided and that the thing to keep in mind in all matters of indifference is edification. The sum of it is this: we are the servants of the brethren, but for this purpose, that we may all together serve the Lord and that the liberty of our conscience shall remain sound. When false brethren wanted to lead the saints into bondage, it was their duty not to yield to them.

'The truth of the Gospel' is to be taken for its genuine purity, or what comes to the same thing, its pure and sound doctrine. For the false apostles did not altogether abolish the Gospel but adulterated it with their own notions, so that it soon began to be false and cloaked. This is always so when we depart in the smallest degree from the simplicity of Christ. How impudent then the Papists are in boasting that they possess the Gospel, for it is not only corrupted by many inventions but more than adulterated by many ungodly dogmas. Let us remember that it is not enough to keep the name of the Gospel and some kind of summary of it,[1] if its genuine purity does not remain unimpaired. Where are the men who, by a pretended moderation, try to reconcile us with the Papists? as if it is right to arrange a settlement in the doctrine of religion as is done with finance or property! We see how Paul would have abhorred this kind of transaction, for he denies that it is the true Gospel if it is not pure.

But from those who seemed to be somewhat (whatsoever they were, it maketh no matter to me: God accepteth not man's person)—they who seemed to be of repute imparted nothing to me: but contrariwise, when they saw that I had been entrusted with the gospel of the uncircumcision, even as Peter with the gospel of the circumcision, (for he that wrought for Peter unto the apostleship of the circumcision, wrought for me also unto the Gentiles); and when they perceived the grace that was given unto me, James and Cephas and John, who were reputed to be pillars, gave to me and Barnabas the right hands of fellowship, that we should go unto the Gentiles, and they unto the circumcision. Only they would that we should remember the poor; which very thing I was also zealous to do. (6-10)

6. *Of those who seemed to be somewhat.* Paul is not satisfied until the Galatians have grasped that he had learned nothing from Peter and the apostles. Porphyry and Julian accuse this holy man of pride, that he claims so much for himself that he cannot bear to learn anything from others; that he boasts of having become a teacher without any master or helper; and that he strives so hard not to appear inferior to anyone. But those who consider how necessary that boasting was will admit that it was holy and utterly praiseworthy. For if he had granted to his opponents that he had profited under the apostles, he would have presented them with two slanders. They would at once have said, 'At last you have made some progress and corrected your past errors and have not repeated your past recklessness.' Thus, first, the whole of his earlier doctrine would have become suspect and the building demolished. Secondly, he would ever afterwards have

[1] I.e. the Creed.

28

possessed less authority because he would have been reckoned an ordinary disciple. We see, therefore, that it was not so much on his own account but from his need to protect his doctrine that he was led to this holy boasting. This was no strife from ambition, for it was not concerned with personalities. But Paul refused to have his apostleship obscured by the greatness of anyone, for the authority of his teaching was bound up with it. If this be not enough to curb those dogs, their barking is at any rate sufficiently checked.

Whatsoever they were. This must be read separately, for the parenthesis was introduced to show his enemies that he took no heed of the opinions of men. This passage is variously expounded. Ambrose thinks it is a passing rebuke of the folly of minimizing Paul by magnifying the apostles, as if he had said, 'May not I just as well object that they were poor illiterate men who knew nothing but how to fish, whereas I was well taught from my boyhood under my master Gamaliel. But I pass over all that, because I know that there is no respect of persons with God.' Chrysostom and Jerome take a harsher view; as if he indirectly threatened even the foremost apostles in this way, 'Whatsoever they may be, they shall not escape the judgment of God if they swerve from their duty. Neither the dignity of their office nor the estimation of men shall exempt them.' But another interpretation seems simpler to me and more accordant to Paul's meaning. He admits that they were first in time, but argues that this does not debar him from being their equal in rank. He does not say that it is nothing to him what they are at present, but speaks of time past, when they were already apostles but he himself outside the faith of Christ. In short, he does not want the matter decided from the past and rejects the proverb that he who comes first has the best right.

No man's person. Besides the interpretations I have mentioned, a third seems reasonable, that in the government of the world there is a place for respect of persons, but not in the spiritual Kingdom of Christ. This is plausible, but it is precisely in respect of worldly government that the Lord says, 'Ye shall not respect persons in judgment' (Deut. 1.17). But I will not enter into that argument, for it has nothing to do with this present passage. Paul simply means that the noble position which the apostles held did not prevent his having been called by God and raised suddenly from being nothing to becoming their equal. Although the difference between them had been great, it was nothing in God's sight, for He does not accept persons and His calling is not influenced by any prejudice. But this may also appear unreasonable. For, granting it to be true (and a truth, moreover, which must be sedulously maintained) that in God's affairs we must not respect persons, how does this apply to Peter and his fellow apostles, who were to be revered, not only for themselves, but for true holiness and spiritual gifts? 'Person' is contrasted to the fear of God and a good conscience; and this is its ordinary sense in Scripture (Acts 10.34; I Pet. 1.17). But piety, righteous zeal, holiness and other similar gifts were the chief grace and honour of the apostles. But here Paul speaks contemptuously, as if they had nothing but the outward appearance.

I reply: Paul is not estimating the apostles at their true value but only from the idle boasting of their adversaries. To advertise their worthless wares they talked big about Peter and James and John and took advantage of the veneration with which the Church regarded them, to degrade Paul. Thus, he is not here treating of the nature of apostles or what must be thought of them apart from this controversy; but he tears off the masks that the false apostles wore. Therefore, just as later on he deals with circumcision, not in its real meaning but according to the false and ungodly opinion that those impostors held of it, so he now declares of the apostles that they were, considered as the masks in which these men excelled in the world, nothing in the sight of God. And this is plain from the words. For why did they prefer them to Paul? Because they came before him. This was a mere pretext. Apart from all this there is no doubt that Paul would have looked up to them, and have admired the gifts of God in them, such was his exceptional modesty. For elsewhere he freely confesses that he was the least of the apostles and unworthy of such an exalted position.

They communicated nothing to me. This can also be read, 'They communicated nothing with me.' For it is the same word that he had used twice before. But the sense is clear. When the apostles had heard Paul's Gospel, they did not put forward their own in opposition (as is common when it is regarded as better and more perfect) but were satisfied with his explanation and simply and unhesitatingly embraced his doctrine. So that not a word passed between them on settled matters. Nor did Paul, as if he were the superior, take the lead in the discussion like a man who dictates the form of the debate to others, but he explained his faith, about which sinister rumours had arisen, and they approved it by their assent.

7. *But, on the contrary*, they immediately *gave him the right hand of fellowship*. They therefore gave their testimony to his teaching unreservedly. For they brought forward nothing to the contrary, as is usually done with disputed points, but acknowledged that he and they held one Gospel in common. And so they accorded him the honour and position of a colleague. One condition of this fellowship was that they distributed the provinces among themselves. They were

therefore equal, and there was no subjection on Paul's side. To give the right hand of fellowship means here to have an agreed fellowship.

When they saw that I had been entrusted with. He denies that he was indebted to the apostles to the extent that he had become an apostle by their will and favour, but says that they allowed him the honour of apostleship lest they should take away what God had given. He always insists that he was created apostle by the gift and appointment of God; but here he adds that he was acknowledged as such by the apostles themselves. Hence it follows that those humbugs were attempting what the apostles dared not do lest they should oppose the election of God.

And here he begins to claim what was proper and peculiar to him above others: the apostleship of the uncircumcision. For Paul and Barnabas differed from the rest in having been marked out to be the apostles of the Gentiles. This had been done by the revelation of God, which the apostles did not merely accept passively but determined to ratify, because not to obey it would have been impious. We see therefore how they distributed the offices among themselves, according to the revelation; namely that Paul and Barnabas should be the apostles of the Gentiles and the others of the Jews.

But this seems to conflict with the command of Christ when He bade the twelve to go into all the world. I reply that that command was not intended for each individual but describes generally the purpose of the office: that salvation must be proclaimed to all nations by the teaching of the Gospel. For the apostles certainly did not travel over the whole world. In fact, it is probable that none of the twelve ever passed into Europe; for what they allege about Peter may, for all I know, be fabulous and is, in any case, quite uncertain.

Yet all of them, it may be objected, still had a ministry both to Gentiles and to Jews. I own that they had, as occasion offered. Each apostle was, I grant, entrusted with the task of publishing the Gospel both among Gentiles and Jews. For the partition was not one that fixed hard and fast boundaries that they must not pass, like those of kingdoms, principalities and provinces. We see that Paul, wherever he went, made it his habit first to offer his labours and ministry to the Jews. Now, as he had a right while among the Gentiles to offer himself as an apostle and teacher to the Jews, so the others were free to bring whatever Gentiles they could to Christ. Peter exercises this right towards Cornelius and others. But as there were other apostles in that district, which was almost completely inhabited by Jews, Paul travelled through Asia, Greece and other distant regions and therefore he was in a special way ordained to be the apostle to the Gentiles. In fact, when the Lord first commanded him to be set apart.

he directed him to leave Antioch and Syria and to go away to far countries for the Gentiles. Ordinarily, therefore, his apostolate was to the Gentiles; extraordinarily, to the Jews. But the others took the Jews for themselves, though on the understanding that, when an opportunity occurred, they would extend their ministry to the Gentiles. This last, however, was for them extraordinary, so to say.

But if Peter's apostleship pertained peculiarly to the Jews, let the Romanists ask by what right they derive from him their succession to the primacy. If the Pope of Rome claims the primacy because he is Peter's successor, he ought to exercise it over the Jews. Paul is here declared to be the chief apostle of the Gentiles; yet they deny that he was bishop of Rome. Therefore, if the Pope would enter into the possession of his primacy, let him assemble Churches from the Jews. For we ought to acknowledge as an apostle him who, by the decree of the Holy Spirit and by the consent of the whole apostolic college, has been publicly proclaimed one. Those who transfer that right to Peter overturn both human and divine ordination. It is unnecessary to explain the well-known metaphor in the words *circumcision* and *uncircumcision* for Jews and Gentiles.

8. *He that wrought effectually*. He declares that the province assigned to him was his by right, for the Lord had displayed His power in his ministry. Now such a manifestation of the divine power, as we have often seen, is like a seal to sign the certainty of, and to confirm, his teaching office. Whether Paul relates God's effectual working to the result of his preaching or to the graces of the Holy Spirit which were then given to believers, is doubtful. I do not take it as the mere outcome but as spiritual power and efficacy, which he has mentioned elsewhere (I Cor. 2.4). The sum of it is that it was no idle bargain that the apostles had arranged among themselves, but a decision which God had sealed.

9. *And when they perceived the grace*. He shows up in its true colours the arrogant contempt of those who cared nothing for the grace of God in him which had won the admiration and respect of the first apostles. For it would be insupportable for them to pretend to be ignorant of what the apostles had seen from the start. This cautions us to yield to the grace of God wherever it is seen, unless we want to fight against the Holy Spirit, who does not wish His gifts to be idle. The grace which the apostles saw had been given to Paul and Barnabas moved them to confirm the fellowship of their ministry.

James and Cephas. I have already said that James was the son of Alphaeus. He could not be the brother of John, whom Herod had killed a little earlier. And that he should be one of the disciples raised above the apostles would be to my mind quite absurd. Luke also shows that he held the primacy among the apostles and ascribes to him the summing up and decision of the case in the Council (Acts 15.13) and afterwards mentions that all the elders of the Church at Jerusalem met with him (Acts 21.18). When he says that *they seemed to be pillars* he is not speaking contemptuously but quoting the general opinion and arguing from this that their acts ought not to be lightly set aside. In a question relating to position, it is surprising that James should be put before Peter. But the reason perhaps is that he presided over the Church at Jerusalem. As to the word 'pillar', we know that, from the nature of things, those who excel in talents or wisdom or other gifts, possess also greater authority. And in the Church of God he who has the greater grace ought to receive the higher honour. It argues ingratitude, even impiety, not to worship the Spirit of God wherever He appears in His gifts. And as a people must not lack a pastor, so the assembly of pastors requires a controller (*moderator*). But always let the rule be followed that he who is first is like a servant.

10. *That we should remember the poor.* It seems that the brethren who were in Judaea laboured under extreme poverty; otherwise they would not have been a charge on other Churches. This may have been caused partly by the various calamities that befell the whole nation and partly by the cruel rage of their own countrymen by whom they were daily stripped of their goods. It was only fair that they should receive help from the Gentiles, who owed them the Gospel, an incomparable blessing. Paul says that he faithfully performed what the apostles had asked of him. And thus he deprives his adversaries of their excuse.

But when Peter came to Antioch, I resisted him to the face, because he was worthy of blame. For before that certain came from James, he did eat with the Gentiles: but when they came, he drew back and separated himself, fearing them that were of the circumcision. And the rest of the Jews dissembled likewise with him; insomuch that Barnabas also was carried away with their dissimulation. But when I saw that they walked not uprightly, according to the truth of the gospel, I said unto Peter before them all, If thou, being a Jew, livest as do the Gentiles, and not as do the Jews, why compellest thou the Gentiles to live as do the Jews? We being Jews by nature, and not sinners of the Gentiles, knowing that a man is not justified by the works of the law, but only through the faith of Jesus Christ, even we have believed in Jesus Christ, that we might be justified by the faith of Christ, and not by the works of the law: because by the works of the law shall no flesh be justified.
(11-16)

11. *When Peter came.* Whoever intelligently considers all the circumstances will, I hope, agree with me in thinking that this happened before the apostles had decided that the Gentiles should not be worried about ceremonies. For Peter would have shrunk from clashing with James or those sent by him, after the verdict had been passed. But now Paul had to go even further to affirm his Gospel in the face of Peter's dissimulation. At first he said that the certainty of his Gospel was not at all dependent on Peter and the apostles, so as to stand or fall by their judgment. Secondly, he said that it had been approved by all without any exception or contradiction, and especially by those who were universally admitted to hold the highest place. Now, as I have said, he goes further, and says that he had blamed Peter for inclining to the other side; and he uses this opportunity to explain the cause of the dispute. From this we see how firm his doctrine was; he not only obtained their willing subscription to it, but steadfastly maintained it against Peter and came off victorious. What reason could there now be for hesitating to receive it as certain and invincible truth?

At the same time Paul deals with another slander: that he was an ordinary disciple, far below the rank of an apostle. For the reproof was a sign of his equality. I agree, of course, that the highest and the lowest are alike to be reproved, and so it does not follow that he who reproves another must be his equal; for this freedom in the lesser towards the greater is allowed by God. But the nature of the reproof deserves notice. Paul did not simply reprove Peter, as one Christian towards another, but he did it officially, as the phrase is; that is, by the right of the apostolic office (*persona*) that he bore.

And here the Roman Papacy is struck down by another thunderbolt. In particular, it is a reproof of the impudence of the Roman Antichrist in claiming that he need not give any reasons for his actions and so exempting himself from the judgment of the universal Church. Without recklessness, without unlawful boldness, but in the exercise of the power granted him by God, this one man reproves Peter in the presence of the whole Church, and Peter obediently submits to correction. The whole debate on those two points was nothing less than the overthrow of the tyrannical primacy which the Romanists prate was founded on divine right. If they wish to have God as their founder, they must write a new Bible. If they do not wish to have Him as an open opponent, these two chapters of the Holy Scriptures must be wiped out.

Because he was worthy of blame. The Greek participle signifies 'blamed'; but I have no doubt that the word was put in place of a noun, for one who deserved a just reproof. Chrysostom's interpretation that the complaint and accusation had first been raised by others is very weak. It was customary for the Greeks to give their participles the force of nouns, and everyone must see that this agrees with this passage. Hence it is easy to see how inept was the invention of Jerome and Chrysostom, who thought that this was a sort of play, pre-arranged and acted by the apostles before the people. They are not supported by the phrase κατὰ πρόσωπον which means that 'to the face', as they say, or 'being present', Peter was chastised and put to silence. Chrysostom's idea that, for the sake of avoiding scandal, they would have talked in private if they had had any differences, is frivolous. For other less serious scandals had to be subordinated to the worst of all, that the Church would be rent, that Christian liberty was in danger, that the grace of Christ was overthrown. This public sin had to be corrected.

The argument on which Jerome chiefly depends is extremely weak. 'Why should Paul,' he asks, 'condemn in another what he takes praise for in himself? For he boasts that to the Jews he became as a Jew' (I Cor. 9.20). I reply that what Peter did was very different. Paul accommodated himself to the Jews only so far as was consistent with the doctrine of liberty. Hence he refused to circumcise Titus, that the truth of the Gospel might not be hurt. But Peter judaized in such a way as to force the Gentiles into slavery and at the same time to undermine Paul's doctrine as if the matter had been already settled. He did not, therefore, keep within the proper limits. For he was more desirous to please than to edify, and looked more to what would gratify the Jews than to what would be expedient for the whole body. Augustine judges more truly in asserting that this was no previously arranged plan, but that Paul opposed the sinful and out-of-place dissimulation of Peter from Christian zeal, in that he saw it would be injurious to the Church.

12. *For before that certain came.* The background of the case is here described. For the sake of the Jews, Peter had withdrawn from the Gentiles so as to drive them from the communion of the Church unless they renounced the liberty of the Gospel and submitted to the yoke of the law. Had Paul been silent here, his whole teaching would have fallen, all the edification his ministry had achieved would have been overthrown. It was therefore necessary that he should rise manfully and fight fiercely. Here we see how cautiously we should moderate our obedience to men, lest an undue desire to please or a dread of giving offence should turn us from the right path. If this could happen to Peter, how much more easily to us, if we are not very careful!

14. *But when I saw that they walked not uprightly.* Some expound

this of the Gentiles, who were perplexed by Peter's example and began to give way. But it fits in better if we understand it of Peter and Barnabas and their followers. The proper approach to the truth of the Gospel was to unite the Gentiles with the Jews in such a way that true doctrine should not be hurt. But to bind the consciences of the godly by an obligation to keep the law and to bury the doctrine of liberty in silence was to purchase unity too dearly.

Paul here uses *the truth of the gospel* in the same sense as before and contrasts it with the disguise with which Peter and the others deformed the Gospel. Accordingly, the struggle was undoubtedly a serious one for Paul. They were perfectly agreed about doctrine; but since Peter now disregarded doctrine and yielded too submissively to the Jews, he is accused of wavering. There are some who excuse Peter on another ground, that, as the apostle of the circumcision, he was bound to care more for the salvation of the Jews. And yet at the same time they admit that Paul also was right to plead the cause of the Gentiles. But it is foolish to defend what the Holy Spirit has condemned by the mouth of Paul. This was no human business matter but involved the purity of the Gospel, which was in danger of being contaminated by Jewish leaven.

Before them all. This example teaches us that those who have sinned publicly must be chastised publicly, so far as it concerns the Church. The aim is that their sin may not, by remaining unpunished, do harm by its example. And elsewhere (I Tim. 5.20) Paul expressly says that this should be observed in regard to elders, because the office they hold makes their bad example more harmful. It was especially useful that the good cause which concerned them all should be frankly defended in the presence of the people, so that Paul might make it quite clear that he did not shrink from the light.

If thou, being a Jew. Paul's speech to Peter consists of two parts. In the first he blames him for his injustice to the Gentiles in forcing them to keep the law, from which he himself wished to be exempted. For apart from every man being bound to keep the law that he lays down for others, Peter sinned more grievously by coercing the Gentiles into Judaism, while he, a Jew, gave himself liberty. For the law was given to Jews, not to Gentiles. So he argues from the less to the greater.

Moreover, Peter's manner of coercion was very harsh and violent, for he refused to have fellowship with the Gentiles unless they were willing to accept the yoke of the law, and this was an unjust condition. Indeed, the whole force of the reproof lies in this word, a fact which neither Chrysostom nor Jerome has noticed. The use of ceremonies for edification was free so long as believers were not deprived of their liberty or laid under any necessity from which the Gospel releases them.

15. *We being Jews by nature.* To some, I know, this seems an anthypophora,[1] as if Paul, speaking for his opponent, forestalls his objection that the Jews had more privileges, as one says. Not that they would claim exemption from the law. For it would have been quite absurd that they to whom the law was given should claim this: though it was right that there should be some distinguishing marks between them and the Gentiles. I do not entirely reject, nor, as will soon appear, do I altogether adopt this interpretation. Others take it as representing Paul's own statement, thus: 'If you were to lay the burden of the law upon the Jews it would be more reasonable, since it is theirs by inheritance.' But nor does this explanation fit in.

Therefore we proceed rather to the second part of his speech, which begins with an anticipation. For there was a distinction between Jews and Gentiles, in that the one were profane and impure, whereas the other were holy, inasmuch as God had chosen them for His people. And the Jews might fight for this superiority. But by a shrewd anticipation Paul turns it to the opposite conclusion. If the Jews, with all their distinctions, were forced to flee to the faith of Christ, how much more necessary was it that the Gentiles should seek salvation through faith? Paul's meaning therefore is: 'We who seem to excel others, who by the benefit of the covenant have always been near to God, even we found no way of obtaining salvation but by believing in Christ. Why then should we lay down another way for the Gentiles? For if the law were necessary or profitable for salvation to its observers, it must have been especially so to us to whom it was given. But if we left it and withdrew to Christ, much less ought the Gentiles to be urged to submit to it.'

The word *sinner* signifies here, as often elsewhere, a profane person or one who is lost and alienated from God. Such were the Gentiles, who had no fellowship with God; whereas the Jews were by adoption the children of God and therefore set apart to holiness. When he says, 'by nature', he does not mean that they were naturally free from the corruption of the human race; for David, who was a descendant of Abraham, confesses that he was begotten of impure seed (Ps. 51.5); but the corruption of nature which bound them had been met by the remedy of sanctifying grace. Now, as the promise made the blessing hereditary, so this benefit is called natural; just as, in Romans, he says that they were sprung from a holy root (11.16).

Therefore, when he says, *we are Jews by nature*, it is equivalent to saying, 'We are born holy; not indeed by our own merit, but because God has chosen us to be His people. We, then, who were by nature Jews, what have we done? We have believed in Jesus Christ. What

[1] Counter-allegation.

37

was the purpose of our believing? That we might be justified by the
faith of Christ. For what reason? Because we were convinced that
a man cannot achieve righteousness by the works of the law.' From
the nature and effect of faith, therefore, he reasons that the Jews are
in no degree justified by the law. For, just as those who want to
establish their own righteousness have not submitted to the righteousness of God, so, on the contrary, those who believe in Christ confess
that they are sinners and renounce the righteousness of works. This
already involves the main question; or rather, in this single proposition
nearly the whole controversy is contained. We must therefore examine
the passage more carefully.

The first thing to be noticed is that we must seek righteousness by
the faith of Christ, because we cannot be justified by works. The
question now is, what is meant by *the works of the law*? The Papists,
misled by Origen and Jerome, think, and in fact assert definitely,
that the dispute relates to shadows and accordingly interpret the
works of the law as ceremonies, as if Paul were not discussing the free
righteousness given us by Christ. For they see no absurdity in maintaining that no man is justified by the works of the law and yet also
that we are accounted righteous in the sight of God by the merits of
works. In short, they hold that this does not refer to moral works.
But the context shows clearly that the moral law is also comprehended
in these words, for almost everything that Paul adds relates to the
moral rather than the ceremonial law. Then again, he continually
contrasts the righteousness of the law to the free acceptance with which
God is pleased to favour us.

But our opponents object that the term 'works' would have been
used without an addition if Paul had not intended to limit it to a
particular kind. I reply that there is an excellent reason for this expression; for if a man were to excel all the angels in holiness, no
reward would be due to works save because God had promised it.
Therefore, that perfect obedience to the law is righteousness and
carries the reward of eternal life derives from God, who declares that
they who have fulfilled it shall live. We shall treat this point more
fully later in its own place. Moreover, the controversy with the Jews
was on the law. Paul therefore prefers to fight hand to hand and to
carry the attack into their own camp rather than harry them here and
there, which might seem like evasion or distrust of his cause. Accordingly he determines to debate about the law.

Their second objection is that the problem was only about ceremonies. This we allow. Why then, they say, should Paul pass from
a particular to the whole? This was the sole cause of the mistake of
Origen and Jerome. They did not think it consonant that, while the

false apostles were contending about ceremonies alone, Paul should cover a wider field. But they did not consider that the very reason for his disputing so keenly was that the doctrine had more serious consequences than at first appeared. Paul was worried not so much about ceremonies being observed as that the confidence and glory of salvation should be transferred to works. Just as, in the dispute over forbidding flesh on certain days, we do not so much regard the importance of the prohibition itself as the snare which is set for consciences. Paul therefore is not wandering from the point when he begins a disputation on the law as a whole, whereas the false apostles were arguing only about ceremonies. Their object in pressing ceremonies was that men might seek a salvation in the observance of the law, which they made out to be a meritorious service. Therefore Paul opposes to them the grace of Christ alone, and not the moral law. And yet this wider discussion does not occupy the whole of the epistle; he comes at length to the specific question of ceremonies. But as the heart of the problem was whether righteousness is to be obtained by works or by faith, this had first to be settled. The Papists today do not like us forcing from them the acknowledgment that men are justified by faith alone; and so they reluctantly admit that the works of the law include moral works. Many of them, however, imagine that by quoting Jerome's gloss they have put up a good defence; but the context will show that the words relate also to the moral law.

16. *But by the faith of Jesus Christ.* He does not merely mean that ceremonies or works of any kind are insufficient without the aid of faith, but he meets their denial with an exclusive statement, as if he had said, 'Not by works but by the faith of Christ alone.' Otherwise his statement would have been trivial and irrelevant. For the false apostles did not reject Christ or faith, but demanded that ceremonies should be joined with them. Had Paul admitted this conjunction, they would have been perfectly at one and therefore he would not have needed to trouble the Church with this unpleasant argument. Let it therefore remain settled that this proposition is exclusive, that we are justified in no other way than by faith, or, which comes to the same thing, that we are justified by faith alone.

From this it is clear how foolish the present day Papists are to quarrel with us about the word 'only', as if we had invented it. Paul was unacquainted with the theology of the Papists, who declare that a man is justified by faith and yet place a part of righteousness in works. Of such semi-righteousness Paul knew nothing. For when he tells us that we are justified by faith because we cannot be justified by works, he takes for granted what is true, that we cannot be justified through the righteousness of Christ unless we are poor and destitute of our own righteousness. Consequently we have to ascribe either nothing or everything to faith or to works. As to the word 'justification' and the way in which faith is the cause of it, we shall see later.

No flesh shall be justified. He had already appealed to the consciences of Peter and the others. Now he confirms it more fully by asserting that it is even so: by the works of the law no mortal will obtain righteousness. The foundation of free righteousness is when we are stripped of our own righteousness. Moreover, when he asserts that no mortal is justified it amounts to this, that all mortals are excluded from the righteousness of the law and that none can possibly reach it.

> *But if, while we sought to be justified in Christ, we ourselves also were found sinners, is Christ a minister of sin? God forbid. For if I build up again those things which I destroyed, I prove myself a transgressor. For I through the law died unto the law. That I might live unto God, I have been crucified with Christ; and it is no longer I that live, but Christ liveth in me: and that life which I now live in the flesh I live in the faith which is in the Son of God, who loved me, and gave himself up for me. I do not make void the grace of God: for if righteousness is through the law, then Christ died for nought.* (17-21)

17. *If, while we sought to be justified.* He now returns to the Galatians. We must beware of connecting this sentence to the one before, as if it were part of the speech to Peter; for what need was there to speak like this to Peter? Nevertheless, this fact has little or no relevance to the matter, and therefore let everyone choose as he will. Moreover, some (Chrysostom among them) read it affirmatively and take it to mean: 'If, while we seek to be justified in Christ, we are not yet fully righteous but still unclean, and if Christ is not sufficient for our righteousness, it follows that Christ is the minister of a teaching which leaves men in sin.' It is as if by this absurd proposition Paul accuses of blasphemy those who attribute a part of righteousness to the law. But as there at once follows the cry of horror that Paul uses only after questions, I think that he said it to remove the apparent absurdity. Therefore, in his customary way, he forestalls them with a question: 'If the consequence of the righteousness of faith is that even we Jews, who were sanctified from the womb, are reckoned guilty and polluted, shall we say that Christ is the author of sin, in that he makes the power of sin vigorous in his people?' This doubt arose from his having said that Jews, by believing in Christ, renounce the righteousness of the law. For even apart from Christ (*remoto Christo*), the Jews, in that they are separated from the ordinary pollution of the Gentiles, seem in a sense to be exempted from the number of sinners. The

grace of Christ places them on a level with the Gentiles and the remedy which is common to both shows that they both had the same disease. This is the force of the particle *also*. 'We ourselves also', he says, meaning not just any sort of men, but the Jews, who stood highest.

God forbid. He rightly rejects the thought. For Christ, by uncovering the sin that lay concealed, is not the minister of sin, as if, by depriving us of righteousness, He opened the gate to sin or even established its dominion. The Jews were mistaken in claiming any holiness for themselves outside Christ, for there was none. Hence the complaint, 'Did Christ come to take the righteousness of the law away from us, to change saints into sinners, to subject us to sin and guilt?' Paul denies it and rebuts the blasphemy with horror. Christ did not introduce sin; He unveiled it. He did not take away righteousness, but stripped the Jews of their false cloak.

18. *For if I build up again.* This reply is twofold. The first part is indirect and tells us that the idea is at variance with his whole teaching, for he had preached the faith of Christ in such a way as to connect with it the ruin and destruction of sin. For John teaches that Christ came not to build up but to destroy the kingdom of sin (I John 3.8). And so Paul declares here that in preaching the Gospel he had restored true righteousness that sin might be destroyed. It was therefore not at all consistent that the same person who destroyed sin should restore righteousness. It is by showing this absurdity that he repels the slander.

19. *For I through the law.* Now follows the direct reply, that we must not ascribe to Christ what is properly the task of the law. It was not necessary that Christ should annihilate the righteousness of the law, for the law itself slays its disciples. To paraphrase: 'You deceive unhappy men by the false notion that they must live by the law, and with that pretext you hold them under the law. And yet you are against the Gospel as annihilating the righteousness which we have by the law. But it is the law which forces us to die to itself; for by threatening our destruction it leaves us nothing but despair and thus drives us away from trusting in it.'

This passage will be better understood by comparing it with Rom. 7. There Paul describes superbly how that no man lives to the law but he to whom the law is dead, that is, is idle and without effect. For as soon as the law begins to live in us, it inflicts a fatal wound by which we die, and at the same time it breathes life into the man who is already dead to sin. Those who live to the law, therefore, have never felt the power of the law or even tasted what it is all about; for the law, when truly understood, makes us die to itself. This is the source of sin, not Christ.

41

To die to the law is to renounce it and to be freed from its dominion, so that we have no confidence in it and it does not hold us captive under the yoke of slavery. Or it might mean that, as it gives us all up to destruction, we find no life in it. This latter view fits in better. For he denies that Christ is the author of evil, because the law is more hurtful than helpful. The law bears within itself the curse which slays us. Hence it follows that the death brought about by the law is truly deadly. With it is contrasted another kind of death, in the life-giving fellowship of the cross of Christ. He says that he is crucified along with Christ that he might begin to live. The common punctuating of this passage obscures its meaning. They read: 'I through the law am dead to the law, that I might live to God.' But the context flows more smoothly thus: 'I through the law am dead to the law,' and then separately, 'That I might live to God I am crucified with Christ.'

That I might live to God. He shows that the kind of death which the false apostles seized on as a ground for quarrel is to be desired. For he means that we are dead to the law, not by any means that we may live to sin, but to God. 'To live to God' sometimes means to regulate our life according to His will, so as to study nothing else in our whole life than to be approved by Him. But here it means to live, so to say, the life of God. In this way the antitheses will agree. For in whatever sense we are said to die to sin, in the same sense we live to God. In short, Paul tells us that this death is not mortal but the origin of a better life. For God rescues us from the shipwreck of the law and by His grace restores us to another life. I will say nothing of other interpretations. This seems to me the apostle's real meaning.

When he says that he had been crucified with Christ, he is explaining how we, who are dead to the law, live to God. Engrafted into the death of Christ, we derive a secret energy from it, as the shoot does from the root. Again, Christ has nailed the hand-writing of the law, which was contrary to us, to His cross. Therefore, being crucified with Him, we are freed from all the curse and guilt of the law. To try and set that deliverance aside is to make the cross of Christ void. But let us remember that we are delivered from the yoke of the law only when we are made one with Christ, as the shoot draws its sap from the root only by growing into one nature.

It is no longer I. The word death is always hateful to man's mind. Having said that we are nailed to the cross along with Christ, he adds that this makes us alive. At the same time he explains what he meant by 'living to God'. He does not live by his own life but is animated by the secret power of Christ, so that Christ may be said to live and grow in him. For, as the soul quickens the body, so Christ imparts life to His members. A remarkable statement, that believers live outside themselves (*fideles extra se vivere*), that is, in Christ. This can only be if they hold true and genuine communication with Him (*veram cum ipso et substantialem communicationem*). Christ lives in us in two ways. The one consists in His governing us by His Spirit and directing all our actions. The other is what He grants us by participation in His righteousness, that, since we can do nothing of ourselves, we are accepted in Him by God. The first relates to regeneration, the second to the free acceptance of righteousness, and this is how I take the passage. But if anyone would rather apply it to both, I will willingly agree.

And the life which I now live in the flesh. There is hardly a sentence here which has not been torn apart by a variety of interpretations. Some expound 'flesh' as the depravity of corrupt nature. But Paul means by it simply the bodily life. For otherwise this objection might be made: 'You live a bodily life; and while this corruptible body performs its functions, while it is supported by food and drink, this is not the heavenly life of Christ. It is therefore an irrational paradox to assert that while you are living an ordinary human life, your life is not your own.' Paul replies that it consists in faith, which implies that it is a secret hidden from the senses of man. The life therefore which we obtain by faith is not visible to the eye, but is inwardly perceived in the conscience by the power of the Spirit. And so the bodily life does not prevent us from possessing the heavenly life by faith. 'He hath made us sit together in heavenly places in Christ Jesus' (Eph. 2.6). Again, 'Ye are fellow-citizens with the saints and of the household of God' (Eph. 2.19). And again, 'Our citizenship is in heaven' (Phil. 3.20). Paul's writings are full of similar statements, that we so live in the world that we also live in heaven; not only because our Head is there, but because, in virtue of union, we have a life in common with Him (John 14.1ff).

Who loved me. This is added to express the power of faith, for it would immediately occur to anyone to ask 'When does faith derive such power as to convey to us the life of Christ?' He therefore declares that the foundation (*hypostasis*) on which faith rests is the love and death of Christ; for it is from this that the effect of faith must be judged. How comes it that we live by the faith of Christ? Because He loved us and gave Himself for us. The love, I say, with which Christ embraced us, led Him to unite Himself to us. And this He completed by His death. By giving Himself for us, He suffered in our person (*in nostra persona passus est*). Moreover, faith makes us partakers of everything that it finds in Christ. This mention of love means the same that John said, 'Not that first we loved him, but he anticipated us by his love' (I John 4.9). For if any merit of ours had

moved Him to redeem us, such a cause would have been stated. But
now Paul ascribes the whole to love; it is therefore free. Let us observe
the order, 'He loved us and gave himself for us.' It is as if he said,
'He had no other reason for dying than because He loved us', and that
when we were enemies, as he says in Rom. 5.10.

He gave himself. No words can rightly express what this means;
for who can find language to declare the excellency of the Son of
God? Yet it is He who gave Himself as the price for our redemption.
Atonement, cleansing, satisfaction and all the fruit that we receive
from the death of Christ are included under the words 'gave himself
up'.

For me is very emphatic. It is not enough to regard Christ as having
died for the salvation of the world; each man must claim the effect
and possession of this grace for himself personally.

21. *I do not reject.* There is great weight in this word, for how
dreadful is the ingratitude of despising the grace of God, so wonderful
in itself and obtained at such a price. Yet he accuses the false apostles
of this sacrilege, for they were not satisfied with Christ alone but
introduced other aids for salvation. For unless we renounce all
others and embrace Christ alone, we reject the grace of God. And
what is left to a man who refuses the grace of God and makes himself
unworthy of it?

For if righteousness. *Gratis* (for nothing) here means 'in vain', that
is, there would have been no value in the death of Christ, or Christ
would have died without any reward. For the reward of His death
is that He has reconciled us to the Father by making atonement for
our sins. Hence it follows that we are justified by His grace, and
therefore not by works. The Papists interpret this of the ceremonial
law. But who cannot see that it covers the whole law? For it is as if
Paul had said, 'If we could produce a righteousness of our own,
Christ has suffered in vain. For He suffered to procure it for us; and
why should we need to get from elsewhere what we could give ourselves? If the death of Christ is our redemption, then we were captives;
if it is payment, then we were debtors; if it is atonement, we were
guilty; if it is cleansing, we were unclean. And so, on the other hand,
he who ascribes his cleansing, pardon, atonement, righteousness or
deliverance to works makes void the death of Christ.

Here, perhaps, someone will object that this argument is of no
weight against those who join the grace of Christ to works; which
no one doubts is what the false apostles did. These two doctrines are
coexistent: that righteousness is by the law, and that we are redeemed
by the death of Christ. I agree, if we concede that a part of righteousness is obtained by works and a part comes from grace. But such a

doctrine (*theologia*) was unknown to Paul, as may easily be proved. His argument against his opponents is either apt or foolish and wrong. If any blasphemer dares to slander him, a powerful defence is at hand, for to be reckoned righteous in the sight of God is not what we men imagine, but what is absolutely perfect.

But we are not now called to plead for Paul against blasphemers who dare to speak against the Holy Spirit. We are concerned with the Papists. They ridicule us when we follow Paul's reasoning that if righteousness is from works, Christ died in vain. They think they have a fine reply, which their Sophists have furnished them with: that Christ merited for us the first grace, that is, the opportunity for meriting, and that the merit of His death concurs with the satisfactions of works for the daily pardon of sins. Let them ridicule Paul, whose teaching we follow. They must refute him before they can refute us. We know that he had to do with men who did not entirely exclude the grace of Christ but ascribed the half of salvation to works. In opposition to them, he argues that if righteousness is by the law, Christ died in vain, and therefore he does not allow one drop of righteousness to works. The Papists differ from them no whit, and so we are free to take over Paul's argument to refute them.

CHAPTER THREE

O foolish Galatians, who did bewitch you, that ye should not obey the truth, before whose eyes Jesus Christ was openly set forth crucified? This only would I learn from you, Received ye the Spirit from the works of the law, or from the hearing of faith? Are ye so foolish? having begun in the Spirit, are ye now perfected in the flesh? Did ye suffer so many things in vain? if it be indeed in vain. He therefore that supplieth to you the Spirit, and worketh miracles among you, doeth he it by the works of the law, or by the preaching of faith? (1-5)

1. *O foolish Galatians.* He mixes, or rather, inserts, a rebuke into his teaching. Some may be surprised that he did not keep it for the end; but without doubt the very important statement he has made roused him to an outburst of passion. For when we hear that the Son of God, with all His blessings, is rejected and that His death is esteemed as nothing, what godly mind will not break out into indignation? He therefore pronounces those who let themselves be involved in such a sacrilege to have been ἀνόητοι, that is, out of their minds. He rebukes them not only for having allowed themselves to be deceived, but for having been carried away, as it were, by some sort of magical enchantment, a far more serious thing. He hints that their fall was more a matter of madness than of folly.

Some think that Paul is referring to the character of this nation, that they had sprung from barbarians and it was difficult to train them. But I think rather that he is simply referring to the thing itself. It is akin to the supernatural that when living in such a clearness of the Gospel they should open the door to the delusions of Satan. He does not only say that they were bewitched and out of their minds because they did not obey the truth but because, when they had been taught so surely, so clearly, so friendly, so powerfully, they so soon fell away. Erasmus preferred the word 'believe'. I do not reject that outright, but my translation fits the context better, since Paul does not accuse them of having rejected the Gospel from the outset but of not having persevered in obedience.

Before whose eyes. As I have already suggested, this is meant to show up their guilt. For the better Christ was known, the more grievous was their crime in forsaking Him. Therefore he tells them that his teaching was so clear that it was not so much mere teaching (*nuda doctrina*) as the living and express image of Christ. They had a know-

46

ledge that could almost have given them a sight of Him. Augustine's interpretation is harsh and far from Paul's intention. He says that Christ was pre-scribed, as if He were to be thrust out from possession. Others read pro-scribed (*proscriptus*), which, if taken as 'openly proclaimed' would not be out of place. The Greeks borrow from this verb the word προγράμματα, for boards on which property for sale was advertised, so that everyone should see it. But the participle *painted* is less ambiguous, and in my opinion, the most appropriate. To show how forceful his preaching had been, Paul first compares it with a picture which showed them the portrait of Christ to the life.

Then, not satisfied with this comparison, he adds, *Christ hath been crucified among you.* By this he suggests that the actual sight of Christ's death could not have affected them more than his preaching. The way some take it, that the Galatians had crucified the Lord afresh and made Him a mockery when they had withdrawn from the purity of the Gospel or, at least, had hearkened and trusted to impostors who crucified Him, seems to me strained. Therefore we will keep to this meaning, that Paul's doctrine had taught them about Christ in such a manner that it was as if He had been shown to them in a picture, even crucified among them. Such a representation could not have been effected by any eloquence or tricks of oratory, had not that power of the Spirit been present, of which he spoke in both the epistles to the Corinthians.

Let those who want to discharge the ministry of the Gospel aright learn not only to speak and declaim but also to penetrate into consciences, so that men may see Christ crucified and that His blood may flow. When the Church has such painters as these she no longer needs wood and stone, that is, dead images, she no longer requires any pictures. And certainly images and pictures were first admitted to Christian temples when, partly, the pastors had become dumb and were mere shadows (*idola*), partly, when they uttered a few words from the pulpit so coldly and superficially that the power and efficacy of the ministry were utterly extinguished.

2. *This only I wish.* He now confirms his cause with fresh arguments. The first is drawn from their experience, when he reminds them what sort of reception the Gospel first had among them. When they heard the Gospel, they received the Spirit. It was not to the law therefore, but to faith that they owed the admission of this blessing. Peter uses the same argument in his defence before the brethren for having baptized uncircumcised persons (Acts 11.4ff). Paul and Barnabas did the same in the debate which was held at Jerusalem on this subject (Acts 15.12). They were therefore certainly ungrateful for not abiding in the doctrine, by the blessing of which they had

received the Holy Spirit. That he gives them a chance to reply is a sign of greater confidence rather than of doubt. For they were convicted by their own experience and forced to acknowledge that it was true.

Faith is here put by metonymy for the Gospel, which is called elsewhere the doctrine of faith (Rom. 3.27), because it exhibits to us the free grace of God in Christ without the merits of works. *The Spirit* I take here for the grace of regeneration, which is common to all believers; though I do not mind if anyone understands it of the special gifts with which the Lord then adorned the preaching of the Gospel.

It may be objected that the Spirit was not given to all in this respect. I reply that it was enough for Paul's purpose that the Galatians knew that the power of the Holy Spirit in His Church had appeared in Paul's teaching and that believers were severally endowed with the graces of the Spirit for the common edification. It may again be objected that those graces were not sure signs of adoption and so do not apply to the present question. I reply that it was enough that the Lord had confirmed Paul's doctrine by the visible gifts of His Spirit. But the other is more straightforward, that they had been distinguished by the common blessing of adoption before those impostors had brought in their additions. As also he says in Eph. 1.13, 'After that ye heard the gospel of the truth of God, ye were sealed with the Spirit, etc.'

3. *Are ye so foolish?* Here also expositors are doubtful and divided as to what he means by *the Spirit* and *the flesh*. In my opinion, he alludes to what he had said about the Spirit, and we might paraphrase: 'As the teaching of the Gospel brought to you the Holy Spirit, your beginning was spiritual. But now you have fallen into a bad state and may be said to have fallen from the Spirit into the flesh.' By the flesh he means either outward and fading things, like ceremonies (particularly when they are separated from Christ), or dead and weak doctrine. And it was all wrong that their progress should not match their splendid beginning.

4. *Have ye suffered so many things?* This is a different argument. Having suffered so much for the sake of the Gospel, were they now to lose it all at one stroke? He asks them reproachfully if they were willing to lose the spoils of the many wonderful battles they had undergone for the faith. If what Paul had delivered to them had not been the true faith, then what they had suffered had been in the rash defence of a bad cause. But they had experienced the presence of God amidst their persecutions. Therefore he charges the false apostles with malice in despoiling the Galatians of such valuable honours. To soften his severity, however, he adds, 'If it be yet in vain'; and so in-

spires their minds with the expectation of something better and rouses them to repentance. For the purpose of all chastisement is not to drive men to despair but to encourage them to a better way.

5. *He therefore that ministereth.* He is not now speaking of the grace of regeneration but of other gifts of the Spirit. For the order itself shows that this is a new argument; for he starts on another argument. He tells them that all the gifts of the Holy Spirit in which they excelled are the fruit of the Gospel, of that Gospel which had been preached among them by his own mouth. Hence they despoiled themselves of those gifts when they left the Gospel and flitted to another kind of teaching. Therefore, as much as they valued the gift (to which the apostle here adds powers, that is, miracles), they ought also to take care to hold fast to the Gospel.

Even as Abraham believed God, and it was reckoned unto him for righteousness. Know therefore that they which be of faith, the same are sons of Abraham. And the scripture, foreseeing that God would justify the Gentiles by faith, preached the gospel beforehand unto Abraham, saying, In thee shall all the nations be blessed. So then they which be of faith are blessed with the faithful Abraham. (6-9)

Having refuted them by facts and experience, he now comes to testimonies from Scripture. First, he brings forward the example of Abraham. Although arguments drawn from examples are not always conclusive, this is one of the most powerful, since neither in the subject nor in the person is there any basis for exception. For there are not many ways to righteousness, and so Abraham is called the father of all believers because he is a pattern common to all. In fact, the universal rule for obtaining righteousness has been prescribed for us in his person.

6. *Even as Abraham.* The conjunctive phrase 'but rather' should be supplied, for having put a question, he determined to remove at once every ground for hesitation. For the words 'even as' refer only to the verse before, that they had received the ministration of the Spirit and of miracles from the hearing of faith. As if he had said that in the grace bestowed on them there was evident a similarity to Abraham.

Believed God. By this quotation he proves both here and in the fourth chapter of Romans that men are justified by faith; for the faith of Abraham was accounted to him for righteousness. We must say briefly what Paul here means first by faith, secondly by righteousness, and thirdly why faith is regarded as the cause of justification. Faith is not taken for any kind of conviction which men may have of the truth of God. If Cain a hundred times had had faith in the God who

denounced punishment against him, it would have availed nothing
for the obtaining of righteousness. Abraham was justified by believing
because, when he received from God a promise of fatherly kindness,
he embraced it as certain. Faith therefore has a relation and respect
to such a Word of God as may enable men to rest and trust in God.

As to the word *righteousness*, we must note Moses' expression.
When he says that it was reckoned to Abraham in righteousness that
he believed, he means that he is righteous who is reckoned as such in
the sight of God. Now, since men have not righteousness laid up in
them, they obtain it by imputation, in that God accepts their faith in
lieu of righteousness. We are therefore said to be justified by faith,
not in that faith infuses into us a habit or quality, but because we are
accepted by God.

But why is faith given such honour as to be called the cause of our
justification? First, we must know that it is only an instrumental
cause. Properly speaking, our righteousness is nothing but God's
free acceptance of us, on which our salvation is founded. But as the
Lord, by testifying His love and grace in the Gospel, communicates
to us that righteousness of which I have spoken, we receive it by faith.
And thus, when we ascribe man's justification to faith, we are not
dealing with the principal cause but only indicating the way in which
men arrive at true righteousness. For this righteousness is not a quality
inherent in men but the pure gift of God and is possessed by faith only.
And that not even as a reward justly due to faith, but because we
receive by faith what God freely gives. All such expressions as the
following come to the same thing: We are justified by the grace of
God; Christ is our righteousness; the mercy of God is the cause of our
righteousness; righteousness has been procured for us by the death
and resurrection of Christ; righteousness is bestowed on us through
the Gospel; we obtain righteousness by faith.

This shows the childishness of the error of trying to reconcile the
propositions that we are justified at the same time by faith and by
works; for he who is righteous by faith is destitute and empty of his
own righteousness and rests on the grace of God alone. And this is
why Paul in Romans concludes that Abraham could not glory before
God, for he had obtained righteousness by faith (Rom. 4.2). For it is
not said that faith was imputed to him as a part of righteousness but
just simply as righteousness. Hence his faith was truly in place of
righteousness for him. Besides, faith looks at nothing but the mercy
of God and Christ dead and risen. All merit of works is therefore
excluded from being a cause of justification when the whole is ascribed
to faith. For faith, inasmuch as it contains the free goodness of God,
Christ with all His blessings, the testimony of our adoption which is

given in the Gospel, is universally contrasted to the law, the merit of
works and human worth. The notion of the Sophists, that it is contrasted only to ceremonies, can be disproved quickly and without
difficulty from the context. Let us therefore remember that those
who are righteous by faith are righteous outside themselves, that is,
in Christ.

This will also refute the idle quibbling of some who evade Paul.
For Moses calls righteousness uprightness, and so he means simply
that Abraham was regarded as an upright man because he believed
God. Today Satan raises up similar giddy spirits who use the tool of
indirect slanders to undermine the certainty of Scripture. But Paul
knew that Moses was not giving grammar lessons to boys but was
speaking of God's decision, and he very properly took the word
righteousness theologically. For it is not in the way that goodness is
held in approbation among men that we are accounted righteous
before God, but only where we render perfect obedience to the law.
For righteousness is contrasted to the breaking of the law even in its
smallest detail; and because we do not have it from ourselves, God
gives it to us freely.

But here the Jews attack Paul for twisting the words of Moses to
suit his own purpose. For Moses is not treating of Christ or of eternal
life but is only speaking of an earthly promise. The Papists are not
very different from the Jews; for, though they do not dare to attack
Paul, they entirely destroy his intention. I reply that Paul takes for
granted what is an axiom for Christians, that whatever promises the
Lord made to Abraham were appendages of that first promise, 'I am
thy God, thy exceeding great reward, and in thy seed shall all nations
be blessed.' And so, when Abraham heard, 'Thy seed shall be as the
sand which is upon the seashore,' he did not confine himself to that
word but included it in the grace of adoption as a part in the whole.
And in the same way, every other promise was received by him as a
testimony of God's fatherly grace, from which he could apprehend
the trust of salvation. Unbelievers differ from the children of God in
that while they also enjoy the benefits of God, they devour them like
cattle and look no higher. The children of God, on the other hand,
knowing that all these benefits have been sanctified by the promises,
acknowledge in them God as their Father. They are always directed,
therefore, to the hope of eternal life, for they begin at the foundation,
that is, the faith of their adoption. Abraham was not justified merely
because he believed that God would multiply his seed, but because he
embraced the grace of God, trusting to the promised Mediator, in
whom, as Paul declares elsewhere, 'all the promises of God are Yea
and Amen' (II Cor. 1.20).

7. *Know ye therefore.* Or, 'ye know', for both readings fit the Greek ending. But it matters little which you read, for the meaning is the same, save that the old translation, which I have followed, has more force. He says that those are of faith who have renounced confidence in works and rely only on the promise of God. If anyone asks by what authority we give this interpretation, I say, by Paul's own word; for in Romans he writes thus, 'To him that worketh it is not given freely but paid as a wage. But to him that worketh not and no wage is due, his faith is reckoned for righteousness (Rom. 4.4-5). To be *of faith*, therefore, is to place one's righteousness and hope of salvation in the mercy of God. That such are the children of Abraham he concludes from the preceding statement. For if Abraham was justified by faith, those who wish to be his children must likewise stand firmly in faith. He has omitted one fact, which may easily be supplied, that there is no place in the Church for any man who is not a son of Abraham.

8. *And the scripture, foreseeing.* He now applies expressly to the Gentiles what he had said in general. The calling of the Gentiles was a new and extraordinary thing. There were doubts as to the way in which they would be called. Circumcision and the observation of the law seemed to be required or otherwise they would be shut out from participation in the covenant. But Paul shows, on the other hand, that by faith they also arrive at this blessing, and by faith they must be engrafted into the family of Abraham. How does he prove this? In that it is said, 'In thee shall all nations be blessed.' These words unquestionably mean that all must be blessed like Abraham, for he is the common model, even the rule. Now, he obtained the blessing by faith, and this is the same way for all.

The word *faithful* is very emphatic. For it is as if he had said that they are blessed, not with Abraham as circumcised, nor as endowed with the works of the law, nor as a Hebrew, nor as relying on his own worth, but with Abraham who by faith alone obtained the blessing. No personal quality is taken into account here, only faith. The word 'blessing' is used variously in Scripture; but here it means adoption into the inheritance of eternal life.

For as many as are of the works of the law are under a curse: for it is written, Cursed is every one which continueth not in all things that are written in the book of the law, to do them. Now that no man is justified by the law in the sight of God, is evident: for, The righteous shall live by faith; and the law is not of faith; but, He that doeth them shall live in them. Christ redeemed us from the curse of the law, having become a curse for us: for it is written, Cursed is every one that hangeth on a tree: that upon the Gentiles might come the blessing of Abraham through Christ Jesus; that we might receive the promise of the Spirit through faith. (10-14)

10. *For as many as are under the works of the law.*[1] It is an argument from contradictions, for the same fountain does not yield both hot and cold. The law holds all men under its curse. From the law, therefore, it is useless to seek a blessing. He calls them *of the works of the law* who put their trust for salvation in those works. Such modes of expression must always be interpreted by the state of the question. Now we know that the controversy here relates to the cause of righteousness. All who wish to be justified by the works of the law are declared to be liable to the curse. But how does he prove this? The sentence of the law is that all who have transgressed any part of the law are accursed. Let us now see if there is any man living who satisfies the law. It is certain that none has been or ever can be found. Every individual is here condemned. The minor and the conclusion are lacking, for the entire syllogism would run thus:

Whoever has come short in any part of the law is cursed.
All are held chargeable of this guilt.
Therefore all are cursed.

This argument of Paul's would not stand if we had sufficient strength to fulfil the law, for there would then be an inconsistency in the minor. Either Paul reasons badly or it is impossible for men to fulfil the law.

An opponent might at once object, 'I admit that all transgressors are accursed. What then? Men will be found who keep the law. For men have a free choice of good and evil.' But Paul here places beyond controversy what the Papists today regard as a detestable doctrine, that men are destitute of the power of keeping the law. And so he concludes boldly that all are cursed because all have been commanded to keep the law perfectly, and this is because, in the present corruption of our nature, the ability is wanting. Hence we conclude that it is accidental that the law should curse, though at the same time perpetual and inseparable. The blessing which it offers us is excluded by our depravity, so that only the curse remains.

11. *But that no man is justified by the law.* He again argues from a comparison of contradictories, thus:

[1] Note that in the Biblical passage Calvin translates *ex operibus* ('of the works'); here he says *sub operibus* ('under the works') and returns to *ex operibus* four lines down. Only the Amsterdam edition reads *ex* for *sub* in the second instance.

If we are justified by faith, then it is not by the law.

But we are justified by faith.

Therefore it is not by the law.

He proves the minor by a passage from Habakkuk, which is also quoted in Rom. 1.17. The major is proved by the difference in the mode of justification. The law justifies him who fulfils all its commands, whereas faith justifies those who are destitute of the merit of works and rely on Christ alone. To be justified by our own merit and by the grace of another are irreconcilable; the one is overthrown by the other. This is the argument as a whole; let us now attend to the separate clauses.

The just shall live by faith. As we expounded this passage in the Epistle to the Romans, it is unnecessary to repeat the exposition here. The prophet certainly opposes the proud confidence of the flesh to true faith. He declares that the just shall live by it, and he means, not that they are supported for a little while and liable to be overwhelmed by imminent storms, but that they shall continue to live and that even in the midst of death they shall not cease to live. There is therefore no substance in the gibes of those mockers who allege that the prophet uses the word faith more broadly than Paul does in this passage. By faith he simply means the quiet assurance of a conscience that relies on God alone. Therefore Paul uses this quotation aptly.

12. *And the law is not of faith.* The law certainly does not conflict with faith; otherwise God would be unlike Himself. But we must always return to the fact that Paul's language is adapted to these particular circumstances. The contradiction between the law and faith lies in the cause of justification. You will more easily unite fire and water than reconcile the two statements that men are justified by faith and by the law. The law is not of faith, that is, it has a method of justifying a man which is completely foreign to faith.

But the man that doeth them. The difference lies in the fact that when a man fulfils the law he is reckoned righteous by a legal righteousness. This he proves by a quotation from Moses. Now what is the righteousness of faith? He defined it in Rom. 10.9: 'If we believe that Christ died for our sins, etc.'

And yet it does not follow that faith is idle or that believers are set free from good works. For the present question is not whether believers ought to keep the law as far as they can (which is beyond all doubt), but whether they obtain righteousness by works; and this is impossible. Moreover, if anyone objects, 'Since God promises life to the doers of the law, why does Paul deny that they are righteous?' the answer is easy. None is righteous by the works of the law, because there is none who does them. We admit that the doers of the law, if there were any, would be righteous. But since that is a conditional agreement, all are excluded from life because none offers the righteousness that he ought. We must bear in mind what I have already said, that to do the law is not to obey it in part, but to fulfil everything that belongs to righteousness. And from such a perfection all are at the furthest remove.

13. *Christ redeemed us.* He had made all who are under the law subject to the curse. Hence the great difficulty that the Jews could not free themselves from the curse of the law. He solves the difficulty by putting forward the remedy. And this further confirms his purpose. For if we are saved because we have been freed from the curse of the law, then righteousness is not by the law. He next adds the way in which we are made free.

It is written, Cursed is everyone that hangeth on a tree. Christ was hanged. Therefore He came under the curse. But it is certain that He did not suffer that punishment on His own account. It follows therefore, either that He was crucified in vain or that our curse was laid upon Him that we might be delivered from it. Now he does not say that Christ was cursed, but something more, that He was a curse, signifying that the curse of all was placed on Him. If this seems harsh to anyone, let him be ashamed also of the cross of Christ, in the confession of which we glory. God was not ignorant of what death His Son would die when He pronounced, 'Cursed is everyone who hangs on a tree.'

But how does it happen, someone may object, that a beloved Son is cursed by His Father? I reply, there are two things to be considered, not only in the person of Christ, but even in His human nature. The one is that He was the unspotted Lamb of God, full of blessing and grace. The other is that He took our place and thus became a sinner and subject to the curse, not in Himself indeed, but in us; yet in such a way that it was necessary for Him to act in our name. He could not be outside God's grace, and yet He endured His wrath. For how could He reconcile Him to us if He regarded the Father as an enemy and was hated by Him? Therefore the will of the Father always reposed in Him. Again, how could He have freed us from the wrath of God if He had not transferred it from us to Himself? Therefore He was smitten for our sins and knew God as an angry judge. This is the foolishness of the cross and the wonder of angels, which not only exceeds but swallows up all the wisdom of the world.

14. *That upon the Gentiles.* He applies in greater detail to his purpose his statement that we are delivered from the curse of the law by Christ; that is, that the blessing promised to Abraham is founded on this and

proceeds from it to the Gentiles. If, to become the heirs of Abraham, the Jews have to be delivered from the law, what is to hinder the Gentiles from obtaining the same benefit? And if that blessing is in Christ alone, it is faith in Christ which makes us partakers of it.

That . . . the promise of the Spirit. I take the promise of the Spirit, according to the Hebrew idiom, as 'the spiritual promise'. Although the promise 'I will pour out my Spirit upon all flesh' (Joel 2.28) relates to the new testament, Paul is referring to another subject in this passage. The Spirit here seems to me to be contrasted to all outward things, not to ceremonies only, but to physical descent, and leaves no room for respect of persons. He shows from the nature of the promise that Jews are no different from Gentiles; for if it is spiritual, it is received by faith alone.

Brethren, I speak after the manner of men: Though it be but a man's covenant, yet when it hath been confirmed, no one maketh it void, or addeth thereto. Now to Abraham were the promises spoken, and to his seed. He saith not, And to seeds, as of many; but as of one, And to thy seed, which is Christ. Now this I say; A covenant confirmed beforehand by God, towards Christ, the law, which came four hundred and thirty years after, doth not disannul, so as to make the promise of none effect. For if the inheritance is of the law, it is no more of promise: but God hath granted it to Abraham by promise. (15-18)

15. *I speak after the manner of men.* By this expression he wanted to put them to shame. It is disgraceful and base that God should have less authority with us than a mortal man. In demanding that God's sacred covenant shall receive no less authority than is given to ordinary human agreements, he does not place God on a level with men. How great a distance there is between God and men is left for their consideration.

Though it be but a man's covenant. This is an argument from the less to the greater. Human contracts are regarded as binding; how much more what God has established? Moreover, where the Latin version reads *testamentum*, Paul's Greek word is διαθήκη. By this the Greeks mean more often 'testament', though also sometimes any sort of contract. In this latter sense, however, the plural is more general. It matters little in the present passage whether you translate it contract or testament. The case is different in the Epistle to the Hebrews, where the apostle undoubtedly refers to testaments (Heb. 9.7). But here I prefer to take it simply for the covenant which God made. For the simile from which the apostle argues would not apply so strictly to a testament as to a covenant. Therefore let us proceed on the assumption that the apostle reasons from human agreements to that solemn covenant which God made with Abraham. If human bargains are so firm that they must not be added to, how much more must this covenant remain inviolable?

16. *Now to Abraham*. Before pursuing his argument he says of the substance of the covenant that it rests on Christ alone. But if Christ is the foundation of the agreement, it follows that it is free; and this is also his meaning in the word *promise*. As the law has regard to men and their works, so the promise concerns the grace of God and faith.

He saith not, And to seeds. To prove that God is there speaking of Christ, he calls attention to the singular number as denoting some particular seed. I have often been surprised that Christians, when they saw this passage so impudently twisted by the Jews, did not withstand them more definitely, instead of passing it over lightly as if it were undisputed territory. And yet their objection is very plausible. For since זֶרַע, or 'seed', is a collective noun, Paul appears to reason unaptly when he contends that a single man is denoted by this word under which all the descendants of Abraham are comprehended in the passage already quoted, 'Thy seed shall be as the sand on the seashore and the stars of heaven.' And so, as if our error had been proved, they triumph over us haughtily.

I am the more surprised that our own side should have been silent, for we do not lack a firm defence to refute their slander. Among Abraham's own sons a division had already begun, in that one of them was cut off from the family. 'In Isaac shall thy seed be called.' Ishmael is not included. Let us come to the second step. Do the Jews admit that Esau's posterity is the blessed seed? No, they contend that their father, though the firstborn, was struck out. And how many nations have sprung from the stock of Abraham who have no share in this calling? The twelve patriarchs were in the end the twelve heads, not because they had descended from the line of Abraham, but because they were ordained by the special election of God. Since the ten tribes were carried away, how many thousands of them have so degenerated that they no longer have a place among the seed of Abraham? Lastly, the tribe of Judah was led into great testing, so that the true succession to the blessing remained among only a few people. And this has been predicted by Isaiah, 'Only a remnant shall be saved' (Isa. 10.21).

So far I have said nothing that the Jews themselves do not acknowledge. Let them answer me then: how is it that the thirteen tribes sprung from the twelve patriarchs were Abraham's seed rather than the Ishmaelites or the Edomites? Why do they alone claim that name and reject the others as a spurious seed? They will, no doubt, boast that they have obtained it by their own merit. Scripture, on the contrary, asserts that all depends on the calling of God. For we must constantly return to the prior choice, 'In Isaac shall thy seed be called' (Gen. 21.12). The uninterrupted succession of this choice must have been in force until Christ, for the Lord afterwards reiterated and so to say post-dated in the person of David the promise made to Abraham. Paul is therefore not relying on the singular to prove that this was said of one man but only to show that the word 'seed' denotes one who was not only born of Abraham according to the flesh but had also been ordained for this by the calling of God. If the Jews deny this, they will only make themselves ridiculous by their obstinacy.

But as Paul also gathers from these words that an agreement had been made in Christ, or to Christ, let us investigate the force of that expression, 'In thy seed shall all nations be blessed.' The Jews quibble that a comparison is meant, as if the seed of Abraham were to be an example in all disastrous omens and prayers, whereas, on the contrary, to curse by Sodom or Israel is to use the word 'Sodom' or 'Israel' in forms of cursing. This, I admit, is sometimes so, but not always. For to bless oneself by God has quite a different meaning, as the Jews themselves allow. Therefore, since the phrase is ambiguous and denotes sometimes a cause and sometimes a comparison, it must be explained by the context where it appears. It is certain that we are all cursed by nature. The blessing was promised to all nations by the hand of Abraham. Do all arrive at it indiscriminately? Certainly not; only those who are gathered to the Messiah. For it is when they are collected into one body under the command and leading of the Messiah that they become one people. Therefore whoever lays aside disputation and inquires into the truth will readily acknowledge that this is not a mere comparison but a cause. From this it follows that Paul had good ground for saying that the agreement was made in Christ or in respect to Christ.

17. *The law, which came four hundred and thirty years after.* If we believe Origen and Jerome and all the Papists, there is no difficulty in refuting this argument. Paul reasons thus: a promise was given to Abraham four hundred and thirty years before the law was produced. Hence the law which came after could not abolish the promise. Therefore he concludes that ceremonies are not necessary. But it may be objected that the sacraments were given to preserve the faith. Why then should Paul separate them from the promise? He does so in order to wage this controversy. He considers the ceremonies in relation to something higher, that is, the effect of justification which the false apostles ascribed to them and their obligation on the conscience. Indeed, he uses ceremonies as an opportunity to discuss the whole subject of faith and works. If the point at issue had no connexion

with obtaining righteousness, with the merit of works or with en-
snaring the conscience, ceremonies would be consistent with the
promise.

What then lies behind this abolition of the promise which the
apostle attacks? Simply that the impostors denied that salvation is
freely promised to men and received by faith. But, as we shall presently
see, they insisted on ceremonies as necessary to deserve salvation. I
return to Paul's own words. 'The law', he says, 'is later than the
promise; therefore it does not revoke it. For an agreement once
ratified must remain unbreakable.' I again repeat that if you do not
understand that the promise is free, this statement will be quite empty,
for the law and the Gospel are not at variance except that, in regard to
justification, either the law justifies a man by the merit of works or
the promise bestows righteousness freely. This is made abundantly
clear when he calls it a *covenant* founded on Christ.

But here the Papists rise to do battle; and they are ready to evade
this argument. 'We no longer require the old ceremonies,' they will
say, 'Let us put them on one side. Nevertheless, a man is justified by
the moral law. For this law was created along with man and preceded
God's covenant with Abraham. Therefore unless Paul's reasoning is
frivolous it holds good only against ceremonies.' I reply, that Paul
took into account this fact, that no reward is due to works except
through the covenant with God. Thus, even though we were to
grant that the law justifies, yet before the law men could not merit
salvation by works since there was no covenant. I affirm nothing but
what the scholastic theologians allow. They do not teach that works
are meritorious of salvation through their intrinsic worth but by the
acceptance of God (as they say) and by reason of the covenant. Consequently, where no divine covenant, no testimony of acceptance
occurs, no works will suffice for righteousness. Therefore Paul's
argument is perfectly logical. He says that God made a twofold
covenant with men, the first through Abraham, the second through
Moses. The former was founded on Christ and so was free. And
therefore the law, which came after, could not bring salvation to men
apart from grace, for else it would make the promise of none effect.
That this is the meaning appears clearly from what immediately
follows.

18. *If the inheritance is of the law.* In case his opponents should
quibble that nothing was farther from their intention than to dissolve
or disannul God's covenant, he anticipates all their subterfuges and
asserts that salvation by the law and by the promise are contraries.
Who will dare to expound this only of ceremonies when Paul comprehends under it whatever opposes the free promise? Beyond all doubt

CC B   59

he excludes works of every kind. Thus in Rom. 4.14, 'if inheritance is by the law, faith is abolished and the promise made of none effect.' Why so? Because salvation would depend on the condition of satisfying the law. Therefore he immediately concludes that it is of faith, so that the promise might be sure. Let us carefully remember why, when the promise is compared with the law, the establishment of the one overturns the other: because the promise has respect to faith and the law to works. Faith receives what is freely given, but to works a reward is paid.

And he immediately adds that *God gave it to Abraham*, not by requiring some sort of reciprocal compensation, but by free promise. For if you take it as conditional, the word *gave* would be utterly inapplicable.

What then is the law? It was added because of transgressions, till the seed should come to whom the promise hath been made; and it was ordained through angels by the hand of a mediator. Now a mediator is not a mediator of one; but God is one. Is the law then against the promises of God? God forbid: for if there had been a law given which could make alive, verily righteousness would have been of the law. But the scripture hath shut up all things under sin, that the promise by faith of Jesus Christ might be given to them that believe. (19-22)

When we hear that the law is powerless to give justification, various thoughts immediately arise, that it is either useless, or opposed to God's covenant, or something of that sort. Indeed, it might occur to us, 'Why should we not say of the law what Jeremiah says of the new testament (Jer. 31.31), that it was given afterwards to correct the weakness of the earlier teaching?' Objections of this kind had to be explained if Paul wished to satisfy the Galatians. First he asks what is the use of the law? Since it came after the promise, it seems to have been intended to supply its defects; and certainly there was doubt whether the promise would have been ineffectual had it not been helped by the law. But we must note that Paul does not speak of the moral law only but of the whole ministry of Moses. The office peculiar to Moses consisted in prescribing a rule of life and ceremonies to be observed in the worship of God, and in adding promises and threats to them. That many promises concerning the free mercy of God and Christ and which belong to faith, are included there, is accidental and quite outside the comparison to be made between the law and the doctrine of grace. You will remember that the question is this: why, after a promise had been made, did Moses intervene with a new contract, that he who does these things shall live in them, but cursed be he that fulfilleth not these things? Was it to produce something better and more perfect?

19. *Because of transgressions.* The law has many uses, but Paul confines himself to one which serves his present purpose. He did not propose to inquire in how many ways the law is of advantage to men. Readers must be put on their guard on this matter; for I see many make the mistake of acknowledging no other use of the law than what is expressed here. But elsewhere Paul himself applies the precepts of the law to teaching and exhortation (II Tim. 3.16). Therefore this definition of the use of the law is not complete and those who acknowledge nothing else in the law are wrong.

Now, what is the meaning of the phrase 'because of transgressions'? Even philosophers speak like this, that the law was made for restraining evil-doers. And there is also the old proverb, 'Good laws have sprung from bad morals.' But Paul's meaning is higher than the words seem to convey. He means that the law was given in order to make transgressions obvious, and in this way to compel men to acknowledge their guilt. As they are naturally too ready to excuse themselves unless they are aroused by the law, their consciences are drugged. Hence the saying of Paul, 'Before the law, sin was in the world, but it was not imputed' (Rom. 5.13). The law came and aroused the sleepers. And this is the true preparation for Christ. 'By the law is the knowledge of sin,' he says (Rom. 3.20). Why? 'That sin might become exceedingly sinful,' as he replies in Rom. 7.13. Thus the law was added because of transgressions, that they might be detected, or, as he says in Rom. 5.20, that it might make them abound.

This passage puzzled Origen, and all to no purpose. For what is absurd in God summoning to His tribunal consciences which would otherwise take pleasure in evil, that they may be humbled by their guilt when He breaks up the torpor which deadened all feeling of His judgment and drags into light the sin which had lurked like a thief in the den of hypocrisy? If anyone objects, 'As the law is the rule of a devout and upright life, why is it said to be given because of transgressions rather than for the sake of obedience?' I answer, however much it may point out true righteousness, yet in this corruption of our nature, its teaching merely increases transgressions until the Spirit of regeneration comes and writes it on the heart. And He is not given by the law but received by faith. This saying of Paul's, let the reader remember, is not philosophical or political, but expresses a purpose of the law which the world has never known.

Till the seed should come. The seed spoken of here is that on which the blessing was founded, and therefore this does not detract from the promise. For *till* signifies 'so long as' the seed is expected. From this it follows that the law had to serve and not be the chief. It was given to rouse men to look for Christ. But it may be asked whether it had to last only until the coming of Christ. For if so, it follows that it is now abolished. I reply that the whole of that administration was temporary and was given for the purpose of keeping the ancient people in the faith of Christ. And yet I do not admit that by the coming of Christ the whole law was abolished. The apostle did not mean this, but only that the mode of government which had been set up, had to receive its accomplishment in Christ, who is the fulfilment of the promise. But we will speak more fully on this subject later.

Ordained by angels. It is a commendation of the law that it was delivered through angels. This is declared by Stephen also (Acts 7.53). The interpretation given by some that Moses and Aaron and the priests are the angels meant here is more ingenious than solid. Moreover, there is nothing surprising that angels, by whom God distributes to us some of the smallest blessings, should have been entrusted also with this office of attending as witnesses at the promulgation of the law.

In the hand of a mediator. Hand usually stands for ministration but, since He made angels His ministers in giving the law, I take 'the hand of a mediator' as the highest rank of ministry. For He was the Head of the embassy and He had angels with Him as His companions. Some think this is said of Moses, as marking a comparison between Moses and Christ. But I agree rather with the ancient expositors, who apply it to Christ. It will be found that this sense agrees better with the context. Yet I differ from the ancients on the meaning of the word. 'Mediator' does not, as they think, signify here one who makes peace, as in I Tim. 2.5, but a messenger employed in publishing the law.

We are thus to understand that since the beginning of the world God has held no communication with men but through the intervention of His eternal Wisdom or Son. Hence Peter says that the holy prophets spoke by the Spirit of Christ (Acts 2.25) and Paul makes Him the Leader of the people in the wilderness (I Cor. 10.4). And certainly the Angel who appeared to Moses can be regarded as none other, for He claims to Himself the peculiar and essential name of God, which is never given to creatures. As He is the Mediator of reconciliation, by whom we are accepted of God, and the Mediator of intercession, through whom the way is opened for us to call upon the Father, so He has always been the Mediator of all teaching, because by Him God has always revealed Himself to men. And he wanted to state this expressly that the Galatians might learn that He who is the foundation of the free covenant held also the primacy in giving the law.

20. *Now, a mediator is not a mediator of one.* Although some philo-

sophize on the twofold nature of Christ, as if Paul's meaning were that it is not one in essence, yet that Paul is speaking of the contracting parties, no man of sound judgment can doubt. And so they commonly expound it that there is no room for a mediator unless one of the parties has something to transact with the other. But they leave undetermined why that statement should have been put in, though the passage deserves particular care. There may perhaps be a prolepsis in which Paul forestalls some wicked thought of a change in the divine purpose. Someone might say to himself, 'Just as men, when they change their minds about contracts, are accustomed to retract them, so has it happened with the covenant of God.' If you take this to be the meaning, then in the former clause Paul would acknowledge that men, who are one party in this contract, are changeable and unsteady, whereas God remains the same, is consistent with Himself and is not altered by the unsteadiness of men.

But when I look at it more closely, I think rather that it marks a distinction between Jews and Gentiles. Christ is not the Mediator of one, since, in external respects, there is a diversity of condition among those with whom, through His agency, God enters into covenant. But Paul asserts that God's covenant must not be assessed like this, as if it contradicted itself or varied on account of differences in men. Now the words are clear. As Christ formerly reconciled God to the Jews in making a covenant, so now He is the Mediator of the Gentiles. The Jews are very different from the Gentiles, for circumcision and the ceremonies have erected a barrier. They were near God when the Gentiles were afar off. But God does not cease to be consistent with Himself. And this is realized when Christ brings those who used to be distinct to one God and causes them also to unite in one body. God is one because He always remains like Himself and in a settled course holds fixed and unalterable what He has once decreed.

21. *Is the law then?* Although when the certainty and steadiness of the divine purpose are known we are bound also to conclude that its results are not contrary to it, yet there was a difficulty to be resolved, arising from the apparent contradiction of the law and the covenant of grace. This may be an exclamation. Expecting no further contradiction now that the point is settled, Paul concludes from what has gone before that no doubt remains, and exclaims, 'Who will now dare to imagine a disagreement between the law and the promises?' But this does not prevent Paul from proceeding to remove difficulties that might still arise. Before answering the question, he expresses in his usual way great disdain for such nonsense, to show the abhorrence which the godly must have for any insult against God. But there is another move here which we must notice. He accuses his adversaries

of making God contradict Himself. For the law and the promises have obviously both proceeded from Him. Therefore whoever alleges any contradiction between them blasphemes against God. But they are contradictory if the law justifies. Thus Paul very appropriately turns against his adversaries the charge which they falsely and slanderously brought against him.

For if there had been a law given. The reply is, as they say, indirect; not immediately and plainly asserting an agreement between the law and the promises, but containing enough to remove the contradiction. At first sight you would say that this sentence is foreign to the context and has nothing to do with the solution of the question. But this is not so. The law would be opposed to the promises if it had the power of justifying. For there would then be two opposing methods of justifying a man and, as it were, two contrary roads towards the attainment of righteousness. But Paul removes this from the law, and therefore the contradiction is removed. 'I would admit,' he says, 'that righteousness is obtained by the law if salvation were found in it.' But what then?

22. *The Scripture hath shut up.* By the word Scripture is chiefly meant the law itself. It shuts up all men under accusation and therefore, instead of giving, it takes away righteousness. The reasoning is most powerful. 'You seek righteousness in the law. But the law itself, with the whole of Scripture, leaves nothing to men but condemnation; for all men and their works are condemned as unrighteous. Who then shall live by the law?' He is alluding to 'He who shall do these things shall live in them.' Shut out by guilt, I say, from life, we seek salvation in the law in vain. By saying *all things* he conveys more than if he had said 'all men'; for it embraces not only men but everything that they have or can put forward.

That the promise by faith. There is no remedy but to strip off the righteousness of works and flee to the faith of Christ. The consequence is certain: if works come into judgment, we are all condemned. Therefore, by the faith of Christ we obtain a free righteousness. This sentence is full of real consolation. For it tells us that, whenever we hear ourselves condemned in Scripture, there is help provided for us in Christ if we betake ourselves to Him. We are lost even though God were silent. Why then does He so often pronounce that we are lost? It is that we may not perish by everlasting destruction but may be struck and confounded by such a horrifying sentence and by faith seek Christ, through whom we pass from death to life. In the word *promise* is a metonymy in which the thing containing is put for the thing contained.

But before faith came, we were kept under the law, shut up under the faith which should afterwards be revealed. So that the law was our schoolmaster to bring us to Christ, that we might be justified by faith. But now that faith is come, we are no longer under a schoolmaster. For ye are all sons of God through faith in Christ Jesus. For as many of you as were baptized into Christ did put on Christ. There is neither Jew nor Greek, there is neither bond nor free, there is neither male nor female: for ye are all one in Christ Jesus. And if ye are Christ's, then are ye Abraham's seed, and heirs according to the promise. (23-29)

23. *Before faith came.* The question proposed is now more fully defined. He explains clearly both the use of the law and the reason why it had to be temporary; for otherwise it would have seemed always unreasonable that there should be delivered to the Jews a law from which the Gentiles were exempt. For if there is but one Church of Jews and Gentiles, why a diversity in its government? Whence or by what right is this new liberty, since the fathers were under subjection to the law? He therefore tells us that the distinction is not one which would interrupt the union and harmony of the Church. We must again remind readers that Paul is not speaking only of ceremonies or of the moral law, but embraces the whole economy by which the Lord governed His people under the old covenant. It became a subject of dispute whether the form of government instituted by Moses had any power to provide righteousness. Paul compares the law first to a prison or guardhouse and then to a *schoolmaster.* Such was the nature of the law, as both metaphors plainly show, that it could be in force only for a certain time.

Faith. He means the full revelation of those things which were hidden under the darkness of the shadows of the law. For he does not deprive the fathers of faith, who lived under the law. We have already spoken of the faith of Abraham. Other instances are cited by the author of the Epistle to the Hebrews. The doctrine of faith, in short, is attested by Moses and all the prophets. But since the clarity of faith was not so openly manifested then, he calls the time of the new covenant the time of faith, but relatively, not absolutely. He at once shows that this was his meaning when he says that they were shut up under the faith which should afterwards be revealed. For this implies that those who were under the custody of the law were partakers of the same faith. The law did not remove them from faith. But, that they might not wander outside the fold of faith, it kept hold of them. There is an elegant allusion, too, to what he had said before, that the Scripture has shut up all under sin. They were besieged on every hand by the curse; but against this siege there were built the prison walls which protected them from the curse. So that he shows the prison of the law to have been in fact beneficent in spirit.

Faith was not yet revealed; not that the fathers lacked light altogether but that they had less light than we. For whereas the ceremonies sketched out an absent Christ, to us He is represented as present. Thus, what they had in a mirror, we today have in substance. However much darkness there might be under the law, the fathers were not ignorant of the road they had to take. The dawn may not be as bright as noonday, but it is sufficient for making a journey, and travellers do not wait until the sun is right up. Their portion of light was like the dawn; it could keep them safe from all error and guide them to everlasting blessedness.

24. *So that the law was our schoolmaster.* This is the second metaphor, and it expresses Paul's purpose still more clearly. A schoolmaster is not appointed for a person's whole life, but only for childhood, as the etymology of the word shows. Besides, in training a boy, the object is to prepare him by childish elements for greater things. The comparison applies in both respects to the law, for its authority was limited to a fixed age and its purpose was to advance its scholars only to the stage where, when the elements had been learned, they could make progress in further education.

And so he says, *unto Christ.* The grammarian trains a boy and then hands him over to someone else who polishes him in the higher disciplines. Thus the law was as it were the grammarian who started its pupils off and then handed them over to the theology of faith for their completion. In this way Paul compares the Jews to children and us to growing youths.

But it may be asked in what the instruction of training by this schoolmaster consisted. First, the law, by displaying the righteousness of God, convinced them of their own unrighteousness. For in the commandments of God, as in a mirror, they could see how far they were from true righteousness. And so they were reminded that righteousness must be sought elsewhere. The promises of the law served the same purpose, for their meaning was this, 'If you cannot obtain life by works but by fulfilling the law, some new and different method must be sought. Your weakness will never allow you to reach it. However much you may desire and strive, you will fall far short of the aim.' On the other hand, the threatenings urged and pressed them to seek refuge from the wrath and curse of God. Indeed, it gave them no rest till they were constrained to seek the grace of Christ.

This was the aim of all the ceremonies; for why were there sacrifices and washings except that men might continually consider their pollution and condemnation? When a man sees his uncleanness before his eyes, and the innocent animal is held out as the image of his own death, how can he indulge in sleep? How can he fail to be roused and desire a remedy? And certainly ceremonies had the power not only of alarming and humbling consciences, but of exciting them to faith in the coming Redeemer. In the whole solemnity of the ceremonial everything that was presented to the eye had impressed on it, as it were, the mark of Christ. The whole law, in short, was nothing but a manifold variety of exercises in which the worshippers were led by the hand to Christ.

That we might be justified by faith. He has already denied the perfection of the law by comparing it to schooling. But it would make men perfect if it bestowed righteousness on them. What remains but that faith shall take its place? And this it does when we, who are destitute of a righteousness of our own, are clothed by it with the righteousness of Christ. Thus the saying is accomplished, 'he hath filled the hungry with good things' (Luke 1.53).

25. *But now that faith is come.* We have already said what the coming of faith is—the brighter revelation of grace after the veil of the temple had been rent. And this, we know, was effected by the manifestation of Christ. He affirms that under the reign of Christ there is no longer a childhood which needs to be ruled by a schoolmaster, and that consequently the law has finished its task. This is another application of the comparison. He had undertaken to prove two things: that the law is a preparation for Christ, and that it is temporary. But here again it may be asked whether the law is so abolished that it has nothing to do with us. I reply that the law, so far as it is a rule of life, is a bridle which keeps us in the fear of the Lord, a spur to correct the slackness of our flesh, in short, so far as it is profitable for teaching, correcting, reproving, that believers may be instructed in every good work, is as much in force as ever, and remains intact.

In what way, then is it abolished? We have said that Paul looks at the law as endued with its qualities; and these are that it gives a reward and a punishment to works; that is, it promises life to those who keep it and curses all its transgressors. It requires from man the highest perfection and precise obedience. It remits nothing, pardons nothing, but calls to reckoning. It does not openly exhibit Christ and His grace but points to Him afar off and enclosed in ceremonies as in wrappings. And I say that all such qualities of the law are abolished according to Paul, so that the office of Moses has ended in so far as it differs in outward aspect from the covenant of grace.

26. *For ye are all the children of God.* That it would be unjust and completely unreasonable for the law to hold believers in perpetual

slavery he proves by the additional argument that they are the children of God. It would not be enough to say that we have passed out of our childhood, unless it were added that we are freemen, for age does not change the state of slaves. The fact of their being the children of God proves their freedom. How? *By faith in Christ*; for to all who believe in Him is given the privilege of being the sons of God. Therefore it is at the same time brought to pass that we are set free by faith when we are adopted by means of it.

27. *As many of you as were baptized.* The greater and sublimer it is that we are the children of God, the farther is it from our senses and the more difficult to believe it. He therefore explains briefly the nature of our conjunction, or rather uniting, with the Son of God, so that we may not doubt that what belongs to Him is communicated to us. He employs the metaphor of a garment, when he says that the Galatians *have put on Christ.* But he means that they are united to Christ in such a way that, in the sight of God, they bear the name and person of Christ and are viewed in Him rather than in themselves. This metaphor or similitude from garments often occurs and has been treated by us elsewhere.

But the argument that they have put on Christ because they have been baptized seems weak, for baptism is far from being efficacious in all. It is absurd to say that the grace of the Holy Spirit should be so bound to the external sign. Both the uniform doctrine of Scripture and also experience seem to be able to confute this statement. I reply that it is customary for Paul to speak of the sacraments in a twofold way. When he is dealing with hypocrites who boast in the bare sign, he then proclaims the emptiness and worthlessness of the outward sign and strongly attacks their foolish confidence. Why? Because he considers, not the ordinance of God, but the corruption of the ungodly. When, however, he addresses believers, who use the signs properly, he then connects them with the truth which they figure. Why? Because he makes no boast of any false splendour in the sacraments, but what the outward ceremony figures he exhibits in fact. Thus, in agreement with the divine appointment, the truth becomes joined to the signs.

If anyone asks whether it is possible that, through the fault of men, the sacrament can cease to be what it figures, the reply is easy. Though wicked men may feel no effect, nothing is detracted from the sacraments and they still retain their nature and power. The sacraments present the grace of God both to the good and to the bad; nor do they deceive in promising the grace of the Holy Spirit; believers receive what is offered. By rejecting it, the ungodly render the offer unprofitable to themselves, but they cannot destroy the faithfulness of God and the true meaning of the sacrament. Therefore, in addressing believers, Paul very properly says that in baptism they put on Christ; just as in Rom. 6.5 he says that we have been planted into His death so as to be also partakers of His resurrection. In this way, what is proper to God is not transferred to the sign and yet the sacraments keep their power, so that they cannot be regarded as empty and cold spectacles. This reminds us of what base ingratitude they are guilty who abuse the saving ordinances of God and not only make them unprofitable to themselves but even turn them to their own destruction.

28. *There is neither Jew nor Greek.* The meaning is that there is no distinction of persons, and therefore it does not matter to what nation or class anyone may belong. Nor is circumcision any more regarded than sex or civil rank. Why? Because Christ makes all one. Whatever other differences there may be, the one Christ suffices to unite them all.

Therefore he says, *Ye are one,* and means by this that the distinction is now removed. His object is to show that the grace of adoption and the hope of salvation do not depend on the law but are contained in Christ alone. The one Christ therefore is all.

Greeks is here put, as usual, for Gentiles, the species for the genus.

29. *Then are ye Abraham's seed.* This is not put in because to be a child of Abraham is better than being a member of Christ, but to check the pride of the Jews, who gloried in their privilege, as if they alone were the people of God. They reckoned nothing higher than to belong to the race of Abraham. Therefore he makes this same distinction common to all who believe in Christ. The conclusion rests on this argument, that Christ is the blessed seed in whom, as we have said, all the children of Abraham are united. He proves this from the common inheritance offered to them all; from which it follows that the promise includes them among the children. But notice that faith is always joined in relation to the promise.

CHAPTER FOUR

But I say, That so long as the heir is a child, he differeth nothing from a bondservant, though he is lord of all; but is under guardians and stewards until the time appointed of the father. So we also, when we were children, were held in bondage under the rudiments of the world: but when the fulness of the time came, God sent forth his Son, born of a woman, set under the law, that he might redeem them which were under the law, that we might receive the adoption of sons. (1-5)

1. *But I say.* Whoever made the division into chapters has mistakenly separated this paragraph from the one before, for it is simply the ἐπεξεργασία[1] in which Paul explains and illustrates the difference between us and the ancient people. He does so by introducing a third comparison, that of the pupil and his tutor. The pupil, although he is free and even lord of all his father's family, is still like a slave, for he is under the government of tutors. But this subjection under a guardian lasts only until the time appointed by the father, after which he enjoys his freedom. In this respect the fathers under the old covenant, being the sons of God, were free. But they were not in possession of freedom, since the law like a tutor kept them under its yoke. The slavery of the law lasted as long as God pleased and He put an end to it at the coming of Christ. Lawyers enumerate various methods by which guardianship is brought to a close; but of them all, the only one that fits this comparison is that which Paul puts here, the appointment by the father.

Let us now examine the individual clauses. Some apply the comparison to any particular man, whereas Paul is speaking of two nations. What they say is, I acknowledge, true, but it has nothing to do with the present passage. The elect, they say, although they are the children of God from the womb, nevertheless remain under the law like slaves until by faith they come to the possession of freedom; but once they have known Christ, they no longer require this kind of tutelage. Granting all this, I still deny that Paul is here treating of individuals; I deny that he distinguishes between the time of unbelief and the calling to faith. The point at issue was this: Since the Church of God is one, how comes it that our condition is different from that of the Israelites? Since we are free by faith, how comes it that they, who had faith in common with us, were not partakers with us of the same

[1] *Investigation* or perhaps *recapitulation.*

freedom? Since we are all equally the children of God, how comes it
that we at this day are exempt from the yoke which they were forced
to bear? The controversy and argument turned on these points and
not on the manner in which the law reigns over each of us before we
are freed by faith from its slavery. Let this be settled first of all, that
Paul here compares the Israelite Church which existed under the old
covenant with the Christian Church, and then we shall be able to
discern the points of agreement and difference. This comparison
contains most useful and rich teaching.

First, we learn that we today have the hope of the same inheritance
as the fathers under the old covenant; for they were partakers of the
same adoption. For Paul does not teach (as some fanatics dream,
among them Servetus) that God chose them for this only to figure to
us the people of God, but that they should be the children of God together with us; and he declares expressly that the spiritual blessing
promised to Abraham belongs to them no less than to us.

Secondly, we learn that in spite of their external slavery their
consciences were free. The obligation to keep the law did not hinder
Moses and Daniel, all the godly kings, priests and prophets and the
whole company of believers from being free in spirit. They so bore
the yoke of the law on their shoulders that they worshipped God with
a free spirit. More particularly, they had been taught about the free
pardon of sins, and their consciences were delivered from the tyranny
of sin and death. Hence we must conclude that they held the same
doctrine as ourselves, were joined with us in the true unity of faith,
placed reliance with us on the one Mediator, called on God as their
Father, and were governed by the same Spirit. All this leads to the
conclusion that the difference between us and the ancient fathers lies
not in substance but in accidents. In all the chief points of the testament or covenant we agree. The ceremonies and all that régime in
which we differ are, so to say, appendages. Besides, we must note
that that age was the infancy of the Church; but now at the advent
of Christ the Church began to grow up, so that it has come to man's
estate.

For Paul's words are clear. But a difficulty arises in that he seems
to contradict himself. In Eph. 4.13 he exhorts us to make daily
progress until we come to an adult age. And in I Cor. 3.1 he reminds
them that he fed them with milk, like children, because they could
not take solid food. And shortly after this he compares the Galatians
to babies (Gal. 4.19). I reply that there he is dealing with particular
men and their own individual faith; but here he is speaking in general
of two bodies without regard to persons. This reply will help us to
resolve a much greater difficulty. For we see the matchless faith of

Abraham and the great light of understanding in the holy prophets. How can we dare to boast that we are superior to such men? Were not they rather the heroes and we the children? To say nothing of ourselves, who among the Galatians would have been found equal to any of those men?

But here, as I have already said, he is not dealing with particular persons but describes the universal condition of both peoples. Some men were endowed with greater gifts; but they were the few and not the whole body. Besides, even had they been numerous, we must consider not what they were inwardly but what was the economy of God in which they were governed. And that was certainly a *paedagogia*, a system of instruction for children. And what are we now? God has broken those chains, governs His Church more freely and does not hold it in such a strict restraint. At the same time, we must note in passing that however much knowledge they were given, it partook of the nature of the period, for a dark cloud continually rested on the revelation which they had. Hence that saying of Christ, 'Blessed are the eyes which see the things that ye see: many kings and prophets have desired to see those things which ye see, and have not seen them; and to hear them and have not heard them' (Luke 10.23-24). We now understand in what respect we are preferred to those who were far above us. For this is not applied to persons, but depends entirely on the economy of the divine administration.

This is a most powerful battering-ram for destroying all the pomps of ceremonies, which are the sole glory of the Papacy. For what else today dazzles the eyes of the simple so that they admire the dominion of the Pope, or at least are moved to some respect for it, but the magnificence of ceremonies, rites, gesticulations and all the cultic apparatus contrived for the express purpose of amazing the ignorant? From this passage it appears that they are false disguises, by which the Church is deformed. I do not now speak of greater and more accursed corruptions which they pretend are the worship of God, imagine to have the power of meriting salvation, and enforce with more severity than the whole divine law, trifles as they are. I only advert to the pretext under the cloak of which our new workmen of today put forward so many abominations. They object, I say, that the masses of the people are far more ignorant than they were among the Israelites and that therefore many helps are needed. They will never be able to prove from this that there must be a *paedagogia* similar to what existed among the people of Israel. For I shall always put forward the objection that the appointment of God is quite different.

If they plead expediency, I deny that they are better judges of what is expedient than God Himself. Let us hold the firm conviction that what God has determined is both the most correct and also the most useful. Therefore the aids which must be sought for the ignorant are not those which the desire of men has been pleased to contrive, but those decreed by God Himself, who unquestionably has omitted nothing that was fitted to assist their weakness. Let this shield be sufficient for repelling any objections: 'The Lord has decided otherwise, and His counsel is sufficient for us without any reasons. Unless perhaps men can devise better aids than those which God Himself has provided and which He afterwards abrogated as useless!' Observe carefully that Paul does not merely say that the yoke which had been laid on the Jews is removed from us, so that we are free to use ceremonies, but expressly lays down a distinction in the government which God has wished to be observed. I acknowledge that we today are free as to all outward matters; but this freedom must not lead to the Church being burdened with a multitude of ceremonies, unless we want Christianity confounded with Judaism. The reason for this we shall afterwards give in the proper place.

3. *Under the elements of the world.* He calls 'elements' either literally, outward and bodily things, or metaphorically, rudiments. I prefer the latter. But why does he say that those things which had a spiritual signification were of the world? It was as if he said that we do not hold the truth naked but as it is enveloped in earthly figures. Therefore he says that what was outward was of the world, even though beneath it there was a heavenly mystery.

4. *When the fulness of the time came.* He proceeds with his comparison and applies to his purpose 'the time appointed by the Father'. But at the same time he shows that the time which had been ordained by the providence of God was seasonable and fit. That is the right season and that is the best method of acting which the providence of God directs. Therefore the right time for the Son of God to be revealed to the world was for God alone to judge and determine. This ought to restrain all curiosity, if any man, not content with the secret purpose of God, should dare to dispute why Christ did not appear sooner. Let readers seek a fuller treatment, if they wish, in the conclusion of the Epistle to the Romans.[1]

God sent forth his Son. Here much is contained in a few words. The Son who was sent, must have existed before. From this is proved His eternal divinity. Christ therefore is the Son of God sent forth from heaven. He says that this same was made of a woman because He put on our nature. So he means that He has two natures. Some texts (*codices*) read born (*natum*), but the other reading is the more received and in my opinion fits in better. He expressly intended to distinguish

---

[1] In his commentary on Rom. 16.25-26.

Christ from the rest of men as having been created of the seed of His mother and not by intercourse of man and woman. For any other sense this would have been trifling and foreign to the subject. The word *woman* is here put for the female sex in general.

Set under the law. Literally it is, 'Made under the law'. But I wanted to express the sense more plainly. Christ the Son of God, who was by right exempt from all subjection, became subject to the law. Why? In our name, that He might obtain freedom for us. A free-man redeemed a slave by constituting himself a surety; by putting the chains on himself, he takes them off the other. In the same way Christ chose to become liable to keep the law that He might obtain exemption for us. Otherwise He would have submitted to the yoke of the law in vain, for it was certainly not on His own account that He did so.

Moreover, we are not so exempted from the law by Christ's benefit that we no longer owe any obedience to the teaching of the law and may do what we please. For it is the perpetual rule of a good and holy life. But Paul is speaking of the law with its appendages. And we are redeemed from subjection to that law because it is no longer what it was once. Now that the veil is rent, freedom has openly appeared; and this is what he goes on to say.

5. That we might receive the adoption. The fathers under the old covenant were sure of their adoption, but did not as yet so fully enjoy their privilege. Adoption, like redemption in Rom. 8.23, is put for actual possession. For as, at the last day, we receive the fruit of our redemption, so now we receive the fruit of our adoption, which the holy fathers did not partake of before the coming of Christ. Therefore those who now burden the Church with an excess of ceremonies, wickedly defraud her of what is justly due to adoption (*lit.* the just debt of adoption).

And because ye are sons, God sent forth the Spirit of his Son into your hearts, crying, Abba, Father. So that thou art no longer a bondservant, but a son; and if a son, then an heir of God through Christ. Howbeit at that time, not knowing God, ye were in bondage to them which by nature are no gods. But now that ye have come to know God, or rather to be known of God, how turn ye again to the weak and beggarly rudiments, whereunto ye desire to be in bondage over again? Ye observe days, and months, and seasons, and years. I am afraid for you, lest by any means I have bestowed labour upon you in vain. (6-11)

6. And because ye are sons. He shows by the following argument that the adoption which he had spoken of belongs to the Galatians:

Adoption by God precedes the testimony of adoption given by the
Holy Spirit.

But the effect is the sign of the cause. And you dare to call God
your Father only by the instigation and incitement of the Spirit of
Christ.

Therefore it is certain that you are the sons of God.
This means, as he often teaches elsewhere, that the Spirit is the earnest
and pledge of our adoption, so that we are surely convinced of God's
Fatherly attitude towards us.

But it will be objected: do not wicked men also carry their rashness
so far as to claim that God is their Father? Do they not often with even
greater boldness boast that God is theirs? I reply that Paul is not here
speaking of idle boasting or of what any man may claim for his own
spirit, but of the testimony of a godly conscience which follows the
new regeneration. This argument can have weight only for believers,
for the reprobate have no experience of this certainty. As the Lord
Himself declares, 'The Spirit of truth, whom the world cannot receive,
because it knoweth him not' (John 14.17). This is implied in Paul's
words.

God hath sent forth. It is not what they themselves in the judgment
of the flesh foolishly venture, but what God declares in their hearts by
His Spirit, that he wants to teach. *The Spirit of his Son* is more apt to
the present context than any other epithet that he could have used.
We are the sons of God because we are endowed with the same Spirit
as His only Son.

And observe that Paul ascribes this to all Christians in common;
for where the pledge of the divine love towards us is wanting, there is
assuredly no faith. Hence it is plain what sort of Christianity there is
in the Papacy, where they accuse of pious presumption any man who
says that he has the Spirit of God. For they imagine a faith without
the Spirit of God and without certainty. This single dogma that they
hold is clear proof that in all the schools of the Papists, the devil, the
father of unbelief, reigns. I acknowledge indeed that the Schoolmen,
when they order that men's consciences shall fluctuate in perpetual
doubt, teach only what natural sense dictates. It is the more necessary
to fix in our mind this dogma of Paul's, that none is a Christian save
he who has been taught by the teaching of the Holy Spirit to call
God his Father.

Crying. I consider that this participle is used to express greater
boldness. Uncertainty does not let us speak calmly, but keeps our
mouth half-shut, so that the half-broken words can hardly escape
from a stammering tongue. 'Crying', on the contrary, is a sign of
certainty and unwavering confidence. 'For we have not received the

spirit of bondage again to fear,' as he says in Rom. 8.15, but of freedom to full confidence.

Abba, Father. The meaning of these words, I have no doubt, is that calling upon God is common to all languages. For it pertains to the present subject that God has the name Father among the Hebrews and the Greeks. As it was foretold by Isaiah, 'Every tongue shall make confession to my name' (Isa. 45.23). Since therefore Gentiles are reckoned among the sons of God, it is evident that adoption comes, not by the merit of the law, but from the grace of faith.

7. *So that thou art no longer a servant.* That is, in the Christian Church there is no longer servitude, but the free state of children. In what respect the fathers under the law were slaves has already been said. Their freedom was not yet revealed, but was hidden under the coverings and yoke of the law. He again speaks of the distinction between the old and new testaments. The ancients were also sons of God and heirs through Christ. But we are so in a different way, for we have Christ present with us and for that reason enjoy His blessings. All this is handled at greater length in Romans. If you look there you will find that I have spoken of what I omit here.[1]

8. *At that time not knowing God.* Here he does not so much teach as rebuke. And he had already proved his point so fully that no doubt remained and they could not evade his reproof. His object is to emphasize their present defection by comparing it with the past. It is not surprising, he says, that formerly you served them as gods which are not gods, for wherever ignorance of God exists there is a dreadful blindness. You were then wandering in darkness; but how disgraceful it is that now, in the midst of light, you should stray so horribly. It follows, then, that the Galatians were less excusable for corrupting the Gospel than they had formerly been for idolatry. This is the sum of it. But here we must observe that, until we have been enlightened in the true knowledge of the one God, we always serve idols, whatever disguise we may cover our false religion with. The legitimate worship of God, therefore, must be preceded by sure knowledge.

He puts *nature* for reality or substance. For whatever men imagine about God is a figment and nothing. In men's opinions idols may be gods; in reality they are nothing.

9. *But now that ye have come to know God.* No words can express the base ingratitude of departing from God when He has once been known. What is it but to forsake voluntarily the light, the life, the fountain of all blessings, as He Himself complains through Jeremiah (2.13). To intensify the blame still more, he corrects himself and says *or rather, come to be known of God.* For the greater God's grace toward,

---

[1] In his commentary on Rom. 6.14ff.

us is, the heavier must be our guilt if we despise it. Paul reminds the Galatians whence the knowledge of God had come to them. He states that they did not obtain it by their own exertions, by their mental acuteness or industry, but because, when they were at the furthest possible remove from thinking about Him, God prevented them with His mercy. What is said of the Galatians may be extended to all, for the words of Isaiah are fulfilled in all, 'I am found by them that sought me not: I have appeared to them that asked not for me' (65.1). The beginning of our calling is the free election of God, by which we are foreordained to life before we are born. On this depends our calling, our faith, the fulfilment of our salvation.

How turn ye again? They could not turn again to ceremonies that they had never practised. He has used the word imprecisely, and merely means that to fall again into wicked superstitions, as if they had never received the truth of God, was completely foolish. When he calls the ceremonies beggarly elements, he views them outside Christ, in fact, opposed to Christ. To the fathers they were not only wholesome exercises and aids to godliness, but efficacious organs of grace. But their whole strength lay in Christ and in the appointment of God. The false apostles on the other hand neglected the promises and wanted to oppose them to Christ, as if Christ alone were not sufficient. That Paul should regard them as worthless is not surprising; but of this I have already spoken. By the word *bondage* he reproves their privation.

10. *Ye observe days.* He adduces as an example one kind of elements, the observance of days. But we must note that he is not condemning the ordinary observance of seasons. The order of nature is fixed and perpetual. How are months and years computed but by the revolution of the sun and moon? What distinguishes summer from winter, or spring from harvest, but the appointment of God—an appointment which He promised to continue to the end of the world (Gen. 8.22)? This common observance serves not only for agriculture and public affairs, but even touches the government of the Church. What sort of observance, then, did Paul reprove? It was that which would bind the conscience by religion, as something that was necessary to the worship of God and which, as he says in Rom. 14.5f, would make a distinction between one day and another.

When certain days are represented as holy in themselves, when one day is distinguished from another on religious grounds, when holy days are reckoned a part of divine worship, then days are improperly observed. The false apostles strongly advocated the sabbath, new moons, and other festivals, because they were observances of the law. When we today make a distinction of days, we do not lay a snare of necessity on the conscience, or distinguish between days as if one were more holy than another, nor do we set them up as religion and the worship of God. We merely give heed to order and harmony. Among us the observance is free and void of all superstition.

11. *Lest I have bestowed labour upon you in vain.* The expression is severe and must have filled the Galatians with alarm. For what hope was left to them if Paul's labour had been in vain. Some are surprised that Paul should be so upset by the observance of days as to call it a subversion of almost the whole Gospel. But if we carefully and rightly weigh the whole, we shall see that he had just cause. For the false apostles not only attempted to lay the Jewish bondage on the neck of the Church, but filled their minds with wicked superstitions. To force Christians to submit to Judaism was in itself no small evil. But it was a far more serious mischief when they set up holidays as meritorious works, in opposition to the grace of Christ, and claimed that God was to be worshipped and propitiated in this way. When such doctrines were received, the worship of God was corrupted, the grace of Christ made void and freedom of conscience suppressed.

Do we wonder that Paul should be afraid that he had laboured in vain? For of what value would the Gospel be any more? Since that same description of ungodliness is now supported by the Papacy, what sort of Christ or what sort of Gospel do they hold? So far as binding the consciences goes, they enforce the observance of days no less severely than Moses did. They consider holy days to be part of the worship of God, just as the false apostles did, and even connect them with the devilish concept of merit. The Papists therefore must be held as much to blame as the false apostles. They are, in fact, worse. Those men wanted to observe days which had been appointed by the law of God; but the Papists command days to be kept as holy which they have rashly stamped with their own seal.

Be as I am; for I am as ye are. Brethren, I beseech you. Ye did me no wrong. But ye know that because of an infirmity of the flesh, I preached the gospel unto you the first time. And that which was a temptation to you in my flesh ye despised not, nor rejected; but ye received me as an angel of God, even as Christ Jesus. Where then is that blessedness of yours? For I bear you witness, that, if possible, ye would have plucked out your eyes and given them to me. So then, am I become your enemy, because I tell you the truth? They zealously seek you in no good way; nay, they desire to shut you out, that ye may seek them. But it is good to be zealously sought in a good matter at all times, and not only when I am present with you. My little children, of whom I am again in travail until Christ be formed in you, yea, I could wish to be present

with you now, and to change my voice; for I am perplexed about you.
(12-20)

12. *Be as I am.* He now speaks more gently, and softens the harshness he had shown; for although it had been more than justified by the wickedness of the crime, yet, because he wanted to do good, he tempers his style to conciliate them. It is the part of a wise pastor to consider, not what those who have erred may justly deserve, but how he can call them back to the way. He must charge them in season and out of season, but with all gentleness and patience, as Paul elsewhere commands (II Tim. 4.2). Following this method, he turns from chiding to entreaties. *I beseech you,* he says, and calls them *brethren,* to assure them that there had been no bitterness in his reproofs.

But what does it mean, *Be as I am?* It refers to his attitude. He takes care to accommodate himself to them, and he wants them to do the same to him. *For I am as ye are*: that is, as I seek nothing but to behave kindly to you, so it is only fair that you should be converted to moderation and behave teachably and obediently to me. And here again pastors are admonished of their duty to come down to the people, as far as possible, and to conform themselves to the minds of those with whom they have to deal, if they want them to be compliant. For it is always true that 'to be loved you must be lovable'.

Ye did me no wrong. He removes the suspicion that might have made his earlier reproofs disagreeable. For if we think that a man is avenging his injuries or a private quarrel, we completely avert our minds from him and twist whatever he says into an unfavourable meaning. Paul therefore forestalls the Galatians and says, 'So far as I am concerned I have nothing to complain of from you. It is not for my own sake, or from any hostility to you that I am angry. And therefore, if I speak strongly, it obviously does not spring from hatred or wrath.'

13. *Ye know that, because of an infirmity of the flesh.* He reminds them of the friendly and respectful way they had received him. And he does so for two reasons. First, to let them know that he loved them, so that they would lend a ready ear to all that he said; and secondly that, as they had begun well, they would go on in the same course. These reminiscences, then, are first a sign of his friendliness and secondly an exhortation to act as they had done at first.

By 'infirmity of the flesh' he means here, as in other places, whatever might make him mean and despised. 'Flesh' signifies his outward appearance, but 'infirmity' means lowness. Such was Paul when he came among them, without pomp, without show, without worldly honours or rank, but mean and of no worth in the eyes of men. Yet all this did not prevent the Galatians from receiving him with the greatest honour. This fact contributes powerfully to his argument. For what was there in Paul to esteem or revere, apart from the power of the Holy Spirit? What excuse then, have they to begin to despise that power? They are next accused of inconsistency, since no subsequent occurrence in Paul's life could entitle them to esteem him less than before. But this he leaves them to think over and only indirectly offers it to their consideration.

14. *My temptation.* That is, 'Although you saw that I was, from the world's point of view, a lowly man, you did not reject me.' He calls it a temptation or trial, because it was not something unknown or obscure and he did not conceal it, as ambitious men are wont to do when they are ashamed of their littleness. It often happens that the unworthy are applauded before their nakedness is espied, but in a day or two they are dismissed with shame and disgrace. But it was very different with Paul, who had not deceived the Galatians, but had told them frankly what he was.

As an angel of God. As every true minister of God ought to be regarded. For as God distributes His graces to us by the activity of angels, so godly teachers are divinely raised up to administer to us the most excellent of all blessings, the doctrine of eternal salvation. Therefore those by whose hands God dispenses to us such a treasure are not undeservedly compared to angels. Then again, they are the messengers of God, by whose mouth God speaks to us. And this argument is found in Mal. 2.7.

But he rises still higher and adds, *even as Christ Jesus.* For the Lord Himself commands that His ministers shall be regarded just as He is. 'He that heareth you heareth me; he that despiseth you despiseth me' (Luke 10.16). Nor is this surprising. For it is in His place that they discharge their embassy. And so they play the part of Him in whose stead they act. These are His praises with which the majesty of the Gospel is commended to us and its ministry adorned. If it be the command of Christ that His ministers shall be thus honoured, it is certain that contempt of them comes from the instigation of the devil. And indeed they can never be despised so long as the Word of God is prized. But the Papists claim this argument in vain, for since they are obviously the enemies of Christ, how absurd that they should steal the feathers of the servants of Christ and advertise themselves as His! Those who want to be honoured as angels must perform the duty of angels. Those who want to be heard like Christ must faithfully bring us His pure Word.

15. *Where then is that blessedness?* He suggests that they had been blessed when they had embraced the instrument of their blessedness

with such dutiful love. But now, by allowing themselves to be
deprived of his ministry to whom they should have attributed whatever they possessed of Christ, they were unhappy. He wants to pierce
them with this rebuke. 'What! Shall all this be lost? Shall it profit
you nothing that you once knew Christ speaking by me? Shall it be
in vain that you were founded in the faith by me? Shall your falling
away now destroy the glory of your obedience before God?' In
short, by despising the pure doctrine which they had embraced, they
throw away of their own accord the blessedness which they had
obtained, and draw upon themselves the destruction in which they
will miserably perish.

For I bear you witness. It is not enough that pastors be respected, if
they are not also loved. Both are necessary; otherwise their teaching
will not have a sweet taste. And he declares that both had been true
of him among the Galatians. He had already spoken of their respect;
he now speaks of their love. To be willing to *pluck out their own eyes*
if necessary was proof of a very extraordinary love, stronger than a
willingness to part with life itself.

16. *So then am I become your enemy?* He now returns to himself and
denies that it was his fault that they had changed their minds. Though
it is a common remark that truth begets hatred, yet truth is never
hateful except through the wickedness and malice of those who cannot
bear to hear it. Therefore he so clears himself of any blame in this
quarrel that he indirectly censures their ingratitude. Yet still his advice
is friendly, not to reject rashly or causelessly their apostle, for they
know him worthy of love whom they had formerly loved dearly.
What can be worse than from a hatred of truth to become an enemy
instead of a friend? And so he says this, not so much to upbraid as to
move them to repentance.

17. *They are paying court to you.* He comes at last to the false apostles
and makes them more odious by his silence than if he had named them.
For we usually suppress the names of those whom it annoys and
offends us to mention. Because they might be deceived by the apparent
zeal of these men, he warns the Galatians against misplaced ambition.
The comparison is taken from the unchaste and dishonourable wooing
of girls in order to seduce them. 'That they are desiring or courting
you ought not to deceive you, for they act, not from a right zeal, but
from a perverse desire to obtain fame.' He contrasts to it the holy
jealousy that he speaks of in II Cor. 11.2.

Yea, they shut you out. He emphasizes their perverse tricks by adding
a correction. They not only court you but, as they cannot possess you
by any other means, they try to stir up strife between us, so that when
you have been, as it were, left abandoned, you will yield to them.

For they see that as long as a godly harmony exists between us, there can be no place for them. This stratagem is common to all the ministers of Satan, of alienating the people from their pastor to draw them to themselves, and having, so to say, disposed of the rival, to take his place. A careful and judicious examination will show that they always begin like this.

18. *But it is good to be honourably wooed.* It is uncertain whether he is speaking of himself or of the Galatians. Good ministers ought to burn with a holy jealousy that they may preserve their Churches in chaste union with their Husband. If we take it of Paul, the meaning will be: 'I confess that I also am jealous of you, but with a different aim and feeling. And this is true as much when I am absent as when I am present, because I do not seek my own advantage.' But I would rather refer it to the Galatians, though it can bear more than one interpretation. For it can be expounded thus: 'They indeed try to alienate you from me, so that, when you have been abandoned, you may turn to them. But you loved me when present; now love me even when absent.' But a more correct opinion is that Paul was using a pun. For, as he had used *aemulari* for courting or soliciting to vice, so here he uses it of imitating or striving after the virtues of another. By condemning debased jealousy, he exhorts the Galatians to engage in a different sort of rivalry and that, too, while he was absent.

19. *My little children.* He uses an even gentler word, for children is better than brethren, and the diminutive is an expression, not of contempt, but of endearment. Nevertheless, at the same time it suggests the tender years of those who ought now to be growing up. The style is abrupt, as is usual in passionate outbursts. Strong feeling, when it cannot express itself adequately, breaks off our words half-uttered, and powerful emotion chokes our utterance.

Of whom I am again in travail. This also comes from the vehement declaration of his love, which for their sakes endured the labour pangs of a mother. It denotes likewise his anxiety. For when a woman has been delivered, she rejoices. Once they had been conceived and brought forth; now, after their fall, they had to be begotten a second time.

Yet he lessens their resentment by saying *Until Christ be formed in you.* For he does not annihilate their former birth, but says that they must again be nourished in the womb, as if they were an immature and unformed embryo. That Christ should be formed in us is the same as our being formed in Christ. For we are born that we may be new creatures in Him. And He, on the other hand, is born in us so that we may live His life. Since the true image of Christ had been deformed through the superstitions introduced by the false apostles,

Paul labours to restore it so that it might shine clearly and unhindered. This is done by the ministers of the Gospel, by giving sometimes milk and sometimes solid food. Indeed, they ought to undertake this in the whole course of their preaching. But Paul here compares himself to a woman in labour, because the Galatians were not yet completely born.

This is a remarkable passage on the efficacy of the ministry. True, it is the work of God that we are begotten and born; but because He employs a minister and preaching as His instruments for that purpose, He ascribes to them what is His, so joining the power of His Spirit with the activity of man. Let us always keep this distinction that, when a minister is contrasted to God, he is nothing and can do nothing but is a useless instrument. But because the Holy Spirit works efficaciously through him, the praise and renown of acting is also transferred to him. Yet it is not what he can do by himself or apart from God, but what God does through him that is described here. If ministers wish to be something, let them labour to form Christ, not themselves. Here he is, as it were, worn out with grief and stops in mid sentence.

20. *I could wish to be present with you now.* This is a very strong protest, the complaint of a father so perplexed by the misconduct of his sons that he is at his wit's end and does not know where to turn. He wishes he had an opportunity of speaking to them personally; for we get a better idea from first-hand knowledge of what to do, because, depending on whether the hearer is affected, on whether he is tractable or stubborn, we can accommodate our conversation. But he wanted to express something more than this by *to change my voice*; that is, he was very ready to assume a variety of forms and even to frame a new language, so long as it fitted the need. Pastors ought to notice this carefully, lest they should be devoted to themselves or their own understanding; they must accommodate themselves, so far as the occasion demands, to the capacity of the people—although in God's affairs they must not swerve from the right path to gain the favour of the people.

Tell me, ye that desire to be under the law, do ye not hear the law? For it is written, that Abraham had two sons, one by the handmaid, and one by a free-woman. But he who was of the handmaid was born after the flesh; but he of the free-woman was through promise. Which things are an allegory: for these women are the two covenants: one from mount Sinai, bearing children unto bondage, which is Hagar. For this Hagar is mount Sinai in Arabia, and correspondeth to the Jerusalem that now is; for she is in bondage with her children. But

83

the Jerusalem that is above is free, which is the mother of us all. (21-26)

21. *Tell me.* After these exhortations to touch their feelings, he follows up his former teaching with a fine illustration. As an argument it is not very strong, but as confirmation of his earlier vigorous reasoning, it is not to be despised.

To be under the law here signifies to come under the yoke of the law, with the condition that God will deal with you according to the covenant of the law and that you in return bind yourself to keep the law. In another sense, all believers are under the law, but here, as we have said, he treats of the law with its appendages.

22. *For it is written.* No man with a choice will be so mad as to despise freedom and choose slavery. But here the apostle teaches us that they who are under the law are slaves. Unhappy men who voluntarily choose this state when God wills to free them! He gives an image of this in the two sons of Abraham, one of whom, born a slave, kept his mother's condition, whereas the other, the child of a free-woman, obtained the inheritance. He afterwards applies the whole story to his purpose and illustrates it gracefully.

In the first place, because their adversaries armed themselves with the authority of the law, he quotes the law on the other side. 'The law' was the name usually given to the five books of Moses. Again, as the story which he cites seems to have nothing to do with the question, he gives it an allegorical interpretation. But he writes that these things are ἀλληγορούμενα. Origen, and many others along with him, have seized this occasion of twisting Scripture this way and that, away from the genuine sense (*a genuino sensu*). For they inferred that the literal sense is too meagre and poor and that beneath the bark of the letter there lie deeper mysteries which cannot be extracted but by hammering out allegories. And this they did without difficulty, for the world always has and always will prefer speculations which seem ingenious, to solid doctrine. With such approbation the licence increased more and more, so that he who played this game of allegorizing Scripture not only was suffered to pass unpunished but even obtained the highest applause. For many centuries no man was thought clever who lacked the cunning and daring to transfigure with subtlety the sacred Word of God. This was undoubtedly a trick of Satan to impair the authority of Scripture and remove any true advantage out of the reading of it. God avenged this profanation with a just judgment when He suffered the pure meaning to be buried under false glosses.

Scripture, they say, is fertile and thus bears multiple meanings. I acknowledge that Scripture is the most rich and inexhaustible fount of all wisdom. But I deny that its fertility consists in the various meanings which anyone may fasten to it at his pleasure. Let us know, then, that the true meaning of Scripture is the natural and simple one (*verum sensum scripturae, qui germanus est et simplex*), and let us embrace and hold it resolutely. Let us not merely neglect as doubtful, but boldly set aside as deadly corruptions, those pretended expositions which lead us away from the literal sense (*a literali sensu*).

But what shall we reply to Paul's assertion? He certainly does not mean that Moses deliberately wrote the story so that it might be turned into an allegory, but is pointing out in what way the story relates to the present case. That is, when we see there the image of the Church figuratively delineated. And an *anagoge* of this sort is not foreign to the genuine and literal meaning, when a comparison was drawn between the Church and the family of Abraham. For as the house of Abraham was then the true Church, so it is beyond doubt that the principal and most memorable events that happened in it are types for us. Therefore, as in circumcision, in sacrifices, in the whole Levitical priesthood there was an allegory, as there is today in our sacraments, so was there likewise in the house of Abraham. But this does not involve a departure from the literal meaning (*a literali sensu*). In a word, it is as if Paul says that there is depicted in the two wives of Abraham a figure of the two covenants, and in the two sons a figure of the two peoples. And Chrysostom indeed acknowledges that in the word allegory is κατάχρησις[1]; which is quite true.

23. *But he who was of the handmaid.* Both were begotten by Abraham according to the flesh. But Isaac was different in that he had the promise of grace. In Ishmael there was nothing beyond nature; in Isaac was the election of God. And this is suggested by his very birth, which was not ordinary but miraculous. Yet he hints at the calling of the Gentiles and the rejection of the Jews. For the latter boast of their ancestry, whereas the former have become the spiritual offspring of Abraham by faith and without human advantages.

24. *These women are the two covenants.* I have preferred to translate it like this so as not to destroy the beauty of the comparison. Paul compares the two διαθῆκαι to the two mothers; but to use *testamentum*, which is neuter, for denoting a mother would be awkward. The word *pactio*[2] is therefore more appropriate. But I have aimed at clarity rather than elegance.

The comparison is now formally introduced. As in the house of Abraham there were two mothers, so are there also in the Church of God. Doctrine is the mother by whom God begets us. It is twofold,

[1] An imprecise use.

[2] *Pactio*, which also means 'covenant', is more appropriate to apply to women because it is a feminine noun.

legal and evangelical. The legal bears children to bondage; hence the
simile of it is Hagar. But Sarah represents the second, which bears
children to freedom. In fact, however, Paul begins higher and makes
our first mother Sinai and our second Jerusalem. So that if anyone
wants to work out the details more finely, he will make the law into
the seed from whence are begotten the children of Sinai and from the
Gospel the children of Jerusalem. But this has nothing to do with the
argument in itself. The two covenants are like mothers from whom
it is sufficient to hold that dissimilar children are born. For the legal
covenant makes slaves and the evangelical covenant free-men.

But all this may seem absurd at first sight; for there is none of God's
children who is not born to freedom; therefore the comparison does
not apply. I answer that what Paul says is true in two respects. The
law formerly brought forth its disciples (that is, the holy prophets and
the other believers) to slavery, yet not to permanent slavery, but
because God had placed them for a time under a schoolmaster. Their
freedom was concealed under the veil of ceremonies and of the whole
economy by which they were governed. To the outward eye appeared nothing but slavery. Paul says the same thing to the Romans
(chapter 8.15), 'Ye have not received the spirit of bondage again to
fear.' Those holy fathers, though inwardly they were free in the sight
of God, yet in outward appearance were no different from slaves and
so are related to their mother's condition. But the doctrine of the
Gospel bestows perfect freedom on its children as soon as they are
born and brings them up in freedom.

I admit that Paul does not speak of that kind of children, as the
context will show. By the children of Sinai, it will afterwards be
explained, are meant hypocrites, who are at last expelled from the
Church of God and deprived of the inheritance. What then is the
bearing of children to bondage, which he is now discussing? It
denotes those who wickedly abuse the law by conceiving nothing but
slavery from it. Not so the godly fathers who lived under the old
testament; for their slavish birth by the law did not prevent them
having Jerusalem for their mother in spirit. But those who cleave to
the bare law and do not know it as a schoolmaster to bring them to
Christ, but rather make it a barrier against coming to Him, are the
Ishmaelites born to slavery.

It will again be objected, why does the apostle say that such are
born of God's covenant and are regarded as in the Church? I reply,
they are not strictly God's children but are degenerate and spurious,
and are disclaimed by God whom they falsely call their Father. They
are regarded as in the Church, not because they are members of it in
reality but because for a time they usurp a place and deceive men by

the mask they wear. The apostle here considers the Church as it is seen in this world. But we shall speak of this later.

25. *Hagar is mount Sinai.* I shall not waste time in refuting other expositions. For Jerome's conjecture that Mount Sinai had two names is trifling. And the philosophizing of Chrysostom about the agreement of the names is no less childish. Sinai is called Hagar, because it is a type or figure; just as the Passover was Christ. The position of the mountain is expressed in contempt. It lies in Arabia, he says, beyond the borders of the Holy Land, which is the symbol of the eternal inheritance. The wonder is that in so straightforward an application they should go so far astray.

And corresponds on the other hand. The old translator renders it 'is joined' (*coniunctus est*); and Erasmus, 'borders on' (*confinis*). I have translated it as above to avoid obscurity. For the apostle certainly does not refer to propinquity or situation but to the comparison, which he treats figuratively. Σύστοιχα denotes things that are so arranged as to have a mutual relation to each other; and συστοιχία, when applied to trees and so on, means that they are set in a regular order. In the same way Mount Sinai is said συστοιχεῖν to that which is now Jerusalem, just as Aristotle writes that rhetoric is the ἀντίστροφος or counterpart to dialectic, by a metaphor borrowed from the lyric, which was usually arranged in two parts, adapted to one another in harmony. In short, συστοιχεῖν means simply to be, so to say, coordinated.

But why does he compare the present Jerusalem with Mount Sinai? Although I once held the opposite opinion, I now agree with Chrysostom and Ambrose, who expound it of the earthly Jerusalem, and indeed that it had then degenerated into a slavish doctrine and worship. This is why he says, *which now is.* It ought to have been a lively image of the heavenly Jerusalem and an expression of its character. But such as it now is, he says, it is related to Mount Sinai. Although the two places are far apart, they are completely and perfectly accordant. This is a severe reproach to the Jews, who had fallen from grace and whose real mother was not Sarah but the spurious Jerusalem, twin sister of Hagar. They were therefore slaves born of a slave, though they haughtily claimed to be the sons of Abraham.

26. *But Jerusalem which is above.* What he calls heavenly is not shut up in heaven, nor are we to seek for it outside the world. For the Church is spread over the whole world and is a pilgrim on the earth. Why then is it said to be from heaven? Because it originates in heavenly grace. For the sons of God are born, not of flesh and blood but by the power of the Holy Spirit. The heavenly Jerusalem, which derives its origin from heaven and dwells above by faith, is the mother of

believers. For she has the incorruptible seed of life deposited in her by which she forms us, cherishes us in her womb and brings us to light. She has the milk and the food by which she continually nourishes her offspring.

This is why the Church is called the mother of believers. And certainly, he who refuses to be a son of the Church desires in vain to have God as his Father. For it is only through the ministry of the Church that God begets sons for Himself and brings them up until they pass through adolescence and reach manhood. This is a title of wonderful and the highest honour. But the Papists are foolish and worse than puerile when they plead this to annoy us. For their mother is an adulteress, who brings forth into death the children of the devil. How foolish is the demand that the children of God should surrender themselves to her to be cruelly slain! Could not the synagogue of Satan at that time have boasted with far more honest claim than Rome today? And yet we see how Paul strips her of every honourable distinction and assigns to her the lot of Hagar.

For it is written, Rejoice, thou barren that bearest not; break forth and cry, thou that travailest not: for more are the children of the desolate than of her which hath the husband. Now we, brethren, as Isaac was, are children of promise. But as then he that was born after the flesh persecuted him that was born after the Spirit, even so it is now. Howbeit, what saith the scripture? Cast out the handmaid and her son: for the son of the handmaid shall not inherit with the son of the free-woman. Wherefore, brethren, we are not children of a handmaid, but of the free-woman. (27-31)

27. *For it is written.* He proves, by a quotation from Isaiah, that the legitimate sons of the Church are born according to the promise. The passage is chapter 54.1ff, where the prophet speaks of Christ's Kingdom and the calling of the Gentiles. And he promises to the barren and the widow a numerous offspring. For this is why he exhorts the Church to sing and rejoice. The apostle's aim, let it be noted, is to deprive the Jews of that spiritual Jerusalem of which Isaiah prophesies. The prophet proclaims that her children shall be gathered out of all the nations, and that, not by any preparation of hers, but by the free blessing of God.

He next concludes that we become the sons of God by promise, after the pattern of Isaac, and that we obtain this honour in no other way. To readers little skilled or practised in Scripture, this conclusion may seem weak, because they do not hold the principle which is most sure, that all the promises, being grounded in the Messiah, are free. It was because the apostle took this for granted that he so fear-lessly contrasted the promise to the law.

29. *As then he that was born after the flesh.* He restrains the fierceness of the false apostles, who impudently triumphed over the godly, those who put all their trust in Christ. For such fierceness disturbed them and they needed comfort. The others also needed to be checked severely. It is not surprising, he tells them, that the children of the law at this day do what Ishmael their father did at first when he trusted to his being the firstborn and harassed Isaac the true heir. His posterity now, with their outward ceremonies, circumcision and the various services of the law, molest and vaunt over the legitimate sons of God with the same disdain.

The Spirit is again contrasted to the flesh, that is, the calling of God to human appearance (as they say). So the disguise is admitted to the followers of the law and of works, but the reality is claimed for those who rely on the calling of God alone and depend upon His grace.

Persecuted. But persecution is nowhere mentioned, except that Moses says that Ishmael was מְצַחֵק, by which participle he means that Ishmael ridiculed his brother Isaac. The explanation of some Jews, that this was a mere smile, is quite discordant; for how cruel it would have been to have avenged so fearfully a simple smile! There is then no doubt that he exasperated the child Isaac by galling re-proaches. But how far this is from persecution! And yet it is not idly or carelessly that Paul enlarges on this. No persecution should distress us so much as to see our calling undermined by the mockeries of the ungodly. Neither blows nor stripes nor nails nor thorns tortured Christ so much as that blasphemy, 'He trusted in God; what good is it to him, for he is deprived of all help?' (Matt. 27.43). There is more venom in this than in all persecutions. For how much worse is it that the grace of the divine adoption should be made void than that this frail life should be taken from us? Ishmael did not persecute his brother with the sword; but he did worse and treated him haughtily by trampling under foot the promise of God. We have a memorable instance of this in the story of Cain and Abel.

This shows us that we ought to be filled with horror, not only at outward persecutions, when the enemies of religion slay us with fire and sword, when they imprison, torture or scourge us, but also when they attempt with their blasphemies to overturn our trust, which rests on the promises of God, when they ridicule our salvation, when they wantonly laugh to scorn the whole Gospel. Nothing ought to wound our minds so deeply as contempt of God and mockery of His grace. Nor is there any kind of persecution more deadly than assaults on the salvation of the soul. We who have been delivered from the

tyranny of the Pope are not today attacked by the swords of the ungodly. But how dull we must be if we are not affected by that spiritual
persecution, when they strive in every way to extinguish the teaching
from which we draw the breath of life, when they attack our faith
with their blasphemies and shake some who are less well informed.
For my own part, I am far more worried by the fury of the Epicureans
than of the Papists. They do not attack us with open force; but the
name of God is dearer to me than my own life and I cannot but be
tortured and anxious when I see this diabolical conspiracy to extinguish
all fear and worship of God, to root out the remembrance of Christ,
or to expose it to the jeers of all the rabble. It is worse than if a whole
country were on fire at once.

30. *Howbeit, what saith the Scripture?* There was some consolation
in the example of our father Isaac that was put forward; but it is even
stronger when he adds that hypocrites, with all their boasting, can
gain nothing more than to be cast out of the spiritual family of Abraham; and that, however much they may harass us insolently for a
time, the inheritance will certainly be reserved for us. Let believers
cheer themselves with the consolation that the tyranny of the Ishmaelites will not last for ever. They seem to have appropriated the
primacy, and, proud that they are the firstborn, they despise us. But
one day they will be declared as abortive Hagar-ites, the sons of a
slave and unworthy of the inheritance.

A most beautiful passage, to prevent us being upset by the pride
of hypocrites or envying their lot, when they hold a temporary
habitation and rank in the Church. Instead, we must patiently look
for the end that awaits them. There are many illegitimate children
or strangers who usurp a place in the Church but do not keep on
holding to the faith; just as Ishmael was proud of his birthright and at
first reigned but was cast out like a foreigner with his posterity.
Some clever people smile at Paul's simplicity in comparing a woman's
spite arising out of a mean brawl to the Judgment of God. But they
overlook God's decree, by which it was made manifest that it was all
governed by the heavenly providence. That Abraham should have
been commanded to humour his wife completely is certainly extraordinary. From this we gather that God used Sarah's services for
confirming His promise. In a word, the casting out of Ishmael was
nothing but the consequence and accomplishment of that oracle. 'In
Isaac shall thy seed be called', not in Ishmael. Although, therefore,
it was the avenging of a woman's quarrel, God did not the less make
His sentence known by her mouth as a type of the Church.

31. *Wherefore, brethren.* He now exhorts the Galatians to prefer to
be children of Sarah rather than of Hagar, and, reminding them that

by the grace of Christ they were born to freedom, to continue in the same state. If we call the Papists Ishmaelites and Hagar-ites and claim that we are the lawful children, they will laugh at us. But let the two subjects in dispute be fairly compared and the most ignorant person will be at no loss to decide.

CHAPTER FIVE

Stand fast therefore in the liberty wherewith Christ hath made us free, and be not entangled again in a yoke of bondage. Behold, I Paul say unto you, that if ye be circumcised, Christ will profit you nothing. For I testify again to every man that is circumcised, that he is a debtor to do the whole law. Ye are brought to nought from Christ, whosoever of you are justified by the law; ye are fallen away from grace. For we through the Spirit by faith wait for the hope of righteousness. For in Christ Jesus neither circumcision availeth anything, nor uncircumcision; but faith working through love. (1-6)

1. *Stand fast therefore.* After saying that they are children of the free woman, he now tells them how precious is this freedom and warns them not to despise or belittle it. And certainly it is an inestimable blessing, for which we should fight even to the death. For we are not talking here about our hearths but about our altars. Many today have not considered the matter and condemn us for ruthlessness when they see us so fiercely and earnestly asserting the freedom of the faith in opposition to the tyranny of the Pope in outward matters. Our adversaries make this a pretext for prejudicing ignorant people against us, as if we only sought licence, the relaxation of all discipline. But wise and experienced persons know that this is one of the most important questions in the doctrine of salvation. For it is not a matter of whether you are to eat this or that food, whether you are to observe or neglect a particular day (as many foolishly think and some accuse us of) but of what is permitted before God, what is necessary for salvation and what it is wrong to omit. In short, the controversy relates to the state of conscience when it comes to the judgment seat of God.

Paul here means liberty from the ceremonies of the law, the observance of which was demanded as necessary by the false apostles. But at the same time let readers remember that such liberty is only a part of what Christ has procured for us. For what a small thing it would be, if He had freed us only from ceremonies. This is a stream which flows from a higher source. It is because He was made a curse that He might redeem us from the curse of the law, because He has revoked the power of the law, so far as it held us liable to the judgment of God under pain of eternal death, because, in a word, He has rescued us from the tyranny of sin, Satan and death. Thus under one species is comprehended the whole genus. But on this we shall speak in the Epistle to the Colossians.

Moreover, Christ won this liberty for us on the cross; the fruit and possession of it are bestowed on us through the Gospel. Paul does well, then, to warn the Galatians not to be entangled again with the yoke of bondage; that is, not to allow a snare to be laid for their consciences. For if men lay an unjust burden on our shoulders, it can be borne; but if they want to bring our consciences into bondage, we must resist valiantly, even to the death. If we let men bind our consciences, we shall be despoiled of an invaluable blessing and at the same time an insult will be offered to Christ, the Author of freedom. But what is the force of *again*, seeing that the Galatians had never lived under the law? It should be taken simply for 'as if'; as if they had not been redeemed by the grace of Christ. Although the law was given to Jews and not to Gentiles, neither has any freedom apart from Christ but only bondage.

2. *Behold, I Paul.* He could not have pronounced a severer threatening than that it would exclude them entirely from the grace of Christ. But what does this mean, that Christ will be of no avail to all who are circumcised? Did Christ profit nothing to Abraham? Certainly He did; for it was in order that Christ might profit him that he received circumcision. If we say that it was in force before Christ's coming, what shall we say of Timothy? We must notice that Paul is not here speaking of the outward surgical act or of the ceremony, but rather is attacking the wicked doctrine of the false apostles, who pretended that it was a necessary part of the worship of God and at the same time made it a ground of confidence as a meritorious work. These devilish devices made Christ nothing; not that the false apostles denied Christ or wished Him to be entirely set aside, but that they made such a division between His grace and the works of the law as to leave only the half of salvation to Him. The apostle asserts that He cannot be divided like this and that He only profits us when we embrace Him in His wholeness.

But do not our modern Papists thrust on us their own inventions in the place of circumcision? The trend of their whole teaching is to mix up the grace of Christ with the merits of works, and this is impossible. Whoever wants to have a half-Christ loses the whole. And yet the Papists think they are very acute when they tell us they ascribe nothing to works except through the mediating grace of Christ. How was the error of the Galatians any different? They did not believe that they had departed from Christ or renounced His grace. And yet they lost Christ when that chief head of the doctrine of the Gospel was corrupted.

The expression 'Behold, I Paul' is very emphatic. He places himself before them and gives his name, lest he should seem to have a doubtful case. And though his authority had begun to lessen among the Galatians, he asserts that it is sufficient to put down every adversary.

3. *For I testify again.* This is a proof by contraries of the next sentence. He who is a debtor to do the whole law will never escape death, but will always be held guilty. For no man will ever be found who satisfies the law. Such an obligation, therefore, means the man's sure damnation. We see then that these two are contradictory: that we are partakers of the grace of Christ; and that we are bound to fulfil the whole law. But then it follows that none of the patriarchs were saved. Then it follows that Timothy was lost, since Paul circumcised him. Woe to us, then, till we have been freed from the law, for where there is circumcision there is subjugation.

But we must observe that Paul was accustomed to speak of circumcision in two ways, as everyone who has read him a fair amount will easily perceive. In Rom. 4.11 he calls it a seal of the righteousness of faith. Thus, under circumcision, he includes Christ and the free promise of salvation. But here he contrasts it with Christ and faith and the Gospel and grace, viewing it simply as a legal agreement founded on the merit of works. From this it is clear, as I have already said, that he does not always speak about circumcision in the same way. And the reason for the difference must be taken into account. I say that when Paul views circumcision in its own nature, he properly makes it a symbol of grace, because this was God's appointment. But when he was dealing with the false apostles, who misused circumcision so as to destroy the Gospel, he does not consider why it was appointed by the Lord, but attacks the corruption that has proceeded from men.

A very striking example occurs here. When Abraham had been given a promise about Christ, about free righteousness and eternal salvation, circumcision was added to confirm the promise. Thus by God's appointment it was a sacrament which would serve faith. Along come the false apostles and make it out to be a meritorious work, and recommend the observance of the law, with circumcision as an initiation into the profession of the law. The apostle is not referring here to the appointment of God but attacking the invention of the false apostles. It will be objected that the abuses of the ungodly, whatever those abuses may be, do not impair the sacred ordinances of God. I reply that circumcision was only a temporary ordinance of God. After the coming of Christ, this sacrament ceased to be a divine institution, because baptism had succeeded to its place. Why then was Timothy circumcised? Not indeed for his own sake, but for the sake of the weak brethren, to whom that point was yielded.

To show more clearly how close are the doctrine of the Papists and that which Paul opposes, it must be noted that the sacraments, received sincerely, are not strictly the works of men but of God. In Baptism or the Lord's Supper we do nothing; we simply come before God to receive His grace. Baptism, from our side, is a passive work (*respectu nostri est opus passivum*). We bring nothing to it but faith, which has all things laid up in Christ. But what say the Papists? They invent the *opus operatum*, by which men merit the grace of God. What is this but to extinguish utterly the truth of the sacrament? We retain Baptism and the Lord's Supper because Christ wished them to be used perpetually. But we bitterly detest those ungodly absurdities, as we should do.

4. *Ye are brought to nought from Christ.* The meaning is: 'If you seek any part of righteousness in the works of the law, Christ has nothing to do with you, and you are separated from grace.' They were not so grossly mistaken that they believed that they were justified by the observance of the law alone; but they wanted to mix Christ with the law. Otherwise Paul would have been threatening them without effect. 'What are you doing? You are making Christ useless to you and annihilating His grace.' We see, then, that the smallest part of righteousness cannot be attributed to the law without renouncing Christ and His grace.

5. *For we through the Spirit by faith.* This is an anticipation of an objection that might easily occur to their minds. 'Will circumcision then be of no use?' 'In Christ,' he replies, 'it is of no value.' Righteousness, therefore, lies in faith and is obtained in the Spirit, without ceremonies.

To *wait for the hope of righteousness* is to put our trust in this or that object, or to decide from whence righteousness is to be hoped for. But the words probably also denote perseverance: 'Let us continue stedfastly in the hope of righteousness which we obtain by faith.' When he says that we obtain righteousness by faith, it applies equally to us and to the patriarchs. All of them, as the Scripture testifies, pleased God by faith; but their faith was wrapped up in the veil of ceremonies. Therefore he distinguishes us from them by the word 'spirit', which is contrasted to outward shadows. He therefore means that bare faith is now sufficient for obtaining righteousness, one which is not adorned with the pomp of ceremonies but is satisfied with the spiritual worship of God.

6. *For in Christ Jesus.* The reason why they now hope for righteousness in the Spirit is that in Christ, or in the Christian Church, circumcision with its appendages is abolished. For by synecdoche, the word 'circumcision' is put for ceremonies. While he declares that they no

longer have any place, he does not allow that they had always been useless. For he says that they were repealed only after the revelation of Christ. This at the same time solves another problem: why does he here speak so contemptuously of circumcision, as if it was of no value? The fact that circumcision was once a sacrament is not the point now. The question is not what its value was before it had been abolished. Under the Kingdom of Christ he pronounces it to be on a level with uncircumcision, since the coming of Christ has put an end to legal ceremonies.

But faith working through love. He contrasts ceremonies and the exercise of love, lest the Jews should be too pleased with themselves, as if they had some special superiority; for towards the end of the epistle he uses, instead of this clause, the words 'a new creature'. Therefore it is as if he had said, 'God does not keep us nowadays under ceremonies; it is enough if we exercise ourselves in love.' But yet this does not set aside our sacraments, which are aids to faith; he is merely confirming what he had formerly taught on the spiritual worship of God.

There would be no difficulty in this passage, had the Papists not dishonestly twisted it to uphold the righteousness of works. When they want to refute our doctrine that we are justified by faith alone, they seize up this weapon: 'If the faith that justifies us be that which works by love, faith alone does not justify.' I reply: they do not understand their own babbling; far less what we teach. It is not our doctrine that the faith which justifies is alone. We maintain that it is always joined with good works. But we contend that faith avails by itself for justification. The Papists themselves, like murderers, tear faith to pieces, sometimes making it *informis* and empty of love, and sometimes *formata*. But we deny that true faith can be separated from the Spirit of regeneration. When we debate justification, however, we exclude all works.

In the present passage Paul does not dispute whether love co-operates with faith in justifying; but, lest he should seem to make Christians idle and like blocks of wood, he indicates the true exercises of believers. When you discuss justification, beware of allowing any mention of love or of works, but resolutely hold on to the exclusive adverb. But that Paul is not here treating of justification or assigning the credit for it partly to love, is easily proved from the fact that by the same argument it would follow that circumcision and ceremonies once justified. For as in Christ Jesus he commends faith with love, so before the coming of Christ ceremonies were required. But this has nothing to do with obtaining righteousness, as the Papists themselves agree. Therefore this must not be supposed about love either.

Ye were running well; who did hinder you, that ye should not obey the truth? This persuasion is not from him that called you. A little leaven leaveneth the whole lump. I have confidence in you in the Lord, that ye will be none otherwise minded: but he that troubleth you shall bear his judgment, whosoever he be. But I, brethren, if I still preach circumcision, why am I still persecuted? then has the stumbling-block of the cross been done away. I would they which trouble you were even cut off. (7-12)

7. *Ye were running well.* He mingles censure for their present defection with praise for their former course, expressly so that they may be covered with shame and return more quickly to the way. When he asks with astonishment who had seduced them from the right way, it is to make them ashamed. I have chosen to translate πείθεσθαι as 'obey' rather than 'believe', because they had already once embraced the purity of the Gospel, but had been led away from obedience.

8. *This persuasion is not.* Before, he had fought them with arguments; now he uses his authority and declares that their persuasion did not come from God. Such an admonition would not have so much weight, were it not supported by personal authority. But Paul had been the preacher who announced their divine calling, and this is why he could speak so boldly to them. And so he does not directly name God, but refers to Him by a circumlocution. As if he had said, 'God is never inconsistent with Himself and it is He who by my preaching called you to salvation. This new persuasion, then, has come from somewhere else. If you wish to have it thought that your calling is from God, beware of lending an ear to those who thrust upon you their new inventions.' Although the Greek participle καλοῦντος is, of course, in the present tense, it is taken indefinitely and I have preferred to translate it 'who hath called you', so as to remove ambiguity.

9. *A little leaven.* I refer this to doctrine, not to men. It warns them how mischievous is the corruption of doctrine, so that they may not overlook it (as is common) as something of little or no danger. Satan goes to work with cunning and does not obviously destroy the whole Gospel but taints its purity with false and corrupt opinions. Many do not consider the seriousness of the evil and therefore make a less determined resistance. The apostle therefore protests that once the truth of God is corrupted, nothing remains sound. He uses the metaphor of leaven, which, however small in quantity, transmits its sourness to the whole mass. We must be very careful not to allow anything to be added to the pure doctrine of the Gospel.

10. *I have confidence in you.* All his anger is again directed against

the false apostles. He traces the evil to them and therefore threatens them with the punishment. He declares that he has good hopes of the Galatians quickly and readily returning to true concord. It gives us courage to learn that good hopes are held of us, for we think it shameful to disappoint those who feel kindly and friendly towards us. But because it was the work of God to bring the Galatians back to the pure doctrine of faith from which they had turned aside, he says that he has confidence in them in the Lord; by which he reminds them that repentance is a heavenly gift and that they must ask it from God.

He that troubleth you. This is a confirmation of the last sentence, for he indirectly imputes a great part of the blame to those impostors who had deceived the Galatians. He almost exempts the Galatians from the vengeance he declares against these others. Moreover, let all who introduce causes of trouble into Churches, who break the unity of faith, who destroy harmony, listen to this, and if they have any right feeling, let them tremble at this word. For God declares by the mouth of Paul that no authors of such scandals will escape unpunished.

The phrase *whosoever he be* is emphatic. For because the impressive language of the false apostles had terrified the ignorant multitude, it became necessary for Paul to proclaim his doctrine with an equal impressiveness and not to spare anyone who dared to raise his voice against it, however eminent he might be.

11. *But I, brethren.* This argument is drawn from the final cause. He says, 'I should be able to avoid the hatred of men and all danger and persecution were I only to mix ceremonies with Christ. The vigour with which I fight them is not for my own sake, nor for my own advantage.' But does it therefore follow that his teaching is true? I answer, that a right attitude and pure conscience in a teacher have no small share in winning assent. Besides, it is not credible that a man would be so mad as willingly to bring distress upon himself. Finally, he casts on his opponents the suspicion that in preaching circumcision they were more interested in their own ease than in serving Christ faithfully. In short, Paul was completely free from ambition, covetousness or regard to personal interest, since he despised favour and applause and laid himself open to the persecutions and fury of the multitude rather than swerve a hair's breadth from the purity of the Gospel.

Then has the stumbling-block of the cross been done away. Paul freely calls the Gospel the Cross or the Word of the Cross, when he wants to contrast its lowly simplicity with the bombast of human wisdom or righteousness. For the Jews, puffed up with a perverted confidence in their righteousness, and the Greeks, with a foolish belief in their

wisdom, despised the meanness of the Gospel. When therefore he
says that now, if the preaching of circumcision be received, the stum-
bling block of the cross will no longer exist, he means that the Gospel
will no longer be harried by the Jews, but will be given a place with
their entire agreement; for they will not take offence at a pretended
and spurious Gospel, compounded of Moses and Christ, but will
tolerate such a mixture, because it will leave them in possession of
their earlier superiority.

12. *I would they were even cut off.* His indignation increases and he
prays for destruction on the impostors by whom the Galatians had
been deceived. The word 'cut off' seems to allude to the circumcision
which they were pressing for. Chrysostom inclines to this view:
'They tear the Church for the sake of circumcision; I wish they were
cut off entirely.' But such a curse does not seem to fit the mildness
of an apostle, who ought to wish that all should be saved and therefore
that not one should perish. I reply that this is true when we have men
in mind; for God commends to us the salvation of all men without
exception, even as Christ suffered for the sins of the whole world.
But godly minds are sometimes carried beyond the consideration of
men to fix their gaze on the glory of God and the Kingdom of Christ.
For to the extent that the glory of God is more excellent than the
salvation of men, it ought to ravish us to a corresponding love and
regard. Believers, earnestly intent on promoting the glory of God,
forget men and the world and would rather that the whole world
should perish than that any part of God's glory should be lost.

Let us remember that this prayer is the result of leaving men completely out of view and looking at God alone. Paul cannot be accused
of cruelty, as if he were opposed to love. Besides, if we compare a
single man or a few persons with the Church, how immeasurably
must she preponderate. It is a cruel mercy that prefers one man to the
whole Church. On one side I see the flock of God in danger; on the
other I see a wolf on the attack, spurred on by Satan. Ought not care
for the Church to swallow up all my thoughts so that I desire to
purchase its salvation with the destruction of the wolf? And yet I
would not wish that any should perish like this; but love and anxiety
for the Church carry me away into a sort of ecstasy, so that I care for
nothing else. Every true pastor of the Church will burn with such a
zeal. The Greek word that I have translated *who trouble you* signifies
to remove from a certain rank or station. To emphasize this he adds
also, desiring not only that they should be degraded but entirely
separated and cut off.

For ye, brethren, have been called unto freedom; only do not give freedom to the flesh as an occasion, but through love serve one another. For the whole law is fulfilled in one word, even in this: Thou shalt love thy neighbour as thyself. But if ye bite and devour one another, take heed that ye be not consumed one of another. But I say, Walk in the Spirit, and ye shall not complete the lust of the flesh. For the flesh lusteth against the Spirit, and the Spirit against the flesh: and these are contrary the one to the other; so that ye may not do the things that ye would. But if ye are led by the Spirit, ye are not under the law. (13-18)

13. *Ye have been called unto liberty.* He now shows how liberty must be used. In I Corinthians we have pointed out that liberty and the use of it are two different things. Liberty lies in the conscience and looks to God. Its use lies in externals and deals not with God only but with men. Having exhorted the Galatians not to allow any diminution of their liberty, he now enjoins them to be moderate in using it. Moreover, he lays down a rule for its lawful use, that it shall not be turned into a pretext or occasion for licence. Liberty is not given to the flesh, which ought rather to be held captive under the yoke, but is a spiritual benefit, of which none but godly minds are capable.

But through love. He explains that the way to restrain liberty from breaking out into unsettled and licentious abuse is if it is ruled by love. Let us always remember that he is not here dealing with how we are free before God but how we may use our liberty among men. An upright conscience submits to no slavery; but the use of, or abstention from, outward slavery is not dangerous. In a word, if we serve one another through love, we shall always have regard to edification; so that we shall not grow wanton, but use the grace of God to His honour and the salvation of our neighbours.

14. *For the whole law.* In this verse an antithesis must be supplied between Paul's exhortation and the doctrine of the false apostles. While they insisted on ceremonies alone, Paul glances in passing at the true duties and exercises of Christians. The present commendation of love is intended to teach the Galatians that it forms the chief part of Christian perfection. But we must see why all the precepts of the law are comprehended under love. The law consists of two tables, the first of which teaches of the worship of God and the duties of godliness, and the second of love. For it is absurd to make a part into the whole. Some avoid this by saying that the first table contains nothing but to love God with our whole heart. But Paul expressly mentions love to our neighbour and therefore a firmer solution must be sought. Piety towards God is, I confess, higher than love of the brethren; and therefore the observance of the first table is more valuable in the sight of God than that of the second. But as God

Himself is invisible, so godliness is something hidden from the human senses. And although the ceremonies were appointed to bear witness to it, they are not certain proofs. It often happens that none are more zealous and regular in observing ceremonies than hypocrites. God therefore wants to make trial of our love to Him by that love of our brother which He commends to us. This is why not here alone, but also in Rom. 13.8 and 10, love is called the fulfilling of the law, not because it is superior to the worship of God, but because it is the proof of it. God, as I said, is invisible; but He represents Himself to us in the brethren and in their persons demands what is due to Himself. Love to men springs only from the fear and love of God. Therefore it is not surprising if by synecdoche the effect includes under it the cause of which it is the sign. But it would be wrong to separate the love of God from the love of men.

Thou shalt love thy neighbour. He who loves will render to every man his right, will do injury or harm to no man and will, so far as he can, do good to all. For what else is the whole of the second table about? This too is the argument that Paul uses in Romans. The word neighbour includes all men living. For we are joined by a common nature, as Isaiah reminds us 'that thou despise not thine own flesh'[1] (Isa. 58.7). The image of God ought to be a specially sacred bond of union. Thus, no distinction is made here between friend and foe, for the wickedness of men cannot annul the right of nature.

The phrase *as thyself* means that as each man is moved to love himself by the impulse of the flesh, so love for our neighbour is commanded to us by God. For they subvert and not interpret the words of the Lord who gather from them (as do all the Sorbonnists) that the love of ourselves is always first in order, because what is ruled is inferior to what rules (*regulatum inferius sit sua regula*). They are asses and have not a spark of love. For if the love of ourselves were the rule, it would follow that it is right and holy and approved by God. But we shall never love our neighbours sincerely and according to the Lord's criterion until we have corrected the love of ourselves. The two affections are opposite and contradictory; for the love (*amor*) of ourselves begets a neglect and contempt of others, it begets cruelty, it is the fount of avarice, of violence, deceit and all kindred vices, it drives us to impatience and arms us with the desire for revenge. The Lord therefore demands that it be changed to love (*charitatem*).

15. *But if ye bite and devour.* From the nature of the subject, as well as from the words, we may conjecture that the Galatians had disputes among themselves; for they differed on doctrine. He now demonstrates from the result how destructive such an evil is in the Church.

[1] Vulgate. Calvin's own translation *ad loc.* is: 'hide not thyself from'.

So it is probable that the Lord punished their ambition, pride and other sins by false doctrine. This may be inferred from what is customary as well as from what is declared by Moses in Deut. 13.3.

By *biting and devouring* he means, to my mind, slanders, accusations, wrangling and other kinds of verbal quarrels as well as acts of injustice arising either from fraud or violence. And what is the end of them? *To be consumed*, he says. But the property of love is a mutual protection and kindness. Would that we always remembered, when the devil tempts us to disputes, that the disagreement of members within the Church can lead to nothing but the ruin and consumption of the whole body. How unhappy, how mad it is, that we who are members of the same body should voluntarily conspire together for mutual destruction!

16. *But I say*. Now follows the remedy. The ruin of the Church is no small evil. Therefore whatever threatens it must be opposed with determination. But by what method? When the flesh does not rule in us, and when we yield ourselves to be ruled by the Spirit of God. He hints that the Galatians are carnal, destitute of God's Spirit and that they lead a life unworthy of Christians. For whence did it come that they attacked one another, but from their being guided by the lust of the flesh? This, he says, is evidence that they do not walk according to the Spirit.

We should mark the word *complete*. By it he means that, although the sons of God are subject to sin while they groan under the burden of the flesh, they are not its subjects or slaves, but strive to resist it. The spiritual man is not free from the lusts of the flesh and their often incitements, but he does not submit to letting them reign over him, which is what completing them is. See chapter 8 of Romans.

17. *For the flesh lusteth*. He warns them of the difficulty, that they may know that they cannot live without a struggle. The difficulty arises from our nature being opposed to the Spirit. The word 'flesh', as we have said in the Epistle to the Romans, denotes the nature of man. For the limited application of it by the Sophists to the lower senses, as they are called, is refuted by many passages. And the antithesis removes all doubt. The Spirit means the renewed nature, or the grace of regeneration. What else then is the flesh but the old man? And so, since the whole nature of man is rebellious and obstinate against the Spirit of God, we must labour and fight and exert our utmost energy to obey the Spirit. We must begin with denial of ourselves. Here we see the compliment that the Lord pays to our nature, that there is no greater agreement between it and righteousness than between fire and water. Now what drop of goodness is to be found in free will?—unless we call something good that is contrary

to God's Spirit. This is what it says in Rom. 8.7, 'All the thoughts of the flesh are enmity against God.'

So that ye may not do the things that ye would. This undoubtedly refers to the regenerate. Carnal men have no battle with their depraved lusts, no true wish to aspire to the righteousness of God. Paul is addressing believers; therefore it must be understood, not of the inclination of nature, but of the holy affections which God gives (*inspirat*) to us by His grace. Paul therefore declares that believers, so long as they are in this life, are not so victorious that they serve God perfectly, however much they strive. The fulfilment does not correspond to their wishes and desires. This argument is treated more fully in Rom. 7.15ff.

18. *But if ye are led by the Spirit.* Although believers stumble in the way of the Lord, let them not be discouraged, because they desire to satisfy the law. They need such a comfort as they find here, when Paul says, 'Ye are not under the law.' (This occurs also in Rom. 6.14.) For it follows from this that what they have lacked hitherto is not reckoned against them, but their duties are accepted by God as if they were full and complete in every respect. Moreover, he is still following the same train of thought. For this is the Spirit whom he had formerly called 'the Spirit of adoption', who, when he makes men free, emancipates them from the yoke of the law. As if he had said, 'Is it your desire once for all to end the controversies in which you are engaged? Walk according to the Spirit. You will then be free from the dominion of the law, which will be only a liberal teaching to warn you; it will no longer hold your consciences bound.' Besides, when the condemnation of the law is removed, freedom from ceremonies follows; for ceremonies are signs of the condition of a slave.

Now the works of the flesh are manifest, which are these; Adultery, fornication, uncleanness, lasciviousness, idolatry, witchcraft, enmities, strifes, jealousies, wraths, factions, seditions, heresies, envyings, murders, drunkenness, revellings, and such like: of the which I forewarn you, as I also did forewarn you, that they which practise such things shall not inherit the kingdom of God. (19-21)

19. *Now the works of the flesh are manifest.* He had set before Christians the aim they should strive after: to obey the Spirit and to resist the flesh. He now draws a picture both of the flesh and of the Spirit. If men knew themselves, they would not need this declaration that they are nothing but flesh. But such is our innate hypocrisy that we never perceive our foulness until the tree has been made known by its fruits.

The apostle therefore now tells us of those sins against which we must fight, that we may not live according to the flesh. He does not enumerate them all, as he himself states at the end; but from those cited the others may be easily ascertained. He puts *adultery* and *fornication* first; then follows *uncleanness*, which applies to every kind of unchastity. *Lasciviousness* is, so to say, an instrument, for the Greek word ἀσέλγεια, which is thus translated, is applied to those who lead wanton and dissolute lives. These four refer to the one principle of unchastity. He adds *the worship of idols*, which is here used for gross superstitions openly practised in the sight of men.

The seven species which follow are closely related and two others are added afterwards. He names *wrath* and *strife*, which differ chiefly in that wrath is brief and strife lasting. *Jealousies* and *envyings* are the causes of hatred. Aristotle makes this distinction between them in the second book of the *Rhetoric*: he who is jealous is grieved that another should excel him, not because the virtue or worth of that person harms him but because he would wish to be superior. The envious man has no desire to excel but chafes at the excellence of others. Therefore he tells us that none but low and mean persons are envious, whereas he ascribes jealousy to lofty and heroic minds. Paul declares both to be a disease of the flesh. From wrath and hatred arise quarrels and uproars. Finally he comes to murders and witchcraft. By *revellings* he means a dissolute life and every kind of intemperance of the appetite. It should be observed that he reckons heresies among the works of the flesh, for it shows clearly that the word flesh has a wider reference than sensuality, as the Sophists imagine. What produces heresies but ambition, which resides, not in the lower senses but in the highest seat of the mind? He says that these works are manifest, lest anyone should think that he would gain anything from evasion. For how does it help to deny that the flesh reigns in us if the fruit betrays the tree?

21. *Of which I forewarn you.* By this solemn threatening he not only intended to alarm the Galatians but also indirectly to rebuke the false apostles who had laid aside a far more useful teaching to squabble about ceremonies. But at the same time he tells us by his example to press home those exhortations and threatenings according to the words, 'Cry aloud, spare not; declare unto my people their transgressions' (Isa. 58.1). What more terrifying thing can be said than that they who walk after the flesh are banished from the kingdom of God? Who will dare view those sins lightly which God so much hates?

But this makes it sound as if all are cut off from hope of salvation; for who is there who does not labour under one or other of these sins? I reply: Paul does not threaten that there shall be excluded from the

Kingdom of God all who have sinned, but all who remain impenitent. The saints themselves are sometimes heavily burdened, but they return to the way. Because they do not surrender, they are not included in this catalogue. All the threatenings of God's judgments call us to repentance, for which pardon is always ready with God; but if we continue obstinate, they will be a testimony against us.

Paul uses κληρονομεῖν as *to possess*, that is, to receive by hereditary right. For it is only by the right of adoption that we obtain eternal life, as we have seen elsewhere.

> *But the fruit of the Spirit is love, joy, peace, longsuffering, kindness, goodness, faithfulness, meekness, temperance: against such there is no law. And they that are Christ's have crucified the flesh, with the passions and the lusts. If we live by the Spirit, by the Spirit let us also walk. Let us not be desirous of vainglory, provoking one another, envying one another.* (22-26)

22. *But the fruit of the Spirit.* Just as earlier he had condemned the whole nature of man as producing nothing but evil and worthless fruits, so he now tells us that all virtues, all good and well-regulated affections, proceed from the Spirit, that is, from the grace of God and the renewed nature which we have from Christ. As if he had said: 'Nothing but evil comes from man; nothing good comes but from the Holy Spirit.' For although there have often appeared in unregenerate men remarkable instances of gentleness, faithfulness, temperance and generosity, it is certain they were all only deceptive masks. Curius and Fabricius were famous for their courage, Cato for temperance, Scipio for kindness and generosity, Fabius for patience. But all this was only in the sight of men and as members of society. In the sight of God nothing is pure but what proceeds from the fountain of all purity.

Here I do not take *joy* in the same sense as in Rom. 14.17, but as that cheerfulness (*hilaritas*) towards our fellow-men which is the opposite of moroseness. Faith is used for truth, and is contrasted with cunning, deceit and falsehood. *Peace* I contrast with quarrels and contentions. *Longsuffering* is gentleness of mind, which disposes us to take everything in good part and not to be easily offended. The rest are clear, for the quality of the mind becomes open from its fruit.

But it may be asked what judgment we are to form of wicked men and idolaters who yet displayed an extraordinary resemblance of the virtues. For from their works they seem spiritual. I reply: as not all the works of the flesh appear in a carnal man, but his carnality is shown by one or another vice, so a man cannot be considered spiritual from a single virtue. Sometimes it will be obvious from other vices that the flesh reigns in him; and this is easily seen in all those whom I have mentioned.

23. *Against such.* Some understand this as meaning simply that the law is not directed against good works, because from evil manners have sprung good laws. But Paul's meaning is profounder and less obvious: where the Spirit reigns, the law has no longer any dominion. By moulding our hearts to His own righteousness, the Lord delivers us from the severity of the law, so that He does not deal with us according to its covenant, nor does He bind our consciences under its condemnation. Yet the law continues to perform its office of teaching and exhorting. But the Spirit of adoption sets us free from subjection to it. He therefore ridicules the false apostles, who enforced subjection to the law but were none the less eager to free themselves from its yoke. Paul tells us that the only way in which this can be done is when the Spirit of God gains the dominion. From which it follows that they had no care for spiritual righteousness.

24. *And they that are Christ's.* He adds this to show that freedom belongs to all Christians, because they have renounced the flesh. Moreover, he reminds the Galatians what is true Christianity in relation to the life, lest they should profess themselves Christians falsely. The word *crucified* is used to indicate that the mortification of the flesh is the effect of Christ's cross. This work does not belong to man, but it is by the grace of Christ that we have been planted into the fellowship of Christ's death, so that we might no longer live to ourselves (Rom. 6.5). If, by true self-denial and the destruction of the old man, we are buried with Christ, we shall enjoy the privilege of the sons of God. Not that the flesh is entirely destroyed, but it ought not to exercise dominion but should yield to the Spirit.

The *flesh* and its *lusts* are put for the root and the fruits. The flesh itself is the depravity of corrupt nature, from which all evils proceed. Now it is clear that the members of Christ are injured if they are still held in bondage to the law, from which all who have been regenerated by His Spirit are set free.

25. *If we live by the Spirit.* Now in his usual way, Paul draws an exhortation out of the doctrine. The death of the flesh is the life of the Spirit. If God's Spirit lives in us, let Him govern all our actions. There will always be many who impudently boast of living in the Spirit, but Paul challenges them to prove their claim. As the soul does not live idly in the body, but gives motion and vigour to every member and part, so the Spirit of God cannot dwell in us without manifesting Himself by the outward effects. By 'life' is here meant the inward power, and by 'walk', the outward actions. Paul means

that works are witnesses to spiritual life. The metaphorical use of the word walk is frequent.

26. *Let us not be desirous of vain glory.* The special exhortations which were necessary for the Galatians are no less important for our own time. Of the many evils existing in our society and particularly in the Church, ambition is the mother. And so he warns us to beware. For κενοδοξία in Paul is nothing but φιλοτιμία, or the desire for honour, by which everyone desires to excel all others. The heathen philosophers do not condemn every desire for glory. But among Christians, whoever is greedy for glory is justly accused of empty and foolish ambition, because he departs from true glory. It is only lawful for us to glory in God. Outside God it is always mere vanity. Mutual provocations and envyings are the daughters of ambition. He who aspires to the highest rank must of necessity envy all others. Hence come detractions, malice, attacks.

CHAPTER SIX

Brethren, even if a man be overtaken in any fault, ye which are spiritual restore such an one in a spirit of meekness; looking to thyself, lest thou also be tempted. Bear ye one another's burdens, and so fulfil the law of Christ. For if a man think himself to be something, when he is nothing, he deceiveth himself. But let each man prove his own work, and then shall he have glorying in himself alone, and not in another. For each man shall bear his own burden. (1-5)

1. *Brethren, even if a man be overtaken.* Just as ambition is a particularly poisonous evil, so also great harm is often done by unseasonable and excessive severity, which goes under the noble name of zeal but frequently springs from pride and from dislike and contempt of the brethren. For very many harass their brethren violently and cruelly, as if their faults were something to taunt them with. The reason is that they would rather scold than correct. Those who sin should be reproved, and it is often necessary to be severe and sharp. Therefore it is right to press them with rebukes even to the point of discourtesy; but the vinegar must be tempered with oil. Therefore he teaches us to show mildness in correcting the faults of brethren and says that no rebukes are godly and Christian which do not savour of meekness.

To gain this object he explains the purpose of godly reproofs, which is, to restore the fallen and make him sound again. This will never be accomplished by violence or by a spirit of accusation, or by fierceness of countenance and words. It remains that we must show a calm and kind spirit if we want to heal our brother. And lest any man should be satisfied with the outward form of kindness, he demands the spirit of meekness; by which he means that only they are fit to chastise a brother who are disposed to kindness in their minds.

He gives another reason for gentleness in correcting brethren when he says, 'if he be overtaken'. If he had fallen through want of consideration or by being deceived, it would be cruel to treat him harshly. Now we know that the devil is always ready with snares and we are deceived by him in a thousand ways. When we see that a brother has fallen, let us consider that he has fallen into the snares of Satan. Let us be moved with compassion, and be the more ready to forgive him. But offences and falls must be distinguished from deep-seated crimes accompanied by a deliberate and obstinate contempt of God. Such wickedness and malignity towards God must be dealt with more severely; for what good would gentleness do? The particle *even if* which he uses implies that not only the weak who have been tempted but those who have yielded to temptation, shall receive pardon.

Ye which are spiritual. This is not spoken in irony; for however spiritual they might be, they were still not completely filled with the Spirit. It is the duty of such to raise up the fallen. For what is the purpose of their superiority except the welfare of the brethren? The more any man is endowed with grace, the more is he bound to devote himself to the edification of the weaker brethren. But because we are so disordered that even in our best duties we fail, he warns us not to be influenced by the flesh.

Considering thyself. It is not without reason that he changes the number, for his admonition is more forceful when he calls each person individually and bids him take stock of himself. 'Whoever thou art,' he says, 'that art a critic of others, look also to thyself.' Nothing is more difficult than to bring us to acknowledge or examine our own weakness. However acute we may be in observing the faults of others, we do not see, as someone says, 'the wallet that hangs behind our own back'. And therefore, to stir us up the more sharply, he uses the singular number.

The meaning could be twofold. As we acknowledge that we are liable to sin, we more readily grant that forgiveness to others which we ourselves wish to be given to us. Some take Paul's words thus, 'Thou who art a sinner and needest the mercy of thy brethren, oughtest not to show thyself cruel or implacable to others.' But I would as soon accept the other expositions, that Paul tells us to beware lest, in correcting others, we ourselves sin. There is a danger here that we must particularly beware of and yet which it is difficult to avoid, since nothing is easier than to exceed due limits. 'Tempt', however, may very properly be taken in the present tense and extended to the whole life. Whenever we have occasion to criticize, let us remember to begin with ourselves and then, conscious of our own weakness, let us be restrained with others.

2. *Bear ye one another's burdens.* It is a very appropriate exhortation to humanity when he calls the weaknesses or vices under which we labour 'burdens'. For nature dictates to us that those who sink under a burden should be relieved. He enjoins us to bear their burdens—not to indulge or overlook the evils by which our brethren are pressed down, but rather to disburden them. And this can only be done by friendly and mild correction. There are many adulterers who would gladly make Christ a pander; thieves who would like to make Him a receiver; wicked criminals of all kinds who would like to make Him their patron: they all want to lay their burdens on the shoulders of

believers. But since he connects bearing with restoring or repairing, the sort or bearing demanded of Christians is unmistakable.

And so fulfil the law of Christ. The word 'law' when applied to Christ represents an argument. There is an implied contrast between the law of Christ and the law of Moses, as if he said, 'If you desire to keep a law, Christ enjoins on you a law which you can only prefer to all others; and that is, to cherish kindness towards each other. He who lacks this has nothing.' On the other hand he says that when everyone compassionately helps his neighbour, the law of Christ is fulfilled. By this he means that everything that is foreign to love is unnecessary; for the composition of the Greek word expresses an absolute completion. But as no man performs in every respect what Paul requires, we are still at a distance from perfection. He who is nearest to it in comparison with others, is yet far distant in respect of God.

3. *For if a man think himself.* There is an ambiguity in the construction, but Paul's meaning is clear. The phrase 'when he is nothing' seems at first sight to mean, 'If anyone who is in other ways nothing claims to be something'; for there are many men of no worth who are yet swollen with a foolish idea of themselves. But the meaning is more general and should therefore be expressed thus, 'Since all men are nothing, he who wishes to appear something and persuades himself that he is somebody, deceives himself.' First, then, he declares that we are nothing; by which he means that we have nothing of our own to boast about, but are destitute of every good thing; so that all our glorying is mere vanity. Secondly, he concludes that those who claim something for themselves deceive themselves. Now since we think there is nothing worse than to be deceived by others, it is completely absurd that we should voluntarily deceive ourselves about ourselves. This thought will make us much more fair to others. Where do fierce insult or haughty sternness come from but from everyone exalting himself and proudly despising others? Let arrogance go and we shall be most moderate towards one another.

4. *But let each man prove his own work.* Paul has beaten down human pride with a powerful blow. But it often happens that we compare ourselves with others and from the low opinion that we form of them set a high price on ourselves. He says that there is no room for such a comparison. 'Let no man', he says, 'measure himself by the standard of another, or be pleased with himself because others displease him more. Let him lay aside all regard to others, examine just his own conscience and inquire what is his own work.' It is not what we gain by detracting from others, but what we have without any comparison, that is truly praiseworthy.

Some think this is ironical, as if Paul were saying, 'You flatter yourself because of the faults of others. But if you consider who you are, you will then have the praise that is your due—namely, none at all.' For there is no man who deserves one bit of praise. Then they expound what follows, 'each man shall bear his own burden', as that it is usual for him to bear it. But the true sense fits better without a figure of speech. For the words mean, 'You will have praise in regard to yourself alone and not by comparison with others.' I know why they like it to be irony, since in the next sentence the apostle annihilates all the glory of men. But here Paul treats of the glorying of a good conscience which the Lord allows to His people and which Paul everywhere praises. This is simply an acknowledgment of the grace of God, which lauds man not at all, but stirs him up to glorify God. This is the reason for praise that the godly find in themselves, and they do not ascribe it to their own merits but to the goodness of God. 'This is our rejoicing,' he says elsewhere, 'the testimony of a good conscience that we have lived faithfully' (II Cor. 1.2). And Christ, 'Enter into thy closet; and when thou hast shut thy door, do thy good deed[1] before thy Father in secret, and thy Father, who is in secret, shall reward thee' (Matt. 6.6). Strictly speaking, this is not an assertion, but he teaches us that if a man is valued for his own worth and not for the lowness of others, the praise is just and substantial. The statement is therefore conditional, as if he said that none are entitled to be regarded as good men who are not found to be so indeed quite apart from comparison with others.

5. *For each man shall bear his own burden.* To destroy our sloth and pride he brings before us the judgment of God, in which each man for himself and without comparison will render an account of his life. For this is what deceives us. Just as a one-eyed man living among the blind thinks he has good sight and a swarthy man among negroes thinks he is white. He affirms that those imaginings will find no place in the judgment of God. There each one will bear his own burden and none will acquit others of their sins. This is the natural meaning of the words.

Let him that is taught in the word communicate unto him that teacheth in all good things. Be not deceived; God is not mocked: for whatsoever a man soweth, that shall he also reap. For he that soweth unto his flesh, shall of the flesh reap corruption; but he that soweth unto the Spirit, shall of the Spirit reap eternal life. And let us not be weary in well-

---

[1] We must probably regard this strange reading as a slip rather than a considered choice. Elsewhere (*Inst.* III.xx.29 and *Comm. on Harmony of Gospels*, Matt. 6.6) he gives the usual reading 'pray'.

*doing: for in due season we shall reap, if we faint not. So then as we
have opportunity, let us do good unto all men, especially unto them
who are of the household of faith.* (6-10)

6. *Let him that is taught.* It seems probable that the teachers and
ministers of the Word were at that time neglected. This reflected the
basest ingratitude. It is disgraceful to defraud of their means of living
those by whom our souls are fed, to refuse an earthly recompense to
those from whom we receive heavenly blessings. But it is and always
has been the world's nature to stuff the stomachs of the ministers of
Satan and hardly and grudgingly to supply godly pastors with their
necessary food. Although we must not be too complaining or too
tenacious of our rights, Paul had to exhort the Galatians to perform
this duty. He was the more willing to do so because he had no private
interest in the matter, but consulted the common benefit of the
Church, without regard to his own advantage. He saw that ministers
of the Word were neglected, because the Word itself was despised.
For it cannot be denied that if the Word be prized, its ministers will
always be treated kindly and honourably. It is a trick of Satan to
defraud godly ministers of support, so that the Church may be deprived of ministers of their sort. An earnest desire to preserve the
ministry led Paul to recommend the care of good and faithful pastors.
'The Word' is here put κατ' ἐξοχήν for the teaching of godliness.
He says that those by whom we are taught in the Word should be
supported. By what right then are the idle bellies of dumb men and
fierce wild beasts, who have nothing in common with the doctrine
of Christ, fed in the Papacy?

In all good things. He does not want them to have an immoderate
and superfluous abundance, but merely that they should not lack any
of the necessary supports of life. Ministers should be satisfied with
frugal fare, and the danger of luxury and pomp must be avoided.
Therefore, so far as their needs demand, let believers regard all their
property as at the disposal of godly and holy teachers. What return
will they make for the inestimable treasure of eternal life which they
receive by their preaching?

7. *God is not mocked.* He adds this to refute the excuses which are
frequently pleaded. One alleges that he has a family to support and
another asserts that he has nothing left over to give or disburse. In
consequence, so many abstain that the few who do their duty are
generally insufficient. Paul denounces these empty pleas for a reason
which the world little considers: that this is a transaction with God.
For he is not concerned here merely with a man's food but with how
much we esteem Christ and His Gospel. This passage bears witness

that the habit of treating faithful ministers with scorn did not originate in our own day. But the taunts of the ungodly will not pass unpunished.

For whatsoever a man soweth. Our liberality is hindered by the idea that whatever passes into the hands of another is lost to ourselves, and also by the fact that we are always anxious about ourselves in this life. Paul meets this idea with the comparison of seed-time and says that when we do good we are sowing seed. We spoke of this in the Second Epistle to the Corinthians, where the same metaphor was used. If only we could be really convinced of this! How readily would we devote ourselves and what we have to our neighbours if our minds were set on the hope of the harvest! Farm workers do nothing more cheerfully than sowing seed. But whereas they wait with patience for nine months to reap a corruptible harvest, we fail to wait for a blessed immortality.

8. *For he that soweth unto his flesh.* The distribution of parts follows the general train of thought. To sow to the flesh is to provide for the needs of the present life without any regard to the future life. Those who do this will gather fruit corresponding to the seed they have sown; they will lay in a store of what will miserably perish. Some explain 'to sow in the flesh' as meaning indulgence in the lusts of the flesh and 'corruption' as meaning destruction. But the former exposition fits the context better. I have not acted without thought in departing from the Vulgate and Erasmus. Paul's Greek words run thus: 'to sow unto the flesh'. And what is this but to be so given up to the flesh as to direct all our energies to pleasing it and looking after it?

But he that soweth unto the spirit. By 'the spirit' I understand the spiritual life, to which they are said to sow who look to heaven rather than to earth and who so direct their lives as to aspire to the kingdom of God. Therefore they will reap in heaven the incorruptible fruit of their spiritual endeavours. He calls them spiritual endeavours on account of their end, although in some cases they are external and relate to the body. This is so here, where he is dealing with the support of pastors. If the Papists try, in their usual way, to build on these words the righteousness of works, we have shown elsewhere how easily their absurdities can be refuted. Although eternal life is a reward, it does not follow that we are justified by works or that works merit salvation. The fact that God so honours the works which He grants us freely as to promise them an undeserved reward is itself of grace.

If a more complete solution is required, then first I deny that in us there are any good works which God rewards except those which we have from His grace. Secondly, I say that the good works which we perform by the guidance and direction of the Holy Spirit are the freely granted fruits of adoption. Thirdly, I say that they are not only unworthy of the smallest and meanest reward but deserve to be wholly condemned, because they are always spattered and stained with many blemishes; and what agreement have pollutions with the presence of God? Fourthly, I say that even if a reward had been promised to works a thousand times, it is due only to the perfect fulfilment of the whole law. And we are all far from that perfection. Now let the Papists go and try to break their way into heaven by the merit of works! We gladly agree with Paul and the whole of Scripture in acknowledging that we can do nothing but by the free gift of God, and yet that the requital made to our works receives the name of reward.

9. *And let us not be weary in doing good.* 'Good' does not here mean uprightness but kindness, and refers to men. He tells us not to be weary in assisting our neighbours, in performing good deeds and in exercising generosity. This precept is especially necessary because we are naturally lazy in the duties of love, and many little stumbling-blocks hinder and put off even the well-disposed. We meet with many unworthy, many ungrateful people. The vast number of the needy overwhelms us; we are drained by paying out on every side. Our warmth is damped by the coldness of others. Finally, the whole world is full of hindrances which turn us aside from the right path. Therefore Paul does well to confirm our efforts, so that we do not faint through weariness.

If we faint not. That is, we shall only reap the fruit which God promises if we persevere to the end. Those who do not persevere are like lazy husbandmen who only plough and sow and leave the work unfinished, when rolling is necessary to prevent the seed being eaten by birds or scorched by the sun or destroyed by the cold. It is worthless to start to do good if we do not press on to the goal.

He says, *in due season*, lest anyone, from a wish to gather the fruit in this life, should deprive himself of the spiritual harvest. Believers must support and restrain their desire by hope and patience.

10. *While we have opportunity.* He continues with his metaphor. Not every season is fitted for tilling and sowing. Active and prudent farmers will push ahead at the right season and will not let it pass out of laziness. Therefore, since God has set aside the whole of the present life for ploughing and sowing, let us make use of the opportunity, lest, through our negligence, the chance be taken away. Beginning with liberality to ministers of the Gospel, Paul now applies his doctrine more widely and tells us to do good to all men, but commends especially the household of faith, that is, believers, because they belong to the same family as ourselves. This metaphor is used to stir us up

to that kind of communication which is necessary among the members of one family. Our common humanity makes us debtors to all; but we are bound to believers by a closer spiritual kinship, which God hallows among us.

Ye see how large a letter I have written unto you with mine own hand. As many as desire to make a fair show in the flesh, they compel you to be circumcised: only that they may not be persecuted for the cross of Christ. For not even they who are circumcised keep the law; but they desire to have you circumcised, that they may glory in your flesh. (11-13)

11. *Ye see.* The Greek word has an ambiguous ending, which could be either imperative or indicative. But the meaning is little affected, if at all. To convince the Galatians more fully of his anxiety and at the same time to make them read it more carefully, he mentions that this long letter had been written by his own hand. The greater the toil he had undertaken for them, the stronger their inducement to read it, not carelessly but with the closest attention.

12. *As many as desire to make a fair show.* First, to make a fair show in the flesh is to catch greedily at popularity, and that not for the sake of edification. The verb is very expressive and means sweet looks and charming words assumed for the purpose of pleasing. He accuses the false apostles of ambition; as if he were saying, 'Do you want to know what they are like who lay the necessity of circumcision upon you, and what they are aiming at and seeking? You are mistaken if you imagine that they are at all motivated by godly zeal. By this bribe they merely want to gain or preserve the favour of men.' For because they were Jews they thought that by this method they would keep the good will, or at least divert the anger, of their own nation. It is the usual practice with ambitious men to fawn meanly on those by whose favour they hope to better themselves; they insinuate themselves into their good graces, so that, when better men have been displaced, they may reign alone. He reveals this wicked design to the Galatians, to put them on their guard.

Only that they may not be persecuted. He again calls the pure preaching of the Gospel *the cross of Christ.* But he is alluding to their fancy of wanting to preach Christ without the cross. The deadly rage which the Jews bore against Paul arose because they could not endure a desertion from their ceremonies. To avoid persecution, these men flattered the Jews. Yet if they had themselves kept the law, it might have been more tolerable. But they disturbed the whole Church for the sake of their own convenience and did not scruple to lay a tyrannical

yoke on men's consciences that they might be quit and freed from
bodily troubles. They corrupted the true preaching of the cross from
a fear of the cross.

13. *For not even they who hold circumcision.*[1] The Vulgate and Erasmus
translate it 'who are circumcised'. But I think Paul is speaking only of
teachers, and not of all in general, and for this reason I would prefer
to render it as I have done, to avoid ambiguity. The meaning therefore
is: 'It is not from zeal for the law that they bind you with the yoke of
ceremonies. For they do not keep the law with their own circumcision. It is no doubt under the pretext of the law that they require
you to be circumcised. But although they have themselves been
circumcised, they do not perform what they bind on others.'

When he says that they do not *keep the law*, it is doubtful whether
this is to be understood of the whole law or just of ceremonies. There
are some who expound it that, because the law is an intolerable
burden, they do not satisfy it. But he rather hints an accusation of bad
faith against them because they despised the law so long as there was
no danger of ill-will.

And even now this disease rages everywhere. You will find many
who, more by ambition than from conscience defend the tyranny of
the Papacy. I speak of our courtly apostles who are attracted by the
smell of a kitchen. They pronounce oracularly that the decrees of the
holy Church of Rome must be reverently observed. And what do they
do all the while? They pay no more heed to the decrees of the Roman
see than to an ass's braying; yet they do not want to run any risks.
In short, Paul had the same kind of conflict with those impostors as
we have now with pretended professors of the Gospel who offer us
a chimaera compounded of Christ and Pope. Paul therefore unmasks
them and says that they are acting insincerely and that they command
circumcision so as to boast to the Jews of the converts they have made.
For this is to glory in the flesh. 'They wish to lead you in triumph,'
he says, 'and they abuse your body that they may seek popularity
when they show your mutilated flesh to the false zealots of the law
as a sign of peace and harmony.'

*But God forbid that I should glory, save in the cross of our Lord Jesus
Christ, through which the world is crucified unto me, and I unto the
world. For in Christ neither is circumcision anything, nor uncircumcision, but a new creature. And as many as shall walk by this rule,
peace be upon them, and mercy, and upon the Israel of God. For the
rest, let no man trouble me: for I bear in my body the marks of the*

[1] Calvin's Biblical text (p. 115) reads: *they who are circumcised*, as the Vulgate
and Erasmus.

*Lord Jesus. The grace of our Lord Jesus Christ be with your spirit,
brethren. Amen. Unto the Galatians, sent from Rome.* (14-18)

14. *But God forbid.* He now contrasts the plots of the false apostles
with his own sincerity, as if he were saying, 'To avoid being compelled to bear the cross, they deny the cross of Christ, purchase the
applause of men with the price of your flesh and end by leading you
in triumph. But my triumph and my glory are in the cross of the Son
of God.' If the Galatians had not been destitute of all common feeling,
ought they not to have detested those whom they saw enjoying
themselves at their expense?

To *glory in the cross of Christ* is to glory in Christ crucified, although
something more is implied. For he means a death full of disgrace and
ignominy which God Himself has cursed; a death which men view
with abhorrence and shame; in that death he says he will glory,
because in it he has perfect happiness. For where the highest good
exists, there is glory. But why not also elsewhere? Although salvation
is revealed in the cross of Christ, what of His resurrection? I answer,
in the cross is contained the whole of redemption and all its parts, but
the resurrection of Christ does not lead us away from the cross. And
note well that he abominates every other sort of glorying as nothing
less than a terrible offence. May God protect us from this plague, this
monstrosity! Such is the meaning of the phrase which Paul frequently
uses, *God forbid.*

By which the world. As σταυρός is masculine, the relative pronoun
may in the Greek be referred either to Christ or to the cross. In my
opinion, however, it is better to refer it to the cross. For by it,
strictly speaking, we die to the world. But what does 'the world'
mean? It is undoubtedly contrasted with the new creature. Whatever
is opposed to the spiritual Kingdom of Christ is the world, because it
belongs to the old man; or, in a word, the world is as it were the
object and aim of the old man.

The world is crucified unto me, says Paul. In the same sense elsewhere
he declares that he counts all things as dung (Phil. 3.8). To crucify
the world is to despise and belittle it.

He adds the converse, *and I unto the world.* By this he means that
he was quite unimportant and indeed nothing at all, because nothing-
ness belongs to the dead. At any rate, he means that by the mortification of the old man he had renounced the world. Some expound it
thus: 'If the world regards me as accursed and outcast, I consider the
world to be condemned and accursed.' This seems to me to be a little
foreign to Paul's meaning, but I leave readers to judge.

15. *For in Christ Jesus.* The reason why he is crucified to the world

and the world to him is that, in Christ, in whom he is engrafted, only a new creature is of any avail. Everything else must be discarded, nay, perish. I am referring to those things which hinder the renewing by the Spirit. This is what he says in II Corinthians: 'If any man is in Christ, let him be a new creature' (II Cor. 5.17). That is, if any man wishes to be considered as within the kingdom of Christ let him be reformed by the Spirit of God; let him not live any longer to himself or to the world, but let him be raised up to a new life. Why he concludes that neither circumcision nor uncircumcision is of any importance has already been mentioned. The truth of the Gospel swallows up and negatives all the shadows of the law.

16. *And as many as shall walk by this rule.* 'May all who hold this rule', he says, 'enjoy prosperity and happiness!' This is both a prayer for them and a token of approbation. He means, therefore, that those who teach this doctrine are worthy of love and goodwill, and on the other hand, those who desert it are not worthy to be heard. He uses the word *rule* to express the sure and continual course which all godly ministers of the Gospel ought to pursue. For as architects in erecting buildings work to a plan, so that all the parts may agree in true proportion and symmetry, so he commits to the ministers of the Word a canon by which to build the Church properly and in order.

This place ought to give great zeal to faithful and honest teachers and to all who let themselves be conformed to this rule, for in it they hear God bless them by the mouth of Paul. We need not dread the thunders of the Pope if God promises us from heaven peace and mercy. The word *walk* can apply both to the minister and the people, although it refers chiefly to ministers. The future sense of the verb is used to express perseverance.

And upon the Israel of God. This is an indirect mockery of the vain boasting of the false apostles, who claimed to be the descendants of Abraham according to the flesh. He therefore makes a double Israel, the one a pretence and visible only to men, and the other visible to God. Circumcision was a mask before men, but regeneration is the truth before God. In a word, he now calls them the Israel of God whom he formerly named the children of Abraham by faith, and thus includes all believers, whether Gentiles or Jews, who were united in the same Church. On the other hand, the Israel of the flesh can claim only the name and the race, and of this he treats in Rom. 9.6ff.

17. *Let no man trouble me.* He now speaks with the voice of authority to restrain his adversaries, for he declares with all the right of his superior power, 'Let them cease to hinder me in the course of my preaching.' He was ready, for the sake of the whole Church, to meet difficulties, but he will not be obstructed by opposition.

To trouble is to oppose so as to upset the progress of any work.

For the rest, that is, as for everything besides the new creature. He means, 'This one thing is enough for me. Other matters are un-important and do not interest me. Let no man worry me about them.' He thus places himself above all men and allows none the right to attack his ministry. Literally, it means 'as to the rest of the remainder'. To my mind, Erasmus was wrong in referring it to time.

For I bear in my body the marks. He shows that the boldness of his authority rested on the marks of Christ which he bore in his body. And what were they? Imprisonment, chains, scourging, blows, stonings and every kind of ill treatment which he had suffered for the testimony of the Gospel. For even as earthly warfare has its decora-tions with which generals honour the bravery of a soldier, so Christ our leader has His own marks, of which He makes good use in decor-ating and honouring some of His followers. These marks, however, are very different from the others; for they have the nature of the cross, and in the sight of the world they are disgraceful. This is suggested by the word 'marks', for it literally means prickings, the marks with which foreign slaves, or fugitives, or malefactors, were branded. Paul therefore speaks quite strictly when he claims to be distinguished by those marks with which Christ is accustomed to honour His most distinguished soldiers. In the view of the world these marks were shameful and disgraceful, but before God and the angels they surpass all the honours of the world.

18. *The grace of Christ be with your spirit.* He prays not only that grace may be bestowed upon them freely, but that they may have a proper feeling of it in their minds. It is only really enjoyed by us when it reaches to our spirit. We ought therefore to ask that God would prepare in our souls a habitation for His grace. Amen.

The Epistle to
THE EPHESIANS

THE THEME OF THE EPISTLE
TO THE EPHESIANS

EPHESUS, well known by a number of names, was a very celebrated city of Asia Minor. How God won there a people for Himself through the labours of Paul, with the commencement and progress of that Church, Luke relates in the Acts. At present, I shall only mention what bears directly on the theme of the Epistle. Paul had instructed the Ephesians in the pure doctrine of the Gospel. While he was a prisoner at Rome, he saw that they needed confirmation and wrote them the present epistle.

The first three chapters are chiefly occupied in commending the grace of God. For immediately after the greeting at the beginning of the first chapter, he treats of God's free election, so that they may acknowledge that they are now called into the Kingdom of God because they had been appointed to life before they were born. And God's wonderful mercy shines forth in the fact that the salvation of men flows from His free adoption as its true and native source. But as the minds of men are slow to grasp so sublime a mystery, he betakes himself to prayer, that God would enlighten the Ephesians in the full knowledge of Christ.

In the second chapter, to magnify His grace by a comparison, he focusses light strongly on the riches of the divine grace. He reminds them how wretched they were before they were called to Christ. For we never become duly sensible of how much we owe to Christ, nor estimate sufficiently His kindnesses towards us, until the unhappiness of our state outside Him has been set before our eyes. His second explanation is that the Gentiles were aliens from the promises of eternal life, with which God had honoured the Jews alone.

In the third chapter he declares that he had been appointed to be peculiarly the Apostle of the Gentiles, so that they who had for a long time been foreigners, might now be engrafted into the people of God. As this was an unusual event and its novelty disturbed many minds, he calls it a 'mystery hidden from the ages', but the dispensation of it had been entrusted to himself.

Towards the close of the chapter, he again prays that God would fill the Ephesians with a sound knowledge of Christ, that they would have no desire to know anything else. His aim is not merely to lead them to gratitude to God for so many favours, and to testify to that gratitude by consecrating themselves wholly to Him, but rather to remove all doubt about his own calling. Paul was probably afraid that the false apostles would shake their faith by insinuating that they had been only half-instructed. They had been Gentiles, and, when they embraced pure Christianity, had not been told anything about ceremonies or circumcision. But those who pressed the Law on Christians were loud in the avowal that those who have not been initiated into God by circumcision were profane. This was their usual song, that no man who is not circumcised should be reckoned among the people of God and that all the rites prescribed by Moses ought to be observed. Accordingly, they accused Paul of making Christ the common Saviour of Gentiles and of Jews without distinction.

They asserted that his apostleship was a profanation of the heavenly doctrine and prostituted the covenant of grace to wicked men without discrimination. He wanted to forewarn the Ephesians, assailed by these calumnies, so that they might not give way. While he argues so earnestly that they were called to the Gospel because they had been chosen before the creation of the world, he forbids them, on the other hand, to imagine that the Gospel had been accidentally brought to them by the will of men, or that it had flown to them by chance. For the preaching of Christ among them was nothing but the announcement of that eternal decree. While he lays before them the unhappy condition of their former life, he tells them at the same time that it was by the singular and wonderful mercy of God that they got clear from so deep a gulf. While he proclaims his own apostolic commission to the Gentiles, he confirms them in the faith which they had once received, because they had been divinely admitted into the communion of the Church. And yet all the sentences contained in this must be viewed as exhortations fitted to stir up the Ephesians to gratitude.

In chapter four he describes the manner in which the Lord governs and protects His Church, which is, by the Gospel preached by men. Hence it follows, that in no other way can it be kept sound, and that this is the aim of true perfection. The apostle's design is to commend to the Ephesians the ministry by which God reigns among us. He afterwards proceeds to the fruits of this preaching—innocence and holiness and all the duties of godliness. Nor does he describe only in general how Christians ought to live, but lays down particular precepts belonging to each particular calling.

CHAPTER ONE

Paul, an apostle of Jesus Christ, through the will of God, to all the saints which are at Ephesus, and the faithful in Christ Jesus: Grace to you, and peace, from God our Father, and the Lord Jesus Christ. Blessed be the God and Father of our Lord Jesus Christ, who hath blessed us with every spiritual blessing in the heavenly places in Christ; even as he chose us in him before the creation of the world, that we should be holy and without blame before him in love: having predestinated us into adoption through Jesus Christ in himself, according to the good pleasure of his will, to the praise of the glory of his grace, wherein he hath made us accepted in the beloved. (1-6)

1. *Paul, an apostle.* As the same form of greeting, or at least very little different, is used in all the epistles, it would be superfluous to repeat here what has been said elsewhere.[1] He calls himself an apostle of Jesus Christ; for all to whom has been given the ministry of reconciliation work as His ambassadors. The word 'Apostle', indeed, is more specialized; for it is not every minister of the Gospel (as we shall see later, in chapter 4.11) that is an apostle. But this subject I have explained more fully in Galatians.[2]

He adds *through the will of God*; for no man ought to take this honour to himself, but should wait for the calling of God, which alone makes lawful ministers. He thus opposes the jeers of wicked men to the authority of God, and removes every occasion of thoughtless strife.

He calls them *saints* whom he afterwards names *the faithful in Christ*. No man, therefore, is a believer who is not also a saint; and, on the other hand, no man is a saint who is not a believer. Most of the Greek copies omit the word *all*; but I was unwilling to strike it out, because it must at least be understood.

3. *Blessed be the God.* He extols sublimely the grace of God toward the Ephesians, to rouse their hearts to gratitude, to set them all aflame, to occupy and fill them with this thought. They who acknowledge in themselves such an outpouring of God's goodness, so full and absolutely perfect, and who exercise themselves in it with earnest meditation, will never embrace new doctrines, which obscure the very grace that they feel so powerfully within themselves. The aim of the apostle, therefore, in asserting the greatness of divine grace

---

[1] In the four preceding commentaries on Romans, I and II Corinthians, and Galatians.   [2] See pp. 8ff.

toward the Ephesians, was to arm them, lest they should let their faith be shaken by the false apostles, as if their calling were doubtful, or salvation were to be sought in some other way. He tells them at the same time, that the full certainty of salvation consists in the fact that through the Gospel God reveals His love to us in Christ. But to confirm the matter more fully, he recalls them to the first cause, to the fountain, the eternal election of God, by which, before we are born, we are adopted as sons. And this so that they may know that they were saved, not by any accidental or unforeseen occurrence, but by the eternal and unchangeable decree of God.

The word *bless* is here used in more than one sense, as referring to God, or as referring to men. I find in Scripture a fourfold signification. Our blessing of God is the praise when we declare His goodness. But God is said to bless us, when He gives our affairs good success, and in His goodness bestows upon us happiness and prosperity; and the reason is, that we are blessed only in His good pleasure. We must note how he expresses the great power which dwells in the very Word of God for the Church and each individual believer. Men bless each other by prayer. Priestly blessing is more than a prayer, because it is a testimony and pledge of the Divine blessing; for the priests received a commission to bless in the name of the Lord. Paul therefore here blesses God with a confession of praise, because He has blessed us, that is, has enriched us with all blessing or grace.

I have no objection to Chrysostom's remark, that the word spiritual conveys an implied contrast between the blessing of Moses and of Christ. The law had its blessings; but in Christ alone is perfection found, because He is the perfect revelation of the Kingdom of God, which leads us directly to heaven. When the body itself is revealed, figures are no longer needed.

When he says, *In the heavenly*, it matters little whether we supply 'Places', or 'Benefits'. He only wanted to express the superiority of that grace which is bestowed on us through Christ, in that its happiness is not in this world but in heaven and everlasting life. The Christian religion, indeed, as we are taught elsewhere (I Tim. 4.8), contains promises not only of the future life but also of the present; but its aim is spiritual happiness, even as the Kingdom of Christ is spiritual. He contrasts Christ and all the Jewish symbols, in which the blessing under the law was contained. For where Christ is, all those things are superfluous.

4. *Even as he chose us.* Here he declares that God's eternal election is the foundation and first cause both of our calling and of all the benefits which we receive from God. If the reason is asked as to why God has called us to participation in the Gospel, why He daily bestows

upon us so many blessings, why He opens to us the gate of heaven, we always have to return to this principle, that He chose us before the world was. The very time of the election shows it to be free; for what could we have deserved, or in what did our merit consist, before the world was made? For what a childish quibble is the sophistry that we were not chosen because we were already worthy, but because God foresaw that we would be worthy. We are all lost in Adam; and therefore, had not God rescued us from perishing by His own election, there was nothing to be foreseen. The same argument is used in Romans, where, speaking of Jacob and Esau, he says, 'For they were not yet born, nor had done any good or evil' (Rom. 9.11). But though they had not yet acted, a certain sophist of the Sorbonne might reply, 'God foresaw what they could do.' This objection has no force in the nature of corrupt men, in whom nothing can be seen but materials for destruction.

When he adds, *In Christ*, it is the second confirmation of the freedom of election. For if we are chosen in Christ, it is outside ourselves. It is not from the sight of our deserving, but because our heavenly Father has engrafted us, through the blessing of adoption, into the Body of Christ. In short, the name of Christ excludes all merit, and everything which men have of themselves; for when he says that we are chosen in Christ, it follows that in ourselves we are unworthy.

That we should be holy. He indicates the immediate, but not the chief design. For there is no absurdity in supposing that one thing may have two objects. The design of building is that there should be a house. This is the immediate aim. But the convenience of dwelling in it is the ultimate aim. It was necessary to mention this in passing; for Paul at once mentions another aim, the glory of God. But there is no contradiction here. The glory of God is the highest end, to which our sanctification is subordinate.

From this we infer that holiness, innocence, and every virtue in men, are the fruit of election. And so once more Paul expressly puts aside every consideration of merit. If God has foreseen in us everything worthy of election, the very opposite would have been said. For he means that all our holiness and innocence of life flow from the election of God. How comes it then that some men are godly, and live in the fear of the Lord, while others give themselves up without reserve to all manner of wickedness? If Paul may be believed, the only reason is, that the latter retain their natural disposition, and the former have been chosen to holiness. The cause certainly does not follow the effect, and therefore election does not depend on the righteousness of works, of which Paul here declares that it is the cause.

Moreover, in this clause he signified that election gives no occasion to licentiousness, as when wicked men blaspheme and say, 'Let us live in any manner we please; for if we have been elected, it is impossible for us to perish.' Paul tells them plainly that it is wicked to separate holiness of life from the grace of election; for God calls and justifies those whom He chooses. The inference, too, which the Catharists, Celestines and Donatists drew from these words, that it is possible for us to be perfect in this life, is without foundation. This is the goal to which we must direct the whole course of our life, but we never reach it till our race is done. Where are the men who dread and avoid the doctrine of predestination as an inextricable labyrinth, who regard it as useless and almost poisonous? No doctrine is more useful, provided it be handled properly and soberly, that is, as Paul does here, when he presents the consideration of the infinite goodness of God, and stirs us up to give thanks. This is the true fountain from which we must draw our knowledge of the divine mercy. If men should evade every other argument, election shuts their mouth, so that they dare not and cannot claim anything for themselves. But let us remember the purpose for which Paul discusses predestination, lest, by reasoning with any other aim, we go perilously astray.

Before him in love. Holiness in the sight of God is that of a pure conscience; for God is not deceived, as men are, by outward pretence, but looks to faith, that is, to the truth of the heart. If you refer the word 'love' to God, the meaning will be, that the only reason why He chose us, was His love for mankind. But I prefer to take it with the latter part of the verse, as denoting that the perfection of believers consists in love; not that God requires love alone, but that it is an evidence of the fear of God, and of obedience to the whole law.

5. *Who hath predestinated us.* What follows heightens still further the commendation of divine grace. The reason why Paul pressed so earnestly on the Ephesians Christ and free adoption in Him, and the eternal election which preceded it, we have already mentioned. But as the mercy of God is nowhere declared more sublimely, this passage deserves our special attention. Three causes of our salvation are mentioned in this clause, and a fourth is shortly afterwards added. The efficient cause is the good pleasure of the will of God; the material cause is Christ; and the final cause is the praise of His grace. Let us now see what he says respecting each.

To the first belongs this whole context: God has predestinated us in Himself, according to the good pleasure of His will, unto adoption, and has made us accepted by His grace. In the word *predestinate* we must again attend to the order. We did not yet exist and therefore there was no merit of ours. Hence the cause of our salvation did not proceed from us, but from God alone. Yet Paul, not yet satisfied with these statements, adds *in himself.* The Greek equivalent of this is, of course, ἐν αὑτῷ; but ἐν αὑτῷ means the same as the phrase he uses here, εἰς αὑτόν. By this he means that God did not seek a cause out of Himself, but predestinated us because such was His will.

But what follows is still clearer: *according to the good pleasure of his will.* The word 'will' was enough, for Paul is accustomed to contrast it to all outward causes by which men imagine that the mind of God is influenced. But that no ambiguity may remain, he uses the contrast 'good pleasure', which expressly sets aside all merit. In adopting us, therefore, the Lord does not look at what we are, and is not reconciled to us by any personal worth. His single motive is the eternal good pleasure, by which He predestinated us. Why, then, are the Sophists not ashamed to mingle with it other considerations, when Paul so strongly forbids us to look at anything else than the good pleasure of God?

Finally lest anything should still be wanting, he adds, ἐχαρίτωσεν ἐν χάριτι. By this he tells us that God embraces us in His love and favour freely and not on a wages basis, just as, when we were not yet born, and when He was prompted by nothing but Himself, He chose us.

The material cause, both of eternal election, and of the love which is now revealed, is *Christ,* whom he names *the Beloved,* to tell us that by Him the love of God is poured out to us. Thus He is the well-beloved, to reconcile us. The highest and last purpose is immediately added, the glorious praise of such abundant grace. Every man, therefore, who hides this glory, is endeavouring to overturn the everlasting purpose of God. Such is the doctrine of the Sophists, which turns everything upside down, lest the whole glory of our salvation should be ascribed undividedly to God alone.

In whom we have redemption through his blood, the forgiveness of sins, according to the riches of his grace; wherein he hath abounded (ex-undavit—overflowed) towards us in all wisdom and prudence; having made known unto us the mystery of his will, according to his good pleasure, which he hath purposed in himself, unto the dispensation of the fulness of times; that he might gather together all things in Christ, both which are in heaven, and which are on earth, even in him: through whom also we have been received into an inheritance, having been foreordained according to the purpose of him who worketh all things after the counsel of his will; that we should be to the praise of his glory, we who have before hoped in Christ. (7-12)

7. *In whom we have redemption.* This still refers to the material cause, for he explains how we are reconciled to God through Christ, in that by His death He has appeased the Father towards us. Therefore we

ought always to direct our minds to the blood of Christ, if we are seeking grace in Him. And he says that by the blood of Christ we obtain redemption, which he immediately calls the forgiveness of sins. By this he means that we are redeemed because our sins are not imputed to us. From this comes the free righteousness by which we are accepted by God, and freed from the bonds of the devil and death. We must note carefully the opposition which defines the manner of our redemption; for so long as we remain liable to the judgment of God, we are bound in wretched chains. Therefore release from guilt is an inestimable freedom.

According to the riches. He returns to the efficient cause: Christ has been given to be our Redeemer because God has abounded in active kindness. And he puts 'riches' here, and the word *overflow*, to magnify that kindness, so that he may fill men's minds completely with wonder at it. He cannot be sufficiently content in celebrating the goodness of God. Would that men's minds were steeped in the richness of grace which is here commended! No place would any longer be found for invented satisfactions and such trifles by which the world imagines it can redeem itself; as if the blood of Christ dried up without subsidiary aid.

8. *In all wisdom.* He now comes to the formal cause, the preaching of the Gospel, by which the goodness of God flows out to us. For by faith is communicated to us Christ, through whom we come to God, and through whom we enjoy the benefit of adoption. He gives to the Gospel the magnificent titles of *wisdom and prudence*, so that the Ephesians may despise all contrary doctrines. The false apostles insinuated themselves under the pretence of teaching something more sublime than the rudiments which Paul conveyed. And the devil, in order to undermine our faith, labours to disparage the Gospel, as far as he can. Paul, on the contrary, builds up the authority of the Gospel, that believers may rest in it safely. 'All wisdom' means full or perfect wisdom.

Because the novelty frightened some, he deals with the mistake in good time and calls it *the secret of the divine will*, and yet a secret which God has now been pleased to reveal. As he formerly ascribed their election to the good pleasure of God, so also now their calling, that the Ephesians may acknowledge that Christ has been made known and the Gospel preached to them, not because they deserved any such thing, but because it pleased God.

Which he hath purposed in himself unto the dispensation. All is wisely and properly arranged. What can be more fair than that His purposes, which are hidden from men, should be known to God alone so long as He wishes to keep them to Himself. Or, again, that it should be in

His own will and power to predetermine the time when they shall be made known to men? Therefore he tells us that the decree in the mind of God to adopt the Gentiles was till now hidden, yet in such a way that He reserved it in His own power until the time of the revelation. If anyone now complains that it was a new and unprecedented occurrence that those who had been strangers to God should be chosen into the Church, is it fair to allow God no more knowledge than men have? In case anyone should ask why one time rather than another was selected, he forestalls their curiosity by calling that which was appointed by God, 'the fulness of times'—the ripe and proper time, as also in Gal. 4.4. Let human presumption restrain itself, and, in judging of the succession of events, let it bow to the providence of God. The word 'dispensation' points in the same direction, for on the judgment of God depends the proper administration of all things.

That he might gather. The Vulgate has *instaurare* (restore). Erasmus has added *summatim.*[1] I have preferred to keep the strict meaning of the Greek word, ἀνακεφαλαιώσασθαι, because it is more agreeable to the context. For to my mind, Paul wants to teach that outside Christ all things were upset, but that through Him they have been reduced to order. And truly, outside Christ, what can we perceive in the world but mere ruins? We are alienated from God by sin, and how can we but be wandering and shattered? The proper state of creatures is to cleave to God. Such an ἀνακεφαλαίωσις as would bring us back to regular order, the apostle tells us, has been made in Christ. Formed into one body, we are united to God, and mutually conjoined with one another. But without Christ, the whole world is as it were a shapeless chaos and frightful confusion. He alone gathers us into true unity.

But why does he include heavenly beings in this reckoning? The angels were never separated from God, nor yet dispersed. Some explain it like this. Angels are said to be gathered together, because men have been united together with them, are conjoined equally with them to God, and obtain a common blessedness with them in this blessed unity. Just as we speak of a whole building being repaired, many parts of which were ruinous or fallen down, though some parts remained entire. This is true. But there is no reason why we should not say that the angels also have been gathered together, not from a scattering, but first that they may cleave to God perfectly and wholly, and then that they may keep this state for ever. For what is the analogy (*proportio*) between the creature and the Creator, without the interposition of the Mediator? So far as they are creatures, they would

[1] It is difficult to render this adverb literally. By *instaurare summatim* Erasmus may be taken as meaning, 'to restore and sum up'.

have been liable to change and to falling and not blessed eternally, had they not been exempted by the benefit of Christ. Who then will deny that angels as well as men have been restored to a steadfast order by the grace of Christ? Men had been lost, but angels were not out of danger. By uniting together both into His own Body, Christ has conjoined them to God the Father, that He might establish a true harmony in heaven and in earth.

11. *Through whom also.* Hitherto he has spoken generally of all the elect; he now begins to make distinctions. He now speaks of himself and of the Jews, or, if you prefer it, of all who were the firstfruits of Christianity; and then he comes to the Ephesians. It did much to confirm them (I speak of the Ephesians), that he reckons them with himself and other believers, who were, so to say, the firstborn in the Church. As if he had said, 'The condition of all the godly is just the same as yours; for we whom God first called owe our acceptance by Him to His eternal election.' Thus he shows that, from first to last as they say, all have obtained salvation by mere grace, because they have been freely adopted according to eternal election.

Who worketh all things. We should note the periphrase by which he describes God as alone doing all things according to His own will, so as to leave nothing to man. In no respect, therefore, does he admit men to share in His praise, as if they brought anything of their own. For God looks at nothing outside Himself by which He is moved to elect us, for the counsel of His own will is the only and proper and (as they say) intrinsic cause of election. By this may be refuted the error, or rather madness, of those who, unless they see a reason in God's works, never cease to attack His design.

That we should be to the praise, etc. He repeats the purpose. For only then does God's glory shine in us, if we are nothing but vessels of His mercy. The word 'glory' denotes, κατ' ἐξοχήν, peculiarly that which shines in the goodness of God; for there is nothing more His own, in which He desires to be glorified, than His goodness.

In whom ye also having heard the word of truth, the gospel of your salvation—in whom having also believed, ye were sealed with the Holy Spirit of promise, which is the earnest of our inheritance, unto the redemption of the possession obtained, unto the praise of his glory. (13-14)

13. *In whom ye also.* He associates the Ephesians with himself, and with the rest of those who were the firstfruits; for he says that they trusted in Christ in like manner. His object is to show that both had the same faith; and therefore he repeats the word 'trusted'. He after-

wards adds that they had been brought to that hope by the preaching of the Gospel.

He applies two epithets to the Gospel, 'the word of truth', and the instrument of the Ephesians salvation. These two deserve our careful attention, for since nothing is more earnestly attempted by Satan than to imbue our minds either with doubt or contempt of the Gospel, Paul furnishes us with two shields, by which we may repel both temptations. Therefore we should set this testimony against all doubts, that the Gospel is not only certain truth, which cannot deceive, but is called, κατ' ἐξοχήν, *the word of truth*, as if, strictly speaking, there were no truth outside itself. If we are ever tempted to despise or dislike the Gospel, let us remember that its power and efficacy lie in bringing us salvation; just as elsewhere he teaches that it is the power of God unto salvation to believers. But here he expresses more, for he tells the Ephesians that, having been made partakers of salvation, they had learned this by experience. Unhappy are those who weary themselves, as the world generally does, in wandering through many winding paths, neglecting the Gospel, and pleasing themselves with gadding imaginations; so long learning and never reaching the knowledge of the truth or finding life! But happy they who have embraced the Gospel and steadfastly abide in it!—for this, beyond doubt, is truth and life.

In whom having also believed. A proof of the certainty he had attributed to the Gospel. And by what better sponsor can it be affirmed than by the Holy Spirit? It is as if he said: 'Having called the Gospel the Word of truth, I will not prove it by the authority of men; for you have the Author Himself, the Spirit of God, who seals the truth of it in your hearts.' This excellent comparison is taken from seals, by which doubt is removed among men. Seals give authenticity both to charters and to wills. Moreover, the seal was especially used on letters to identify the writer. In short, a seal distinguishes what is genuine and certain from what is unauthentic and fraudulent. This office Paul ascribes to the Holy Spirit, not only here, but also in chapter 4.30, and in II Cor. 1.22. Our minds never become so firm that the truth of God prevails with us against all the temptations of Satan, until the Holy Spirit has confirmed us in it. The true conviction which believers have of the Word of God, of their own salvation, and of all religion, does not spring from the feeling of the flesh, or from human and philosophical arguments, but from the sealing of the Spirit, who makes their consciences more certain and removes all doubt. The foundation of faith would be frail and unsteady if it rested on human wisdom; and therefore, as preaching is the instrument of faith, so the Holy Spirit makes preaching efficacious.

But here he seems to subject the sealing of the Spirit to faith. If so, faith precedes it. I answer, the effect of the Spirit in faith is twofold, corresponding to the two chief parts of which faith consists. It enlightens the intellect (*mens*) and also confirms the thinking (*animus*). The commencement of faith is knowledge; its completion is a firm and steady conviction, which admits of no opposing doubt. Each, I have said, is the work of the Spirit. No wonder, then, if Paul should declare that the Ephesians not only received by faith the truth of the Gospel, but also were confirmed in it by the seal of the Holy Spirit.

He calls Him *the Spirit of promise* from His effect. For He brings it to pass that the promise of salvation is not made to us in vain. For as God promises in His Word that He will be to us a Father, so by the Holy Spirit, He gives us the testimony of His adoption.

14. *Which is the earnest.* He uses this term twice in II Cor. 1 and 5. The metaphor is taken from transactions which are so confirmed by the giving of a pledge, that no room is left for a change of mind. Thus, when we have received the Spirit of God, we have God's promises confirmed to us, and we are not afraid that He will retract. Not that the promises of God are in themselves weak; but, because we never rest in them confidently until they are supported by the testimony of the Spirit. The Spirit, then, is the earnest of our inheritance, that is, of eternal life, unto redemption, that is, until the day of complete redemption comes. So long as we are in this world we need this earnest, because we fight in hope; but when the possession itself shall have been revealed, the necessity and use of the earnest will cease.

For the symbol of a pledge lasts only till both parties have fulfilled the contract; and, accordingly, he says later, *until the day of redemption* (Eph. 4.30). But he is speaking of the day of judgment, for though we are already redeemed by the blood of Christ, the result of that redemption is not yet visible; for every creature groans, desiring to be delivered from corruption. And we ourselves also, who have received the firstfruits of the Spirit, long for the same freedom; for we have not yet obtained it, except by hope. But we shall enjoy it in reality, when Christ shall appear in judgment. In this sense Paul uses the word *redemption* in Rom. 8.23, and so also the Lord, when He says 'Lift up your heads, for your redemption draweth nigh' (Luke 21.28).

Περιποίησις, which we have translated by the Latin *acquisitam haereditatem* (the possession obtained) is not the Kingdom of Heaven, or a blessed immortality, but the Church itself. This is added for their consolation, that they might not think it hard to cherish their hope till the day of Christ's coming, or think it a shame if they are yet partakers of the promised inheritance; for such is the common lot of the whole Church.

To the praise of his glory. The word *praise,* as a little before, is used as 'proclamation'. His glory may sometimes be concealed, or obscure. And so Paul says that in the Ephesians God had given proofs of His goodness, that His glory might be celebrated and openly made known. Those therefore, who slighted the calling of the Ephesians, were also hating and slighting the glory of God.

His frequent mention of the glory of God ought not to be thought superfluous, for what is infinite cannot be spoken of too much. This is particularly true in commending the Divine mercy, to whose meaning no truly godly person will ever be able to do justice in words. All godly tongues will be as ready to utter His praises as their ears will be open to hear them. For if men and angels combined their eloquence on this theme, it would still fall far short of its greatness. We may also observe, that there is no stronger refutation to shut the mouths of the ungodly, than by showing that we defend, but they obscure, the glory of God.

I also, having heard of the faith in the Lord Jesus, which is among you, and of your love unto all the saints, cease not to give thanks for you, making mention of you in my prayers; that the God of our Lord Jesus Christ, the Father of glory, may give unto you the spirit of wisdom and revelation in the knowledge of him: the eyes of your understanding being enlightened; that ye may know what is the hope of his calling, and what the riches of the glory of his inheritance in the saints, and what is the exceeding greatness of his power to us-ward who believe, according to the working of the strength of his might. (15-19)

15. *Wherefore I also.* This thanksgiving was not only a testimony of his love for the Ephesians. Paul also tells them what judgment he had formed of them, and congratulated them before God, that it was so good. Observe here, that under faith and love Paul sums up the whole perfection of Christians. He says 'faith in Christ', because He is properly the aim and object (as they say) of faith. Love ought to embrace all men, but here the saints are especially mentioned; because love, properly ordered, begins with them, and then flows to all others. If our love ought to look to God, the nearer any man approaches Him, the higher the place he should hold.

16. *Making mention of you.* To thanksgiving, as his custom is, he adds prayer, in order to excite them to additional progress. It was necessary that the Ephesians should understand that they had entered upon the proper course, lest they should turn aside to some new kind of doctrine: and yet also that they should know that they must proceed

farther; for nothing is more dangerous than satiety of spiritual benefits. However strong may be our virtues, let us always aim at further progress.

But what does Paul wish for the Ephesians? The spirit of wisdom, and the enlightening of the eyes of their understanding. And did they not possess these? Yes; but at the same time they needed increase, that, being endowed with a larger measure of the Spirit, and being more and more enlightened, they might more clearly and fully hold what they already held. The knowledge of the godly is never so pure but that some bleariness troubles their eyes and obscurity hinders them. But let us examine the words in detail.

The God, he says, *of our Lord Jesus Christ*. For the Son of God became man in such a manner that he had God in common with us. As He testified, 'I ascend to my God, and your God' (John 20.17). And the reason why He is our God, is that He is Christ's God, whose members we are. Let us remember, however, that this belongs to His human nature; so that His subjection takes nothing away from His eternal divinity.

He calls Him *the Father of glory*. This title emerges from the former; for the glorious Fatherhood of God is shown in subjecting His Son to our condition, that, through Him, He might be our God. 'The Father of glory' is a well-known Hebrew idiom for 'the glorious Father'. I do not disapprove the joining of these two phrases: that He is the glorious Father of Christ, and reading the word 'God' separately.

The Spirit of wisdom and revelation is here put, by metonymy, for the grace which the Lord bestows upon us by his Spirit. But let us observe that the gifts of the Spirit are not the endowments of nature. Until the Lord opens them, the eyes of our heart are blind. Until we have been taught by the Spirit our master, all that we know is folly and ignorance. Until the Spirit of God has made it known to us by a secret revelation, the knowledge of our Divine calling exceeds the grasp of our minds.

Where we translate *In the knowledge of him*, it can also be read, 'In the knowledge of himself.' Both renderings fit in well. For he that knows the Son knows also the Father. But I prefer my rendering, as keeping to the strict meaning of the relative pronoun.

The word 'heart' is the rendering of the Vulgate; it is also the reading of some Greek manuscripts. It is not very important, for the Hebrews frequently use it of the rational part of the soul; though more strictly, being the seat of the affections, it means the will or the appetitive part of the soul. But I have preferred the more usual reading.

And what the riches. He proclaims the excellence of this, so that the comparison may remind us how unfit we are for this sublime knowledge; for the power of God is no small matter. He says that this great power had been exerted towards the Ephesians, and that not simply but surpassingly. Moreover, it laid them under constant obligations to follow His calling. He extolls the grace of God towards them, lest they should shrink from it with contempt or dislike. With splendid praises he declares to us that faith is such a wonderful work and gift of God, that it cannot be sufficiently praised. Paul does not throw out hyperboles without discrimination; but when he treats of faith, which is superior to the world, he raises us to the admiration of heavenly power.

19. *According to the working, etc.* Some refer this only to the word 'believe', which comes immediately before it; but I rather take it as the greatness of the power, so that it is a new amplification, as if he said: 'in that greatness of power appears the efficacy of the strength of His might', or, if you prefer it, 'the greatness of power is an instance and evidence of the efficacy of the power'. The repetition of the word δυνάμις seems superfluous. But in the first place it is restricted to one class, in the second it has a general application. Paul, we find, is never satisfied in proclaiming our calling. And certainly the wonderful power of God is displayed when we are brought from death to life, and when, from being the children of hell, we become the children of God and heirs of eternal life.

Foolish men imagine that this language is sheer exaggeration; but the godly, who are engaged in daily struggles of conscience, easily see that there is not a word here that is not perfectly true. As the importance of the subject cannot be too strongly expressed, so Paul spoke sublimely because of our unbelief and ingratitude. Either we never think highly enough of the treasure offered to us in the Gospel, or, if we do, we cannot persuade ourselves that we are capable of it, because we perceive nothing in us that corresponds to it, but everything adverse. Hence Paul both strove to magnify the glory of Christ's kingdom among the Ephesians and also to impress their minds with a deep sense of the Divine grace. And that they might not be cast down by the thought of their own unworthiness, he exhorts them to consider the power of God; as if he had said that their regeneration was the work of God, yet extraordinary, in which He displayed wonderfully His infinite power.

There are three words here on which we may remark. *Strength* is like the root, *power* the tree, and *efficacy* the fruit, of the stretching out of the Divine arm which appears in action.

Which he wrought in Christ, when he raised him from the dead, and made him to sit at his right hand in the heavenly places, far above all

*rule, and power, and might, and dominion, and every name that is
named, not only in this world, but also in that which is to come; and he
put all things under his feet, and gave him to be the head over all things
to the church, which is his body, and the fulness of him that filleth all
in all.* (20-23)

20. *Which he wrought in Christ.* The Greek word is ἐνέργησεν, from
which ἐνέργεια is derived. Therefore this is equivalent to saying in
English, 'According to the efficacy which he effected.' But my translation comes to the same thing, and is less harsh.

He very rightly enjoins us to contemplate this power in Christ;
for in us it is still concealed. For the power of God is made perfect in
weakness (II Cor. 12.9). In what do we surpass the children of the
world, but in that our condition seems somewhat the worse? Though
sin does not reign, it continues to dwell in us, and death is still strong.
Blessedness is shut up in hope, not perceived by the world. The
power of the Spirit is a thing unknown to flesh and blood. The
thousand distresses to which we are liable render us more contemptible than other men.

Christ alone, therefore, is the mirror in which we can contemplate
that which the weakness of the cross obscures in us. When our minds
are roused to trust in righteousness, salvation, and glory, let us learn
to turn them to Christ. We still lie under the power of death; but
He, raised from the dead by heavenly power, has the dominion of
life. We struggle under the bondage of sin, and, surrounded by endless
miseries, we fight a hard warfare, but He, sitting at the right hand of
the Father, obtains the highest government in heaven and earth, and
triumphs gloriously over the enemies whom He has subdued and
vanquished. We lie here despised and lowly; but to Him has been
given a name which angels and men revere, and devils and wicked
men dread. We are oppressed here by the scantiness of all our gifts:
but He has been appointed by the Father to be the sole Judge and
Dispenser of all things. For these reasons, it is to our good to transfer
our thoughts to Christ, that in Him, as in a mirror, we may see the
glorious treasures of Divine grace, and the immeasurable greatness of
that power which has not yet been manifested in ourselves.

And made him to sit at his right hand. This passage shows more
plainly than any other what 'the right hand of God' means. It does
not mean some particular place, but the power which the Father
bestowed on Christ, that in His name He might administer the government of heaven and earth. It is idle, therefore, to quibble, as some do,
that Stephen saw Him standing, whereas Paul here writes that He sat.
It does not refer to bodily posture, but denotes the highest power of

ruling, with which Christ has been invested. This agrees with Paul's words: 'Above all principality etc.', for the whole of this description is added explanatorily to express the meaning of 'the right hand'.

God the Father is said to have raised Christ to His right hand in that He has made Him to share in His government; for by Him He exercises all His power. The metaphor is borrowed from earthly princes, who confer on their general the honour of sitting beside them. Since the right hand of God fills heaven and earth, it follows that the Kingdom and power of Christ are everywhere diffused. They are wrong, therefore, who attempt to prove from His session at the right hand of God, that He dwells only in heaven. His humanity, it is very true, is in heaven and not in earth; but that argument is beside the point. For what follows, *In heavenly places*, does not mean that the right hand of God is confined to heaven. He wants us to know that Christ is raised to the height, to the heavenly glory of God, that He has obtained the highest place in blessed immortality among the Angels.

21. *Far above all principality*. There is no doubt that by all these names he refers to the Angels, who are so called, because it is by their agency that God exercises His power, might and dominion. For inasmuch as He communicates to the creatures what belongs to Himself, He is wont to ascribe to them His own name; which is why they are called אֱלֹהִים, gods. Now although from the diversity of names we conclude that there are various orders, yet to investigate them more minutely, to fix their number, and determine their ranks, would not merely be foolish curiosity, but also ungodly rashness and dangerous.

But why did he not simply call them angels? I answer, Paul enhanced these titles to magnify the glory of Christ; as if he had said, 'There is nothing so sublime or excellent, by whatever name it may be called, that is not subject to the majesty of Christ.' There was an ancient superstition, common to both Jews and Gentiles, of imagining many things about angels, which drew away their minds from God and from the true Mediator. Therefore Paul everywhere takes care to prevent this imaginary glory of angels from dazzling men's eyes, and so obscuring the brightness of Christ; and yet his utmost diligence could not prevent the cunning of the devil from succeeding in this matter. For we see how the world departed from Christ through a wrong preoccupation with angels. It was unavoidable that the pure conception of Christ should disappear among inventions about angels.

Above every name. Name is here taken for 'largeness', or 'excellence'; and 'to be named' means to enjoy celebrity and praise.

The age that is to come is expressly mentioned, to indicate that the excellence of Christ is not temporal, but eternal; and that it is not limited to this world, but flourishes also in the Kingdom of God. For this reason, too, Isaiah calls Him 'the everlasting Father' (Isa. 9.6). In short, all the glories of men and angels are put in their place, to give way to the glory of Christ, so that it alone may shine above them all unequalled and without let.

22. *And gave him to be the head.* That is, He was made the Head of the Church, so that He should have the administration of all things. But he means that it was not a bare title that He was appointed Head of the Church, but that there was committed to Him the entire command and government of the universe. The metaphor of Head denotes the highest authority. I am unwilling to dispute about a name, but these modern flatterers of the Roman idol drive us to it by their wickedness. For since Christ is called the sole Head, all others, whether angels or men, are forced into their proper place as members; so that He who holds the highest place is still one of the members under the common Head. And yet they are not ashamed to make a to-do that the Church will be ἀκέφαλον, unless it has one head on earth besides Christ. What a wicked sacrilege it is that they give Christ so little honour that, if He alone obtains the honour His Father has bestowed on Him, the Church is supposed to be dismembered! But let us listen to the apostle, who declares that the Church is His Body; by which he means that those who refuse to submit to Him are unworthy of its communion; for on Him alone the unity of the Church depends.

23. *The fulness of him.* This is the highest honour of the Church, that, unless He is united to us, the Son of God reckons Himself in some measure imperfect. What an encouragement it is for us to hear, that, not until He has us as one with Himself, is He complete in all His parts, or does He wish to be regarded as whole! Hence in I Corinthians, when Paul uses the metaphor of the human body, he includes under the single name of Christ the whole Church (12.12).

But, lest this should be taken to mean that Christ would lack something if He were separated from us, Paul at once adds: *That filleth all in all.* His wish to be filled, and, in some respects, made perfect in us, arises from no want or poverty; for He brings all things to pass in us and in all the creatures. And His goodness appears the greater in His making us out of nothing, that He on His side may be and live in us. There is no absurdity in limiting the word 'all' to the present context; for, although Christ performs all things by His will and power, yet Paul is here speaking particularly of the spiritual government of the Church. There is nothing, indeed, to hinder us from referring it to the universal government of the world; but to limit it to the case in hand is the more probable interpretation.

CHAPTER TWO

And you when ye were dead through your trespasses and sins; wherein aforetime ye walked according to the age of this world, according to the prince of the power of the air, the spirit that now worketh in the sons of disobedience: among whom we also all once lived in the lusts of our flesh, doing the desires of the flesh and of the mind; and were by nature children of wrath, even as others. (1-3)

1. *And you when ye were dead.* An *epexergasia* of the former statements—that is, an exposition and clarification. To apply more effectually to the Ephesians the general declaration of grace, he reminds them of their former condition. This application has two parts. 'You were once lost; but now God, by His grace, has rescued you from destruction.' But by struggling to heighten each of these parts, he makes a break in his argument by a hyperbaton.[1] There is some difficulty in the language, but the meaning is clear. Only we must refer what he says to both those parts. Now of the first, we see that he says that *they were dead*, and states at the same time the cause of the death, namely, *sins*. He does not mean only that they were in danger of death; but he declares that it was a real and present death by which they were overwhelmed. As spiritual death is nothing else than the alienation of the soul from God, we are all born dead, and we live dead until we are made partakers of the life of Christ; hence also John: 'The hour now comes, when the dead shall hear the voice of the Son of God, and they that hear shall live' (John 5.25).

The Papists, who are eager to seize every opportunity of weakening the grace of God, say that outside Christ we are half-dead. But it was not for nothing that the Lord Himself and also this apostle shut us out from life completely while we remain in Adam, and declare that regeneration is the new life of the soul, by which it rises from the dead. Some kind of life, I acknowledge, does remain in us, while we are still strangers to Christ; for unbelief does not extinguish every sense, or the will, or the other faculties of the soul. But what has this to do with the Kingdom of God? What has it to do with the blessed life, when everything we think and wish is death? Let this, then, stand fast, that the union of our soul with God is the true and only life; and that outside Christ we are altogether dead, because sin, the cause of death, reigns in us.

[1] An inversion for the sake of emphasis.

2. *Wherein aforetime ye walked.* From the effects or fruits he proves that sin once reigned in them; for, unless sin proceeds into outward acts, men are not sufficiently aware of its power.

When he adds, *according to the age of this world,* he implies that the death which he had mentioned rages in the nature of man and is a universal disease. He does not mean that course of the world which God has ordained, nor the elements, such as the heaven, and earth, and air, but the depravity with which we are all infected; so that sin is not peculiar to a few, but engrasps the whole world.

According to the prince. He goes farther, and explains the cause of our corruption to be the dominion which the devil has over us. A more severe condemnation of mankind could not have been pronounced. What does he leave to us, whom he declares to be the slaves of Satan, and subject to his will, so long as we live outside the Kingdom of Christ? Our condition, therefore, though many are pleased with it (or, at least, little displeased), ought certainly to horrify us. Where is now the free-will, the guidance of reason, the moral virtue, about which Papists babble so much? What will they find that is pure or holy under the tyranny of the devil? But they are shrewdly taking care of themselves when they abominate this doctrine of Paul's as the worst heresy. But I say, that there is no obscurity in these words, and that all men who live according to the world, that is, to the inclinations of their flesh, fight under the command of Satan.

As is usual in Scripture, he calls him the devil in the singular. As the children of God have one Head, so have the wicked; for each forms a body. Therefore he assigns to one the dominion over all the evil, so as to represent ungodliness as one mass. As to his attributing to the devil power in the air, that will be considered in Chapter Six. At present, we shall only notice the foolish nonsense of the Manichees in endeavouring to form from this passage two principles, as if Satan could do anything against God's will. Paul does not allow him the supreme rule, which belongs to the will of God alone, but merely a tyranny which he exercises by God's permission. What is Satan but God's executioner to punish man's ingratitude? This is implied in Paul's language, for he says that he is powerful only with unbelievers and thus exempts the children of God from his power. If this is so it follows that Satan does nothing but by the will of a superior, and that he is not αὐτοκράτωρ.

Nevertheless, we infer at the same time that ungodly men have no excuse that they are driven by Satan to commit all their crimes. How does it come that they are subject to his tyranny, but because they are rebels against God? If none are the slaves of Satan but those who are freed from God and who refuse to yield obedience to Him, let them blame themselves for having so bad a master.

By *the children of disobedience*, he means, according to the Hebrew custom, the obstinate. Unbelief is always accompanied by disobedience; so that it is the source and mother of all stubbornness.

3. *Among whom we also*. Lest he should seem to slander the former character of the Ephesians, or as a Jew to despise the Gentiles, he associates himself and his race with them. This is not said in hypocrisy, but in a sincere confession of glory to God. Yet it may seem strange that he should admit that he had walked in the lusts of the flesh, when on other occasions he claims that his life had been throughout irreproachable. I reply, this applies to all who have not yet been regenerated by the Spirit of Christ. However praiseworthy in appearance the life of some may be, because their lusts do not break out in the sight of men, there is nothing pure or incorrupt save from the fountain of all purity.

Now we must note his definition of *walking according to the lusts of the flesh*, that is, doing the desires of the flesh and of the mind, or in other words, living according to the will of our nature and mind. 'The flesh' means here the disposition, or what is called the inclination of the nature. He adds the word διανοιῶν, that which proceeds from the mind. 'The mind' includes reason, such as exists in men by nature. 'Lusts' does not refer only to the lower appetites, or what is called the sensual part, but extends to the whole.

And were by nature children of wrath. He pronounces all men without exception, both Jews and Gentiles (as Gal. 2), to be guilty until they are set free by Christ. So that outside Christ there is no righteousness, no salvation, and, in short, no excellence. By 'children of wrath' understand simply those who are lost and deserving of eternal death. 'Wrath' means the judgment of God; so that 'the children of wrath' signifies those who are condemned before God. Such, Paul here tells us, had been the Jews, and all who had been eminent in the Church; and they were so by nature, that is, from their very origin, and from their mother's womb.

This is a remarkable passage against the Pelagians and all who deny original sin. What dwells naturally in all is certainly original; but Paul teaches that we are all naturally liable to condemnation. Therefore sin dwells in us, for God does not condemn the innocent. The Pelagians quibbled that sin spread from Adam to the whole human race, not by derivation, but by imitation. But Paul affirms that we are born with sin, as serpents bring their venom from the womb. Others who deny that this is really sin, are no less at variance with Paul's language; for where condemnation is, there must surely be sin.

It is not with blameless men, but with sin, that God is angry. Nor is it wonderful that the depravity which is inborn in us from our parents is reckoned as sin before God; for while the seed is still hidden, He perceives and condemns it.

But one question here arises. Why does Paul subject the Jews to wrath and curse, like the rest, when they were in fact the blessed seed? I answer, they have a common nature. Jews differ from Gentiles only in that, by the grace of the promise, God delivers them from destruction; but the remedy was still to come. Another question is, since God is the Author of nature, how comes it that He is not to blame, if we are lost by nature? I answer, nature is twofold: the first was created by God, the second is the corruption of it. This condemnation, therefore, which Paul speaks of does not proceed from God but from a depraved nature. For we are not now born such as Adam was at first created, but we are the adulterous seed of degenerate and sinful man.

But God, who is rich in mercy, for his great love wherewith he loved us, even when we were dead in sins, quickened us together with Christ; (by grace have ye been saved); and raised us up with him, and made us sit in the heavenly places in Christ Jesus; that in the ages to come he might shew the exceeding riches of his grace in kindness towards us in Christ Jesus. (4-7)

4. *But God, who is rich in mercy.* Now follows the second cause, the substance of which is, that God had delivered the Ephesians from the destruction to which they were formerly bound over; but he uses different words. 'God, who is rich in mercy,' he says 'has quickened you together with Christ.' He means that there is no other life of the soul than that which is breathed into us by Christ: so that we begin to live only when we are engrafted into Him, and enjoy a common life with Him. From this we gather what he formerly meant by death. For that death and this resurrection are opposed to one another. To be made partakers of the life of the Son of God, so that we are animated by the same Spirit, is an incomparable benefit.

On this ground he praises the mercy of God, meaning by its riches, that it had been poured out liberally and superbly. Although he here ascribed the whole of our salvation to the mercy of God, a little after he more precisely places it in His free goodness, when he adds that this was done because of His great love. For he means that God was moved by this single consideration. Just as also John says, 'Not that we first loved Him, but he first loved us' (I John 4.10, 19). The particle *even* is emphatic, as in Rom. 6.

5. *By grace ye have been saved.* I do not know whether this has been inserted by another hand, but, as it is perfectly agreeable to the con-

text, I am willing to receive it as written by Paul. We see that he is never satisfied with proclaiming the richness of grace, and accordingly emphasizes the same thing with many words, that everything in our salvation must be ascribed to God. And certainly he who duly weighs the ingratitude of men will not complain that this parenthesis is superfluous.

6. *And made us sit in the heavenly places.* What he declares of the resurrection and the session in heaven, is not yet seen with the eyes. Yet, as if those blessings were already in our possession, he states that they have been conferred on us, so that he may declare the change in our condition, when we were led from Adam to Christ. It is as if he said that we had been transferred from the deepest hell to heaven itself. And certainly, although, as respects ourselves, our salvation is still hidden in hope, yet in Christ we possess blessed immortality and glory.

Therefore he adds, *in Christ*, because what he speaks of does not yet appear in the members, but only in the Head; yet, because of the secret union, it belongs truly to the members. Some render it, 'through Christ'; but, for the reason mentioned, 'in Christ' fits the context better. And from this we should gather the richest consolation—that of everything which we now lack, we have a sure pledge and firstfruits in the Person of Christ.

7. *That in the ages to come.* He repeats the final cause, that God should be glorified; and this so that the Ephesians might exercise themselves persistently in it and therefore be the more sure of their salvation as they knew that its cause was the more righteous. He likewise adds that it was the will of the Lord to hallow in all ages the remembrance of so great goodness. This makes even more hateful those who attacked the free calling of the Gentiles; for they were trying to crush immediately what was meant to be remembered through the ages. But we are admonished by it that the mercy of God, who was pleased to admit our fathers into His people, deserves to be held in everlasting remembrance. The calling of the Gentiles is an astonishing work of divine goodness, which ought to be handed down from parents to children, and to grandchildren, that it may never be blotted out of men's minds by silence.

The riches of his grace in kindness. He now demonstrates or confirms by repetition that the love which God shows to us in Christ springs from mercy. 'That he might shew', he says, 'the richness of his grace.' How? 'In kindness towards us', as the tree in its fruit. Not only, therefore, does he assert that the love of God was free, but also that God displayed in it the richness of His grace—and that not ordinary but outstanding.

It is to be noted, also, that the word *Christ* is repeated; for we must expect no grace, no love, from God, except through His mediation.

For by grace have ye been saved through faith; and that not of yourselves: it is the gift of God: not of works, lest any man should boast. For we are his work,[1] created in Christ Jesus for good works, which God afore prepared that we should walk in them. (8-10)

8. *For by grace have ye been saved.* This is, so to say, the inference from the former statements. For he treated of election and of free calling, so as to reach the conclusion that they had obtained salvation by faith alone. First, he asserts that the salvation of the Ephesians was entirely the work, the free work, of God; but they had obtained this grace by faith. On one side, we must look at God; and, on the other, at men. God declares that He owes us nothing; so that salvation is not a reward or recompense, but mere grace. Now it may be asked how men receive the salvation offered to them by the hand of God? I reply, by faith. Hence he concludes that here is nothing of our own. If, on the part of God, it is grace alone, and if we bring nothing but faith, which strips us of all praise, it follows that salvation is not of us.

Ought we not then to be silent about free-will, and good intentions, and invented preparations, and merits, and satisfactions? There is none of these which does not claim a share of praise in the salvation of men; so that the praise of grace would not, as Paul says, remain whole. When, on man's side, he places the only way of receiving salvation in faith alone, he rejects all other means on which men are accustomed to rely. Faith, then, brings a man empty to God, that he may be filled with the blessings of Christ. And so he adds, *not of yourselves*; that, claiming nothing for themselves, they may acknowledge God alone as the Author of their salvation.

9. *It is the gift of God.* Instead of what he had said, that their salvation is of grace, he now affirms that it is the gift of God. Instead of what he had said, 'Not of yourselves,' he now says, *Not of works.* Hence we see that he leaves nothing to men in procuring salvation. For in these three phrases, he embraces the substance of his long argument in the Epistles to the Romans and to the Galatians, that righteousness comes to us from the mercy of God alone, is offered to us in Christ and by the Gospel, and is received by faith alone, without the merit of works.

From this passage it is easy to refute the idle quibble by which Papists attempt to evade the argument. Paul, they tell us, is speaking about ceremonies when he tells us we are justified without works. But

---

[1] *Opus* can mean 'workmanship' (as AV) and this would be the smoother rendering here. But I have preferred 'work' to preserve the link with Calvin's characteristic concept of the *opus dei*.

it is quite certain that he is not dealing with one sort of works, but rejects the whole righteousness of man, which consists in works—nay, the whole man, and everything that he has of his own. We must observe the contrast between God and man, between grace and works. Why should God be contrasted with man, if the controversy only concerned ceremonies?

The Papists are compelled to own that Paul here ascribes to the grace of God the whole glory of our salvation; but then they think up another idea, that this was said because God bestows 'the first grace'. But they are really foolish to imagine that they can succeed in this way, since Paul excludes man and his faculties, not only from the start of obtaining salvation, but completely from salvation itself.

But they are even more foolish to overlook the conclusion: *lest any man should boast.* Some room must always remain for human boasting so long as merits are of any avail apart from grace. Paul's statement cannot stand, unless the whole praise is rendered to God alone and to His mercy. But they commonly misinterpret this text, and restrict the word 'gift' to faith alone. But Paul is only repeating his earlier statement in other words. He does not mean that faith is the gift of God, but that salvation is given to us by God, or, that we obtain it by the gift of God.

10. *For we are his work.* By setting aside the contrary, he proves what he says, that we are saved by grace, that no works are of use to us in meriting salvation, for all the good works which we possess are the fruit of regeneration. Hence it follows that works themselves are a part of grace. When he says that we are the work of God, it is not to be taken of general creation, by which we men are born, but he asserts that we are new creatures who are formed to righteousness by the Spirit of Christ and not by our own power. This applies only to believers, who, although they are born of Adam wicked and perverse, are spiritually regenerated by the grace of Christ, and begin to be new men. Everything in us that is good, therefore, is the supernatural work of God. And an explanation follows; for he adds that we are God's work because we have been created, not in Adam, but in Christ, and not to any kind of life, but to good works.

What remains now for free-will, if all the good works which proceed from us have been received from the Spirit of God? Let godly readers weigh carefully the apostle's words. He does not say that we are assisted by God. He does not say that the will is prepared, and has then to proceed in its own strength. He does not say that the power of choosing aright is bestowed upon us, and that we have afterwards to make our own choice. This is what those who weaken God's grace (so far as they can) are accustomed to babble. But he says that we are God's work, and that everything good in us is His creation. By which he means that the whole man is formed by His hand to become good. It is not the mere power of choosing aright, or some indefinable preparation, or assistance, but the right will itself, which is His workmanship. Otherwise Paul's argument would be pointless. He means to prove that man does not in any way procure salvation for himself, but obtains it freely from God. The proof is that man is nothing but by divine grace. Whoever, then, makes the very smallest claim for man, apart from the grace of God, allows him to that extent ability to procure salvation.

Created to good works. They stray far from Paul's thought, who twist this text for the purpose of injuring the righteousness of faith. Ashamed to deny outright, and aware that they would do so in vain, that we are justified by faith, they take refuge in this kind of subterfuge: we are justified by faith, because faith, by which we receive the grace of God, is the commencement of righteousness; but we become righteous by regeneration, because, being renewed by the Spirit of Christ, we walk in good works. Thus they make faith the door by which we enter into righteousness, but imagine that we attain it by works; or, at least, they define righteousness as uprightness, when a man is reformed to a good life. I do not care how old this error may be; but they err who support it by this text.

We must look to Paul's design. He intends to show that we have brought nothing to God, by which He might be obliged to us; he shows that even the good works which we do have come from Him. Hence it follows that we are nothing, except through His pure liberality. Now when those men infer that we are justified half by works, what has this to do with Paul's intention, or with the subject which he handles? It is one thing to discuss in what righteousness consists, and another thing to follow up the doctrine that it is not from ourselves, with this argument, that there is nothing of our own in good works, but we have been formed by the Spirit of God to all that is good, and that through the grace of Christ. When Paul defines the cause of righteousness, he dwells chiefly on this point, that our consciences will never be at peace till they rest on the forgiveness of sins. He deals with nothing of this sort here. His whole object is to prove that we are what we are completely by the grace of God.

Which God afore prepared. Do not apply this, as the Pelagians do, to the teaching of the law; as if Paul meant that God commands what is just, and lays down a proper rule of life. Rather, he emphasizes what he had begun to teach, that salvation does not proceed from ourselves. He says, that, before we were born, the good works were prepared by God; meaning, that in our own strength we are not able to lead a holy life, but only so far as we are adapted and formed by the hand of God. Now, if the grace of God forestalled us, all ground of boasting has been taken away. Let us carefully observe the word 'prepared'. Paul shows from the order itself that, with respect to good works, God owes us nothing. How so? Because they were drawn out of His treasures, in which they had long before been laid up; for whom He called, them He justifies and regenerates.

Wherefore remember, that aforetime ye the Gentiles in the flesh, who are called Uncircumcision by that which is called Circumcision, in the flesh made by hands; that at that time ye were separate from Christ, alienated from the commonwealth of Israel, and strangers from the tables of the promise, having no hope and without God in the world: but now, in Christ Jesus ye that once were far off are made nigh by the blood of Christ. (11-13)

11. *Wherefore remember.* He always comes to the basic principle, marks it out clearly, and emphasizes it more strongly. He again bids the Ephesians remember what they had been before their calling. This consideration showed them that they had no cause for pride. He afterwards points out the method of reconciliation, that, satisfied with Christ alone, they might not imagine that they needed other aids. The first clause may be thus summed up: 'Remember that, when you were uncircumcised, you were aliens from Christ, from the hope of salvation, from the Church and from the Kingdom of God; so that you had no connection with God.' And the second: 'But now engrafted into Christ, you are at the same time reconciled to God.' What is implied, and what effect the remembrance of it ought to produce in their minds, I have said above.

Gentiles in the flesh. He first recalls that they had lacked the marks of God's people. For circumcision was a token by which the people of God were marked out and distinguished from others, and uncircumcision was the mark of a profane man. Since, therefore, God usually connects His grace with the sacraments, he deduces from their want of the sacraments that they were also not partakers of grace. The argument is, of course, not always true, though it does hold as to God's ordinary dispensation. Hence the verse: 'Adam was cast out lest he should take of the tree of life, and live' (Gen. 3.22-24). If he had eaten the whole tree, he would not, by merely eating it, have recovered life. But by taking away the sign, the Lord took away the thing also. And so Paul holds out uncircumcision to the Ephesians as a sign of pollution. He takes from them the symbol of sanctification, and so deprives them also of the thing signified.

They are deceived, therefore, who think that all this is said to throw contempt on outward circumcision. At the same time, I acknowledge that the qualifying phrase, *in the flesh made by hands*, points out a twofold circumcision, so as to blunt the glory of the Jews, who boasted in vain in the literal circumcision, and also to free the Ephesians from all scruples on their own account, since they knew they had the chief thing—nay, the whole truth of the outward sign. He calls it 'Uncircumcision in the flesh', because they bore in their body the sign of their pollution; but, at the same time, he suggests that their uncircumcision was no longer a drawback, for they had been spiritually circumcised by Christ.

This can be read either joined: 'in the flesh made by hands', or separated so that he first calls it fleshly, and then, made by men's hands. Moreover, he contrasts this kind of circumcision with that of the Spirit, which is in the heart, which in Col. 2.11 he also calls 'the circumcision of Christ'.

By that which is called. 'Circumcision' can be taken here either as a collective noun for the Jews themselves, or literally for the thing itself; and then the meaning would be, that they were called the Uncircumcision, because they lacked the sacred symbol, that is, by way of distinction. This latter sense is sanctioned by the qualifying phrase; but the substance of the argument is little affected.

12. *That at that time ye were separated from Christ.* He now declares that the Ephesians had been banished, not only from the outward tokens, but from everything necessary to the salvation and happiness of men. But because Christ is the foundation of all the promises and of hope, he says, first, that they were separated from Him. But for him who has not Christ, nothing remains but destruction. For on Him the commonwealth of Israel was founded; and in whom but in Himself could the people of God be collected into the unity of a holy body?

The same might also be said of *the tables of the promise.* On one great promise all the others depend, and without it they become empty: 'In thy seed shall all nations be blessed' (Gen. 22.18). Hence the verse, 'All the promises in him are yea and Amen' (II Cor. 1.20). Take away the covenant of salvation, and there remains no hope. I have translated διαθήκας here as *the tables*, which are commonly called instruments. For God made His covenant with Abraham and his posterity, that He would be their God for ever, by a solemn rite. Tables of this covenant were confirmed by the hand of Moses, and intrusted, as a peculiar treasure, to the people of Israel, for they did not belong to the Gentiles.

And without God in the world. But neither the Ephesians, nor any other Gentiles, were ever completely destitute of all religion. Why, then, are they called by Paul ἄθεοι, for ἄθεος, strictly speaking, is one who has no sense of the Divinity, and ridicules any idea of the divine. Certainly we do not usually call superstitious persons ἄθεοι, but those who are touched with no feeling or religion, who in fact desire to see it utterly obliterated. I answer, Paul spoke quite rightly, for he regarded all the notions about false gods as nothing. And indeed all idols must become nothing, since they are nothing among the godly. Those who do not worship the true God, however many sorts of worship they may have, however many ceremonies they may tire themselves with, are without God. For they adore what they know not. Let it be carefully observed, that the Ephesians are not charged with ἀθεϊσμός as Diagoras and his like, who were branded with that reproach. But it was those who imagined themselves to be very religious who are charged with that crime; seeing that an idol is a forgery and a deception, not the Divinity.

From what had been said before, the conclusion will be easily drawn that outside Christ there are only idols. For he now separates from God those whom he had at first declared to be without Christ; and indeed as John says, 'Whosoever hath not the Son, hath not the Father' (II John 1.9). Let us know, therefore, that all who do not keep this way wander from the true God. Someone may ask, 'Did God never reveal Himself to any of the Gentiles?' I answer, no manifestation of God apart from Christ was ever made among the Gentiles, any more than among the Jews. For it was not to one age or to one nation that He said, 'I am the way'; but He declares that it is through Him that all come to God (John 14.6).

13. *But now in Christ Jesus.* We must either supply the verb, so that the sense will be: 'now that ye have been received in Christ Jesus', or connect it with the phrase following, 'through the blood of Christ', which will be a still clearer exposition. In either case, the meaning is that the Ephesians, when they were far off from God and from salvation, had been reconciled to God through Christ, so that now they were nigh in His blood. For the blood of Christ has taken away the quarrel which existed between them and God, and from being enemies had made them sons.

For he is our peace, who made both one, and brake down the middle wall of partition, the enmities in his flesh, and abolished the law of commandments contained in ordinances; that he might create in himself the twain into one new man, so making peace; and might reconcile them both in one body unto God by the cross, having slain the enmity thereby. (14-16)

He now extends to the Jews the blessing of reconciliation, and says that all are united to God through the one Christ. By this he refuted the false confidence of the Jews, who, despising the grace of Christ, boasted that they were the people holy to God and the chosen inheritance. For if Christ is our peace, it follows that all who are outside Him are at enmity with God. This is a beautiful title of Christ: the Peace between God and men. Let no one doubt that God is favourable to him if he remains in Christ.

In particular he says, *Who made both one*. This distinction was necessary. They thought all communication with the Gentiles inconsistent with their superiority. To beat down this pride, he tells them that they and the Gentiles have been united into one body. Put all these things together, and you will frame the following syllogism:

If the Jews wish to have peace with God, they must have Christ as their Mediator.
But Christ will not be their peace in any other way than by making out of them and the Gentiles one body.
Therefore, unless the Jews admit the Gentiles to fellowship, they have no connexion with God.

And brake the middle wall of partition. To understand this passage, we must observe two things. The Jews were for a certain time separated from the Gentiles by the appointment of God; and ceremonies as open symbols testified to that separation. Passing over the Gentiles, God had chosen a peculiar people to Himself. A wide distinction was thus made, because the Jews were the household of the Church, and the others were foreigners from the Church. This is what Moses said in his Song: 'When the Most High divided to the nations, when he set the bounds of the people, he set his cord in Jacob' (Deut. 32.8, 9). Thus you see that bounds were fixed by God to mark off one people from the rest; and hence arose the enmity which Paul here mentions. For a segregation was made between them, when the Gentiles were rejected and God chose only the Jews and sanctified them, freeing them from the common pollution of mankind. The ceremonies were afterwards added, which, like walls, enclosed the inheritance of God, lest it should be open to all or confused with other possessions; and thus the Gentiles were excluded from the Kingdom of God.

But now, the apostle says, the enmity is removed and the wall broken down. By extending the blessing of adoption beyond the limits of Judaea, Christ has now made us all to be brethren. And so is fulfilled the prophecy: 'Japheth shall dwell in the tents of Shem' (Gen. 9.27). Paul's words are now clear. The middle wall prevented Christ from collecting together Jews and Gentiles. Therefore He broke down the wall. The reason why it is broken down is then added: to abolish the enmity by the flesh of Christ. The Son of God, by assuming a nature common to all, has consecrated in His own Body a perfect unity.

The law of commandments contained in ordinances. He now expresses more plainly what he had metaphorically understood by the word 'wall', saying that the ceremonies, by which the distinction was declared, had been abolished through Christ. For what were circumcision, sacrifices, washings and abstaining from certain kinds of food, but symbols of sanctification, reminding the Jews that their lot was different from that of the rest; just as today the white cross and the red cross distinguish the French from the Burgundians. Paul means not only that the Gentiles are equally admitted to the fellowship of grace, so that they no longer differ from the Jews, but that the mark of difference has been taken away; for ceremonies have been abolished. Just as, if two contending nations were brought under the dominion of one prince, he would not only desire that they should live in harmony, but would remove the badges and marks of their former enmity. Or just as when a pledge is discharged, the handwriting is torn up—a metaphor which Paul employs on this very subject in Col. 2.14.

Some connect the phrase, *in ordinances*, with *abolished*; but they are mistaken. This is how he usually speaks of the ceremonial law, in which the Lord not only enjoined upon the Jews a simple rule of life, but also bound them by various statutes. From this we may infer that Paul is here treating exclusively of the ceremonial law; for the moral law is not a wall of partition separating us from the Jews, but it includes teaching which concerns us no less than the Jews. From this passage we can refute the error of some, that circumcision and all the ancient rites, though not binding on the Gentiles, still remain today for the Jews. On this principle there would still be a middle wall of partition between us, which is proved to be false.

That he might create in himself. When he says, 'in himself', he turns the Ephesians away from the diversity of men, lest they should seek unity elsewhere than in Christ. However much the two might differ in their former condition, in Christ they have become one man. And it is not for nothing that he adds, *into one new man*. For he means (what he teaches more fully elsewhere[1]) that in Christ neither circumcision, nor uncircumcision, avails anything, that nothing external is of any value, but that a new creature holds the first and last place. Therefore there is one spiritual regeneration which joins us. If then we are all renewed by Christ, let the Jews cease to congratulate themselves on their ancient conditions, and let them, both for them-

[1] The reference is probably multiple—to I Cor. 7.19, Gal. 5.6 and 6.15.

selves and for others, allow Christ to be in all (as he says elsewhere).[1]

16. *And might reconcile both.* He asserts that we are not only set at peace among ourselves, but have been brought back into favour with God. And this means that the Jews have no less need of a Mediator than the Gentiles. Without this, neither the Law, nor ceremonies, nor their descent from Abraham, nor all the advantages they had been given would be of any avail. For all are sinners; and forgiveness of sins can be obtained only through the mediating grace of Christ.

He repeats, *in one body*, to teach the Jews that to cultivate unity with the Gentiles will be well-pleasing to God.

By the cross. The word cross is added to denote the sacrifice of expiation. Sin is the cause of the enmity between God and us; and until it is abolished, we shall never be in God's favour. It has been blotted out by the death of Christ, in which He offered Himself to the Father as an expiatory Victim. There is another reason, indeed, why he mentions the cross here, for it is through the cross that all ceremonies have been abolished.

Accordingly it follows, *slaying the enmity thereby*, for this ought indubitably to be referred to the cross. Yet the phrase may admit of two senses—either that Christ, by His death, has reconciled the Father to us and taken away His anger, or that, by redeeming both Jews and Gentiles alike, He has brought them into one flock. The latter appears to me the more probable, as it agrees with a former clause, 'abolishing in His flesh the enmity'.

And he came and preached peace to you that were far off, and peace to them that were nigh. For through him we both have access in one Spirit unto the Father. So then ye are no more strangers and foreigners, but citizens with the saints, and of the household of God, being built upon the foundation of the apostles and prophets, Christ himself being the chief corner-stone; in whom the whole building, fitly framed together, groweth unto an holy temple in the Lord: in whom also be ye builded together for an habitation of God in the Spirit. (17-22)

All that he had taught of the reconciliation made by Christ would have been of no service, if it had not been proclaimed through the Gospel. And therefore he adds that the fruit of this peace has now been offered both to Jews and to Gentiles. Hence it follows that Christ came to save Gentiles as well as Jews. For the preaching of the Gospel, which is appointed indiscriminately for both, is a sure testimony to this. The same order is followed in II Cor. 5.20: 'He made him to be sin for us who knew no sin.' And then: 'He hath committed

---

[1] Eph. 1.23.

to us the ministry of reconciliation. And so we are ambassadors for Christ. He first declares that the cause of salvation lies in the death of Christ.' Then he describes the manner in which Christ communicates to us Himself and the benefit of His death. But here Paul dwells chiefly on the circumstance that the Gentiles are united with the Jews in the Kingdom of God. Having already represented Christ as common to both, he now makes them fellows in the Gospel, meaning that although they had the law, they needed the Gospel also; and God had bestowed upon the Gentiles equal grace. Those; therefore, whom God joined together in an equal participation of grace, let not man put asunder. The words 'afar off' and 'nigh' do not refer to distance of place. The Jews, by reason of the covenant, were nigh to God. The Gentiles who were banished from the Kingdom of God, so long as they had not the promise of salvation, were afar off.

17. *And preached peace.* Not indeed by His own lips, but through the apostles. It was necessary that Christ should rise from the dead before calling the Gentiles to the fellowship of grace. Hence that saying, 'I am not sent but to the lost sheep of the house of Israel' (Matt. 15.24). He forbade the apostles to carry their first embassy to the Gentiles while He was still in the world (Matt. 10.5). Therefore He proclaimed the Gospel to the Gentiles through His apostles as by trumpets. What they did, not only in His name, and by His command, but as it were in His own person, is justly ascribed to Him alone. We too speak as if Christ Himself exhorted you by us. The faith of the Gospel would be weak indeed, were we to look only to men. Its whole authority comes from recognizing men as God's instruments, and hearing Christ speak to us by their mouth. Observe also, that the Gospel is the message of peace, by which God declares Himself favourable to us, and brings down to us His fatherly love. Take away the Gospel, and war and enmity remain between God and men; and, on the other hand, the proper effect of the Gospel is to give peace and calmness to the conscience, which would otherwise be tormented by wretched disquiet.

18. *For through him we both have access.* This is an argument from the effect; a declaration of peace that access to God is open to us. For the ungodly, lulled into a profound sleep, sometimes deceive themselves by a false notion of peace, but can only rest when they have brought on a forgetfulness of the divine judgment, and keep themselves at the greatest possible distance from God. Paul had good reason, therefore, to add this definition of evangelical peace, that we may know that it does not lie in a stupefied conscience, in false confidence, in proud boasting, in ignorance of our own wretchedness, but in cloudless tranquillity, which desires the sight of God as something

lovely rather than fearful. Now, it is Christ who opens the door to us, yea, who is Himself the door. Moreover, as this door has two leaves and is open both to Jews and Gentiles, it follows that God is open to both to reveal His fatherly love.

He adds, *in one Spirit*, by whose direction and guiding we come to Christ, and by whom we cry, 'Abba, Father'; for from this arises boldness to approach. The Jews had various means of approaching to God; now all have but one way, to be ruled by the Spirit of God.

19. *So then ye are no more strangers.* He alludes to what he had said, that the Ephesians were formerly strangers from the covenant. For now he addresses them alone. So it is as if he said, 'Your condition is changed; for from being foreigners, God has made you citizens of His church.' And he praises with many words the honour which God had bestowed on them. He calls them *citizens with the saints*; secondly, *the household of God*; and lastly, stones properly fitted into the building of the temple of God. The first title is taken from the comparison of the Church to a state, which occurs very frequently in Scripture. It is a great honour that those who were formerly profane and unworthy to be partners with the godly, have now the rights of citizens along with Abraham, with all the holy patriarchs, and prophets, and kings, nay, with the angels themselves. Yet the second is not less, that God had admitted them into His own family. For the Church is God's House.

20. *Being built.* The third honour expresses the manner in which the Ephesians and all others become the household of God and citizens with the saints. That is, if they are founded on the doctrine of the apostles and prophets. We are thus enabled to distinguish between a true and a false Church. This is of the first necessity. For no imagination is more dangerous, and a slip is easily made. Hardly any Churches boast more loudly of the name than those which bear a false and empty title; as may be seen in our own times. To guard us against mistakes, Paul points out the mark of a true Church.

Foundation unquestionably here refers to doctrine; for he does not mention patriarchs or godly kings, but only those who held the teaching office, and whom God had appointed to build His Church. And so Paul teaches that the faith of the Church ought to be founded on this doctrine. What, then, must we think of those who rest entirely on the inventions of men, and yet accuse us of desertion because we embrace the pure doctrine of God? But the manner in which it is founded must be noted; for strictly, Christ is the only foundation, since He alone supports the whole Church. He alone is the rule and standard of faith. But in Christ the Church is founded by the preaching of doctrine. Hence, the prophets and apostles are called master-builders. It is therefore as if Paul said that the prophets and apostles never meant to do anything but found the Church on Christ.

We shall find this to be true, if we begin with Moses. For Christ is the end of the law, and the sum of the Gospel. Let us remember, therefore, that if we wish to be reckoned among believers, we must rest on no others: if we wish to progress well in the Scriptures, everything must be directed to Him. We are also taught where to seek the Word of God in the prophets and apostles. So that we may learn how to combine them, he shows their mutual accord; for they have a common foundation, and labour together in building the temple of God. For the teaching of the prophets has not become superfluous because we have the apostles as teachers; but they both perform one and the same work.

I say that just as the Marcionites in ancient times expunged the word 'prophets' from this passage, so today there are fanatics who have the Marcionite spirit. They clamour that the law and the prophets have nothing to do with us, since the Gospel has put an end to them all. The Holy Spirit everywhere declares that He has so spoken to us by the mouth of the prophets, that He wishes to be heard in their writings. It is of no small consequence in maintaining the authority of our faith when we see that all the servants of God, from first to last, are so perfectly agreed that their harmony itself clearly demonstrates that it is one God who speaks in them all. The beginning of our religion must be sought from the creation of the world. In vain do Papists and the Turks, and other sects, boast of their antiquity, for they are the degenerate offspring of true and pure religion.

Christ himself being the chief corner-stone. Those who transfer this honour to Peter, and maintain that the Church is founded on him, are so shameless as to pervert this text to support their error. They object that Christ is called the chief corner-stone in comparison with others; and that there are many stones on which the Church is supported. But the solution is easy. The apostles use various metaphors according to the circumstances, but still with the same meaning. The constant factor is that no other foundation can be laid. He does not therefore mean here that Christ is merely a corner, or a part of the foundation; for then he would contradict himself. What then? He wants to form Jews and Gentiles into one spiritual building. They were like two separate walls; but he places Christ in the middle of the corner to join the two, and this is the meaning of the metaphor.

Immediately after, he declares sufficiently that he is very far from limiting Christ to any one part of the building, when he says: *In whom the whole building groweth.* If this be true, what will become of Peter? When Paul in Corinthians calls Him the Foundation, he does not mean that the Church is begun by Him and completed by others, but merely makes this distinction so as to compare his own labours with those of other men. It had been his part to found the Church at Corinth, and to leave to his successors the completion of the building.

As to the present passage, he teaches that all who are framed together in Christ are the temple of God. There is first required a fitting together, that believers may comprehend and accommodate themselves either to other by mutual communication; otherwise there would not be a building, but a confused mass. The chief symmetry consists in unity of faith. Next follows progress or increase. Those who are not so united in faith and love as to progress in Christ, have a profane building, which has nothing in common with the temple of God.

Groweth unto an holy temple. Elsewhere individual believers are called temples, but here the temple of God is said to consist of them all. Both statements are just and appropriate. For God so dwells in each of us, that He wants us all to be embraced in a holy unity, and that thus He should form one out of many. Therefore, he who on his own is a temple, is, when joined to others, a stone of a temple. And this is said so as to commend unity.

22. *In whom also be ye builded together.* The Greek ending, like that of the Latin (*coædificamini*), is ambiguous. For both the imperative and indicative mood would fit, and the context will admit either. But I prefer the imperative. It is, I think, an exhortation to the Ephesians to grow more and more in the faith of Christ, after having been once founded in it, and thus to be a part of that new temple which through the Gospel was then being built by God in every part of the world.

He repeats the word *Spirit* for two reasons. First, to remind them that all human powers are of no avail without the operation of the Spirit; and secondly, to contrast the spiritual mode to all outward and Jewish means.

CHAPTER THREE

*For this cause, I Paul, the prisoner of Jesus Christ, am an ambassador
for you Gentiles, if ye have heard of the dispensation of the grace of God
which was given me to you-ward: how that by revelation he made
known unto me the mystery; as I wrote a little earlier; whereby, when
ye read, ye may understand my knowledge in the mystery of Christ,
which in other ages was not made known unto the sons of men, as it is
now revealed unto his holy apostles and prophets by the Spirit; that
the Gentiles are fellow-heirs, and fellow-members of the body, and
fellow-partakers of his promise in Christ by the gospel.* (1-6)

1. *For this cause.* Paul's imprisonment, which ought to have helped
to confirm his apostleship, was undoubtedly represented by his adversaries unfavourably. He therefore points out to the Ephesians
that his chains proved and declared his calling. For the only reason
for his imprisonment was that he had preached the Gospel to the
Gentiles. His strong and unshaken firmness was no small confirmation
to the Gentiles that he had discharged his office properly.

To strengthen his authority still more, he speaks of his prison
proudly, and says, *I am an ambassador.* In the sight of the world and
of the ungodly, this was a foolish boasting; but for the godly, it was
dignified and faithful. For the glory of Christ not only obliterates the
ignominy of the chains, but converts what was a reproach into the
highest glory. If he had simply said, 'I am a prisoner,' this would not
have conveyed the idea of his being an ambassador. Imprisonment
has no claim to this honour, being usually the mark of wickedness
and crime. But the chains of a prisoner of Jesus Christ surpass in
honour the crowns and sceptres of kings, to say nothing of the insignia
of an ambassador. Not that they seem so in the sight of men, but it
is our task to decide the real case. So highly ought the name of
Christ to be revered by us, that what men consider to be the greatest
reproach, should be to us the greatest honour.

And Paul commends his persecutions to the Ephesians when he
says that they were endured for the Gentiles. And it must have been
very moving for them to hear that it was for their sake that he was in
trouble and peril.

2. *If ye have heard.* It is probable that, while Paul was at Ephesus,
he had said nothing on these subjects, because there was no necessity
to do so. For no controversy had taken place among them about the

calling of the Gentiles. If he had mentioned them before, he would now have reminded the Ephesians about them, instead of referring only, as he now does, to common report and to his own epistle. He did not raise unnecessary disputes of his own accord. It was only when the wickedness of his adversaries made it necessary, that he undertook the defence of his ministry. *Dispensation* is here used for a divine order or command, or, as it is generally called, a commission.

3. *That by revelation.* Lest it should seem that in his apostleship he had acted rashly, and was now paying the penalty of his rashness, he insists earnestly that God was the Author of his actions, and because, on account of its newness, it had few supporters, he calls it *a mystery.* By this name he removes the dislike of His actions which might arise. He was not so concerned with himself in all this as with the Ephesians, who greatly needed to be assured that, through the certain purpose of God, they had been called by Paul's ministry. Lest what was little known should become suspect, he sets the word mystery in opposition to the perverse judgments and opinions which were then prevalent in the world.

Moreover, he says that the mystery was made known to him by revelation. He dissociates himself from those fanatics who ascribe to God and to the Holy Spirit their own idle dreams. The false apostles also claim their revelations, but falsely. Paul was persuaded that his revelation was true, could prove it to others, and certainly speaks of it as a well testified fact.

As I wrote a little before. This either reminds them of what he had touched on in the second chapter, or refers to another epistle, which appears to be the general opinion. If the former exposition be adopted, it will be best to translate it, 'I wrote in few words'; for he had only glanced at the subject in passing. But as the latter is, as I have said, the prevailing interpretation, I have followed it in my version. The phrase, ἐν ὀλίγῳ, which Erasmus has translated 'in a few words', appears rather to refer to time. So that there would be an implied comparison between the present and the former writings. But there would be no point at all in drawing attention to brevity; for a more concise expression than this passing glance could not be imagined. By speaking of a little time, he seems purposely to appeal to their remembrance of a recent event, though I do not insist on this point.

There is more difficulty in the next verse: πρὸς ὃ δύνασθε ἀναγινώσκον-τες νοῆσαι, etc. Erasmus renders it, 'from which things, when ye read, ye may understand'. But Greek syntax will not, in my judgment, permit the translation of ἀναγινώσκειν τι as 'to read'. I leave it to the reader's consideration whether a more appropriate meaning would not be 'Giving heed to (or knowing) which things, ye may understand.' The particle would then be connected with the preposition πρός. If, however, you take ἀναγινώσκοντες as separate and absolute, the meaning will be, 'By reading you may understand according to what I have written'; taking the phrase πρὸς ὃ as equivalent to καθ' ὃ, but I put this forward merely as a conjecture on a doubtful point.

If we adopt the almost universal view, that the apostle had formerly written to the Ephesians, this is not the only epistle which we have lost. And yet there is no truth in the sneers of the ungodly, that the teaching of Scripture has been mutilated, or has in some part become imperfect. If we consider aright Paul's earnestness, his watchfulness and care, his zeal and fervour, his kindness and readiness in helping the brethren, we can easily guess that he would write many epistles, both public and private, to various places. Those which the Lord foresaw to be necessary for His Church He consecrated by His providence for everlasting remembrance. Let us know then, that what is left is enough for us, and that its smallness is not accidental; but that the body of Scripture, which is in our possession, has been controlled by the wonderful counsel of God.

My knowledge in the mystery. We can deduce from such frequent repetition how necessary is the certainty of calling, both in people and ministers. But Paul looks more to others than to himself. He had everywhere indeed been blamed for making the Gospel common to Jews and Gentiles. But he was not so much worried on his own account, as because he saw that there were many whose faith was shaken because the slanders of wicked men made them doubt his apostleship. It was for this that he so frequently reminded the Ephesians that he knew the will and command of God.

What he had formerly simply called a mystery, he now calls *the mystery of Christ.* He means that it had to remain hidden until it was revealed by His coming; just as the prophecies of His kingdom can be called 'prophecies of Christ'. We must first explain the word 'mystery', and then consider why he said it remained unknown in all ages. The mystery was that the Gentiles were to come into the fellowship of promise, and so become partakers of life in Christ, and that by the Gospel. When this name is given to the Gospel, it has other meanings, which do not apply to the present passage. The calling of the Gentiles, then, was the mystery of Christ; that is, it was to be fulfilled under the reign of Christ.

But why does he affirm that it was not known, when it had been foretold by so many predictions? For the prophets everywhere declare that people shall come from all the world to worship God; that an altar shall be erected both in Assyria and in Egypt, and that all alike shall speak the language of Canaan. They mean by these words that

the worship of the true God and the same profession of faith will be
spread abroad everywhere. Christ's Kingdom shall stretch from east
to west, and all nations of the earth shall be subject to Him. We see
also that the apostles quote many testimonies to this purpose, not
only from the later prophets, but also from Moses. How then could
that be hidden which had been proclaimed by so many heralds?
Why does Paul pronounce all without exception to have been in
ignorance? Shall we say that the prophets spoke of what they did not
know, and uttered sound without meaning?

I reply, the words of Paul must not be understood as if there had
been no knowledge at all on these subjects. There had always been
some in the nation who acknowledged that, at the advent of the
Messiah, the grace of God would be proclaimed throughout the
whole world, and who looked for the restoration of the human race.
The prophets themselves prophesied out of the certainty of revelation,
but they left the time and manner undetermined. They knew that
some communication of the grace of God would be made to the
Gentiles, but when, how or by what means, was quite hidden from
them. There was a remarkable instance of this sort of ignorance in
the apostles. They had not only been taught about it by the predictions
of the prophets, but had heard the distinct statement of their Master,
'Other sheep I have which are not of this fold: them also I must
gather in: and there shall be one fold and one shepherd' (John 10.16).
And yet the novelty of the matter prevented them from understanding
it fully. In fact, even after they had received the command, 'Go
preach to every creature' (Mark 16.15), and, 'Ye shall be witnesses to
me from Samaria to the uttermost nations' (Acts 1.8), they dreaded
and recoiled from the calling of the Gentiles as a monstrosity, because
its mode was still unknown to them. Before the actual event arrived,
they had dark and confused apprehensions of Christ's words; for the
ceremonies were a kind of veil over their eyes. Therefore there is
nothing absurd in Paul calling this a mystery, and saying that it had
been hidden; for it was not known that ceremonies had been repeated
and that in this was the access.

As it is now revealed. Lest he be accused of arrogance in claiming to
know what none of the patriarchs, prophets, or holy kings had known,
he reminds them, first, that he shared this knowledge with others and
was in the company of the leading doctors of the Church; and,
secondly, that it was the gift of the Holy Spirit, who has a right to
bestow it on whom He pleases. For there is no other measure of
knowledge than that which He assigns to us.

In these few words, he expresses the election of the Gentiles into
the people of God, so as to show on what condition this should take

place—that they shall be placed on a level with the Jews, to form one body. That the novelty may give no offence, he states that this must happen through the Gospel, the preaching of which was certainly new and hitherto unheard, but yet all the godly confessed that it came from heaven. Why is it surprising then, if, in renewing the world, God should follow an unusual method?

Whereof I was made a minister, according to the gift of the grace of God, which was given me according to the working of his power. Unto me, who am the least of all saints, is this grace given, that I should preach among the Gentiles the unsearchable riches of Christ; and to make all men see what is the fellowship of the mystery, which from all ages hath been hid in God, who created all things by Jesus Christ: to the intent that now, unto the principalities and powers in the heavenly places, might be made known through the church the manifold wisdom of God, according to the eternal purpose which he purposed in Christ Jesus our Lord: through whom we have boldness and access in confidence through the faith in him. Wherefore I ask that ye faint not at my tribulations for you, which is your glory. (7-13)

7. *Of which I was made.* Having declared the Gospel to be the instrument of communicating grace to the Gentiles, he now connects this command to his office, and thus applies to himself his statement. But lest he should seem to be claiming for himself more than is proper, he affirms first that it is the gift of the grace of God; and then that this gift contained the power of God; as if he had said, 'Do not look at what I have deserved; for in His free kindness, the Lord made me an apostle of the Gentiles, not for any excellence of mine, but by His own grace. Do not look at what I formerly was; for it is the Lord's to exalt men from nothing. To produce something great out of nothing, is the working of His power.'

8. *To me, who am the least.* He minimizes himself and all he has, as much as possible, to exalt the grace of God the more highly. And by this acknowledgment he forestalls the objections which his adversaries might bring against him: 'Who is this man, that God should have raised him above all the rest? What special gifts does he possess that he should be chosen before all the others?' Therefore he takes away all such comparisons of worth and ability, when he confesses that he is the least of all.

He is not speaking insincerely when he so lowers himself. Most men profess a feigned humility, while inwardly they swell with pride; in word they acknowledge themselves to be the least, while they wish to be regarded as supreme, and think themselves entitled to the highest honour. Paul is sincere in admitting his insignificance; indeed, he elsewhere speaks of himself far more meanly. 'For I am not worthy to be called an apostle' (I Cor. 15.9). Again, when he calls himself the chief of sinners (I Tim. 1.15).

But let us observe that, when he speaks of himself as the meanest of all, he is reckoning what he was in himself, and apart from the grace of God. As if he said that his lowness did not prevent him from being appointed the apostle of the Gentiles, while others were passed by. For when he says it was given to him, he means that it was a special gift, and speaks relatively. Not that he alone had been elected to that office, but that he held the primacy among the doctors of the Gentiles, a title which he employs elsewhere as peculiar to himself.

By *the unsearchable riches of Christ* he means the boundless and unbelievable treasures of grace, which God had suddenly and unexpectedly bestowed on the Gentiles. He therefore tells the Ephesians how eagerly the Gospel should be embraced, how highly esteemed. On this we have spoken in the Epistle to the Galatians. And certainly, although he held the office of apostleship in common with others, it was an honour peculiar to himself to be appointed apostle to the Gentiles.

9. *What is the fellowship of the mystery.* The proclamation is called the fellowship, because it is the will of God that men shall share in His purpose, which had formerly been hidden. And he uses an apt metaphor when he says, φωτίσαι πάντας, as if in his apostleship the grace of God shines with full light.

Which hath been hid in God. As before, he evades the prejudice of novelty. And especially he declares that it was hidden in God, so as to oppose the rashness of men, who think it unworthy that they should be ignorant of anything whatever. As if God had not the right to keep His purposes concealed in His own power until He wishes to communicate them to men! What presumption, what madness it is, not to admit that God is wiser than we! Let us remember, therefore, that our rashness must be suppressed whenever the boundless height of the Divine foreknowledge is set before us. This, too, is the reason why he calls them 'the unsearchable riches of Christ', meaning that this subject, though it exceeds our grasp, deserves reverence and admiration.

Who created all things in Christ. This is not so properly understood of the first creation as of spiritual restoration. It is no doubt true that by the Word of God all things were created, as it is said in many places. But the context demands that it be understood of that renewal which is contained in the blessing of redemption. Unless, perhaps, anyone would rather draw the argument from creation to renewal in this way: 'By Christ as God, the Father created all things. It is not surprising, then, if by the same Mediator all the Gentiles are now restored into the whole.' I have no objection to this view. He uses a

similar argument in II Cor. 4.6: 'For God, who commanded the light
to shine out of darkness, is the same who hath shined in your hearts.'
From the creation of the world he concludes that it is the office of
God to lighten the darkness; but what was there physically visible, he
ascribes to the Spirit when he speaks of the Kingdom of Christ.

10. *That now to the principalities and powers.* Some think it absurd
to say that this was spoken of angels, because such ignorance does not
belong to those who are permitted to behold the brightness of God's
countenance. They choose rather to refer it to devils, but rashly; for
what wonderful thing would the apostle declare of the Gospel or of
the calling of the Gentiles if he said it was now first made known to
devils? But it is certain that he labours to magnify as much as possible
the mercy of God towards the Gentiles, and the worth of the Gospel.
And to do this he declares that in the preaching of the Gospel is set
out the manifold grace of God, which had never been made known
even to the heavenly angels. Whence it follows that the wisdom of
God which was manifested by uniting Jews and Gentiles in the fellowship of salvation, should be more than wonderful to men.

He calls it πολυποίκιλον, because men are accustomed to measure
it erroneously by one particular idea and ignore the whole and the
individual parts. The Jews thought, for example, that the wisdom
of God was confined to the dispensation under the law, with which
they were acquainted and familiar. But, by publishing the Gospel
to all men indifferently, God has brought forth another instance and
token of His wisdom. Not that it was new wisdom, but that it was
more full and manifold than our limited capacity could grasp. Let
us know, then, that the knowledge, whatever it may be, which we
have acquired, is only a slight portion. And if the calling of the
Gentiles is known and revered by the angels in heaven, how shameful
that it should be rejected or despised by men upon earth!

The inference which some draw from this, that angels are present
in our assemblies, and make progress along with ourselves, is a groundless speculation. We must always keep in view the purposes for which
God appointed the ministry of His Word. If angels, who enjoy the
sight of God, do not walk in faith, neither do they need the outward
administration of the Word. Preaching, therefore, serves the need
only of men, among whom alone it is used. Paul's words mean that
the Church, gathered from Jews and Gentiles alike, is a mirror in
which angels contemplate the wonderful wisdom of God which they
did not know before. They see a work new to them, whose mode
was hid in God. In this way, and not by learning anything from the
lips of men, do they progress.

11. *According to the eternal purpose.* We see how carefully he guards

against the objection that there can be a change in the purpose of God. For the third time he repeats that the decree was eternal and ever-fixed, but it must be enacted in Christ, because in Him it was purposed. Thus he declares that the proper time for publishing this decree belongs to the kingdom of Christ. Literally, it is 'according to the purpose which he made'. But I take 'to make' as 'to purpose', because he is talking not only of the execution of the decree, but of the appointment itself, which, though it preceded all ages, was kept in the bosom of God till the manifestation of Christ.

12. *Through whom we have boldness.* He means that the honour of reconciling the Father to the whole world must be given to Christ. He commends this grace from its effects; for just as faith is common also to the Gentiles, so it admits them into the presence of God. But whenever Paul joins us to God through Christ and faith in Him, there is an implied contrast, which shuts up every other approach and excludes all other ways of union. But here we have remarkable and most valuable teaching, for Paul expresses elegantly the power and nature of faith, and the confidence necessary for the true invocation of God. It is not surprising that the Papists quarrel so much with us about the effects and offices of faith, for they do not understand the meaning of the word faith, which they could learn from this passage, if they were not prejudiced by their false ideas.

First, Paul calls it 'the faith of Christ', meaning that faith ought to contemplate what is exhibited to us in Christ. Hence it follows that a bare and confused knowledge about God must not be taken for faith, but that which is directed to Christ, in order to seek God in Him; and this can only be done when the power and office of Christ are understood. He says that first confidence and then, as its result, boldness, are begotten of faith. Thus there are three steps to be taken. First, we believe the promises of God; next, by resting in them, we conceive confidence, so that we may have a good and quiet mind. From this follows boldness, which enables us to banish fear, and to entrust ourselves courageously and steadfastly to God.

Those who separate faith from confidence act like men trying to take heat or light from the sun. I acknowledge, indeed, that, in proportion to the measure of faith, confidence is small in some and greater in others; but faith will never be found without these effects or fruits. A trembling, hesitating, doubting conscience will always be a sure proof of unbelief; but a firm, steady conscience, victorious against the gates of hell, will be the sure proof of faith. To trust in Christ as Mediator, and to rest with assurance in God's fatherly love, to dare boldly to promise ourselves eternal life, and not to tremble at death or hell, this is, as they say, a holy presumption.

It should also be noted that he says, *access in confidence*. For the children of God differ from the ungodly in that, whereas these men rest supinely in forgetfulness of God, and are never at ease but when they remove to the greatest possible distance from God, His children have peace with God, and approach Him cheerfully and freely. We infer, likewise, from this passage that confidence is necessary in true invocation, and thus becomes the key that opens to us the gate of the kingdom of heaven. Those who doubt and hesitate will never be heard, as James says (Jas. 1.6, 7). The Sophists of the Sorbonne, when they enjoin hesitation, do not know what it is to call upon God.

13. *Wherefore I ask that ye faint not*. Now you see why he had earlier mentioned his chains. It was to prevent them from being discouraged when they heard of his persecution. O heroic heart, which drew from prison and from death itself, comfort for those who were not in danger! He remembers his *tribulations* for the Ephesians, because they brought edification for all the godly. How powerfully is the faith of the people confirmed, when a pastor does not hesitate to seal his doctrine by the surrender of his life! And accordingly he adds, *which is your glory*. His preaching was so lustred, that all the Churches among whom he had taught had good reason to glory that their faith was ratified by the best of all pledges.

For this cause I bow my knees unto the Father of our Lord Jesus Christ, from whom every family in heaven and on earth is named, that he would give to you, according to the riches of his glory, to be strengthened with power through his Spirit in the inward man; that Christ may dwell in your hearts through faith; that ye, being rooted and grounded in love, may be able to comprehend with all the saints what is the breadth and length and depth and height; to know, I say, the love of Christ, which passeth knowledge, that ye may be filled unto all the fulness of God. (14-19)

14. *For this cause*. He mentions his prayers for them, not only to testify his love for them, but also that they themselves may pray. For the Word is sown in vain, unless the Lord fertilizes it by His blessing. Therefore let pastors learn from Paul's example, not only to admonish and exhort people, but also to seek from the Lord success for their labours, that they may not be unfruitful. Yet it should not be an excuse for idleness when they hear that nothing will come of their industry and labour unless the Lord bless it, but all their care and diligence will be useless. They ought, on the contrary, to labour the more earnestly in sowing and watering, provided they ask and look for the increase from the Lord.

By this are refuted the slanders of the Pelagians and Papists, who argue, that, if the grace of the Holy Spirit alone enlightens our minds, and forms our hearts to obedience, all teaching will be superfluous. For we are enlightened and renewed by the Holy Spirit so that the teaching may be strong and effective, so that light may not be set before the blind, nor the truth sung to the deaf. Therefore the Lord alone acts upon us in such a way that He acts by His own instruments. It is therefore the duty of pastors diligently to teach, of the people earnestly to attend to teaching, and of both, to flee to the Lord lest they weary themselves in unprofitable exertions.

When he says, *I bow my knees*, he indicates the thing by the sign. Not that prayer always requires kneeling, but because this sign of reverence is commonly employed, especially where prayer is not perfunctory, but serious.

15. *From whom every family.* The relative, 'of whom', may apply both to the Father and to the Son. I do not approve of Erasmus' restricting it expressly to the Father. For readers ought to have been allowed a liberty of choice; in fact, the other interpretation seems far more probable. The apostle alludes to that relationship which the Jews had with each other through their common father Abraham, who was the first of their line. But since, on the contrary, he wishes to remove the distinction between Jews and Gentiles, he says not only that all men have been brought into one family and one race through Christ, but that they are even made of one family (*contribules*) with the angels.

It will not fit in if anyone interprets it of God Himself, for the objection is obvious, that God formerly passed by the Gentiles, and adopted the Jews as His peculiar people. But when we apply it to Christ, it becomes what Paul says; for all come and blend together into one that they may be brethren under one God the Father. Let us therefore understand that, under the auspices of Christ, a relationship has been consecrated between Jews and Gentiles, because, by reconciling us to the Father, He has at the same time made us all one. Jews have no longer any reason to boast that they are the posterity of Abraham, or that they belong to this or that tribe, so that they can despise the rest as profane, and claim the honour of being the holy people. There is but one family which ought to be reckoned, both in heaven and on earth, both among angels and among men—if we belong to the Body of Christ. For outside Him there is found nothing but dispersion. He alone is the bond of our union.

16. *That he would give to you.* Paul wishes them to be strengthened, although he had already given their godliness no small praise. But believers have never advanced so far as not to grow still more. The highest perfection of the godly in this life is an earnest desire to pro-

gress. This confirming he declares to be the work of the Spirit. From this it follows that it does not come from man's own capacity. For just as the beginning of all good comes from the Spirit of God, so also the increase. That it is received from divine grace is evident from his using the word 'give'. This the Papists will not admit, for they say that second graces are paid to us, according as each has deserved it, by making good use of the first grace. But let us acknowledge with Paul that it is the gift of the grace of God, not only that we have begun to run well, but that we advance; not only that we have been born again, but that we grow from day to day.

And to assert the grace of God more plainly, he says, *According to the riches of his glory*. This may be expounded in two ways: either, 'according to his glorious riches', so that the genitive, in the Hebrew manner, is equivalent to an adjective; or, 'according to his rich and abundant glory'. The word 'glory' will thus be put for 'mercy', as in 1.6. I prefer the second sense.

In the inward man. For Paul the inward man means the soul and whatever belongs to the spiritual life of the soul; just as the outward is the body, with everything that belongs to it, health, honours, riches, vigour, beauty, and such like. 'Though our outward man perish, yet our inward man is renewed day by day' (II Cor. 4.16); that is, if in the world we decay, the spiritual life becomes more and more vigorous. Paul therefore does not wish the saints to be strengthened so that they may excel and flourish in the world, but that, with respect to the Kingdom of God, their souls may be strong with the power of God.

17. *That Christ may dwell*. He explains the nature of the strength of the inward man. For since the Father placed in Christ the fulness of all gifts, so he who has Christ dwelling in him can want nothing. They are mistaken who hope the Spirit can be obtained apart from obtaining Christ; and they are equally foolish and absurd who dream that Christ can be received without the Spirit. Both must be believed. We are partakers of the Holy Spirit to the extent that we share in Christ; for the Spirit will be found nowhere but in Christ, on whom He is said to have rested for that purpose. Nor can Christ be separated from His Spirit; for then He would be, so to say, dead, and empty of His power. Paul well defines those who are endowed with the spiritual power of God as those in whom Christ dwells. Also, he points out that part which is the true seat of Christ, our hearts, to show that it is not enough for Him to be on our tongues or flutter in our brains.

He dwells, he says, *by faith*. He also expresses the method by which so great a benefit is obtained. A remarkable praise of faith, that through it the Son of God is made our own, and has His dwelling with us. By faith we not only acknowledge that Christ suffered for us and rose from the dead for us, but we receive Him, possessing and enjoying Him as He offers Himself to us. This should be noted carefully. Most consider fellowship with Christ and believing in Christ to be the same thing; but the fellowship which we have with Christ is the effect of faith. The substance of it is that Christ is not to be viewed from afar by faith but to be received by the embrace of our minds, so that He may dwell in us, and so it is that we are filled with the Spirit of God.

That ye may be rooted and grounded in love. He recounts the fruits of this dwelling: love, the knowledge of the divine grace and of His love exhibited to us in Christ. Hence it follows that this is the true and substantial virtue of the soul; so that, whenever he treats of the perfection of the saints, he teaches that it consists of these two parts. He uses two metaphors which express how firm and constant our love ought to be. Many have a slight tinge of love; but it easily fades or is removed, because its roots are not deep. But Paul wants it to be thoroughly fixed in our minds, so as to resemble a well-founded building or deeply-planted tree. The simple and true meaning is that we ought to be so deeply rooted in love, and our foundation so firmly laid in its depths, that nothing will be able to move us. They are idle who infer from Paul's words that love is the foundation and root of our salvation. Paul is not discussing here, as anyone can see, on what our salvation is founded, but what a firm and strong hold love ought to have on us.

18. *May be able to comprehend.* The second fruit is that the Ephesians should perceive the greatness of Christ's love to men. Such an apprehension or knowledge springs from faith. By making all the saints their fellows, he shows that it is the most excellent blessing that can be obtained in the present life, that it is the highest wisdom, to which all the children of God aspire. What follows is sufficiently clear in itself, but has hitherto been obscured by a variety of interpretations. Augustine is very pleased with his subtlety, which has nothing to do with the subject. For he seeks here I know not what mystery in the figure of the cross; he makes the breadth to be love, the height, hope, the length, patience, and the depth, humility. All this pleases us with its subtlety, but what has it to do with Paul's meaning? No more, certainly, than the opinion of Ambrose, that it denotes the shape of a sphere. Leaving aside the views of others, I shall state what all will acknowledge to be simple and true.

By these dimensions Paul means nothing other than the love of Christ, of which he speaks afterwards. The meaning is, that he who knows it truly and perfectly is in every respect a wise man. As if he had said, 'In whatever direction men may look, they will find nothing in the doctrine of salvation that should not be related to this.' The love of Christ contains within itself every aspect of wisdom. The meaning will be clearer if we paraphrase it like this: 'That ye may be able to comprehend the love which is the length, breadth, depth, and height, that is, the complete perfection of our wisdom.' The metaphor is taken from mathematics, denoting the whole from the parts. Almost all men are infected with the disease of desiring useless knowledge. Therefore this admonition is very useful: what is necessary for us to know, and what the Lord desires us to contemplate, above and below, on the right hand and on the left, before and behind. The love of Christ is held out to us to meditate on day and night and to be wholly immersed in. He who holds to this alone, has enough. Beyond it there is nothing solid, nothing useful, nothing, in short, that is right or sound. Go abroad in heaven and earth and sea, you will never go beyond this without overstepping the lawful bounds of wisdom.

Which surpasseth knowledge. Thus elsewhere: 'The peace of God, which surpasseth all understanding, shall keep your hearts' (Phil. 4.7). For man to approach to God he must be raised above himself and the world. This is why the Sophists refuse to admit that we can be certain of the grace of God. For they measure faith by the perception (*apprehensione*) of the human senses. But Paul contends that this knowledge (*scientia*) is superior to all knowledge (*notitia*) and justly, for, if the faculties of man could reach it, Paul's prayer that God would bestow it must have been unnecessary. Let us remember, therefore, that the certainty of faith is knowledge (*scientia*), but it is acquired by the teaching of the Holy Spirit, not by the acuteness of our own intellect. If readers desire more on this, let them consult the *Institutio*.[1]

That ye may be filled. He now declares in one word what he meant by the various dimensions, that he who has Christ has everything necessary for perfection in God; for 'the fulness of God' means this. Men imagine that they are complete in themselves, but only because they swell with waste matter or wind. There are some wicked and ungodly madmen who interpret 'the fulness of God' as 'full divinity', as if men became equal with God.

Now unto him that is able to do exceeding abundantly above all that we ask or think, according to the power that worketh in us, unto him be glory in the church through Jesus Christ throughout all ages, world without end. Amen. (20-21)

He now breaks out into thanksgiving, which also contains an ex-

[1] *Inst.* III.ii, esp. 14-16, 33-37.

169

hortation to hope. Moreover, his thanksgiving aims at stirring up the Ephesians more and more to prize the value of the grace of God.

Glory, he says, *be to God through Christ*—that is, because God's mercy is poured out on the Gentiles through Him. He adds *in the Church*, by which he means that God's grace in the calling of the Gentiles ought to be celebrated among the believers wherever the Church had spread. Perpetuity is put here to increase its greatness.

Who is able. This refers to the future, and therefore to the doctrine of hope; and indeed we cannot give God proper or sincere thanks for favours received, unless we are convinced that His goodness to us will be without end. When he says that God is able, he does not mean power apart (as they say) from the act, but power which is exerted and which we actually perceive. Believers ought always to connect it with the work, when it is a matter of the promises made to them and their own salvation. For whatever God can do, He unquestionably will do, if He has promised it. This he confirms both by former or present instances, which the efficacy of the Spirit exerted in them.

'According to what we already perceive in ourselves'; for every benefit which God bestows upon us is evidence to us of His grace, love and power, from which we ought to conceive a stronger confidence for the future. The expressions *exceeding abundantly* and *above all that we ask or think*, should be noted, so that there should not be excessive fear in true faith. For however many blessings we expect from God, His infinite liberality will always exceed all our wishes and our thoughts.

CHAPTER FOUR

I therefore, the prisoner in the Lord, beseech you to walk worthily of the vocation to which ye are called, with all lowliness and meekness, with long-suffering, forbearing one another in love; endeavouring to keep the unity of the Spirit in the bond of peace. There is one body, and one Spirit, even as ye are called in one hope of your calling; one Lord, one faith, one baptism, one God and Father of all, who is above all things[1] and through all and in you all. (1-6)

These three chapters contain only moral precepts. For he exhorts them to mutual agreement and takes occasion also to treat of the government of the Church, as having been framed by the Lord to maintain the bond of unity among us.

1. *I therefore, the prisoner in the Lord.* He claims (as we saw elsewhere)[2] a greater authority from his chains, which seem to make him contemptible. For it was the seal of the honourable embassy which he had obtained. Whatever is of Christ, though in the eyes of the world it may be disgraceful, ought to be received by us with the highest respect. The apostle's prison is more to be revered than all the pomps and triumphs of kings.

To walk worthily. This is a general statement and preface from which flows what follows. He had formerly discussed calling; now he tells them to be teachable towards God, and not be unworthy of such great grace.

When he descends to particulars, he puts humility first. The reason is, that he was about to speak of unity; and humility is the first step to reach it. This again produces meekness, which makes us patient. And by bearing with our brethren we keep that unity which would otherwise be broken a hundred times a day. Let us remember, therefore, that, in cultivating brotherly kindness, we must begin with humility. Whence come impudence, pride, and insult towards brethren? Whence come quarrels, taunts, and reproaches, except from every one loving himself too much, and pleasing himself too much? He who lays aside haughtiness and ceases to please himself, will become meek and easy. And whoever is endued with such moderation will overlook and tolerate many things in the brethren. Let us carefully observe this order and arrangement. It will be useless to

---

[1] *Margin: or* all men (*omnes*).
[2] In his commentary on 3.1. See p. 157.

enjoin patience unless we tame men's minds and correct their wildness, useless to preach on meekness, unless we have begun with humility.

When he says, *in love*, he means what he says elsewhere, that the true nature of love lies in patience. Where love rules and flourishes, we shall put up with a great deal from one another.

Moreover, with good reason he commends patience, that the unity of the Spirit may continue. Innumerable offences arise daily, which might stir up quarrels among us, particularly since the human spirit struggles under such peevishness. Some take *the unity of the Spirit* as the spiritual unity which the Spirit of God effects in us. There can be no doubt that He alone makes us of one mind, and thus makes us one. But I interpret it more simply of harmony of mind. This unity, he tells us, is composed by *the bond of peace*; for disputes frequently give rise to hatred and resentment. We must live at peace, if we would wish kindness to continue among us.

4. *There is one body.* He expresses more clearly how perfect should be the unity of Christians: that it may so flourish from every part that we shall grow together into one body and one soul. These words denote the whole man. As if he said, we ought to be united, not in part only, but in body and soul. He supports this by the powerful argument that we are all called to one inheritance and one life. From this it follows that we cannot obtain eternal life without living in mutual harmony in this world. For God invites all with His one voice, so that they may be united in the same agreement of faith, and study to help one another. If only this thought were implanted in our minds, that there is set before us this law that the children of God can no more disagree among themselves than the Kingdom of heaven can be divided, how much more carefully we should cultivate brotherly kindness! How much we should hate all quarrels, if we duly reflected that all who separate from their brethren, estrange themselves from the Kingdom of God! And yet, strangely enough, while we forget our mutual brotherhood, we go on claiming to be the sons of God. Let us learn from Paul that none are at all fit for that inheritance who are not one body and one spirit.

5. *One Lord.* In I Cor. 12.5 he simply denotes by the word 'Lord', the government of God. But here, as he shortly afterwards expressly speaks of the Father, he means strictly Christ, who has been appointed by the Father to be our Lord, and to whose government we cannot be subject, unless we are of one mind. Whenever you read this word 'one' here, understand it as emphatic, as if he said 'Christ cannot be divided; faith cannot be rent; there are not various baptisms, but one common to all; God cannot be divided into parts.' Therefore it behoves us to cultivate among ourselves a holy unity, composed of

many bonds. Faith, and baptism, and God the Father, and Christ, ought to unite us, so that we coalesce, as it were, into one man. All these arguments for unity ought to be pondered more than they can be explained. I have been content to point out the apostle's meaning briefly, and leave the fuller treatment to my sermons. The unity of faith, which is here mentioned, depends on the one eternal truth of God, on which it is founded.

One baptism. They are mistaken who infer from this that Christian baptism is unrepeatable, for the apostle does not mean this, but that one baptism is common to all, so that, by means of it, we are initiated into one soul and one body. But if that argument has any force, a much stronger one will be that the Father, and Son, and Holy Spirit, are one God; for it is one baptism, which is sanctified by the triune Name. What reply will the Arians or Sabellians be able to make to this argument? Baptism possesses such force as to make us one; and in baptism, the Name of the Father, and of the Son, and of the Holy Spirit, is invoked. Will they deny that it is one Godhead who is the foundation of this holy and mystic unity? We must necessarily acknowledge that the ordinance of baptism proves the three Persons in one essence of God.

6. *One God and Father.* This is the main argument, from which all the rest flow. Whence comes faith? Whence baptism? Whence the government of Christ, under whose guidance we are united, save because God the Father, pouring Himself forth to each of us, employs these means for gathering us to Himself? The two phrases, ἐπὶ πάντων καὶ διὰ πάντων, can be taken either in the neuter or the masculine. Either meaning will apply sufficiently well, or rather, in both cases the meaning will be the same. For although God by His power upholds, and cherishes, and rules all things, yet Paul is not now speaking of the universal, but only of the spiritual government which pertains to the Church. By the Spirit of sanctification, God pours Himself forth through all the members of the Church, embraces all in His government, and dwells in all. But God is not inconsistent with Himself, and therefore we cannot but be united together into one.

This is the spiritual unity mentioned by Christ in John 17.11. This is indeed true, in a general sense, not only of all men but of all creatures. 'In him we are, and move, and live' (Acts 17.28). And again, 'I fill all things' (Jer. 23.24). But we must attend to the context. Paul is now dealing with the mutual conjunction of believers, which has nothing in common either with the ungodly or with the brute beasts. To this we must limit what he says about God's government and presence. It is for this reason, also, that he uses the word Father, which applies only to the members of Christ.

But unto each one of us was the grace given according to the measure of
the gift of Christ. Wherefore he saith, When he ascended on high, he
led captivity captive, and gave gifts unto men. (Now this, He ascended,
what is it but that he also descended first into the lower parts of the
earth? He that descended is the same also that ascended above all
the heavens, that he might fill all things.) (7–10)

7. *But to each one.* He now describes the manner in which God
guards and preserves the mutual conjunction among us, in that He
gives none such perfection as to be sufficient or to be satisfied with
himself on his own and apart from others. A certain measure is
alloted to each; and it is only by communicating with each other that
they have sufficient for maintaining their condition. He discusses the
diversity of gifts in I Cor. 12.4, but very nearly with the same object.
For there he teaches that such a diversity, so far from injuring the
harmony of believers, rather avails to promote and strengthen it.

This verse may be thus summed up: 'On no one has God bestowed
all things, but each has received a certain measure, so that we need one
another; and by bringing together what is given to them individually,
they help one another.'

By the words *grace* and *gift* he reminds us that, whatever gifts we
may possess, we ought not to be proud of them, because they lay us
under deeper obligations to God. Moreover, he makes Christ their
Author. For as he first of all began with the Father, so, as we shall see,
he wishes to collect us and all that we have, into Christ.

8. *Wherefore he saith.* To accommodate it to his argument, Paul
has twisted this quotation somewhat from its true meaning. Wicked
men charge him with having abused Scripture. The Jews go still
further, and, to make their accusations more plausible, maliciously
pervert the natural meaning of this passage. What is said of God, they
transfer to David or to the people. 'David, or the people,' they say,
'ascended on high, when, buoyed up with many victories, they became
superior to their enemies.' But a careful examination of the Psalm
will show that it is to be applied strictly to God alone.

The whole Psalm is in the nature of an *epinicion*, which David
sings to God on account of the victories granted to him; but, taking
occasion from the things wrought through his hand, he mentions in
passing the wonderful things that the Lord had done for His people.
His object is to show the glorious power and goodness of God in the
Church; and among other things he says, 'Thou hast ascended on
high.' The flesh imagines that God lies idle and asleep, unless He
openly executes His judgments. In the judgment of men, when the
Church is oppressed, God is somehow humbled; but, when He

stretches out His avenging arm for her deliverance, He then seems to rouse Himself, and to ascend His judgment seat. This mode of expression is sufficiently common and familiar; and, in short, the deliverance of the Church is here called the exaltation of God.

But although Paul saw that David was hymning his triumph for all the victories which God had wrought for the salvation of His Church, he very properly accommodated this verse about the ascension of God to the person of Christ. The greatest triumph which God ever won was when Christ, after subduing sin, conquering death, and putting Satan to flight, rose majestically to heaven, that He might exercise His glorious reign over the Church. So far there is no ground for the objection that Paul has twisted this quotation from the meaning of David. David is contemplating in the continued existence of the Church the glory of God; but no ascension of God more triumphant or memorable will ever occur than that when Christ was raised to the right hand of the Father, that He might subject all principalities and powers to Himself and might become the everlasting Guardian and Protector of the Church.

He led captivity. 'Captivity' is a collective noun for captive enemies; and so he simply means that God reduced His enemies to subjection; which was more fully accomplished in Christ than in any other way. He has not only overthrown Satan, and sin, and death, and all hell, but out of rebels He makes for Himself every day an obedient people, when He tames by His Word the wantonness of our flesh. On the other hand, His enemies (that is, all the ungodly) are held bound by chains of iron, when by His power He restrains their fury within the limits which He permits.

There is rather more difficulty in what follows. For where the Psalm says that God has received gifts, Paul reverses it to *gave*, and thus seems to translate it into the opposite meaning. But there is no absurdity here; for Paul is not accustomed to quote the exact words of Scripture, but is content to indicate the passage, and then give the substance of it. Now, it is certain that the gifts which David mentions were not received by God for Himself, but for His people; and accordingly it is said a little earlier in the Psalm, that the spoil had been divided among the families of Israel. Since therefore the purpose in receiving was to give, Paul has not at all departed from the substance, however much he may have changed the words.

Yet I incline to a different opinion: that Paul purposely changed the word, and did not take it out of the Psalm, but adapted an expression of his own to the present occasion. Having quoted from the Psalm a few words on Christ's ascension, he adds in his own language, 'and gave gifts', to draw a comparison between the minor and the major.

Paul wants to show that this ascension of God in the Person of Christ was far greater than in the ancient triumphs of the Church; because it is more excellent for a conqueror to dispense all his bounty freely to all, than to gather spoils from the vanquished.

The exposition of some, that Christ received from the Father what He would distribute to us, is forced, and utterly foreign to the argument. No solution in my judgment, is more natural than this, that having briefly pointed to this place in the Psalm, Paul allowed himself the liberty of adding what is not in the Psalm, yet nevertheless is true of Christ—in which the ascension of Christ is more excellent and wonderful than those ancient glories of God which David enumerates.

9. *Now this, he ascended.* Here again the slanderers criticize Paul's reasoning as trifling and childish, in that he attempts to apply to the real ascension of Christ what was spoken figuratively about a manifestation of the Divine glory. Who does not know, they say, that the word 'ascend' is metaphorical? His conclusion, *that he had first to descend,* has therefore no weight.

I reply that he does not here argue in the manner of a logician, as to what necessarily follows, or can be inferred, from the words of the prophet. He knew that what David spoke about God's exaltation was metaphorical. But neither can it be denied that he suggests that God had been in a sense humbled for a time, for he declares that He is now exalted. Paul rightly makes this inference. And at what time did God descend lower than when Christ emptied Himself? If ever there was a time when, after seeming to be laid low ingloriously, God exalted Himself magnificently, it was when Christ was raised from our weak condition, and received into the heavenly glory. So we ought not to inquire minutely into the literal exposition of the Psalm, since Paul merely alludes to the prophet's words, just as elsewhere he accommodates a verse of Moses to his own object, in Rom. 10.6. But apart from the fact that Paul does not apply it to the Person of Christ improperly and unsuitably, the end of the Psalm shows clearly enough that what he says there belongs to Christ's kingdom. Not to mention other things, it contains a clear prophecy of the calling of the Gentiles.

Into the lower parts. Some foolishly twist this to either limbo or hell, whereas Paul is only dealing with the condition of the present life. The argument that they take from the comparative degree is too weak. A comparison is drawn, not between one part of the earth and another, but between the whole earth and heaven; as if he had said, 'From that lofty habitation He descended into our deep gulf.'

10. *Above all the heavens.* It is as if he said, 'Beyond this created world.' When Christ is said to be in heaven, we must not take it that He dwells among the spheres and numbers the stars. Heaven denotes

a place higher than all the spheres, which was appointed to the Son of God after His resurrection. Not that it is strictly a place outside the world, but we cannot speak of the Kingdom of God except in our own way. But those who consider that the expressions, 'high above all heavens', and 'ascended into heaven', mean the same thing, infer that Christ is not separated from us by distance. But they do not reflect that when He is placed above the heavens or in the heavens, all the circumference beneath the sun and the stars, and thus beneath the whole frame of the visible world, is excluded.

That he might fill all things. To fill often means 'to perfect', and it could have that meaning here; for, by His ascension into heaven, Christ took possession of the domination given to Him by the Father, that He might rule and govern all things by His power. But it will be more judicious in my judgment to connect these two apparent contradictions, which are nevertheless perfectly consistent. When we hear of the ascension of Christ, it instantly comes to our minds that He is removed far from us; and so indeed He is, with respect to His body and human presence. But Paul tells us that He is removed from us in bodily presence in such a way that He nevertheless fills all things, and that by the power of His Spirit. Wherever the right hand of God, which encompasses heaven and earth, is displayed, the spiritual presence of Christ is shed abroad and He is present by His boundless power; although His body must be contained in heaven, according to the statement of Peter (Acts 3.21).

We see that the allusion to a seeming contradiction improves the sentence. He ascended—but that He, who was formerly contained in a little space, might fill heaven and earth. But did He not fill them before? In His divinity, I own, He did; but He did not exert the power of His Spirit, nor manifest His presence, as after He had entered into the possession of His Kingdom. 'The Spirit was not yet given, because Jesus was not yet glorified' (John 7.39). And again, 'It is expedient for you that I go away; for, if I go not away, the Comforter will not come' (John 16.7). In a word, when He began to sit at the right hand of the Father, He began also to fill all things.

And he gave some to be apostles; and some, prophets; and some evangelists; and some, pastors and doctors; for the renewal of the saints, unto the work of the ministry, unto the building up of the body of Christ: till we all come to the unity of the faith, and of the knowledge of the Son of God, unto a full-grown man, unto the measure of the age of the fulness of Christ: that we may be no longer children, tossed to and fro, and carried about with every wind of doctrine, by the sleight of men, by cunning craftiness, for the trickery of imposture. (11-14)

He returns to the dispensation of the graces he had mentioned and declares more fully what he had touched on briefly, that out of this variety arises unity in the Church, as various tones in music make a sweet melody. He commends the external ministry of the Word from the usefulness which it yields. The sum of it is that because the Gospel is preached by certain men appointed to that office, this is the economy by which the Lord wishes to govern His Church, that it may remain safe in this world, and ultimately obtain its complete perfection.

Now, we might be surprised that, when he is speaking of the gifts of the Holy Spirit, Paul should enumerate offices instead of gifts. I reply, whenever men are called by God, gifts are necessarily connected with offices. For God does not cover men with a mask in appointing them apostles or pastors, but also furnishes them with gifts, without which they cannot properly discharge their office. Therefore He who has been appointed an apostle by God's authority does not bear an empty and useless title; for he is endued at the same time with both the command and the faculty. Let us now examine the words in detail.

11. *And he gave.* He first declares that the fact that the Church is ruled by the preaching of the Word, is not a human invention, but the appointment of Christ. The apostles did not create themselves, but were chosen by Christ; and today true pastors do not rashly thrust themselves forward at their own will, but are raised up by the Lord. In short, he teaches that the government of the Church by the ministry of the Word is not contrived by men, but set up by the Son of God. As His own inviolable decree, it demands our assent, and those who reject or despise this ministry injure and rebel against Christ its Author. It is Himself who gave them; for if He does not raise them up, there will be none. Another inference is that no man will be fit or equal for so distinguished an office who has not been formed and made by Christ Himself. That we have ministers of the Gospel is His gift; that they excel in necessary gifts is His gift; that they execute the trust committed to them, is likewise His gift.

Some, apostles. That he assigns one name and office to some, another to others, he refers always to that diversity of the members from which the completeness of the whole Body is formed, so that he removes emulation and envy and ambition. For what corrupts the right use of gifts is when each man is devoted to himself, when each man pleases himself, when the lesser envy the greater. He therefore tells them, that something is given to each, that what each has received is not held for himself alone, but to be put in the common pool. We have already spoken in I Cor. 12 about the offices which he here reviews. Here I shall only say what the exposition of the passage seems to demand. Five sorts of offices are mentioned, though on this point, I am aware, there is a diversity of opinion; for some consider the two last make but one office. But omitting the opinions of others, I will say what it seems to me.

I take the word 'apostles' not generally and according to its etymology, but in its peculiar signification, for those whom Christ particularly selected and exalted to the highest honour. Such were the Twelve, to whose number Paul was afterwards added. Their office was to publish the doctrine of the Gospel throughout the whole world, to plant churches, and to erect the Kingdom of Christ. So they had no churches of their own committed to them; but they had a common mandate to preach the Gospel wherever they went.

Next to them were the *evangelists*, who held a kindred office, but of an inferior rank. In this class were Timothy and those like him; for, while Paul associates him with himself in his salutations, he does not make him a fellow in the apostleship, but claims this name as peculiarly his own. Therefore the Lord used them as subsidiaries to the apostles, to whom they were next in rank.

To these two classes Paul adds *prophets*. By this name some understand those who possessed the gift of predicting future events, like Agabus. But, for my own part, as doctrine is the present subject, I would rather explain it, as in I Cor. 14, to mean outstanding interpreters of prophecies, who, by a unique gift of revelation, applied them to the subjects on hand; but I do not exclude the gift of foretelling, so far as it was connected with teaching.

Some think that *pastors and doctors* denote one office, because there is no disjunctive particle, as in the other parts of the verse, to distinguish them. Chrysostom and Augustine are of this opinion. For what we read in the Ambrosian commentaries is too childish and unworthy of Ambrose. I partly agree with them, that Paul speaks indiscriminately of pastors and teachers as if they are one and the same order; nor do I deny that the name doctor does, to some extent, belong to all pastors. But this does not move me to confound two offices, which I see to differ from each other. Teaching is the duty of all pastors; but there is a particular gift of interpreting Scripture, so that sound doctrine may be kept and a man may be a doctor who is not fitted to preach.

Pastors, to my mind, are those to whom is committed the charge of a particular flock. I have no objection to their receiving the name of doctors, if we realize that there is another kind of doctor, who superintends both the education of pastors and the instruction of the whole Church. Sometimes he can be a pastor who is also a doctor, but the duties (*facultates*) are different.

It should be observed, also, that, of the offices which Paul enumer-

179

ates, only the last two are perpetual. For God adorned His Church with apostles, evangelists and prophets, only for a time, except that, where religion has broken down, He raises up evangelists apart from Church order (*extra ordinem*), to restore the pure doctrine to its lost position. But without pastors and doctors there can be no government of the Church.

Papists have reason to complain, that their primacy, of which they boast, is here assailed and insulted. The discussion is on unity. Paul assembles not only the reasons which establish it among us but also the symbols by which it is nourished. He comes at length to the government of the Church. If he was aware of a primacy with one seat, was it not his duty to exhibit one ministerial head placed over all the members, under whose auspices we are collected into a unity? Certainly, either Paul's oversight is inexcusable, in leaving out the most appropriate and powerful argument, or we must acknowledge that this primacy is alien to the appointment of Christ. In fact, he plainly overturns this fictitious primacy, when he ascribes superiority to Christ alone, and subjects the apostles, and all the pastors, to Him, in such a way that they are colleagues and comrades of one another. There is no passage of Scripture which more strongly overturns that tyrannical hierarchy, in which one earthly head is set up. Cyprian followed Paul and defined briefly and clearly what is the lawful monarchy of the Church. There is, he says, one episcopate, a part in which is held by individuals collectively (*in solidum*). This episcopate he claims for Christ alone. He assigns a part in its administration to individuals, and that collectively, lest one should exalt himself above others.

12. *For the renewing of the saints.* In my version I have followed Erasmus, not because I accept his opinion, but that readers may choose which they prefer when they compare his version with the Vulgate and with mine. The Vulgate had *consummationem* (perfecting). Paul's Greek word is καταρτισμός, which signifies literally the mutual adaptation (*coaptationem*) of things which should have symmetry and proportion; just as, in the human body, there is a proper and regular combination of the members; so that the word is also used for 'perfection'. But as Paul intended to express here a just and orderly arrangement, I prefer the word constitution (*constitutio*). For strictly, Latin speaks of a commonwealth, or kingdom, or province, as constituted, when confusion gives place to the regular and lawful state.

To the work of the ministry. God might Himself have performed this work, if He had chosen; but He has delegated it to the ministry of men. This is intended to anticipate an objection: 'Cannot the Church be constituted and properly ordered, without the works of men?'

Paul teaches that a ministry is required, because such is the Will of God.

In place of what he had said, 'the constitution of the saints', he now puts, *the edifying of the body of Christ*, but with the same sense. Our true completeness and perfection consists in our being united into the Body of Christ. He could not have commended the ministry of the Word more highly than by ascribing this effect to it. What is more excellent than to form the true Church of Christ, that it may be established in its right and perfect soundness? But this work, so admirable and divine, the apostle here declares to be accomplished by the external ministry of the Word. From this it is plain that those who neglect this means and yet hope to become perfect in Christ are mad. Such are the fanatics, who invent secret revelations of the Spirit for themselves, and the proud, who think that for them the private reading of the Scriptures is enough, and that they have no need of the common ministry of the Church.

If the Church is built up by Christ alone, it is also for Him to prescribe the way in which it shall be built. But Paul clearly states that, according to the command of Christ, we are not properly united or perfected but by the outward preaching, when we suffer ourselves to be ruled and taught by men. This is a universal rule, which covers both the highest and the lowest. The Church is the common mother of all the godly, which bears, nourishes, and governs in the Lord both kings and commoners; and this is done by the ministry. Those who neglect or despise this order want to be wiser than Christ. Woe to their pride! We do not deny that we can be perfected by the power of God alone without human assistance. But we are now dealing with what is the will of God and the appointment of Christ, and not what the power of God can do. In employing men's work for accomplishing their salvation, God has conferred on men no ordinary honour. And the best way to promote unity is to assemble to the common teaching as to the standard of a leader.

13. *Till we all come.* He now extends his earlier commendation of the ministry. He had already said that by the ministry of men the Church is governed and ordered, so as to be perfect in every respect. Lest anyone should think that this is necessary only for a single day, he tells them that it must be so right to the end. Or, to speak more plainly, he tells us that the use of the ministry is not temporal, as if it were a preparatory school (*paedagogia*), but constant, so long as we live in the world. The enthusiasts dream that the ministry becomes useless as soon as we have been led to Christ. The proud men, who want to know more than is proper, despise it as being childish and elementary. But Paul protests that we must persevere in this course

till all our deficiencies are supplied; that is, that we must so progress till death under the mastership of Christ alone, that we are not ashamed to be the disciples of the Church, to which Christ has committed this duty.

In the unity of the faith. But ought not the unity of the faith to reign among us from the very commencement? It does reign, I acknowledge, among the sons of God, but not so perfectly as to make them come together. Such is the weakness of our nature, that it is enough if every day brings some nearer to others, and all approach together to Christ. The expression, 'coming together', denotes that closest union to which we still aspire, and which we never reach until this flesh, which is always involved in many remnants of ignorance and unbelief, shall have been laid aside.

What follows, on *the knowledge of the Son of God*, I regard as an explanation. For the apostle wanted to explain what is the nature of true faith, and when it exists; that is, when the Son of God is known. For to Him alone faith ought to look, on Him depend, in Him to rest and terminate. If it tries to go farther, it will disappear, for it will no longer be faith, but a delusion. Let us remember that true faith is so contained in Christ, that it neither knows, nor desires to know, anything beyond Him.

Unto a perfect man. This must be read in apposition; as if he had said, 'What is the highest perfection of Christians? And why is this so?' Full manhood is in Christ. For foolish men do not seek their perfection in Christ as they should. It ought to be a principle among us, that everything outside Christ is hurtful and destructive. Whatever man is in Christ, he is, in every respect, perfect.

The age of fulness means full or mature age. No mention is made of old age, for in this progress there is no place for it. Whatever grows old tends to decay; but the vigour of this spiritual life is continually growing.

14. *That we may be no longer children.* As he had spoken of that full-grown age towards which we proceed throughout the whole course of our life, so now he tells us that, during such a progress, we ought not to be like children. He thus sets an intervening period between childhood and maturity. Those are children who have not yet taken a step in the way of the Lord, but still hesitate, who have not yet determined what road they ought to choose, but move sometimes in one direction and sometimes in another, always doubtful, always wavering. But those are thoroughly founded in the doctrine of Christ who, although not yet perfect, have so much wisdom and vigour as to choose what is best, and proceed steadily in the right course. Thus the life of believers, longing constantly for their ap-

pointed state, is like adolescence. So when I said that in this life we are never men, this ought not to be pressed to the other extreme, as they say, as if there were no progress beyond childhood. After being born in Christ, we ought to grow, so as not to be children in understanding. Hence it appears what kind of a Christianity there is under the Papacy, when the pastors labour to the utmost of their power to keep the people in absolute infancy.

Tossed to and fro, and carried about. In two elegant metaphors he illustrates the wretched hesitation of those who do not rest firmly on the Word of the Lord. The first is taken from small ships, buffeted by the waves in the open sea, holding no fixed course, guided neither by skill nor design, but carried away by the storm. Then he compares them with straws, or other light things, which are carried hither and thither as the wind blows them, and often in opposite directions. So, I say, must these unsteady people be moved whose basis is not God's eternal truth. This is the just punishment against all who look to men rather than to God. Paul declares, on the contrary, that faith, which rests on the Word of God, stands unshaken against all the attacks of Satan.

With every wind of doctrine. In a beautiful metaphor he calls all the doctrines of men, by which we are drawn away from the simplicity of the Gospel, 'winds'. God gave us His Word, in which when we have struck root we stay unmoved; but men lead us astray in all directions by their inventions.

When he adds, *By the cunning of men*, he means that there will always be impostors, who menace and attack our faith; but, if we are armed with the truth of God, they will fail. Both parts of this must be carefully noted. When new sects or ungodly tenets spring up, many become alarmed. But Satan can never rest without striving to darken by his lies the pure doctrine of Christ, and God wants to try our faith with these struggles. When we hear, on the other hand, that the best and readiest remedy against every error is to bring forward that doctrine which we have learned from Christ and His apostles, this surely is no ordinary consolation.

From this it is clear how great and accursed is that wickedness of the Papacy in removing from the Word of God all certainty, and in denying any other firmness to faith except a dependence on the authority of men. They teach that, if anyone is in doubt, it is in vain to consult the Word of God: he must abide by their decrees. But we who have embraced the law, the prophets, and the Gospel, let us not doubt that we shall receive the fruit which Paul declares—that all the impostures of men will not harm us. They attack us, indeed, but they will not prevail. We must, I acknowledge, seek for sound doctrine from the Church, for God has committed it to her charge. But when Papists under the guise of the Church bury doctrine, they give sufficient proof that they have a devilish synagogue.

The Greek word κυβεία, which I have translated *cunning*, is taken from dice players, who use many cheating tricks, many arts of deception. He adds πανουργία, meaning that the ministers of Satan are skilled in tricks; and he continues that they keep watch in order to ensnare. All this should rouse and sharpen our carefulness not to neglect to profit in the Word of God, lest we fall into the snares of our enemies, and endure the severe punishment of our sloth.

But, speaking truth in love, may grow up through all things into him which is the head, even Christ; from whom the whole body fitly framed and knit together through every joint of the supply, according to the working in the measure of each several part, maketh the increase of the body, unto the edifying of itself in love. (15-16)

15. *But, speaking truth.* He has already taught that we ought not to be children, destitute of reason and judgment. To confirm it, he now enjoins us to grow in truth. This is what I have already said, that although we have not arrived at man's estate, we are at any rate, older boys (*pueri maiores*). The truth of God ought to be so firm within us, that all the contrivances and attacks of Satan shall never move us from our position; and yet, as we have not hitherto attained full and complete strength, we must make progress until death.

He points out the aim of this progress, that Christ alone may be chief among us, and that in Him alone we may be strong and tall. Again, you see here that no man is excepted; all are forced into their rank, to submit themselves to the body.

What, then, is the Papacy but a deformed hump which destroys the whole symmetry of the Church, when one man, setting himself up against the Head, exempts himself from the number of the members? The Papists deny this, and pretend that the Pope is only a ministerial head. But they cannot escape by this quibble. The tyranny of their idol is altogether contrary to that order which Paul here commends. In a word, Christ alone must increase and all others must decrease, so that the Church may be well ordered. Whatever increase we obtain must be regulated in proportion as we remain in our own place, and serve by exalting the Head.

When he bids us give heed to the truth in love, he uses the preposition 'in', in the Hebrew way for 'with'. For he does not want individuals to be devoted to themselves, but to join a diligence for truth with a care for mutual fellowship, that they may progress peaceably. Such, by Paul's warrant, must be the nature of this harmony, that men shall not neglect the truth, or disregard it, to combine together according to their own will. This refutes the wickedness of the Papists, who lay aside the Word of God, and try to force us to do what they want.

16. *From whom the whole body.* He confirms by the best of reasons that all our increases should tend to exalt more highly the glory of Christ. It is He who supplies us with all things; He who keeps us unharmed, so that we cannot be safe except in Him. For as the whole tree draws sap from the root, so he teaches that all the vigour which we possess flows to us from Christ. There are three things to be noted here. The first is what I have already said. All the life or health which is diffused through the members flows from the Head; so that the members are only assistants. The second is, that, by the distribution, the limited share of each demands a communication between them. The third is, that, without mutual love, the body cannot be healthy. And so he says that through the members, as through conduits, is supplied from the Head all that is necessary for the nourishment of the Body. Again he says that while this connexion is in force, the Body is alive and healthy. Moreover, he attributes to each member its proper mode.

Lastly, he shows that the Church is built up by love: *to the edifying of itself.* This means that no increase is of use which does not correspond to the whole body. That man is mistaken who desires his own separate growth. For what would it profit a leg or an arm if it grew to an enormous size, or for the mouth to be stretched wider? It would merely be afflicted with a harmful tumour. So if we wish to be considered in Christ, let no man be anything for himself, but let us all be whatever we are for others. This is accomplished by love; and where love does not reign, there is no edification of the Church, but a mere scattering.

This I say therefore, and testify in the Lord, that ye no longer walk as also other Gentiles walk, in the vanity of their mind; being darkened in their understanding, alienated from the life of God because of the ignorance that is in them, because of the blindness of their heart: who having ceased to be touched by sorrow, gave themselves up to lasciviousness, to work all uncleanness with greediness. (17-19)

17. *This I say therefore.* After dealing with the government which Christ has appointed for the edification of His Church, he now tells them what fruits his teaching ought to yield in the lives of Christians; or, if you prefer it, he begins to explain minutely the nature of that edification which ought to follow from doctrine.

He first recalls them from the vanity of unbelievers, arguing from

contraries. For those who have been taught in the school of Christ
and enlightened by the doctrine of salvation, to follow vanity and be
no different from the unbelievers and the blind on whom no light of
truth has ever shone, would be quite absurd. Wherefore he very
properly concludes from what he has said, that their life should
demonstrate that they had not become the disciples of Christ in vain.
To make his exhortation more earnest, he beseeches them by the name
of God, telling them that, if they despised this instruction, they must
one day render account.

As also other Gentiles walk. He means those who had not yet been
converted to Christ; but, at the same time, he tells the Ephesians how
necessary it was that they should repent, since by nature they are like
lost and condemned men. It was as if he said, 'The miserable and
shocking condition of other Gentiles incites you to a change of mind.'
He wants to differentiate believers from unbelievers, and points out,
as we shall see, the causes of this difference. As to the former, he
condemns their mind for vanity. And let us remember that he speaks
generally of all who have not been born anew of the Spirit of Christ.

He declares their mind to be vain. Now, this is what holds the
primacy in the life of man, is the seat of reason, presides over the will,
and restrains vicious desires. So that it is called 'the Queen' by the
theologasters of the Sorbonne. But Paul makes it consist of nothing
but vanity; and, as if he had not spoken strongly enough, he gives no
better title to her daughter, διάνοια. For thus I interpret this word;
for, though it signifies thought (*cogitatio*), yet, as it is put in the singular,
it refers to the faculty itself. Plato, near the end of the sixth book of
the *Republic*, assigns it an intermediate place between νοήσις καὶ πίστις;
but his teaching is too confined to geometry to admit of application
to this passage. Having formerly asserted that men see nothing, Paul
now adds that they are blind in reasoning, even on the highest matters.

Let men now go and be proud of free-will, whose guidance is here
marked with such disgrace. But experience, so it seems, is openly
opposed to this opinion; for men are not so blind that they see nothing,
nor so vain that they have no judgment. I reply, as to the Kingdom
of God, and all that relates to the spiritual life, the light of human
reason differs little from darkness; for, before it has shown the way[1]
it is extinguished; and its perspicacity is worth no more than blindness,
for before it comes to harvest, it is gone. For true principles are like
sparks, but these are choked by the depravity of nature before they
are put to their true use. For example, all know that there is a God and
that we ought to worship Him; but such is the vice and ignorance
that reigns in us, that from this confused knowledge we pass at once

[1] French: *voye*; not Latin: *vita* (life), a misprint for *via*.

to an idol, and worship it in the place of God. And even in the worship of God, we go astray, particularly in the first table of the law.

As to the second objection, our judgment does indeed agree with the rule of God in regard to outward actions; but concupiscence, the fount of all evils, is hidden from us. Besides, we note that Paul does not speak merely of the natural blindness which is within us from the womb, but refers also to a still grosser blindness, by which, as we shall see, God punishes former transgressions. Finally, the reason and understanding which men possess make them without excuse in the sight of God; but, so long as they are allowed to live according to their own disposition, they can only wander and slip and stumble in their purposes and actions. Hence it appears what estimation and value false worship has in the sight of God, when it proceeds from the gulf of vanity and the labyrinth of ignorance.

18. *Alienated from the life of God.* 'The life of God' can be taken in two ways, either what is accounted life in the sight of God (as the glory of God, John 12.43), or that life which God communicates to His elect by the Spirit of regeneration. Whichever you take, the meaning is the same and not different. Our ordinary life as men is nothing more than an empty image of life, not only because it quickly passes, but also because, while we live, our souls, not cleaving to God, are dead. We know that there are three degrees of life in this world. The first is universal life, which consists only in motion and sense, and which we share with the beasts. The second is human life, which we have as the children of Adam. And the third is that supernatural life, which believers alone obtain. And all of them are from God, so that each of them may be called the life of God. As to the first, Paul, in his sermon in Acts 17.28, says, 'In him we have our being, and move, and live.' And Ps. 104.30: 'Send forth thy Spirit, and they shall be created; and thou wilt renew the face of the earth.' Of the second, Job 10.12: 'Thou hast granted me life, and thy visitation hath preserved my spirit.'

But the regeneration of believers is here called, *par excellence*, the life of God, because then does God properly live in us, and we enjoy His life, when He governs us by His Spirit. Of this life all mortal men who are not new creatures in Christ are declared by Paul to be destitute. So long, then, as we remain in the flesh, that is, in ourselves, how wretched must be our condition! From this we may estimate all the moral virtues, as they are called; for what sort of actions will that life produce which Paul affirms is not the life of God? Before anything good can begin to proceed from us, we must first be renewed by the grace of Christ. This will be the commencement of a true, and so to say, vital life.

We ought to attend to the reason which is at once added: *Because of the ignorance*. For, as the knowledge of God is the true life of the soul, so, on the contrary, ignorance is the death of it. And lest it should be believed that ignorance is an accidental evil (as philosophers judge that errors come from elsewhere), Paul shows that its root is in the blindness of their heart; by which he intimates that it dwells in their very nature. The first blindness, therefore, which occupies the minds of men, is the punishment of original sin; because Adam, after his rebellion, was deprived of the true light of God, in the absence of which there is nothing but fearful darkness.

19. *Who had ceased to be touched with sorrows*. Having spoken of natural sins, he comes to the worst of all evils, brought upon men by their own wrong-doing, that having become deadened, and sorrow extinguished in their conscience, they abandon themselves to all iniquity. We are by nature corrupt and prone to evil; nay, we are wholly devoted to evil. Those who are destitute of the Spirit of Christ are tender to themselves and slacken the reins, till by offence after offence, they bring down upon themselves the wrath of God. Yet the Lord pricks their consciences, but without effect; rather it hardens them against all admonition. Because of such obstinacy, they deserve to be altogether rejected by God.

The sign of this rejection is the insensibility we have mentioned. Untouched by any fear of judgment when they offend God, they go on securely, and fearlessly delight and please and flatter themselves. They feel no shame, they care nothing for their honour. The torment of a guilty conscience, tortured by dread of the divine judgment, may be compared to the porch of hell; but such security and sluggishness is a deadly whirlpool. As Solomon says, 'When the wicked is come to the deep, he despiseth it' (Prov. 18.3).[1] Paul is right, therefore, to exhibit that dreadful example of divine vengeance, in which men forsaken by God, having laid conscience to sleep, destroyed all fear of the divine judgment, and dismissed feeling, throw themselves with brute-like violence into all wickedness. This is not universal. God restrains even many of the reprobate by His infinite goodness lest the world should be imbroiled in final confusion. The consequence is that such outright lust, such unrestrained intemperence, does not appear in all. But it is enough that the lives of some present such a sight (*speculum*), so that we also may fear lest anything similar should happen to us.

Lasciviousness I take for that wantonness with which the flesh riots in intemperance and licentiousness, when not controlled by the Spirit of God. *Uncleanness* is put for all kinds of gross sin. Finally he

---

[1] Septuagint and Vulgate: *depth of sin*.

adds, *with greediness.* The Greek word often signifies covetousness, and is so expounded by some in this passage; but not very fittingly. Depraved and wicked desires are insatiable, and therefore Paul joins to them as an appendage, *greediness,* which is the contrary of moderation.

> *But ye did not so learn Christ; if so be that ye heard him, and were taught in him, even as truth is in Jesus: that ye lay aside, as concerning your former manner of life, the old man, which is corrupted after the lust of deceit; and that ye be renewed in the spirit of your mind; and put on the new man, which after God is created in righteousness and holiness of truth.* (20-24)

He now shows the antithesis of the Christian life, so as to make it evident how unworthy it is for a godly man to get himself mixed up with the uncleannesses of the Gentiles. Because the Gentiles walk in darkness, they do not distinguish between right and wrong; but those on whom the truth of God shines ought to live differently. That those to whom the vanity of the sense is their rule of life, should be involved in foul lusts, is not surprising; but the doctrine of Christ teaches us to renounce our natural dispositions. He whose life differs nothing from that of unbelievers, has learned nothing of Christ; for the knowledge of Christ cannot be separated from the mortification of the flesh.

Again, to excite their attention and earnestness the more, he not only says that they had heard Christ, but speaks more strongly, *ye have been taught in him*; as if he had said that this doctrine had not been slightly pointed out, but properly delivered and explained.

21. *As the truth.* In this clause he reproves that evanescent knowledge of the Gospel, with which many are vainly filled who know nothing of newness of life. They think that they are exceedingly wise, but the apostle says it is a false and mistaken opinion. He lays down a twofold knowledge of Christ, one which is true and genuine, and the other counterfeit and spurious. Not that there really are two kinds; but most men falsely persuade themselves that they know Christ, whereas they know nothing but what is carnal. Just as in II Corinthians he says, 'If any man be in Christ, let him be a new creature' (II Cor. 5.17), so here he denies that any knowledge of Christ, which is not accompanied by mortification of the flesh, is true and sincere.

22. *That ye lay aside.* He demands from a Christian man repentance, or newness of life, which he places in denial of ourselves and the regeneration of the Holy Spirit. Beginning with the first, he enjoins us to lay aside, or put off, the old man. He often uses the metaphor of garments, and we have touched on this elsewhere.[1] *The old man,* as

[1] In his Commentary on Rom. 13.14 etc.

we have taught in the sixth chapter of Romans, and other passages,[1] means the natural disposition which we bring from our mother's womb. In two persons, Adam and Christ, he describes to us what may be called two natures. As we are first born of Adam, the depravity of nature which we derive from him is called the old man; and as we are born again in Christ, the amendment of this sinful nature is called the new man. In a word, he who wishes to put off the old man must renounce his nature. Those who suppose that the apostle alludes in the words 'old' and 'new' to the Old and New Testaments, are bad philosophers.

To make it more evident that this exhortation to the Ephesians was not superfluous, he reminds them of their former life. As if he said, 'Before Christ revealed Himself to you, the old man reigned in you; and therefore, if you desire to cast him away, you must renounce your former life.'

Which is corrupted. He describes the old man from the fruits, that is, from the depraved desires, which lure men to destruction; for his word, 'corrupt', relates to the word 'old age', for old age is next door to corruption. Beware then of understanding lusts, as the Papists do, only as the gross and visible lusts, whose wickedness is plain to all men; but comprehend under the word also those things which, instead of being censured, are sometimes applauded, such as ambition, cunning, and everything that proceeds either from self-love or from distrust.

23. *And be renewed.* The second part of the rule of a godly and holy life is to live, not by our own spirit, but by the Spirit of Christ. But what is meant by *the spirit of your mind*? I take it simply, as if he said, 'Be renewed, not only in respect to the lower appetites or desires, which are manifestly sinful, but also to that part of the soul which is reckoned most noble and excellent.' And here again, he brings forward that Queen which philosophers almost adore. There is an implied contrast between the spirit of our mind and the divine and heavenly Spirit, who begets in us another and a new mind. How much there is in us that is sound or uncorrupted may be easily gathered from this, which enjoins us to correct chiefly the reason or mind, in which there seems to be nothing but the virtuous and laudable.

24. *And that ye put on the new man.* We may explain it thus, 'Put on the new man, which is simply being renewed in the spirit, or inwardly. And be totally renewed, beginning with the mind, which appears to be the part most untouched by any sin.' What is added about the creation may refer either to the first creation of man, or to the reformation effected by the grace of Christ. Both expositions will

[1] In his Commentary on Rom. 6.6 etc.

be true. Adam was at first created in the image of God, so that he might reflect, as in a mirror, the righteousness of God. But that image, having been wiped out by sin, must now be restored in Christ. The regeneration of the godly is indeed, as is said in II Cor. 3.18, nothing else than the reformation of the image of God in them. But there is a far more rich and powerful grace of God in this second creation than in the first. Yet Scripture only considers that our highest perfection consists in our conformity and resemblance to God. Adam lost the image which he had originally received, therefore it is necessary that it shall be restored to us by Christ. Therefore he teaches that the design in regeneration is to lead us back from error to that end for which we were created.

In righteousness. If you take righteousness in general as uprightness, holiness will be something higher, the purity by which we are consecrated to God. I am rather inclined to make the distinction that holiness pertains to the first table of the law, and righteousness to the second, as in the song of Zacharias, 'That we may serve him in holiness and righteousness, all the days of our life' (Luke 1.74, 75). Plato also teaches correctly that ὁσιότης (holiness) lies in the worship of God, and that the other part, righteousness, relates to men. The genitive, of truth, is put in the place of an adjective, and refers to both righteousness and holiness. He warns us that both ought to be sincere; because we have to do with God, whom no pretence will deceive.

Wherefore, putting away falsehood, speak ye truth each man with his neighbour: for we are members one of another. Be ye angry, and sin not: let not the sun go down upon your wrath: neither give place to the devil. Let him that stole, now not steal: but rather let him labour, working with his hands the thing that is good, that he may have whereof to give to the needy that asks him. (25-28)

25. *Wherefore, putting away falsehood.* From this head of doctrine, that is, from the righteousness of the new man, all godly exhortations flow, like streams from a spring. For if all the precepts for life were collected, they would do little without this principle. Philosophers have another method; but, in the doctrine of godliness, this is the only way to appoint one's life. Now, therefore, follow particular exhortations, which Paul draws from the general doctrine. And first he places true righteousness and holiness in the truth of the Gospel. He now argues from the general to the particular, that they should be truthful to one another. *Lying* is here put for every kind of fraud, deceit, or cunning; and *truth* for simplicity. He demands sincere communication between them in all their affairs. He adds also this confirmation: *for we are members one of another.* For it is a monstrosity that members

should not agree among themselves, even that they should act deceit-
fully towards each other.

26. *Be ye angry.* Whether the apostle had in mind the fourth Psalm
is uncertain. For these words occur in the Greek translation. But
some prefer 'tremble'. The Hebrew verb רְגַז signifies both to be
agitated by anger or by fear. As to the context of the Psalm, the sense
will be appropriate. 'Be not like madmen, who rush fearlessly in any
direction, but let the dread of being accounted foolhardy keep you
in awe.' For in Gen. 45.24 the word is read for 'strive' or 'quarrel'.
Therefore he wants them to be troubled by striving with their own
spirits and so to cease from furious troubles.

In my opinion, Paul merely alludes to the passage for this reason.
There are three faults by which we offend God in being angry. The
first is when we are angry from slight causes, and often from none, or
are moved by private injuries or offences. The second is when we
go too far, and are carried into intemperate excess. The third is when
our anger, which ought to have been directed against ourselves or
against sins, is turned against our brethren. Most appropriately,
therefore, did Paul, when he wished to describe the limitation of anger,
employ the well-known passage, *Be ye angry, and sin not.* This we do,
if we seek the object of our anger in ourselves rather than in others,
if we pour out our indignation against our own faults. As to others,
we ought to be angry at their faults rather than at their persons, nor
ought we to be excited to anger by private offences; but zeal for the
glory of the Lord should inflame our anger. Lastly, our anger ought
to be allowed to subside, lest it should mix itself with the violent
affections of the flesh.

Let not the sun go down. It is scarcely possible, however, but that we
shall sometimes give way to wrong and sinful wrath, which is the
propensity of the human heart to evil. Paul therefore comes to a
second remedy, that we shall at least quickly suppress our anger, and
not suffer it to harden by continuance. The first was, 'Be ye angry,
and sin not'; but, as the great weakness of human nature renders this
exceedingly difficult, the next remedy is not to cherish wrath too long
in our minds, or allow it time to become strong. He enjoins accordingly, 'let not the sun go down upon it'; by which he means that if
we happen to be angry, we must endeavour to be appeased before
the sun has set.

27. *Neither give place.* I know how some expound this. Erasmus,
using the word 'slanderer', shows plainly that he understood it of
malicious men. But I have no doubt that Paul was warning us to
beware lest Satan should take possession of our minds, like an enemy-
occupied fortress, and do whatever he pleases. We feel every day how

incurable is the disease of long-continued hatred, or at least, how difficult it is to cure it. What is the cause of this, but that, instead of resisting the devil, we yield up to him the possession of our hearts? Therefore, before our heart is filled with the poison of hatred, anger must be dislodged in good time.

28. *Let him that stole.* This concerns not only the grosser thefts which are punished by laws, but those of a more concealed nature, which do not fall under the judgment of men; every kind of depredation by which we seize the property of others. But he does not simply bid us to abstain from unjust or unlawful seizure of goods, but also to assist our brethren, as far as lies in our power. 'You who stole must not only gain your living by lawful and harmless toil, but must give to others.' First he prescribes this rule to us, that we may not supply our wants at the expense of our brethren, but may support life by honest labour. Then love leads us much farther. No one may live to himself alone, and neglect others. All must devote themselves to supplying other's necessities.

But it may be asked whether Paul obliges all men to labour with their hands? This would be too harsh. I reply, the meaning of the words is simple, if it be duly considered. He prohibits every man to steal; but many plead want. He obviates that excuse by telling them rather to labour with their hands. As if he had said, 'No condition, however hard or disagreeable, can excuse any injury to another, or more, from helping the necessities of his brethren.'

He amplifies this latter clause. It contains an argument from the greater to the less. *The thing which is good.* As there are many occupations which do little to help the chaste delights of men, he recommends them to choose those which yield advantage to their neighbours. We need not wonder at this, for if those voluptuous sort of trades which can only bring corruption were denounced by the heathens, Cicero among them, as shameful, would an apostle of Christ reckon them among the lawful callings of God?

Let no corrupt speech proceed out of your mouth, but that which is good to the use of edifying, that it may give grace unto the hearers. And grieve not the Holy Spirit of God, by whom ye were sealed unto the day of redemption. Let all bitterness, and wrath, and anger, and clamour, and evil-speaking, be put away from you, with all malice. (29-31)

29. *No filthy speech.* He first takes away all filthy language from the words of believers, comprehending by this name all amatory enticements which are wont to infect men's minds with lust. Not satisfied with the removal of the vice, he commands them to frame

their words for edification, as in Colossians: 'Let your speech be seasoned with salt etc.' (Col. 4.6). Here a different phrase is used: *that which is good to the use of edifying*, he says; which means simply, 'if it be useful'. The genitive, 'of use', may no doubt in the Hebrew idiom be resolved as an adjective, so that it may be 'useful edification'. But when I consider how frequently and how extensively the metaphor of edifying occurs in Paul, I prefer the former exposition. 'The edification of use', I interpret as the progress of our edification, for to edify is to move forward. He adds how this is done, by giving *grace to the hearers*, meaning by the word 'grace', comfort, admonition, and everything that aids salvation.

30. *And grieve not.* Since the Holy Spirit dwells in us, to Him every part of our soul and of our body ought to be consecrated. But if we give ourselves up to anything unclean, it is as if we drive Him away from His lodging. To express this more familiarly, he ascribes human affections, joy and grief, to the Holy Spirit. 'Endeavour', he says, 'that the Holy Spirit may dwell cheerfully in you, as in a pleasant and joyful dwelling, and give Him no occasion for grief.' Some expound it differently, that we grieve the Holy Spirit in others, when we offend by filthy language, or in any other ways, godly brethren who are led by the Spirit of God. For godly ears not only dislike what is contrary to godliness but are wounded with deep sorrow when it is heard. But what follows shows that Paul's meaning was different.

By whom ye were sealed, he says. Because God has sealed us by His Spirit, we vex Him when we do not follow His guidance, but pollute ourselves with ungodly passions. No language can adequately express the gravity of this statement, that the Holy Spirit rejoices and is glad in us, when we are obedient to Him in all things, and neither think nor speak anything but what is pure and holy; and, on the other hand, is grieved when we give place to anything that is unworthy of our calling. Now, let any man reckon what shocking ungodliness there is in piercing the Holy Spirit with such sorrow as to compel Him to withdraw from us at last. The same mode of speaking is used in Isa. 63.10, but in a different sense; for the prophet merely says that they provoked the Spirit of God, just as we are accustomed to speak of provoking the mind of a man. *By whom ye are sealed.* For the Spirit of God is like a seal, by which we are distinguished from the reprobate, and which is impressed on our hearts that we may be assured of the grace of adoption.

He adds, *Unto the day of redemption*, that is, till God conducts us into the possession of the promised inheritance. It is usually called the day of redemption, because we shall then be at length delivered out of all our afflictions. We have already said enough elsewhere about each phrase, and especially about the second in Rom. 8.23 and about the former in I Cor. 1.30. Though the word 'sealed' can be explained differently here, in that God has as it were impressed His Spirit as His mark upon us, that He may reckon among His children those whom He sees to bear that mark.

31. *Let all bitterness.* As he had before condemned anger, he repeats the same judgment, but connects it with the things (*accidentia*) by which it is usually accompanied, such as noisy disputes and brawls. Between ὀργήν and θυμόν there is little difference, except that the former refers sometimes to power, and the latter to action. But here there is no difference, except that the former is a more sudden attack. To good purpose he removes *malice*, that the others may be corrected. By this word he means that depravity of mind which is opposed to humanity and fairness, and which is usually called malignity.

And be ye kind one to another, tender-hearted, forgiving each other, even as God also in Christ forgave you. (32)

32. *And be ye kind one to another.* To bitterness he contrasts kindness, which is a good nature in face, word and manners. And as this virtue will never reign among us, unless συμπάθεια also flourishes, he commends mercy to us. This will lead us not only to sympathize with the distresses of our brethren, as if they were our own, but to be so imbued with true humanity that we are no less affected by everything that happens to them, than if we were in their situation. The contrary of this is cruelty, when men are so iron-hearted and barbarous that they see the sufferings of others without any concern whatever.

Forgiving each other. Some interpret this as beneficence. Erasmus accordingly renders it 'bountiful' (*largientes*). And the meaning of the word will allow this; but the context induces us to prefer another view, that we should be ready to forgive. It may sometimes happen that men are kind and tender-hearted, and yet, when they are undeservedly injured, do not so easily forgive injuries. That those, whose kindness of heart in other respects disposes them to humanity, may not fail through the ingratitude of men, he exhorts them to show themselves forgiving to one another. To make his exhortation the stronger, he holds out the example of God, who has forgiven to us, through Christ, far more than any mortal man can forgive to his brethren. See Col. 3.5ff.

CHAPTER FIVE

Be ye therefore imitators of God, as beloved children; and walk in love,
even as Christ also loved us, and gave himself for us an offering and a
sacrifice to God for an odour of a sweet smelling. (1-2)

1. *Be ye therefore imitators.* He follows up and confirms the same
statement by the fact that children ought to be like their father. He
reminds us that we are the children of God, and that therefore we
ought, as far as we can, to represent Him in beneficence. We see that
the division of chapters is particularly unhappy, as it has separated
statements which are closely related. Therefore, let us grasp this
argument: If we are the children of God, we ought to be imitators of
Him. Christ also declares that we cannot be the children of God unless
we show kindness to the unworthy (Matt. 5.44, 45).

Having set before us the imitation of God, he does the same with
Christ. For He is our true model. 'Embrace each other with that love
with which Christ has embraced us,' he says. For what we perceive
in Christ is our true rule.

2. *And gave himself.* It was a remarkable proof of the highest love
that forgetful, as it were, of Himself, Christ spared not His own life,
that He might redeem us from death. If we wish to be partakers of
this benefit, we must be moved similarly towards our neighbours.
Not that any of us has reached such perfection; but we must aim and
strive according to our measure.

When he adds, *a sacrifice of a sweet smell*; it is first a commendation
of the grace of Christ. Then also it bears directly on the present subject. No language, indeed, can fully express the fruit and efficacy of
Christ's death. We hold that this is the only price by which we are
reconciled to God. This doctrine of the faith holds the highest rank.
But the more we hear that Christ has acted for us, the more are we
bound to Him. Besides, we may infer from Paul's words that, unless
we love one another, none of our duties will be acceptable to God. If
the reconciliation of men effected by Christ was a sacrifice of a sweet
smell, we, too, shall become unto God a sweet savour when this holy
perfume is shed upon us. To this applies the saying of Christ, 'Leave
thy gift before the altar, and go and be reconciled to thy brother'
(Matt. 5.24).

But fornication, and all uncleanness, or covetousness, let it not even be

*named among you, as becometh saints; nor filthiness, nor foolish talking,
or jesting, which are not befitting; but rather grace. For this ye know,
that no fornicator, nor unclean person, nor covetous man, who is an
idolater, hath any inheritance in the kingdom of Christ and God. Let
no man deceive you with empty words: for because of these things
cometh the wrath of God upon the disobedient sons.*[1] *Be not ye therefore
partakers with them.* (3-7)

3. *But fornication.* This chapter has many parallels in Colossians,
which an intelligent reader can compare without my help. He enumerates three things here, which he wants to be so alien to Christians,
that not even their name shall be heard, as is the case with unknown
things. By *uncleanness* he means all foul and impure lusts. This word
differs from *fornication*, as the genus from the species. Thirdly, he puts
covetousness, which is nothing but an immoderate cupidity. To this
precept he adds the authoritative declaration that he demands nothing
from them but that which *becometh saints*, by which word he excludes
from the number and fellowship of the saints all the covetous and
fornicators, and impure.

To those three he adds another three. *Filthiness*, by which word I
understand all that is indecent or inconsistent with the modesty of the
godly. *Foolish talking*, by which word I understand conversations that
are either out of place and pointless and fruitless or even ungodly and
harmful by their emptiness. Moreover, as idle talk is often concealed
under the garb of *jesting*, and wit, he expressly condemns pleasantry,
which is so agreeable as to seem a praiseworthy virtue, as a part of
foolish talking. The Greek word εὐτραπελία is often used by heathen
writers in a good sense, for that sharp and salty pleasantry in which
able and intelligent men may properly indulge. But as it is exceedingly
difficult to be witty without becoming biting, and as wit itself carries
in it a sort of affectation not at all in keeping with godliness, Paul
very properly recalls us from it. Of all three, he declares that they are
not befitting, that is, that they are inconsistent with the duty of
Christians.

But rather grace. Others prefer '*giving of thanks*'; but I like Jerome's
interpretation. For Paul had to contrast something general in our
words with those vices. For if he had said, 'While they delight in idle
or abusive talk, do you give thanks to God,' it would have been too
limited. The Greek word εὐχαριστία admits of our translating it
'grace'. And the meaning will be: 'All our words ought to be filled
with true sweetness, and grace; and this will be so if we mingle the
useful with the sweet.'

[1] *Margin: or* unbelieving sons.

5. *For this ye know*. Lest they should be enticed by the allurements of those vices which he reprehended and receive his admonitions hesitatingly or carelessly, he alarms them by the weighty and severe threat, that these vices shut against us the Kingdom of God. By appealing to their own conscience, he intimates that there was nothing doubtful in this. If it seems harsh or inconsistent with God's goodness that all who have incurred the guilt of fornication or covetousness are excluded from the inheritance of the Kingdom of heaven, the answer is easy. The apostle does not deny pardon to the fallen who have recovered, but pronounces sentence on the sins themselves. After addressing the Corinthians in the same language, he adds: 'And such were some of you; but now ye are justified' (I Cor. 6.11). Where there is repentance and therefore reconciliation with God, men cease to be what they were. But let all fornicators, or unclean or covetous persons, so long as they are such, know that they have nothing in common with God, and are deprived of all hope of salvation.

He says *the kingdom of Christ and of God*, because God gave it to His Son that we may obtain it through Him.

Nor covetous man, who is an idolater. Covetousness, as he says elsewhere, is the worship of idols (Col. 3.5)—not that which is so often condemned in Scripture, but another sort. All covetous men must deny God, and put wealth in His place; such is the blind madness of their wretched cupidity. But why does Paul attribute to covetousness alone what belongs no less to other carnal passions? Why is covetousness denoted by this disgraceful name rather than ambition or vain self-confidence? I answer that this disease is widely spread, and infects the minds of many like a contagion, but it is not reckoned a disease, but rather praised in the common estimation. Paul attacks it more harshly in order to tear from our hearts the false opinion.

6. *Let no man deceive you*. There have always been ungodly dogs who refused and mocked the threatenings of the prophets. We see such in our own day. In all ages, indeed, Satan employs sorcerers like this, who by unholy scoffs run away from God's judgment, and who lull as if with a charm consciences not grounded in the fear of God. 'This is a trivial fault,' they say. 'Fornication is a mere game to God. Under the law of grace God is not so cruel. He has not formed us to be our own executioners. The frailty of nature excuses us.' And so on. Paul, on the contrary, exclaims that we must guard against that sophistry by which consciences are ensnared to their ruin.

For because of these things. If you expound the present tense as the future after the Hebrew idiom, this will be a declaration of the last judgment. But I agree with those who take the word *cometh* indefinitely for 'is accustomed to come', as reminding them of the ordinary judgments of God which were taking place before their own eyes. And certainly, if we were not blind and slothful, God testifies by sufficiently numerous examples of punishment that He is the just avenger of such crimes, privately chastising individuals, and publicly showing His anger against cities, and kingdoms, and nations.

And it is to be noted that he says *upon the unbelievers* or *rebels*. He is now addressing believers, not so much to frighten them with their danger, as to rouse them that they may learn to behold reflected in the reprobate, as in mirrors, the dreadful judgments of God. For God does not make Himself terrible to His children, so that they avoid Him, but in a fatherly way draws them to Himself so far as He can. From this he concludes that they must not involve themselves in the harmful fellowship of the ungodly, whose ruin is foreseen.

> *For ye were once darkness, but are now light in the Lord; walk as children of light; (for the fruit of the light is in all goodness and righteousness and truth;) proving what is acceptable unto God. And have no fellowship with the unfruitful works of darkness, but rather even reprove them. For the things which are done by them in secret, it is a shame even to speak of. But when all things are reproved they are made manifest by the light: for whatsoever doth make manifest is light. Wherefore he saith, Awake, thou that sleepest, and arise from the dead, and Christ shall give thee light. (8-14)*

8. *For ye were once darkness.* He adds confirmations to the precepts, to give them weight. Having spoken of unbelievers, and warned the Ephesians not to become partakers of both their crimes and their destruction, he confirms by an added reason, that they ought to differ widely from their life and actions. At the same time, lest they should be ungrateful to God, he refreshes their remembrance of their own past life. 'You ought', he says, 'to be very different from what you once were; for out of darkness God has made you light.' He calls 'darkness' the whole nature of man before regeneration; for where the brightness of God does not shine, there is nothing but fearful darkness. Light, again, is the name given to those who are enlightened by the Spirit of God; for immediately afterwards in the same sense, he calls them *children of light*, and draws the inference that they ought to walk in light, because by the mercy of God they had been rescued from darkness. Observe that we are said to be *light in the Lord*, because, while we are outside Christ, all is under the dominion of Satan, whom we know to be the prince of darkness.

9. *For the fruit of the light.* He introduces this parenthesis, to point out the road in which the children of light ought to walk. He does not give a complete description, but only touches on a few parts of a

holy and godly life as examples. To comprehend everything under one head, he recalls them to the Will of God; as if he said, 'Whoever desires to live uprightly and out of danger of erring, let him resolve to obey God, and to take His Will as the rule.' To live by His commands alone is, as he says in Rom. 12.1, a reasonable service of God, and as in the other place, 'Obedience is better than sacrifice' (I Sam. 20.22). It is surprising that the word 'Spirit' (πνεύματος) should have crept into many Greek manuscripts, since 'the fruit of the light' fits in better. Paul's meaning indeed is not affected; for it will still be: 'Believers must walk as in the light, because they are children of the light.' This is done, when they do not live according to their own will, but devote themselves entirely to obedience to God; when they undertake nothing but by His command. Besides, such obedience is testified by its fruits, as *goodness, righteousness, truth,* and the like.

11. *And have no fellowship.* As the children of light dwell in the midst of this darkness, that is, in the midst of a perverse and crooked generation, there is good reason for warning them not to get involved in wicked actions. It is not enough that we do not, of our own accord, undertake anything wicked. We must beware of joining or assisting those who do wrong. In short, we must abstain from all fellowship or consent, or advice, or approbation, or help of any sort; for in all these ways we have fellowship. And lest any one should imagine that he has done his duty by not conniving, he expressly bids us to reprove them; and this is opposed to all dissimulation. When he sees that God is openly offended, every man will vindicate himself from guilt, but very few will guard against an assumption of approval; nearly all will dissimulate. But rather than that the truth of God shall not stand firm, let a hundred worlds perish.

The word *reprove* relates to the metaphor of darkness. For ἐλέγχειν strictly means to bring forward what was formerly unknown. Therefore, because the ungodly flatter themselves in their vices, which they wish to be concealed or to be reckoned virtues, Paul commands that they be reproved. He calls them *unfruitful*; not only because they are not useful, but also are harmful in themselves.

12. *Which are done by them in secret.* He wishes to show the point of reproving the ungodly. He says that so long as they are hidden from the eyes of men, they will let themselves commit any sin, however shocking to be mentioned. As it is said in the common proverb, 'Night has no shame'. Why is this, but that, sunk in the darkness of ignorance, they neither see their own wickedness, nor think that it is seen by God and by angels? But their eyes are opened by God's word like a torch brought in. Then they begin to blush and be ashamed. By their warnings the saints enlighten blind unbelievers,

and drag forth from their concealment into the light of day those who were sunk in ignorance.

It is as if he said, 'When unbelievers keep their houses shut, and are withdrawn from the view of men, *it is shameful even to say* how worthlessly and wickedly they rush into all licentiousness.' Would they lay aside all shame, and give the rein to themselves, if darkness did not give them courage, as if what is done in secret is done unpunished? But if you reprove them, it is like bringing in a light, that they may be ashamed of their own baseness. Such shame comes from an awareness of baseness, and is the first step to repentance. We have this also in I Cor. 14.23ff: 'If there come in an unbeliever into your assembly, he is reproved by all, he is judged by all; and the secrets of his heart are made manifest; and so, falling down on his face, he worships God.' Or he may be just using a metaphor. Erasmus, by changing the word 'reprove', has corrupted the whole meaning; for Paul's object is to show that it will not be in vain if the works of unbelievers are reproved.

13. *But when all things.* For the participle, read here in the middle voice, can be translated both passively and actively. The Vulgate prefers the passive sense. If this is followed, the word light will be equivalent, as formerly, to 'full of light' (*lucidus*), and the meaning will be that evil works, which had been concealed, will stand out plainly when they have been made manifest by the Word of God. If we take it actively, there are still two possible expositions. First: Whatever manifests is light. Secondly: That which manifests anything or everything is light; taking the singular as standing for the plural number. There is no problem, as Erasmus feared, about the article; for the apostles are not usually very strict about supplying every article, and even among elegant writers this would be allowable. I judge that this was Paul's meaning; for I follow the context. He had exhorted them to reprove the evil works of unbelievers, and thus to rescue them from darkness; and he now adds, that what he enjoins upon them is the proper business of light, *to make manifest*. It is light, he says, which makes all things manifest. Hence it followed that they were unworthy of the name, if they did not bring to light what was involved in darkness.

14. *Wherefore he saith.* Interpreters are at great pains to discover the passage of Scripture which Paul seems to quote and which is nowhere to be found. I shall state what I think. He first introduces Christ speaking by His ministers; for this is the ordinary message which ought every day to be heard from the preachers of the Gospel. What other object have they than to raise the dead to life? As it is said, 'The hour is coming, and now is, when the dead shall hear the

voice of the Son of God, and they that hear shall live' (John 5.25). Let us now consider the context. Paul had said that unbelievers must be reproved, that, being brought forth to the light, they may begin to acknowledge their wickedness. He therefore represents Christ as speaking because this Voice is constantly heard in the preaching of the Gospel, 'Arise, thou that sleepest.' But yet, I have no doubt that he alludes to the prophecies which foretell Christ's Kingdom; such as that of Isaiah, 'Arise, shine, O Jerusalem, for thy light is come, etc.' (Isa. 60.1). Let us therefore endeavour, as far as lies in us, to rouse the sleeping and dead, that we may bring them to the light of Christ.

When he adds, *And Christ shall give thee light,* he does not mean that when we have risen from death, His light begins to shine upon us, as if we prevented His grace. But Paul simply shows that, when Christ enlightens us, we rise from death to life; and he says this to confirm the former statement, that unbelievers must be recalled from their blindness in order to be saved. Where some manuscripts (*codices*) read, instead of ἐπιφαύσει, ἐφάψεται, that is, 'he shall touch'; it is an evident error and I reject it without more ado.

Look, therefore, that ye walk precisely, not as unwise, but as wise, redeeming the time, because the days are evil. Wherefore be ye not foolish, but understand what the will of the Lord is. And be not drunk with wine, wherein is riot; but be filled with the Spirit; speaking to yourselves in psalms and hymns and spiritual songs, singing and making melody in your hearts to the Lord; giving thanks always for all things even in the name of our Lord Jesus Christ to God the Father. (15-20)

15. *Look therefore.* If believers should drive away the darkness of others by their own brightness, how much less ought they to be blind as to their own plan of life? What darkness shall conceal those on whom Christ, the Sun of righteousness, has arisen? They ought to live as if they were in a crowded theatre, for they live under the eye of God and of the angels. Let them, I say, stand in awe of these witnesses, though they may be concealed from all mortals. Dismissing the metaphor of darkness and light, he enjoins them to regulate their life precisely, *as wise men,* that is, those who have been educated by the Lord in the school of true wisdom. For this is our understanding, that we have God for our Guide and Instructor, to teach us His own will.

16. *Redeeming the time.* By a consideration of the time he confirms his exhortation. He says that *the days are evil,* that is, everything is full of scandal and corruption; so that it is difficult for the godly, who walk among so many thorns, to remain unhurt. Since the age is so

corrupt, the devil appears to have seized tyrannical power; so that time cannot be dedicated to God without being in some way redeemed. And what shall be the price of its redemption? To withdraw from the endless allurements which would easily pervert us; to extricate ourselves from the cares and delights of the world; and, in a word, to renounce every hindrance. Let us be eager to recover the opportunity in every way; more, to let the numerous offences and arduous toil, which many are in the habit of alleging as an apology for indolence, rather sharpen our vigilance.

17. *Wherefore be ye not unwise.* He who exercises himself day and night in the meditation of the law will easily triumph over the difficulties which Satan can put in his way. Whence comes it that some wander, others fall, others stumble, others go backward, but because we allow ourselves to be gradually blinded by Satan, and lose the will of God, which we ought constantly to be exercised in remembering? And observe, that Paul defines *wisdom* to be *understanding what the will of the Lord is.* 'How shall a young man direct his way?' asks David. 'By attending to thy word, O Lord' (Ps. 119.9). He speaks of youths, but this is also the wisdom of the aged.

18. *And be not drunk with wine.* When he forbids them to be drunk, he forbids all excessive and immoderate drinking. So that it is as if he said, 'Be not intemperate in drinking.' At the same time he warns them of the evil that comes from drunkenness, that is, ἀσωτία, by which word I understand wantonness and dissoluteness of every kind; for to translate it 'luxury', would weaken the sense. He means, therefore, that drunkards soon slip into immodesty and are not restrained by shame; that where wine reigns, wantonness will rule; and consequently, that all who have any regard to moderation or decency ought to flee and abominate drunkenness.

The children of this world are accustomed to drink a lot as an excitement to mirth. Against such carnal joy he sets that holy joy with which the Spirit of God gladdens us. He also recounts its opposite effects. What does drunkenness bring forth? Abandoned licentiousness, so that men rejoice in unbridled, unbecoming merriment.

And to what does spiritual joy lead, when we are filled with it? *To hymns and psalms, praises of God and thanksgivings.* These are truly pleasant and delightful fruits. 'The Spirit' here means joy in the Holy Spirit. In the words, *be ye filled,* there is an allusion to deep drinking, with which it is indirectly contrasted. *Speaking to themselves* means among themselves. For he does not enjoin each one to sing inwardly, but when he adds, *singing in your hearts,* it is as if he had said, 'From the heart and not only on the tongue, like hypocrites.' The difference between hymns and psalms, or between psalms and songs is not easy to determine. But I will say something about it in Col. 4.[1] The adjective 'spiritual' fits the argument; for the songs most frequently used are almost always on trifling subjects, and far from being chaste.

20. *Giving thanks always.* He means that this is a pleasure which ought never to bore us by custom; an exercise of which we ought never to weary. The innumerable benefits which we receive from God yield fresh cause of joy and thanksgiving. At the same time, he warns believers that it will be ungodly and disgraceful laziness, if they shall not all through their life study and practise the praises of God.

Subject yourselves one to another in the fear of Christ.[2] Wives, be in subjection unto your own husbands, as unto the Lord. For the husband is the head of the wife, as Christ also is the head of the church, being himself the saviour of the body. Moreover, as the church is subject to Christ, so let the wives also be to their husbands in every thing. Husbands, love your wives, even as Christ also loved the church, and gave himself up for it; that he might sanctify it, cleansing it by the washing of water in the word; that he might present it to himself a glorious church, not having spot or wrinkle or any such thing; but that it should be holy and blameless. Even so ought husbands to love their wives as their own bodies. (21-28)

21. *Subject yourselves.* God has so bound us to each other, that no man ought to avoid subjection. And where love reigns, there is a mutual servitude. I do not except even kings and governors, for they rule that they may serve. Therefore it is very right that he should exhort all to be subject to each other.

But as nothing is more contrary to the human spirit than to submit to others, he recalls us to the fear of Christ, who alone can tame our fierceness, that we may not refuse the yoke, and subdue our pride, that we may not be ashamed of serving our neighbours. It does not much affect Paul's meaning, whether we take the fear of Christ actively or passively, that is, let us submit to our neighbours, because we fear Christ; or because the minds of all the godly ought to be filled with such fear under the reign of Christ. Some manuscripts (*codices*) read 'the fear of God'. This may have been changed by some one who thought that the other phrase, the fear of Christ (though it is in fact more appropriate) was too harsh.

22. *Wives.* He comes now to the various groups; for, besides the universal bond of subjection, some are more closely bound to each other, according to their respective callings. Society consists of groups, which are like yokes, in which there is a mutual obligation of parties. The first yoke is the marriage between husband and wife; the second

---

[1] In fact, Col. 3. See p. 253.   [2] *Margin: or God.*

yoke binds parents and children; the third connects masters and servants. So in society there are six different classes, for each of which Paul lays down its peculiar duties. He begins with wives, whom he commands to be subject to their husbands, in the same way as to Christ. Not that the authority is equal, but wives cannot obey Christ unless they yield obedience to their husbands.

The reason follows. Christ has appointed the same order between husband and wife as He holds with His Church. This comparison ought to impress us more than if he had spoken merely of the appointment of God. For he states two things. God has set the husband over the wife; and an image of this headship (*praefectura*) is found in Christ, who is the Head of the Church, as the husband is of the wife.

23. *And he is the saviour of the body.* Some think that the pronoun refers to Christ; but others, to the husband. It applies better, in my opinion, to Christ, but yet in relation to the present subject. The resemblance ought also to hold in this, that as Christ presides over His Church for her salvation, so nothing is more useful or good to the wife than to be subject to her husband. To refuse that subjection, in which they can be saved, is to choose destruction.

The particle 'but', which follows, can be expounded as an anticipation, that it is peculiar to Christ to be the Saviour of the Church. Nevertheless, let wives know that their husbands, though they cannot claim equality with Christ, have authority over them, after the example of Christ. But the other interpretation is more correct; for the conjunction ἀλλά does not move me much; Paul uses it for 'moreover' (*caeterum*).

25. *Husbands, love your wives.* From husbands, on the other hand, is required love; but by giving them the example of Christ, he implies that this should be no ordinary love. If they have the honour to bear His image, and in a sense to represent His Person, they ought to imitate Him also in their duty.

And gave himself for it. This is intended to express the vehemence of love which husbands owe to their wives; though he then makes it an occasion to commend the grace of Christ. Let husbands imitate Christ in this respect, that He did not hesitate to die for the Church. That He redeemed the Church by His death is a power peculiar to Himself, and it is not given to men.

But now he adds, *That he might sanctify*, that is, that He might separate it to Himself; for so I take the word 'sanctify'. This is accomplished by the forgiveness of sins and the regeneration of the Spirit.

26. *Cleansing it with the washing of water.* He now adds the outward symbol to the inward and secret sanctification. For this is a visible confirmation of it, as if he had said that a pledge of that sanctification

is presented to us by baptism. Yet a sound interpretation is needed here, lest, as has often happened, men in their perverted superstition make an idol out of the sacrament. When Paul says that we are washed by baptism, he means that God there declares to us that we are washed and at the same time performs what it figures. For unless the reality (*rei veritas*) or, which is the same thing, the presentation (*exhibitio*) were connected with baptism, it would be improper to say that baptism is the washing of the soul. At the same time, we must beware of transferring to the sign, or to the minister, what belongs to God alone—that is, to imagine that the minister is the author of the washing, or that water cleanses the pollutions of the soul, which only the blood of Christ can accomplish. In short, we must beware of giving any portion of our trust to the element or to man; for the true and proper use of the sacrament is to lead us by the hand directly to Christ and settle us in Him.

Some try to weaken this eulogy of baptism, in case too much is attributed to the sign if it is called the washing of the soul. But they are wrong; for, in the first place, the apostle does not say that it is the sign that cleanses, but declares that this is the work of God alone. It is God who cleanses, and the praise for this must not be transferred to the sign or even shared with the sign. But there is no absurdity in saying that God uses the sign as an instrument. Not that the power of God is shut up in the sign, but He distributes it to us by this means on account of the weakness of our capacity. Some are offended at this, thinking that it takes from the Holy Spirit what is peculiar to Him, and which is everywhere ascribed to Him in Scripture. But they are mistaken; for God so acts by the sign, that its whole efficacy depends upon His Spirit. Nothing more is attributed to the sign than to be an inferior instrument, useless in itself, except so far as it derives its power from elsewhere.

Equally groundless is their fear, that by this interpretation the freedom of God will be restrained. The powerful grace of God is not confined to the sign, and God may, if He pleases, freely bestow it without the aid of the sign. Besides, many receive the sign who are not made partakers of grace; for the sign is common to all, to the good and to the bad alike; but the Spirit is bestowed only on the elect, and the sign, as we have said, has no efficacy without the Spirit. The Greek participle καθαρίσας is in the past tense, as if he had said, 'After having washed.' But, as Latin has no active participle in the past tense, I chose rather to disregard the tense, and not translate it 'having been washed' (*mundatam*); which would have modified something of far greater importance, namely, that to God alone belongs the office of cleansing.

In the word. This is far from being a superfluous addition; for, if the Word is taken away, the whole power of the sacraments is lost. What else are the sacraments but seals of the Word? This single consideration will drive away any superstition. How comes it that superstitious men are bemused by signs, but because their minds are not directed to the Word, which would lead them to God? Certainly, when we look to anything else than the Word, there is nothing sound, nothing pure. But one madness springs from another, and at length the signs, which were consecrated by the authority of God for the salvation of men, became profane, and degenerated into gross idolatry. The only difference, therefore, between the sacraments of the godly and the inventions of unbelievers, lies in the Word.

Now the Word here means the promise which explains the force and use of the sign. Hence it appears, that there is no legitimate use of the signs in the Papacy. They boast indeed, of having the Word, but it is a sort of incantation; for they mutter it in an unknown tongue, as if it were addressed to dead matter, and not to men. No explanation of the mystery is made to the people; and this is enough to make the sacrament like a dead element. 'In the word' is equivalent to 'by the word'.

27. *That he might present it to himself.* He declares what is the aim of baptism and of our washing. It is, that we may live holy and unblameable to God. For Christ washes us, not that we may return to rolling in our pollution, but that we may retain through our life the purity which we have once received. This is described in metaphorical language appropriate to his argument.

Not having spot or wrinkle. As the wife's beautiful figure is a cause of love, so Christ adorns the Church His bride with holiness as a pledge of His good-will. This metaphor alludes to marriage; but he afterwards lays aside the figure, and says plainly, that Christ has reconciled to Himself the Church, that it may be holy and without blame. The true beauty of the Church consists in this conjugal chastity, that is, in holiness and innocence.

By the word 'present' Paul implies that the Church ought to be holy, not in the opinion of men but in the eyes of the Lord. For he says, 'that He might present it to Himself', not 'that He might show it to others', though the fruits of that secret purity appear afterwards in outward works. Pelagians used this passage to prove a perfection of righteousness in this life; but they have been wisely refuted by Augustine. For Paul does not state what has been done, but for what purpose Christ has cleansed the Church. Now, when a thing is said to be done that another may afterwards follow, it is idle and wrong to infer that this latter thing, which ought to follow, has been already done.

Yet we do not deny that the holiness of the Church is already begun; but they do ill to establish perfection where there is a daily progress.

Even so ought husbands to love their wives as their own bodies. He that loveth his wife loveth himself. For no man ever hated his own flesh; but nourisheth and cherisheth it, even as Christ also the church: because we are members of his body, of his flesh, and of his bones. For this cause shall a man leave his father and mother, and shall cleave to his wife, and they two shall become one flesh. This mystery is great: but I speak in regard of Christ and of the church. Nevertheless, let every one of you severally love his wife even as himself; and let the wife see that she fear her husband. (28-33)

28. *He that loveth his wife.* He now takes an argument from nature itself, to exhort husbands to love their wives. In every man, he says, there is by very nature a love of self. But no man can love himself without loving his wife. Therefore, the man who does not love his wife is a monster. He proves the minor: marriage was appointed by God with the purpose that the two should become one; and that this unity may be the more holy, he says that it is recommended by the consideration of Christ and His Church. This is the sum, and his argument is to a certain extent valid to the whole of human society. To show what man owes to man, Isaiah says, 'despise not thine own flesh' (Isa. 58.7). But this refers to our common nature. Between a man and his wife there is a far closer relation; for they not only are united by a resemblance of nature, but by the bond of marriage are unified into one man. Whoever considers seriously the design of marriage cannot but love his wife.

29. *Even as Christ also the church.* He proceeds to establish the rights of marriage on Christ and His Church; for a more powerful example could not have been adduced. And first he speaks of the unique love of a husband for his wife as exemplified by Christ; and an instance of that unity which belongs to marriage is declared to exist between Himself and the Church. This is a remarkable passage on the mystical communication which we have with Christ.

30. He says that *we are members of him, of his flesh, and of his bones.* First, this is no exaggeration, but the simple truth. Secondly, he does not simply mean that Christ partook of our nature, but wants to express something deeper καὶ ἐμφατικώτερον.

He refers to Moses' words in Gen. 2.24. What does it mean then? As Eve was formed out of the substance of her husband Adam, and thus was a part of him, so, if we are to be the true members of Christ, we grow into one Body by the communication of His substance. In short, Paul describes our union to Christ, a symbol and pledge of which is given to us in the holy Supper. Some assert that it is a twisting of this passage to refer it to the Lord's Supper, when no mention is made of the Supper, but only of marriage; but they are very mistaken. Although they teach that the death of Christ is commemorated in the Supper, they do not admit a communication such as we assert from the words of Christ. We quote this passage against them. Paul declares that we are of the members and bones of Christ. Do we wonder, then, if in the Supper He offers His body to be enjoyed by us, to nourish us unto eternal life? Thus we teach that the only representation in the Supper is that whose truth and effect are taught by Paul.

31. *For this cause.* He joins two things together. For he so treats of the spiritual union between Christ and His Church that at the same time he extends it to the common law of marriage. The quotation from Moses relates to the general rule of marriage. He immediately adds that this is fulfilled *in Christ and the church.* He readily embraces every opportunity for proclaiming the benefits of Christ, but he adapts his teaching to the present subject. It is uncertain whether Moses introduces Adam as using these words, or gathers the doctrine in His person from the creation-story. Nor does it matter much which you take; for in both cases it will be an oracle of God, enjoining the duties which husbands owe to their wives.

When he says, *He shall leave his father and cleave to his wife*, it is equivalent to saying, 'Let him rather leave his father than not cleave to his wife.' The marriage bond does not set aside the other duties of mankind, nor are the appointments of God so inconsistent with each other, that a man cannot be a good and faithful husband without ceasing to be a dutiful son. It is a question of degree. Moses draws the comparison to express better the righteous and sacred union between husband and wife. For the obligation of a son towards his father is an inviolable law of nature. And when the bonds of a husband towards his wife are preferred to this, their force is the better understood. He who wants to be a good husband will not cease to show that he is his father's son; but he will prefer marriage as the most holy of all ties.

And they two shall become one flesh. That is, they shall be one man, or, to use a common phrase, they shall constitute one person; which certainly would not hold true with regard to any other relationship. All depends on this, that the wife was formed of the flesh and bones of her husband. Such is the union between us and Christ, that in a sense He pours Himself into us. For we are not bone of His bone, and flesh of His flesh, because, like ourselves, He is man, but because, by the power of His Spirit, He engrafts us into His Body, so that from Him we derive life.

32. *This mystery is great.* He concludes with wonder at the spiritual

union between Christ and the Church. For he exclaims that this is a great mystery. By which he implies that no language can do it justice. It is in vain that men fret themselves to comprehend, by the understanding of the flesh, its manner and character; for here God exerts the infinite power of His Spirit. Those who refuse to admit anything on this subject beyond what their own capacity can reach, are very foolish. When they deny that the flesh and blood of Christ are offered (*exhiberi*) to us in the Lord's Supper, they say: 'Define the manner or you will not convince us.' But I am overwhelmed by the depth of this mystery, and with Paul am not ashamed to acknowledge in wonder my ignorance. How much more satisfactory is this than to undervalue by my carnal sense what Paul declares to be a deep mystery! Reason itself teaches us this; for whatever is supernatural is clearly beyond the grasp of our minds. Let us therefore labour more to feel Christ living in us, than to discover the nature of that communication.

How wonderful is the acuteness of the Papists, who conclude from the word 'mystery' that marriage is one of the seven sacraments, as if they could change water into wine. They enumerate seven sacraments, while Christ has instituted no more than two; and, to prove that matrimony is one of them, they produce this passage. On what ground? Because the Vulgate uses the word *sacramentum* as a translation of the word 'mystery', which the apostles use. As if this word did not frequently in Latin writers denote 'mystery', or as if Paul did not use the word in this same epistle, when speaking of the calling of the Gentiles. But the present question is whether marriage has been appointed as a solemn symbol of the grace of God, to declare and represent to us something spiritual, such as Baptism or the Lord's Supper. They have no ground for such an assertion, unless it be that they have been deceived by the doubtful signification of the word, or rather by their ignorance of the Greek language. For if someone had told them that the word used by the apostle is 'mystery', no mistake would ever have occurred.

We see then the hammer and anvil with which they fabricated this sacrament. But they have also shown their laziness by not attending to the correction which is immediately added, *But I speak in regard of Christ and the church.* He wanted particularly to enter a caveat, in case anyone should understand him as speaking of marriage; so that he has spoken more plainly than if he had uttered the sentence without any exception. The great mystery is that Christ breathes into the Church His own life and power. But who would make a sacrament out of this? Therefore we see that this blunder arose from the grossest ignorance.

33. *Nevertheless, let every one.* Having digressed a little from the argument, though the very digression aided his design, he adopts the method usually followed in short precepts, and summarizes what he wants to see in them: that husbands love their wives, and wives fear their husbands; understanding by *fear* that reverence which will make them submissive. For there will be no willing subjection that is not preceded by reverence.

CHAPTER SIX

Children, obey your parents in the Lord: for this is right. Honour thy father and mother, (which is the first commandment with promise,) that it may be well with thee, and thou mayest live long on the earth. And, ye fathers, provoke not your children to wrath; but nurture them in the discipline and correction of the Lord. (1-4)

1. *Children, obey.* He uses the word 'obey' instead of 'honour'. But why does he restrict the genus to the species? It is because obedience is the evidence of that honour which children owe to their parents. He therefore demands it the more earnestly. It is likewise more difficult; for the human mind recoils from subjection and only with difficulty suffers itself to be forced under the control of another. Experience shows how rare this virtue is; for do we find one among a thousand that is obedient to his parents? There is, then, a synecdoche in Paul's teaching here, but it is the most important part, and is accompanied by all the others.

In the Lord. Besides the law of nature (*naturae legem*), which is received by all nations, he teaches that the obedience of children is decreed by the authority of God. Hence it follows that parents are to be obeyed, so long only as duty towards God does not suffer, for this holds first place. If the appointment of God is the rule by which the submission of children is to be demanded, it would be all wrong for them to be led away from God Himself by it.

For this is right. This is added to restrain the fierceness which, we have already said, appears to be natural to almost all men. He proves it to be right, because the Lord has commanded it; for it is not lawful to dispute or call in question the appointment of Him whose will is the most sure rule of goodness and righteousness. Moreover, that he should derive obedience from honour is not surprising; for God does not care for ceremonies. The precept, 'Honour thy father and mother', comprehends all the duties by which the sincere affection and respect of children to their parents can be expressed.

2. *Which is the first commandment.* The promises annexed to the commandments are intended to attract us, so that we may obey the more cheerfully. Therefore Paul uses a seasoning, so to say, to render the submission which he enjoins on children more pleasant and agreeable. He does not merely say that God has offered a reward to him who obeys his father and mother, but that such an offer is peculiar to

this commandment. If each of the commandments had its own promises, there would have been no force in the commendation bestowed here. But this is the first commandment, Paul tells us, which God has been pleased to confirm by a remarkable promise as it were with a seal. There is a difficulty here; for the second commandment likewise contains a promise, 'I am God, who shew mercy etc.' (Exod. 20.5, 6). But this is universal, applying indiscriminately to the whole law, and cannot be said to be annexed to that commandment. Paul's assertion still holds true, that no other commandment but that which enjoins the obedience due by children to their parents is distinguished by a promise.

The promise is of a long life; from which we understand that the present life is not to be despised among the gifts of God. Of this and such subjects readers may learn in the *Institutio*.[1] Here I will only note briefly that the reward promised to the obedience of children is very appropriate. Those who show kindness to their parents from whom they received life, are assured by God that it will be well with them in their life.

3. *On the earth.* Moses expressly mentions the land of Canaan (Exod. 20.12). For the Jews there could be no happy or desirable life outside it. But as the same blessing of God is today shed on the whole world, Paul has properly left out the mention of a place, the particular discrimination of which lasted only till the coming of Christ.

4. *And, ye fathers.* Parents, in their turn, are exhorted not to irritate their children with immoderate harshness. This would excite hatred, and would lead them to throw off the yoke altogether. Accordingly, in Colossians he adds, 'lest they be discouraged' (Col. 3.21). Kind and liberal treatment keeps children in reverence for their parents, and increases the readiness and cheerfulness of their obedience, while a hard and unkind severity rouses them to obstinacy, and destroys their dutifulness. But Paul goes on to say, 'let them be kindly cherished'. For the word ἐκτρέφειν unquestionably conveys the idea of gentleness and friendliness. But, on the other hand, lest there should be too much indulgence, as sometimes happens, he tightens the rein as it were, and adds, *in the discipline and correction of the Lord.* For God does not want parents to be so fond towards their children that they corrupt them by sparing them. Let their kindness be tempered, so as to keep them in the discipline of the Lord, and correct them also when they go astray. That age requires frequent admonition and forcing with the rein, in case it should run riot.

Servants, be obedient unto them that according to the flesh are your

[1] *Inst.* III.x.

masters, with fear and trembling, in singleness of your heart, as unto
Christ; not in the way of eye-service, as menpleasers; but as servants
of Christ, doing the will of God from the heart; with good will serving
the Lord, and not men: knowing, that whatsoever good thing each one
doeth, the same shall he receive from the Lord, whether he be bond or
free. And, ye masters, perform your reciprocal duties to them, and
forbear threatening: knowing that their Master and yours is in heaven;
neither is there respect of persons with him. (5-9)

5. *Servants, be obedient.* He exhorts servants the more earnestly
because the trouble and bitterness of their condition makes it harder
to be borne. And he does not speak merely of outward obedience,
but rather of willing *fear;* for it is very rare for anyone willingly to
yield himself to the control of another. Now, he is not speaking of
paid servants, as we have them today, but those in ancient times,
whose slavery was perpetual, unless, by the kindness of their masters,
they were set free. Their masters bought them with money, to use
them for the dirtiest tasks, and by law they had the power of life and
death over them. It is these whom he commands to obey their
masters, lest they should imagine that carnal freedom had been procured for them by the Gospel.

But as some of the worst men were coerced by the dread of punishment, he distinguishes between Christian and ungodly servants, by
their attitude. *With fear and trembling,* he says; that is, with the careful
respect which springs from singleness of heart. But because it is
difficult to get so much deference for a mere man, without the obligation of a superior necessity, he bids them to look to God. Hence it
follows, that it is not enough if their obedience satisfy the eyes of men;
for God requires truth and sincerity of heart. He declares that when
they serve their masters faithfully, they obey God; as if he had said,
'Do not suppose that it was by the will of men that you were thrown
into slavery. It is God who has laid upon you this burden, who has
contracted you out to your masters. He who conscientiously endeavours to render what he owes to his master, discharges his duty
not to man only, but to God.'

He contrasts *good will* with the suppressed indignation which swells
the minds of slaves. Though they dare not openly break out or give
signs of obstinacy, their dislike of the authority is so strong, that it is
with the greatest unwillingness and reluctance that they obey their
masters.

Whoever reads the accounts of the character and manners of slaves,
scattered through the writings of the ancients, will soon see that the
number of injunctions here given does not exceed that of the diseases

which prevailed among this class, and which it was of importance to
cure. But this teaching applies also to servants and maids of our own
times. It is God who appoints and regulates society. As the condition
of servants is much more tolerable, they ought to consider themselves
far less excusable, if they do not endeavour, in every way, to behave
as Paul tells them.

When he calls them *masters according to the flesh*, he softens the
harshness of slavery. For he means that their spiritual freedom, which
they should especially seek, remained untouched.

He mentions ὀφθαλμοδουλεία; because flattery is common among
almost all servants, but, as soon as their master's back is turned, they
indulge freely in contempt, or even ridicule. Paul therefore enjoins
the godly to keep at the greatest distance from such deceitful pretences.

8. *Whatsoever good thing.* A powerful consolation! If they have to
deal with ungrateful or cruel masters, God will accept their services
to unworthy men as rendered to Himself. When servants consider
the pride and arrogance of their masters, they often think that their
labour is thrown away and become lazy. But Paul tells them that
their reward is laid up with God for services which appear to be ill
bestowed on unfeeling men; and that there is no reason, therefore,
why they should be led aside from their straight course. He adds that
no distinction is to be made between a slave and a free man. The
world is wont to set less value on the labours of slaves. He says that
it is not so with God, but they are as precious to Him as the duties of
kings. For the outward station is set aside and each is judged according
to the integrity of his heart.

9. *And ye masters.* The laws granted masters great freedom. Whatever had thus been sanctioned by the civil code was regarded by many
as right in itself. To such an extent did their cruelty sometimes
proceed, that the Roman emperors were forced to restrain their
tyranny. But even had no imperial edicts ever been issued for the
protection of slaves, God allows masters no more than is consistent
with the rule of love. When philosophers want to temper excessive
severity to slaves with complete fairness, they teach that masters ought
to treat them no differently from hired servants. But they only go
for utility, that is, what is advantageous to the head of the family,
and fits society. Paul takes a very different principle. He lays down
what is lawful according to the Divine appointment, and how far
they, too, are debtors to their servants.

First he says, 'Do the same things,' which I have translated 'Perform
your reciprocal duty.' For what he says in Colossians: τὸ δίκαιον καὶ
τὴν ἰσότητα (that which is just and equal), is what, in this passage, he
calls *the same things* (τὰ αὐτά). And what is this but the law of analogy,

as they call it? The state of masters and servants is not indeed equal; but there is a certain mutual right between them; that is, servants are bound to their masters; and thus on the other hand, the difference in rank being remembered, masters lie under certain obligations to their servants. This analogy is wrongly assessed, because men do not test it by the law of love, which is the only true standard. This is what Paul means by the term 'the same things'; for we are all ready enough to demand what is due to ourselves; but when our own duty comes to be performed, every one tries to plead exemption. It is chiefly, however, among the powerful and aristocrats that injustice of this sort rules.

Forbearing threatenings. Every kind of insult, arising from the pride of masters, is comprehended in a single word; as if he forbade them to domineer and look fierce, and seemed constantly threatening some evil against their servants, when they tell them to do something. Threatenings, and every kind of barbarity, begin with masters treating servants like cattle, as if they had been born for their sake alone. Under this one kind he forbids all insulting and barbarous treatment.

Their Master and yours. A very necessary warning. For there is nothing which we will not dare against those subject to us, if they have no ability to resist, and no means of obtaining their rights, if no avenger, no protector appears, none who will be moved by compassion to listen to their complaints. It happens here, in short, as is commonly said, that impunity is the mother of licence. But Paul here reminds them, that, while masters rule over their servants, they have the same Master in heaven, to whom they must render an account.

And there is no respect of persons. A regard to persons blinds our eyes, so as to leave no room for rights or justice; but Paul affirms that it is of no value in the sight of God. By 'persons' is meant anything about a man which is irrelevant to the real case, and which we take into account in judging, as when kinship, beauty, rank, wealth, friendship, and everything of this sort gain our favour, while the opposite qualities produce contempt and sometimes hatred. As these irrelevant feelings arising from the sight of a person have the greatest possible influence in human judgments, those who are invested with power flatter themselves, as if God would countenance such corruptions. 'Who is he that God should regard him, or defend his interest against mine?' Paul, on the contrary, asserts that masters are mistaken if they suppose that their servants will be of little or no account before God, because they are so before the world. For God cares nothing for persons, and the cause of the meanest man will not be a whit less regarded by him than that of the loftiest monarch.

Finally, my brethren, be strong in the Lord, and in the power of his might. Put on the whole armour of God, that ye may be able to stand against the wiles of the devil. For our wrestling is not against flesh and blood, but against principalities, against powers, against the world-rulers of the darkness of this age, against spiritual wickednesses in heavenly places. Wherefore take unto you the whole armour of God, that ye may be able to withstand in the evil day, and having done all, to stand. (10-13)

10. *Finally.* He resumes his general exhortations, and first he bids them to be strong, to summon up courage and vigour; for there is always much to enfeeble us, and we are ill fitted to resist. But because we are weak, an exhortation would be cold unless the Lord were present, and stretched out His hand to give help, in fact, unless He supplied the whole power; and therefore he adds, *in the Lord.* As if he had said, 'You cannot reply that you lack the ability; for I only require you to be strong in the Lord.' And then in explanation he adds, *in the power of his might,* which greatly increases our confidence, particularly as it shows the help which God is accustomed to bestow upon believers. If the Lord aids us by His extraordinary power, we have no reason to be irresolute in battle. But someone will say, 'What purpose did it serve to bid the Ephesians be strong in the Lord's power, which was certainly not at their command?' I answer, there are two clauses here which must be considered. He exhorts them to courage, but then reminds them to ask from God a supply of what in themselves they lack; and at the same time promises that, if they ask for it, the power of God will be displayed.

11. *Put on the whole armour.* God has furnished us with more than one kind of help, provided we are not lazy in taking up what is offered. But we nearly all sin in using the grace offered to us carelessly and hesitantly; just as if a soldier, about to meet the enemy, should take his helmet but neglect his shield. To correct this security, or, rather indolence, Paul borrows a comparison from the military art, and bids us put on the whole armour of God. By which he means that we ought to be prepared on all sides, so as to want nothing. The Lord offers us arms for repelling every kind of attack. It remains for us to apply them to our use, and not leave them hanging on the rack or the wall. To make us more vigilant, he tells us that we must not only engage in open warfare, but that we have a crafty and insidious foe, who attacks us secretly in ambushes; for that is the sense of the word μεθοδείας ('wiles') which he uses.

12. *For our wrestling is not.* He impresses their danger on them by telling them the nature of the enemy, which he illustrates by a com-

parison, *not against flesh and blood.* He means that our difficulties are far greater than if we had to fight against men. There we resist human strength, sword is opposed to sword, man contends with man, force is met by force, and skill by skill; but here the case is very different, for our enemies are such as no human power can withstand. This is the sum of it. By 'flesh and blood' he means men, who are so named to contrast them with spiritual assailants. As if he said, 'Our struggle is not bodily.'

Let us remember this statement when men's injuries provoke us to revenge. For our nature carries us wildly away against the men themselves; but this foolish desire will be restrained as by a tight rein by the consideration that the men who annoy us are nothing more than darts thrown by the hand of Satan. While we are employed in overcoming them, we lay ourselves open to be wounded on all sides. To wrestle against flesh and blood will not only be useless, but very harmful. We must go straight to the enemy, who attacks and wounds us from his concealment, who slays before he is seen.

But let us return to Paul. He puts before us a formidable enemy, not to overwhelm us with fear, but to sharpen our diligence and earnestness. For there is a middle course to be observed. When the enemy is neglected, he does his utmost to oppress us with sloth, and afterwards discourages us by terror; so that, before we have been touched, we are vanquished. By speaking of the power of the enemy, Paul labours to keep us more zealous. He had already called him the devil, but now uses a number of epithets, so that his readers may understand that this is not an enemy to be despised.

He names *principalities and powers*, to strike us with alarm; yet not to fill us with dismay, as I said, but to arouse us to caution. He then calls them κοσμοκράτορας, that is, princes of the world; and in explanation he adds *of the darkness of the age.* He means that the devil reigns in the world, because the world is nothing but darkness. Hence it follows that the corruption of the world gives a place to the kingdom of the devil. For he could not reside in a pure and sound creature of God. It all arises from the sinfulness of men. By 'darkness', as is well known, he means unbelief and ignorance of God, with their consequences. As the whole world is covered with darkness, the devil is the prince of this world.

By calling it *wickednesses*, he not only accuses the malignity and depravity of the devil, but reminds us that we need great care not to be overcome by him. For the same reason, the adjective *spiritual* is applied; for, when the enemy is invisible, the danger is greater. There is emphasis, too, in the following phrase, *in heavenly* places; for the higher place from which we are attacked and assaulted causes us greater trouble and difficulty. And thus our life is menaced from above.

In old times the Manichees misused this passage to prove their wild notion of two principles; but it is easily refuted. They supposed the devil to be ἀντίθεον (an antagonist god), whom the righteous God would not subdue without great exertion. For Paul does not ascribe to devils a principality, which they seize without the consent, and exercise against the opposition, of God, but one which, as Scripture everywhere teaches, God, in righteous vengeance, allows them against the wicked. The question here is, not what power they have in opposition to God, but how frightening they should be to us, to keep us on our guard. Nor do these words countenance the belief that the devil has created and keeps for himself the middle region of the air. Paul does not assign to them a fixed territory, which they hold and control, but merely indicates that they are engaged in hostility, and are higher in place.

13. *Wherefore take unto you.* He does not infer that we must throw away our spears because our enemy is so powerful, but that we must pluck up spirit for the battle. In fact, the exhortation contains a promise of victory. For, by saying *that ye may be able*, he implies that we shall certainly stand, if we only put on the whole armour of God, and fight valiantly to the end. Otherwise, we might be broken by the number and variety of the contests.

Therefore he adds, *in the evil day, and having done all.* By the first expression he rouses them from security, that they may prepare themselves for hard, troublesome, and dangerous conflicts, and, at the same time, animates them with the hope of victory; for amidst the greatest dangers they will win through. In the second clause he extends this confidence to the whole course of life. There will be no danger where the power of God will not prevail; nor will any who are so armed to fight against Satan, fail in mid-course.

Stand therefore, having girded your loins with truth, and having put on the breastplate of righteousness; and having shod your feet with the preparation of the gospel of peace; withal, taking the shield of faith, wherewith ye shall be able to quench all the fiery darts of the evil one. And take the helmet of salvation, and the sword of the Spirit, which is the word of God: with all prayer and supplication praying at all seasons in the Spirit, and watching thereunto with all perseverance and supplication for all the saints; and for me, that utterance may be given unto me, in opening my mouth boldly, to make known the mystery of the gospel, for which I am an ambassador in chains; that in it I may speak boldly, as I ought to speak. (14-20)

14. *Stand therefore.* Now he declares the arms which he ordered

them to wear. We must not, however, inquire too minutely into the meaning of each word; for an allusion to a soldier's kit is all that was intended. Nothing can be more idle than the great pains which some have taken to discover why righteousness is made a breastplate, instead of a girdle. Paul's design was to touch briefly on what was chiefly required in a Christian man, and to adapt it to the comparison which he had already made.

Truth, by which he means a sincere mind, he compares to a belt. Now, a belt was, in ancient times, one of the most important parts of military armour. He looks therefore to the fountain of sincerity; for the purity of the Gospel ought to purge us from all guile, and to cleanse our hearts from all pretence.

Secondly, he recommends *righteousness*, and desires that it should be a breastplate to protect the chest. Some imagine that this refers to free righteousness, or the imputation of righteousness, which consists of remission of sins. But to my mind this would be irrelevant here; for Paul is dealing with innocence of life. He wants us to be adorned, first, with integrity, and next with a devout and holy life.

15. He alludes, if I mistake not, to soldier's boots; for they were always reckoned among his armour, and were never in domestic use. The meaning is that as soldiers covered their legs and feet against cold and other injuries, so we must be shod with the Gospel, if we would pass unhurt through the world. It is clear that he calls it *the gospel of peace*, from its effects; for it is the embassy of our reconciliation to God, and it alone quietens our conscience. But what does the word 'preparation' mean? Some expound it as an injunction to be prepared for the Gospel. But I interpret it as the effect of the Gospel, that we should lay aside every hindrance and be prepared both for journey and for battle. By nature we are slow and sluggish. Moreover, a rough road and many obstacles delay us, and we are discouraged by the smallest opposition. On these accounts, Paul holds out the Gospel as the best instrument for undertaking and performing the expedition. Erasmus' circumlocution, 'that ye may be prepared' (*ut sitis parati*), is not really appropriate.

16. *Taking the shield of faith.* Though faith and the Word of God are one, Paul assigns to them two offices. I call them one, because the Word is the object of faith and cannot be applied to our use but by faith. And again, faith is nothing, and can do nothing, without the Word. But Paul, neglecting so subtle a distinction, allowed himself to speak freely on the military armour. In I Thess. 5.8 he gives both to faith and to love the name of breastplate. From this it is clear that he only wanted to say that he who possess the virtues here described is well-armed on every hand.

And yet it is not without reason that he compares the chief instruments of warfare, a sword and a shield, to faith and the Word of God. In the spiritual combat, these two hold the highest rank. By faith we repel all the attacks of the devil, and by the Word of God the enemy himself is slain outright. In other words, if the Word of God shall be efficacious in us through faith, we shall be more than sufficiently armed both for repelling and for putting to flight the enemy. And those who take from a Christian people the Word of God, do they not despoil them of their necessary armour, so that they perish without a struggle? There is no man of any rank who is not bound to be a soldier of Christ. But who can fight unarmed and swordless?

Wherewith ye shall be able to quench all the darts. He speaks imprecisely. For he ought to have used 'catch' or 'shake off' or something similar. Yet *quench* is far more expressive; for it applies to the adjective he used; as if he said, 'The darts of Satan are not only sharp and penetrating, but, what is more deadly, they are fiery. Faith will not only blunt their edge, but also quench their heat.' For 'this is the victory that overcometh the world', as John says (I John 5.4).

17. *And take the helmet of salvation.* In the passage in Thessalonians that I have quoted, he calls 'the hope of salvation' a helmet, which I take in the same sense. The head is protected by the best helmet, when, uplifted by hope, we look up to heaven to that salvation which is promised us. It is only therefore through hoping, that salvation is a helmet.

18. *With all prayer.* Having put armour on the Ephesians, he now enjoins them to fight by prayer. This is the true method. To call upon God is the chief exercise of faith and hope; and it is in this way that we obtain from God every blessing. Prayer and supplication differ little, except that supplication is the species, prayer the genus.

He exhorts them to persevere in prayer, when he says *with all perseverance.* For by this he tells us that we must press on cheerfully, lest we faint. With unabated ardour we must continue our prayers, though we do not immediately obtain what we desire. If some prefer 'earnestness', I would not object.

But what is the meaning of *at all seasons?* Having already spoken of continued application, does he repeat it? I think not. When everything flows on prosperously, when we are easy and cheerful, we have hardly any thought of praying; in fact, we never flee to God, unless driven by distress. Paul therefore desires us to let no season pass, without remembering to pray; so that praying at all seasons is the same as praying both in prosperity and in adversity.

For all saints. There is not a moment of our life at which our wants ought not to urge us to prayer. But there is another reason for praying without ceasing—that the necessities of our brethren ought to touch us. And when is it that some members of the Church are not in distress, and needing our assistance? If, at any time, we are cold in prayer or more negligent than we ought to be, because we do not feel the pressure of immediate necessity, let us instantly reflect how many of our brethren are worn out by varied and heavy afflictions, are weighed down by deep anxiety, or are reduced to the worst distress. If we are not roused from our lethargy, we must have hearts of stone. Here someone may ask whether we are to pray for believers only? I reply: although Paul commends the godly to the Ephesians, he does not exclude others. And yet in prayer, as in other offices of love, our first care unquestionably is owed to the saints.

19. *And for me.* He enjoins the Ephesians to remember to pray for him particularly. Hence we infer that there is no man so richly endowed with gifts as not to need this kind of assistance from his brethren, so long as he is in this world. Who could be better exempted from this necessity than Paul? Yet he entreats the prayers of his brethren, and not hypocritically, but from an earnest desire of their aid. Now let us hear what he wishes that they should ask for him: that it may be given him to open his mouth. What then? Was he dumb, or restrained by fear from confessing the Gospel? By no means; but he was afraid lest his splendid commencement should fail in the future. Besides, he burned with such zeal in proclaiming the Gospel that he was never satisfied with himself. And indeed, if we consider the weight and importance of the subject, we shall all acknowledge that we are very far from being equal to it.

Accordingly he adds, *as I ought to speak*; meaning that to testify to the Gospel as it deserves is a work of rare virtue. Weigh every word here carefully. He says, *with boldness*; by which he means that fear hinders our freedom in preaching Christ openly and fearlessly; whereas a free and undisguised confession is demanded from the ministers of Christ. Paul does not ask for himself quickness in debate, or the knack of quibbling, that he may escape his enemies by ambiguities. He desires an open mouth, to make a clear and strong confession; for when the mouth is half shut, it utters doubtful and confused sounds. *In opening my mouth*, that is, with perfect freedom, without the smallest fear.

But this seems to have been a sign of unbelief in Paul, when he doubts his steadfastness, and implores the intercession of others. Not so. He does not, like unbelievers, seek a remedy which is contrary to the will of God, or inconsistent with His Word. The only aids on which he relies are those which he sees to be allowed by the Lord and therefore promised and approved. The Lord commands that believers shall pray for one another. It is then no small comfort for each of them to hear that the care of his salvation is enjoined on the rest, and to be told by God Himself that the prayers of others on his behalf are not poured out in vain. Would it be lawful to refuse what the Lord Himself has offered? Each believer, no doubt, ought to have been satisfied with the promise of God, that as often as he prayed he would be heard. But if, to the heap of His kindness, God were pleased to add that He will listen to the prayers of others in our behalf, should this kindness be rejected, and not rather embraced with open arms?

Let us therefore remember that it was not from distrust or doubt that Paul sought refuge in the intercessions of his brethren, but he eagerly desires them because he wished to lose nothing which the Lord had given him. The Papists are ridiculous to conclude from Paul's example that we ought to pray to the dead. For Paul was writing to the Ephesians, to whom he could communicate what I have said. But what intercourse have we with the dead. As well might they argue that we ought to invite angels to our feasts and entertainments, because among men love is nurtured by such offices.

But that ye also may know my affairs, how I do, Tychicus, a beloved brother and faithful minister in the Lord, shall make known to you all things: whom I have sent unto you for this very purpose, that ye might know my state, and that he might comfort your hearts. Peace be to the brethren, and love with faith, from God the Father, and the Lord Jesus Christ. Grace be with all them that love our Lord Jesus Christ in sincerity. Amen. (21-24)

21. *But that ye also may know.* Uncertain or false reports frequently perturb not only weak minds, but sometimes also thoughtful and steady persons. To prevent this danger, Paul sends *Tychicus*, from whom the Ephesians would receive full information. In this we see the godly solicitude which Paul had for the churches. When death stood constantly before his eyes, neither the dread of death, nor anxiety about himself prevented him from making provision for the most remote churches. Another would have said that he had more than enough to do with his own affairs. Others ought to run to his assistance, rather than expect the smallest relief from him. Not so Paul. He sends men in every direction to strengthen the churches which he had founded.

He praises Tychicus, that his statements may have more authority. But it is doubtful whether he calls him *a faithful minister in the Lord* in regard to the public ministry of the Church, or to the private loyalty which he had shown him. This uncertainty arises from these two expressions being connected, 'a beloved brother and faithful minister in the Lord'. The former relates to Paul, and so may the second be supposed to do. I rather interpret it of the public ministry; for I do not think it probable that Paul would have sent any man who had not such a reputation in the Church as would impress the Ephesians with his presence.

23. *Peace be to the brethren.* I take the word peace, as in the salutations, to mean prosperity. Yet if anyone shall prefer to view it as harmony, because, immediately afterwards, he mentions love, I do not object; in fact, the context seems to flow better. He wishes the Ephesians to be in accord and quiet among themselves; and this, he at once says, may be obtained by benevolence and agreement in faith. For love causes men to restrain themselves in peace; and faith produces love and is its bond. From this prayer we note that faith and love, as well as peace itself, are gifts of God bestowed upon us through Christ, nay, that they come from Christ along with the Father their Author.

24. *Grace be with all.* The meaning is, 'May God bestow His favour on all who love Jesus Christ with a pure conscience!' The Greek word, which I follow Erasmus in translating *sincerity*, is literally 'uncorruptedness'. This deserves attention on account of the beauty of the metaphor. Paul intended to suggest that, when the heart of man is empty of all hypocrisy, it will be free from all corruption. Moreover, this prayer ought to be regarded as an oracle, that we know God is favourable to us when with a sincere heart we love His Son, in whom He shows us a testimony and pledge of His love towards us. But let there be no hypocrisy. For the greater part, although not unwilling to profess the Gospel, invent a shadow of Christ and worship Him with counterfeit homage. Would there were not so many instances today to bear witness that Paul's demand for sincere purity in the love of Christ was necessary.

The Epistle to
THE PHILIPPIANS

THE THEME OF THE EPISTLE
TO THE PHILIPPIANS

It is generally known that Philippi was a city of Macedonia, situated on the borders of Thrace, on the plains of which Pompey was defeated by Caesar, and Brutus and Cassius afterwards by Antony and Octavius. Thus Roman civil wars made this place famous by two memorable engagements. When Paul was called into Macedonia by an oracle he first founded a church in that city (as Luke relates in Acts 16.12). It not only persevered steadfastly in the faith, but also, in process of time, as this Epistle bears witness, both grew in numbers and progressed in virtue.

The occasion of Paul's writing to the Philippians was this. They had sent to him by Epaphroditus, their pastor, such things as he needed in prison for sustaining life, and for other and extraordinary expenses. And no doubt Epaphroditus explained to him at the same time the whole state of the Church, and as a sort of adviser told him of what they needed to be admonished. It seems, however, that attempts had been made upon them by false apostles, who wandered about everywhere to spread corruptions of sound doctrine; but as they had stood firm in the truth, the apostle commends their steadfastness. But mindful of human frailty and warned, perhaps, by Epaphroditus that they required to be strengthened in good time lest they should fall away, he appends such admonitions as he knew to be suitable to them.

And first, to win their confidence, he declared his respectful love towards them. He goes on to speak of himself and his bonds, lest they should be dismayed on seeing him a prisoner and in danger of his life. He shows them, accordingly, that the glory of the Gospel is so far from being lessened by this fact, that it is rather an argument in its confirmation, and at the same time stirs them up by his own example to be prepared for every event. He concludes the first chapter with a short exhortation to unity and patience.

As, however, ambition is almost always the mother of dissensions, and so opens the door for new and strange doctrines, at the commencement of the second chapter he entreats them earnestly to put humility and modesty first. For this he uses various arguments. And that he may the better hold them, he promises to send Timothy to them shortly; more, he expresses a hope of visiting them himself. He afterwards excuses the delay of Epaphroditus.

In the third chapter he attacks the false apostles and sets aside both their empty boastings and the doctrine of circumcision which they urged. Over against all their inventions he sets Christ alone; against their arrogance, his former life and present course, in which a true image of Christian devotion shone forth. He says, also, that the aim of perfection, for which we must strive during our whole life, is to have fellowship with Christ in His death and resurrection; and this he attests by his own example.

He begins the fourth chapter with particular admonitions, but soon goes on to generalities. He closes the Epistle with a declaration of his gratitude to the Philippians, that they may not think that what they had given for relieving his necessities had been ill bestowed.

CHAPTER ONE

Paul and Timothy, servants of Jesus Christ, to all the saints in Christ Jesus which are at Philippi, with the bishops and deacons: grace to you and peace, from God our Father and the Lord Jesus Christ. I thank my God in every remembrance of you, always in every prayer of mine for you all, making request with joy, for your fellowship in the gospel from the first day until now; being confident of this very thing, that he which hath begun a good work in you, will perfect it until the day of Jesus Christ. (1-6)

1. *Paul, etc.* Paul is accustomed to use titles which would win credit for himself and his ministry; but there was no need of lengthy commendations with the Philippians, who had known him and acknowledged him without controversy as a true Apostle of Christ. For they had persevered in the calling of God steadfastly and in an even tenor.

Bishops. He names the pastors separately, for the sake of honour. Moreover, we may infer from this, that the name 'bishop' is common to all the ministers of the Word, inasmuch as he assigns several to one Church. Therefore, bishop and pastor are synonymous. And this is one of the passages which Jerome quotes for proving it in his epistle to Evagrius, and in his exposition of the Epistle to Titus. Afterwards the custom prevailed that only the one whom the presbyters in each Church appointed over their college was called bishop. This originated in a human custom and rests on no Scriptural authority. I acknowledge indeed, that, as the minds and manners of men are, order cannot be maintained among the ministers of the Word without one presiding over the others. I speak of individual bodies, not of whole provinces, far less of the whole world. Now, although we must not contend for words, it would be better for us in speaking to follow the Holy Spirit, the Author of tongues, than to change for the worse forms of speech disposed by Him. For from the corrupted signification of the word this evil has resulted, that, as if all presbyters were not colleagues, called to the same office, one of them, under the cloak of a new name, usurped dominion over the others.

Deacons. This name may be taken in two ways: either for administrators and curators of the poor, or for elders (*pro senioribus*), who were appointed for the regulation of morals. As, however, it is more usual in Paul in the former sense, I understand it rather as stewards, who superintended the distributing and receiving of alms. For the rest,[1] consult the preceding commentaries.

3. *I give thanks.* He begins with rejoicing on two accounts: that he may by this token show his love to the Philippians; and secondly, that, by praising their past life, he may exhort them also to perseverance in the future. He gives also another sign of his love, the solicitude which he exercised in supplications. We must note, however, that, whenever he mentions things that are joyful, he immediately breaks forth into thanksgiving, a practice which ought also to be common among us. We must also notice what he gives thanks to God for: the fellowship of the Philippians in the Gospel of Christ. For it follows from this, that it ought to be ascribed to the grace of God. When he says, *in every remembrance of you,* he means, 'As often as I remember you.'

4. *Always in every prayer.* Connect the words like this: 'Always making request for you all in every prayer of mine.' For as he had said before that the remembrance of them was an occasion of joy to him, so he now adds that they come into his mind as often as he prays. He afterwards says that it is with joy that he makes request for them. *Joy* refers to the past; prayer to the future. For he rejoiced in their happy beginnings and desired their perfection. Thus it becomes us always to rejoice in the blessings received from God in such a way as to remember to ask from Him what we still lack.

5. *For your fellowship.* He now passes over the other clause and states the nature of his joy—that they had come into the fellowship of the Gospel, that is, had become partakers of the Gospel, which, as we know, is accomplished by means of faith. For the Gospel is nothing to us, in respect of possessing it, until we have received it by faith. At the same time the word 'fellowship' can be referred to the common society of the saints, as though he had said that they had been gathered together with all the children of God in the faith of the Gospel.

When he says, *from the first day,* he praises their readiness in having shown themselves teachable immediately the doctrine was set before them. The phrase *until now* denotes perseverance. Now we know how rare a virtue it is to follow God immediately He calls us, and to persevere steadfastly unto the end. For many are slow and backward to obey, and still more fail through fickleness and inconstancy.

6. *Persuaded of this very thing.* His confidence in them for the future furnishes an additional reason for joy. But someone will say, 'Why should men dare to promise themselves for tomorrow amidst so great an infirmity of nature, amidst so many impediments, roughnesses and precipices?' Paul assuredly did not derive this confidence from the

---

[1] I.e. the greetings.

steadfastness or excellence of men, but simply from the fact that God had declared His love to the Philippians. And undoubtedly the true recognition of God's benefits is when we conceive from them occasion of hoping well as to the future. For as they are testimonies at once of His goodness and of His fatherly benevolence towards us, what ingratitude it would be to receive from this no confirmation of hope and good courage. In addition to this, God is not like men, who are wearied or exhausted by doing good. Therefore, let believers exercise themselves in constant meditation upon the benefits of God, that they may encourage and confirm hope for the future, and always ponder in their mind this syllogism:

God does not forsake the work which His own hands have begun, as the Prophet bears witness. (Ps. 138.8; Isa. 64.8) We are the work of His hands. Therefore He will complete what He has begun in us.

When I say that we are the work of His hands, I do not refer only to creation, but to the calling by which we are adopted as His sons. For it is a sign to us of our election, that the Lord has called us effectually to Himself by His Spirit.

It is asked, however, whether anyone can be certain as to the salvation of others, for Paul here is not speaking of himself but of the Philippians. I answer, that the assurance which a man has of his own salvation is very different from what he has as to another. For the Spirit of God is a Witness to me of my calling, as He is to each of the elect. For others we have no testimony, except from the outward efficacy of the Spirit; that is, in so far as the grace of God shows itself in them, so that we become aware of it. There is therefore a great difference, because the assurance of faith remains shut up within, and does not spread to others. But wherever we see any apprehensible tokens of Divine election, we ought immediately to be stirred up to a good hope, both in order that we may not be despiteful towards our neighbours and withhold from them an equitable and humane judgment of charity, and also that we may be grateful to God. This, however, is a general rule both as to ourselves and others, that, distrusting our own strength, we depend entirely upon God alone.

Until the day of Jesus Christ. The chief thing to understand here is, 'until the end of the conflict'. Now the conflict is terminated by death. But because the Spirit is accustomed to speak like this in the Scriptures about the last coming of Christ, it would be better to extend the advancement of the grace of God to the resurrection of the flesh. For although those who have been freed from the mortal body no longer contend with the lusts of the flesh and are, so to say, out of range, yet there will be no absurdity in speaking of them as in progress, inasmuch as they have not yet reached the point to which they aspire, and do not yet enjoy the felicity and glory which they have hoped for. In short, the day has not yet dawned which will reveal the treasures hidden in hope. And in truth, when hope is treated of, our eyes must always be focussed on the blessed resurrection, as their object.

Even as it is right for me to think this of you all, because I have you in my heart; inasmuch as, both in my bonds, and in the defence and confirmation of the gospel, ye all are partakers of my grace. For God is my witness, how I long after you all in the heart[1] of Jesus Christ. And this I pray, that your love may abound yet more and more in knowledge and all discernment; so that ye may approve the things that are excellent; that ye may be sincere, and without offence, till the day of Christ; being filled with the fruits of righteousness, which are through Jesus Christ, unto the glory and praise of God. (7-11)

7. *As it is right.* For our understanding of the gifts of God is niggardly if we do not reckon as children of God those in whom there shine forth true signs of piety, which are the marks by which the Spirit of adoption manifests Himself. Paul accordingly says that justice itself dictates that he should hope well of the Philippians for all time, inasmuch as he sees them to be joined with himself in participation of grace. It is not without consideration that I have translated this passage differently from Erasmus, as the judicious reader will easily perceive. For he states what opinion he has of the Philippians, which was the ground of his hoping well of them. He says, then, that they are partakers of the same grace, in his bonds and in the defence of the Gospel.

To have them in his heart is to reckon them as such in the inmost affection of his heart. For the Philippians had always assisted Paul according to their ability, so as to connect themselves with him as comrades for maintaining the cause of the Gospel, so far as they could. Thus, although they were absent in body, yet, on account of the dutifulness which they showed by every service in their power, he recognizes them as in bonds along with him. 'I have you, therefore, in my heart'; that is, sincerely and without pretence, assuredly with no slight or doubtful opinion. As what? as *partakers of grace.* In what? *In my bonds,* by which the Gospel is defended. As he acknowledged them to be such, it was right to hope well of them.

Of my grace and in the bonds. It would be ludicrous in the eyes of the world to consider a prison as a benefit from God; but if we reckon

---

[1] *In visceribus,* and so throughout Calvin's comments.

aright, it is no common honour that God confers upon us, when we suffer persecution for His truth. For it was not said in vain, 'Blessed shall ye be, when men shall afflict and harass you with all kinds of reproaches for my name's sake' (Matt. 5.11). Let us therefore remember also, that we must readily and cheerfully embrace the fellowship of the cross of Christ as a unique grace from God. To 'bonds' he adds *the defence and confirmation of the gospel*, that he may the better express the honourableness of the service which God has enjoined upon us in placing us in opposition to His enemies, to bear testimony to His Gospel. For it is as though He had entrusted to us the defence of His Gospel. And truly it was when they were armed with this considera-tion that the martyrs were able to despise all the rage of the ungodly, and to rise superior to every kind of torture. And would that there were present to the minds of all that are called to confess their faith, that they have been chosen by Christ to act as advocates in His cause! For were they sustained by such consolation, they would be more courageous than to be so easily turned aside to treacherous desertion.

Here, however, some one will inquire whether the confirmation of the Gospel depends on the steadfastness of men. I answer, that the truth of God is in itself too firm to require external support. For though we should all be liars, God nevertheless remains true. But there is no absurdity in saying that weak consciences are confirmed in it by such helps. The kind of confirmation, therefore, which Paul mentions, has a relation to men; as we learn from our own experience that the slaughter of so many martyrs has had at least this result, that the Gospel has been, as it were, sealed by them in our hearts. Hence that saying of Tertullian, that their blood is the seed of the Church; which I have imitated in a certain poem: 'But that holy blood, the champion of God's honour, will be a seed to bring forth children.'

8. *For God is my witness.* He now declares more explicitly his love for them, and to prove it, uses an oath; and that on good grounds, because we know how dear in the sight of God is the edification of His Church. It was, too, of the first importance that Paul's love should be thoroughly made known to the Philippians. For it will in no small degree win credit for the teaching, when the people are persuaded that they are loved by the teacher. He calls God as witness to the truth, for He alone is the Truth, and as witness of his affection, for He alone is the Searcher of hearts. In the expression *I long after*, he puts the species for the genus, and it is a token of love that we long after the things which are dear to us.

In the heart. He places *the heart of Christ* in opposition to carnal affection, to intimate that his love is holy and godly. For he that loves according to the flesh has respect to his own advantage, and may from time to time change his mind according to the variety of circumstances and seasons. Now he teaches us by what rule the affections of believers ought to be ordered, that, renouncing their own will, they may give the helm to Christ. And unquestionably, true love can flow only from the heart of Christ, and this should be a goad to prick us not a little, that Christ in a manner opens His heart, that so He may cherish mutual love between us.

9. *This I pray, that your love.* He returns to the prayer which he had simply touched on in one word in passing. He explains, accordingly, the sum of those things which he asked from God for them, that they also may learn to pray from his example, and may aspire to progress in those gifts. Some take the love of the Philippians for the Philippians themselves, as the illiterate are accustomed to say, 'Your reverence', 'Your lordship'. But this is absurd. For no such instance occurs in Paul, nor had such fooleries come into use. Besides, the statement would be less complete and, apart from this, the simple and natural meaning of the words suits admirably well. For the true growth of Christians is when they progress in knowledge and understanding and in love. Hence the particle *in*, according to the Hebrew idiom, is taken here for 'with', as I have also translated it, unless perhaps anyone would prefer to explain it as 'by', so as to denote the instrument or formal cause. For the more we progress in knowledge, the more ought our love to increase. The meaning then would be, 'That your love may increase according to the measure of knowledge.' *All knowledge* means what is full and complete, not a knowledge of all things.

10. *That ye may approve.* This is the definition of Christian wisdom, to know what is good or expedient, not to torture the mind with empty subtleties and speculations. For the Lord does not want His believers to employ themselves fruitlessly in learning what is of no profit. From this you may gather what you should think of the Sorbonnist theology, to which you may devote your whole life without gaining any more edification in the hope of a heavenly life or more spiritual advantage than from the demonstrations of Euclid. Even if it had taught nothing false, it well deserves to be detested in that it is a pernicious profanation of spiritual doctrine. For 'Scripture is useful', as Paul says (II Tim. 3.16), but there you will find nothing but cold chop-logic.

That ye may be sincere. This is the good which we get from knowledge, not that everyone may cunningly look after his own interests, but that we may live with a pure conscience in the sight of God.

There follows *and without offence.* The Greek word ἀπρόσκοποι is ambiguous. Chrysostom expounds it actively, that as he had desired that they should be pure and upright in the sight of God, so he now wants them to lead an honourable life in the sight of men, that they may not injure their neighbours by bad examples. This exposition I do not reject: the passive signification, however, suits the context better, in my opinion. For he desires wisdom for them, that they may with unhindered step go forward in their calling until the day of Christ. As on the other hand it happens through ignorance that we frequently slip, stumble and wander aside. And how many stumbling-blocks Satan ever and anon throws in our way, either to stop our course altogether, or to impede it, we all know from our own experience.

11. *Filled with the fruits of righteousness.* This pertains to the outward life, for a good conscience produces its fruits in works. Hence he wishes them to be fertile in good works, to the glory of God. He says that such fruits are by Christ, because they flow from the grace of Christ. For the beginning of our well-doing is when we are sanctified by His Spirit, for He rested upon Him that we might all draw of His fulness. And as Paul here uses a similitude from trees, we are wild olive-trees and unproductive, until we are engrafted into Christ, who by His living root makes us fruitbearing trees, according to that saying, 'I am the vine, ye are the branches' (John 15.1). At the same time he shows the aim: that we may serve the glory of God. For there is no life, however excellent in appearance, that is not corrupted and stinking before God, if it is not directed towards this object.

Paul's speaking here of the righteousness of works is not at all inconsistent with the free righteousness of faith. For it does not follow that there is righteousness wherever there are fruits of righteousness, inasmuch as there is no righteousness in the sight of God except full and complete obedience to the law, which is not found in any of the saints. Nevertheless they bring forth according to their measure the good and sweet fruits of righteousness; and for this reason, that, as God begins righteousness in us through the regeneration of the Spirit, so what is lacking is supplied through the remission of sins, yet so that all righteousness depends on faith.

But I would have you know, brethren, that the things which happened unto me have fallen out rather unto the progress of the gospel; so that my bonds in Christ are manifest throughout the whole Praetorium, and in all other places; and many of the brethren in the Lord, being confident through my bonds, are much more abundantly bold to speak the word of God without fear. Some indeed preach Christ even through envy and strife; and some also of good will. The one, I say, proclaim Christ of contention, not sincerely, thinking to raise up affliction to my bonds;

but the other of love, knowing that I am set for the defence of the gospel.
(12–17)

12. *But I would have you know.* We all experience in ourselves how
much the flesh is offended by the lowliness of the cross. We allow,
indeed, Christ crucified to be preached to us; but when He appears
with His cross, then, as though struck at its novelty, we either avoid
or abhor Him; and that not only in our own persons, but also in the
persons of those who deliver to us the Gospel. It may have happened
that the Philippians were somewhat discouraged at the persecution of
their apostle. And it is possible that those bad workmen, who looked
for every opportunity, however small, of doing harm, did not refrain
from triumphing over the calamity of the holy man, and so making
his Gospel contemptible. If, however, they failed in this attempt,
they might easily slander him as hated by the whole world, and at the
same time make the Philippians afraid lest, by an unfortunate associa-
tion with him, they should needlessly incur hatred among all. For
such are the usual tricks of Satan. The apostle forestalls this danger
when he states that the Gospel had been advanced by his bonds. The
aim, therefore, of this account is to encourage the Philippians, that they
may not be put off by his persecution.

13. *So that my bonds.* He puts *in Christ* for 'in the affairs', or 'in the
cause of Christ', for he means that his bonds had become famous, so
as to promote the honour of Christ. The exposition of some, 'Through
Christ', seems forced. I have also preferred 'famous' (*illustria*) to
'manifest' (*manifesta*), for they had ennobled the Gospel by their fame.
To paraphrase: 'Satan, indeed, has attempted it, and the ungodly
have thought it would turn out that the Gospel would be destroyed;
but God has frustrated these attempts and expectations. And that in
two ways; for whereas the Gospel was previously obscure and unknown, it has come to be well known; and not only so, but it has
even become notable in the Praetorium, no less than in the rest of the
city.'

The Praetorium I understand as the hall and palace of Nero, which
Fabius and writers of that age call the Augustale. For as 'praetor' was
at first a general name, and denoted all magistrates who held the chief
rule (hence it came that the dictator was called the sovereign praetor),
it consequently became customary to use the praetorium in war to
mean the tent, either of the consul, or of the leader, while in the city
it was the palace of Caesar, from the time that the Caesars took
possession of the monarchy. Apart from this, the bench of the praetor
is also called the Praetorium.

14. *Many of the brethren.* By this example, we are taught that the

troubles of the saints, suffered for the Gospel, are a ground of confidence to us. It would indeed be a dreadful spectacle, and such as might tend rather to dishearten us, if we saw nothing but the cruelty and rage of the persecutors. When, however, at the same time the hand of the Lord appears and makes His people unconquerable under the infirmity of the cross, and causes them to triumph, then relying on this, we ought to venture farther than we had been accustomed, having already a pledge of our victory in the persons of our brethren. The knowledge of this ought to overcome our fears, that we may speak boldly in the midst of dangers.

15. *Some indeed.* Here is another result of Paul's bonds, that not only were the brethren heartened to confidence by his example, some by maintaining their position, others by becoming more eager to teach, but even those who wished him evil were on another account stirred up to publish the Gospel.

16. *Some, I say, from contention.* An epexegesis,[1] in which he declares more fully the foregoing statement; for he repeats that there are two classes of men who are stirred up by his bonds to proclaim Christ. The one is motivated by contention, that is, by a depraved attitude, the other by godly zeal, for they want to maintain along with him the defence of the Gospel. The former, he says, do not proclaim Christ purely, because theirs was not a right zeal. For this does not refer to doctrine, because it is possible that the man who teaches most purely may, nevertheless, not be of a sincere mind. Now, that this impurity was in the mind and did not show itself in doctrine, may be inferred from the context. Paul assuredly would not willingly see the Gospel corrupted; yet he declares that he rejoices in the preaching of those persons, even though it was not simple or sincere.

It is asked, however, how such preaching could harm him. I answer, that many explanations are unknown to us, because we are not acquainted with the circumstances of the times. It is asked farther, 'Since the gospel can only be preached by those who understand it, what induced them to persecute the doctrine which they commended?' I answer, that ambition is blind; nay, it is a raging beast. Hence it is not surprising if false brethren snatch a weapon out of the Gospel for harassing good and godly pastors. Paul, assuredly, says nothing here of which I have not myself had experience. For there are living at this very day those who have preached the Gospel with no other design than that they might gratify the rage of the wicked by persecuting godly pastors. As to Paul's enemies, it is important to observe, if they were Jews, how mad their hatred was, so as even to forget the reason why they hated him. For while they made it their aim to destroy him,

---

[1] An addition for the sake of clarification.

they did it by promoting the Gospel, the very cause of their hostility. But they imagined, no doubt, that the cause of Christ would stand or fall with the person of one man. If, however, they were envious persons, who were carried away by ambition to thwart him, we ought to acknowledge the wonderful goodness of God, who gave such a happy outcome to their perverse efforts.

17. *That for the defence.* Those who truly loved Christ reckoned that it would be a disgrace to them if they did not associate themselves with Paul as his companions in maintaining his cause. And we must act in such a way as to give a helping hand, as far as we can, to the struggling servants of Christ. Observe, again, this expression, 'For the defence of the Gospel'. For since Christ confers upon us so great an honour, what excuse shall we have, if we are traitors to His cause, or what may we expect, if we betray it by our silence, but that He shall in return desert our cause, who is our sole Advocate, or Patron, with the Father?

What then? only that in every way, whether in pretence or in truth, Christ is proclaimed, and therein I rejoice, yea, and will rejoice. For I know that this shall turn to my salvation, through your prayer and the supply of the Spirit of Jesus Christ, according to my earnest expectation and hope, that in nothing shall I be put to shame, but that with all boldness, as always, so now also Christ shall be magnified in my body, whether by life, or by death. For to me Christ is gain in life and in death. (18-21)

18. *Only that in every way.* As the wicked outlook of those of whom he has spoken might detract from the acceptableness of the doctrine, he says that it ought to be reckoned of great importance that they nevertheless promoted the cause of the Gospel, whatever their attitude might be. For God sometimes accomplishes a wonderful work through wicked and vicious instruments. Accordingly, he says that he rejoices in a happy result of this sort; because the one thing that pleased him was to see the kingdom of Christ increasing. Just as when we heard that that impure dog Carolus was sowing the seeds of pure doctrine in many hearts at Avignon and elsewhere, we gave thanks to God, who had made use of that most profligate and worthless villain for His glory. And today we rejoice that the progress of the Gospel is advanced by many who yet had another purpose. But though Paul rejoiced in the increase of the Gospel, yet, had the matter been in his hand, he would never have ordained such ministers. We ought, therefore, to rejoice if God accomplishes anything that is good by means of the wicked; but they ought not on that account to be

either placed by us in the ministry, or looked upon as Christ's lawful ministers.

19. *For I know.* As some published the Gospel to raise hatred against Paul and kindle against him the more the rage of his enemies, he tells them beforehand that their wicked attempts will do him no harm, because the Lord will turn them to a contrary end. 'Though they plot my hurt, yet I trust that all their attempts will have no other effect but that Christ will be glorified in me; and this is salutary to me.' For it is evident from what follows, that he is not speaking of the safety of the body. But whence this confidence on the part of Paul? It is from what he teaches elsewhere (Rom. 8.28) that all things contribute to the good of God's true worshippers, even though the whole world, with the devil, its prince, should conspire together for their ruin.

Through your prayer. That he may spur them on more sharply to pray, he declares that he is confident that the Lord will give it them through their prayers. Nor does he pretend; for he who puts his help in the prayers of the saints relies on the promise of God. Nevertheless, nothing is detracted from the unmerited goodness of God, from which come our prayers and entreaties.

And the supply. Let us not suppose that, because he joins these two together, they are alike. The statement must therefore be explained in this way, 'I know that all this will turn out to my salvation, through the administration of the Spirit, you also helping by prayer'; so that the supply of the Spirit is the efficient cause, while prayer is a subordinate help. We must also observe the meaning of the Greek word, for ἐπιχορηγία is the supply of what is lacking, just as the Spirit of God pours into us everything of which we are destitute.

He calls Him, too, *the Spirit of Jesus Christ,* to signify that if we are Christians, He is common to all of us, inasmuch as He was poured upon Him in all fulness, that, according to the measure of His grace, He might give out, so far as is expedient, to each of His members.

20. *According to my expectation.* Should anyone object, 'From what do you derive that knowledge?' he answers, 'From hope.' For as it is certain that God does not on any account want to frustrate our hope, hope itself ought not to be wavering. Let then the godly reader carefully observe this adverb, 'according to', that he may be assured in his mind that it is impossible but that the Lord will match our expectation, inasmuch as it is founded on His own Word. Now, He has promised that He will never be wanting to us even in the midst of all tortures, if we are at any time called to confess His name. Let, therefore, all the godly hope after Paul's example, and they will not be put to shame.

With all confidence. We see that, in hoping, he does not indulge carnal desires, but submits his hope to the promise of God. *Christ,* he says, *will be magnified in my body, whether by life or by death.* By expressly mentioning the body, however, he means that, amongst the conflicts of the present life, he is in no wise doubtful as to the issue, for we are assured of this by God. If, therefore, we give ourselves up to the good pleasure of God, and have in our life the same object as Paul had, we hope, in whatever way, for a prosperous issue and shall no longer have occasion to fear lest any adversity befall us. For if we live and die to Him, we are His in life and in death (Rom. 14.8). He expresses the way Christ is to be magnified: by full confidence. Hence it follows that through our fault He is cast down and lowered (so far as it is in us to do this) when we give way through fear. Are not those then ashamed who reckon it a light offence to tremble in confessing the truth? But how ashamed should they be, who are so shamelessly impudent that they dare to excuse even renunciation?

He adds, *as always,* that they may confirm their faith from past experience of the grace of God. Thus, in Rom. 5.4, he says, 'Experience begets hope.'

21. *For to me.* Interpreters have hitherto, in my opinion, given a wrong translation and exposition to this passage; for they make this distinction, that Christ was life to Paul, and death was gain. But I make Christ the subject in both clauses, so that He is declared to be gain to him both in life and in death; for it is common in Greek to leave the word πρός to be understood. Besides that this meaning is less forced, it also agrees better with the foregoing statement, and contains a more complete doctrine. He asserts that it is indifferent to him, and is all one, whether he lives or dies, because, having Christ, he deems both to be *gain.* And assuredly it is Christ alone who makes us happy both in death and in life. Otherwise, if death is miserable, life is no whit happier; so that it is difficult to determine whether it is more advantageous to live or to die outside Christ. On the other hand, let Christ be with us, and He will bless our life as well as our death, so that both will be happy and desirable for us.

But if to live in the flesh, is worthwhile, what I shall choose I wot not. For I am in a strait betwixt the two, having a desire to be set free, and be with Christ; for it is far better: yet to abide in the flesh is more needful for your sake. And having this confidence, I know that I shall abide and continue with you all, for your progress and joy of faith; that your rejoicing may abound in Christ Jesus for me, by my coming to you again. (22-26)

22. *But if to live in the flesh.* As men in despair are perplexed as to

whether to prolong their life any further in miseries, or to end their troubles by death, so Paul, on the other hand, says in a spirit of contentment that he is so well prepared for death or for life, because the condition of believers in both cases is blessed, so that he is at a loss which to choose.

If it is worth while; that is, 'If I believe that there will be greater advantage from my life than from my death, I do not see which of them I ought to prefer.' He puts *to live in the flesh,* contemptuously, from comparing it with a better life.

23. *For I am in a strait.* Paul did not desire any other wages for his life than of promoting the glory of Christ and doing good to the brethren. Hence he reckons that the only value of his life is the welfare of the brethren. But for himself personally, it would be, he knows, better to die soon, because he would be with Christ. By his choice, he shows with what love he burned. It is not a question here of earthly advantages, but of spiritual benefit, which is on good grounds supremely desirable to the godly. Paul, however, as if forgetful of himself, does not merely hold himself undetermined, lest he should be inclined to his own good rather than to that of the Philippians, but at length concludes that a regard for them preponderates in his mind. And this is truly to live and die in Christ, when, with indifference to ourselves, we are carried and borne away whithersoever Christ calls us.

Having a desire to be set free and to be with Christ. These two things must be read together. For death of itself will never be desired, because such a desire conflicts with natural feeling; but it is desired for some particular reason, or with another view. Persons in despair have recourse to it because they are weary of life. Believers willingly hasten to it, because it is a deliverance from the bondage of sin, and a passing into the Kingdom of heaven. What Paul now says is this, 'I desire to die, because by this means I will arrive at union with Christ.' Believers do not cease to regard death with horror, but when they turn their eyes to that life which follows death, they easily overcome their dread by that consolation. Unquestionably, everyone that believes in Christ ought to be so courageous as to lift up his head at the mention of death, joyful at this messenger of his redemption. From this we see how many are Christians only in name, since the greater part, on hearing the name of death, are not merely alarmed but rendered almost lifeless, as though they had never heard a single word about Christ. O good conscience! how strong and effective you are! But faith is the foundation of a good conscience; more, it is itself goodness of conscience.

To be set free. This expression is to be observed. Profane men call death the destruction of man, as if he altogether perished. Paul here reminds us that death is the loosing of the soul from the body. And this he expresses better immediately afterwards, explaining what condition awaits believers after death, that they dwell with Christ. We are with Christ even in this life, inasmuch as the kingdom of God is within us, and Christ dwells in us by faith and has promised that He will be with us even unto the end of the world. But that presence we enjoy only by hope. Hence as to our senses, we are said to be absent from Him (see II Cor. 5.6). This passage will refute the mad fancy of those who dream that souls sleep when separated from the body; for Paul openly declares that we enjoy Christ's presence on being set free.

25. *And having this confidence.* Some, reckoning it absurd that the apostle should confess that he was disappointed of his expectation, think that he was afterwards freed from bonds, and travelled through many countries of the world. Their fears, however, are groundless. For the saints are accustomed to regulate their hope according to the Word of God, so as not to anticipate more than God has promised. Thus, when they have a sure token of God's will, they rely also upon a sure persuasion, which admits of no doubt. Of this nature is the assurance of the perpetual remission of sins, of the aid of the Spirit for the grace of final perseverance (as it is called), and of the resurrection of the flesh. Of this nature, too, was the assurance of the prophets respecting their prophecies. As to other things, they hope only conditionally, and hence they subject all events to the providence of God, who, they allow, sees more clearly than they. *To remain* means here to stay for a little while. 'To continue' means to remain for a long time.

26. *That your glorying.* Where he says ἐν ἐμοί, I have translated it *as to me*, because the preposition is used twice, but in different senses. No one assuredly will deny that I have faithfully expressed Paul's mind. The rendering of some, 'through Christ', I do not approve of. For 'in Christ' is put in place of 'according to Christ', or 'Christianly', to show that it was a holy kind of glorying. For otherwise we are commanded to glory in God alone. Hence the malevolent might object against Paul, 'How is it lawful for the Philippians to glory in you?' He anticipates this calumny by saying that they will do this according to Christ, glorying in a servant of Christ to the glory of the Lord, and that for the sake of the doctrine rather than of the individual, and in opposition to the false apostles; just as David, by comparing himself with hypocrites, boasts of his righteousness.

Only let your manner of life be worthy of the gospel of Christ: that whether I come and see you, or be absent, I may hear of you, that ye stand fast in one spirit, with one soul striving together for the faith of the gospel; and in nothing affrighted by your adversaries: which is to them an evident token of perdition, but to you of salvation, and that from God. Because to you it hath been granted in the behalf of Christ, not only to believe on him, but also to suffer for his sake; having the same conflict which ye saw in me, and now hear to be in me. (27–30)

27. *Only let.* We use this form of expression, when we want to pass on to a new subject. Thus it is as though he had said, 'But the Lord will provide for me; but as for you. . . . Whatever may happen to me, see that you yourselves go forward in the right course.' When he speaks of a pure and honourable conversation as being worthy of the Gospel, he hints on the other hand that those who live otherwise harm the Gospel.

That whether I come. As Paul's Greek phrase is elliptical, I have made use of 'I see', instead of 'seeing'. If you do not like this, you may supply the principal verb, 'I may learn', in this sense: 'Whether, when I shall come and see you, or whether I shall, when absent, hear about your condition, I may learn either way, by being present or by a messenger, that you stand in one spirit.' We need not, however, worry over the words, when the meaning is plain.

Stand in one spirit. This is one of the main virtues of the Church, and hence it is the one means of preserving its healthiness, inasmuch as it is ruined by dissensions. But although Paul wanted by this antidote to provide against novel and strange doctrines, yet he requires a twofold unity, of spirit and soul. The first is, that we agree among ourselves; the second, that we be united in heart. For when these two terms are connected, spirit denotes the understanding, and soul the will. Moreover, agreement comes first in order; and then from it springs union of will.

Striving together for the faith. The strongest bond of concord is when we have to fight together under the same banner; for this has often been the occasion of reconciling even the greatest enemies. Hence, in order that he may confirm unity among the Philippians, he tells them that they are fellow-soldiers, who, having a common enemy and a common warfare, ought to have their minds united together in a holy league. The Greek phrase which Paul used is ambiguous. The Vulgate renders it *collaborantes fidei* (labouring together with the faith). Erasmus has *adiuvantes fidem* (helping the faith), as if they gave help to the faith to the best of their ability. As, however, the dative in Greek is put for the ablative of instrumentality (that language having no ablative), I have no doubt that the apostle's meaning is this: 'Let the faith of the Gospel unite you, more especially as it is a common armour against the same enemy.' In this way the particle σύν, which

others refer to faith, I refer to the Philippians, and this is better, if I
am not mistaken. First, everyone knows how effectual an inducement
it is to concord, when we have to fight together; and further, we
know that in the spiritual warfare we are armed with the shield of
faith for repelling the enemy; more, faith is both our suit of armour
and our victory. Hence he added this clause, to show what is the end
of a godly union. The wicked also conspire together for evil, but
their agreement is accursed. Let us, therefore, fight with one mind
under the banner of faith.

28. *And in nothing affrighted.* The second thing that he commends
to the Philippians is fortitude of mind, that they may not be upset by
the rage of their adversaries. At that time the most cruel persecutions
raged almost everywhere, because Satan strove with all his might to
check the commencement of the Gospel, and was the more enraged
impotently in proportion as Christ put forth powerfully the grace of
His Spirit. He therefore exhorts the Philippians to stand undaunted
and not be alarmed.

Which is to them an evident token. This is the proper meaning of the
Greek word, and there was no compulsive reason for others to render
it 'cause'. For the wicked, when they wage war against the Lord,
give a token of their ruin, already by a trial-fight, as it were, and the
more fiercely they rejoice over the godly, the more do they prepare
themselves for ruin. The Scripture assuredly nowhere teaches that
the afflictions which the saints endure from the wicked are the cause
of their salvation, but Paul elsewhere also calls them a manifest token
or proof (II Thess. 1.5), and instead of ἔνδειξιν, which we have here
he there uses ἔνδειγμα. This, therefore, is an extraordinary consolation,
that when we are assailed and harassed by our enemies, we have
evidence of our salvation. For persecutions are seals of adoption to
the children of God, if they endure them with fortitude and calmness.
The wicked give a token of their condemnation, because they stumble
against a stone by which they shall be annihilated.

And that from God. This is restricted to the last clause, that a taste
for the grace of God may allay the bitterness of the cross. No one
will naturally perceive in the cross a sign or evidence of salvation, for
they are apparently contrary. Hence Paul recalls the Philippians to
another consideration, that God by His blessing turns into an occasion
of salvation things that might otherwise seem to make us miserable.
He proves it from this, that the bearing of the cross is the gift of God.
Now it is certain that all the gifts of God are salutary to us. 'To you,'
he says, 'it is given, not only to believe in Christ, but also to suffer for
Him. Hence even the sufferings themselves are testimonies of the
grace of God; and, since it is so, you have from this source a token of

salvation.' Oh, if this conviction were fixed in our minds, that persecutions are to be reckoned among God's benefits, what progress would be made in the doctrine of godliness! And yet, what is more certain than that it is the highest honour of the Divine grace, that we suffer for His name either reproach, or imprisonment, or miseries, or tortures, or even death, for in that case He decorates us with His insignia. But more will be found who will order God and His gifts to be gone, rather than embrace the cross readily when it is offered to them. Woe, then, to our stupidity!

29. *To believe.* He wisely joins faith with the cross by an inseparable connexion, that the Philippians may know that they have been called to the faith of Christ on condition that they endure persecutions for His Name; as though he had said that their adoption can no more be separated from the cross than Christ can be torn asunder from Himself. Here Paul clearly testifies that faith, as well as constancy in enduring persecutions, is a free gift of God. And certainly the knowledge of God is a wisdom too high for us to reach by our own acuteness, and our weakness shows itself in daily experiences, when God withdraws His hand for a little while. That he may the better declare that both are free, he says expressly that they are given to us for Christ's sake, or at least on the basis of Christ's grace; by which he excludes every idea of merit.

This passage is also against the scholastic dogma that subsequent gifts of grace are rewards for our merit in making a right use of previous ones. I do not deny, indeed, that God rewards the right use of His gifts of grace by bestowing grace more largely upon us, provided only you do not place merit, as they do, in opposition to His free liberality and the merit of Christ.

30. *Having the same conflict.* He confirms also by his own example what he had said, and this adds no little authority to his doctrine. By the same means, too, he shows them that there is no reason for them to be troubled by his bonds, if they behold the outcome of the conflict.

CHAPTER TWO

*If there is therefore any consolation[1] in Christ, if any comfort of love, if
any fellowship of the Spirit, if any bowels and mercies, fulfil ye my joy,
that ye think the same thing, having the same love, being of one accord,
of one mind; doing nothing through strife or vain-glory; but in lowliness
each esteeming other better than himself; not looking every man to his
own things, but every man also to the things of others.* (1-4)

1. *If there is therefore.* There is great tenderness in this exhortation,
in which by all means he entreats the Philippians mutually to cherish
harmony among themselves, lest, if they are rent asunder by inward
contentions, they should be exposed to the impostures of the false
apostles. For in disagreements there is invariably a door opened for
Satan to disseminate wicked teaching, whereas agreement is the best
defence for repelling it.

As the word παράκλησις is often taken as 'exhortation', the commencement of the passage might be expounded in this way: 'If an
exhortation which is delivered in the name and by the authority of
Christ has any weight with you.' The other meaning, however,
corresponds better with the context: 'If there is among you *any consolation of Christ,* by means of which you may alleviate my griefs, and
if you would afford me *any consolation* and relief, which you assuredly
owe me out of love; if you consider that *fellowship of the Spirit,* which
ought to make us all one; if any feeling of humanity and mercy resides
in you, to move you to relieve my miseries, fulfil ye, etc.' From this
we may infer how great a blessing is unity in the Church, and with
what care pastors should attend to it. We must also at the same time
notice how he humbles himself by beseechingly imploring their pity,
when he could have used his paternal authority to demand respect
from them as his sons. He knew how to exercise authority when it
was necessary; but at present he prefers to use entreaties, because he
knew that these would be better fitted to gain an entrance into their
affections, and because he was aware that he had to do with docile
and compliant people. In like manner the pastor must be ready to
assume different characters for the sake of the Church.

2. *Fulfil ye my joy.* Here we may see how little care he had for
himself, so long as all went well with the Church of Christ. He was
kept shut up in prison and bound with chains; he was reckoned guilty

---

[1] *Margin: or* exhortation.

244

on a capital charge; before his eyes were tortures, near at hand was the executioner; yet none of this prevented him from rejoicing wholeheartedly, provided he sees that it is well with the churches. Now he reckons the chief need for the prosperous condition of the Church is for mutual agreement and brotherly harmony to reign there. Thus the Psalm teaches us similarly, that our crowning joy is the remembrance of Jerusalem (Ps. 137.6). But if this were the perfection of Paul's joy, the Philippians would have been worse than cruel if they had tortured the mind of this holy man with a twofold anguish by disagreement among themselves.

That ye think the same thing. The sum is this—that they be united in thought and will. For he places agreement in doctrine and mutual love; and afterwards, repeating the same thing, in my opinion, he tells them to be of one mind, and to think the same thing. The expression τὸ αὐτό implies that they must accommodate themselves to each other. Hence the beginning of love is harmony of outlook; but that is not sufficient, unless men's hearts are at the same time joined together in love. Yet it would not be absurd to translate it thus: 'That ye may be of the same mind, so as to have mutual love, to be of one accord, of one mind'; for participles are sometimes used in place of infinitives. I have followed, however, what seemed to me less forced.

3. *Nothing through strife.* These are two most dangerous pests for disturbing the peace of the Church. 'Strife' is aroused when everyone wants to guard obstinately his own opinion; and when it has once begun to rage it rushes headlong along the road it has entered on. 'Vain-glory' tickles men's minds, so that everyone is delighted with his own inventions. Hence the only way of guarding against dissensions is when we avoid strifes by deliberating and acting peacefully, especially if we are not motivated by ambition. For ambition is a fan for all strifes. *Vain-glory* means any glory of the flesh; for what have men to glory of in themselves that is not vanity?

But by humility. For both diseases he brings forward one remedy, submission, and with good reason, for it is the mother of modesty, the effect of which is that, yielding up our own right, we defer to others, and are not easily thrown into disorder. He defines true humility: when everyone esteems himself less than others. Now, if anything in our whole life is difficult, this is the worst. Hence it is not surprising if humility is so rare a virtue. For, as one says, 'Everyone has in himself the mind of a king, by claiming everything for himself.' What pride! Afterwards from a foolish admiration of ourselves arises contempt of the brethren. And so far are we from what Paul here enjoins, that one can hardly endure that others should be on the same level; for there is no one that is not eager to be on top.

245

But it is asked, how is it possible that one who really is superior to others can reckon those to be above him whom he knows to be far beneath him? I answer, that this altogether depends on a right estimate of God's gifts and our own infirmities. For however anyone may possess outstanding endowments, he ought to consider that they have not been conferred upon him that he might be self-complacent, that he might exalt himself or even esteem himself. Let him instead employ himself in correcting and detecting his faults, and he will have abundant cause for humility. In others, on the other hand, he will regard with honour whatever there is of excellence, and will in love bury their faults. The man who will observe this rule, will have no difficulty in preferring others before himself. And this, too, Paul meant when he added that they ought not to have every one a regard to themselves, but to their neighbours, or that they ought not to be devoted to themselves. Hence it is quite possible that a godly man, even though aware that he is superior, may nevertheless hold others in greater esteem.

Have this mind in you, which was also in Christ Jesus; who, being in the form of God, would not have thought it robbery to be equal with God; but emptied himself, taking the form of a servant, and was made in the likeness of men: and was found in fashion as a man. He humbled himself, I say, becoming obedient unto death, even the death of the cross. Wherefore also God highly exalted him, and gave him the name which is above every name: that in the name of Jesus every knee should bow, of things in heaven, and things on earth, and things of the world below; and that every tongue should confess that Jesus is Lord, to the glory of God the Father. (5-11)

5. *Have this mind.* He now commends humility from the example of Christ, to which he had before exhorted them in words. There are, however, two clauses, in the first of which he persuades us to imitate Christ, because this is the rule of life: in the second, he invites us to it, as being the road by which we attain true glory. Hence he exhorts every one to have the same attitude that was in Christ. He afterwards declares what a pattern of humility has been set before us in Christ. I have kept the passive form of the verb, though I do not disapprove the translation given by others, because there is no difference in meaning. I merely wished readers to see the very form of expression which Paul employed.

6. *Being in the form of God.* This is not a comparison of similarities, but of greater and less. Christ's humility consisted in abasing Himself from the highest pinnacle of glory to the lowest ignominy: our humility consists in not exalting ourselves by a false estimation. He

yielded voluntarily: all that is required of us is that we do not assume
to ourselves more than we ought. Hence he sets out with this, that,
inasmuch as He was in the form of God, He reckoned it not unlawful
for Him to show Himself in that form; yet He emptied Himself.
Since, then, the Son of God descended from so great a height, how
absurd that we, who are nothing, should be uplifted with pride!

The form of God means here His majesty. For as a man is known
by the appearance of his form, so the majesty which shines forth in
God is His figure. Of if you prefer a more apt similitude, the form
of a king is the equipage and magnificence which shows him to be a
king, his sceptre, his crown, his robe, his attendants, his judgment-
throne, and other emblems of royalty. The form of a consul was his
purple-bordered toga, his ivory chair, his lictors with rods and hatchets.
Christ, then, before the creation of the world, was in the form of God,
because from the beginning He had His glory with the Father, as He
says in John 17.5. For in the wisdom of God, before He assumed our
flesh, there was nothing mean or contemptible, but a magnificence
worthy of God. Being such as He was, He could with perfect right
show Himself equal with God; but He did not manifest Himself to
be what He was, nor did He openly assume in the view of men what
was His of right.

Thought it not robbery. There would have been no wrong done
even if He had appeared *in His equality with God.* For when he says,
he would not have thought, it is as though he had said, 'He knew, indeed,
that this was lawful and right for him,' that we might know that His
abasement was voluntary, not of necessity. Hitherto it has been
translated in the indicative, 'he thought', but the context requires the
subjunctive. It is also quite usual for Paul to employ the past indicative
for the subjunctive, by leaving the so-called potential particle ἄν, to
be supplied, as in Rom. 9.3, ηὐχόμην, for 'I would have wished'; and
in I Cor. 2.8, εἰ γὰρ ἔγνωσαν, 'if they had known'. Everyone, however,
will see that Paul has treated hitherto of Christ's glory, which tends to
enhance His abasement. Accordingly he mentions, not what Christ
did, but what it was allowable for Him to do.

Moreover, he is utterly blind who does not perceive that His
eternal divinity is clearly set forth in these words. Nor is Erasmus
modest enough in attempting, by his quibbles, to explain away this
passage, as well as others like it. He acknowledges everywhere that
Christ is God; but how does his orthodox confession help me if my
faith is not supported by any Scripture authority? I acknowledge,
certainly, that Paul does not mention here Christ's divine essence; but
it does not follow from this, that the passage is not sufficient to overthrow the impiety of the Arians, who pretended that Christ was a

created God, and inferior to the Father, and denied that He was con-
substantial. For where can there be equality with God without
robbery, except only in the essence of God? For God always remains
the same who cried by Isaiah, 'I live; I will not give my glory to
another' (Isa. 48.11).

Form means figure or appearance, as they commonly say. This, too,
I readily grant; but will there be found, apart from God, such a form,
that is neither false nor forged? As, then, God is known by His
powers, and His works are witnesses of His eternal divinity (Rom.
1.20), so Christ's divine essence is rightly proved from Christ's majesty,
which He possessed equally with the Father before He humbled
Himself. As to myself, at least, not all the devils would wrest this
passage from me, inasmuch as there is in God a most solid argument
from His glory to His essence, which two things are inseparable.

7. *Emptied himself.* This emptying is the same as the abasement,
as to which we shall see afterwards. The expression, however, is
used ἐμφατικοτέρως for being brought to nothing. Christ, indeed,
could not renounce His divinity, but He kept it concealed for a time,
that under the weakness of the flesh it might not be seen. Hence He
laid aside His glory in the view of men, not by lessening, but by con-
cealing (*supprimendo*) it.

It is asked, whether he did so as man? Erasmus agrees. But where
was the form of God before He became man? Hence we must reply,
that Paul speaks of the whole Christ, as He is God manifested in the
flesh, but, nevertheless, this emptying belongs only to His humanity;
as if I should say of man, 'Man being mortal, he is quite senseless if he
thinks of nothing but the world,' I refer indeed to the whole man; but
I ascribe mortality only to a part of him, namely, to the body. As,
then, Christ is one Person consisting of two natures, it is with right
that Paul says that He who was the Son of God, in reality equal to
God, nevertheless refrained from His glory when in the flesh He
manifested Himself in the appearance of a servant.

It is asked, secondly, how He can be said to be emptied, who,
nevertheless, proved Himself throughout by miracles and powers to
be the Son of God, and in whom, as John testifies, there was always
to be seen a glory worthy of the Son of God? (John 1.14). I answer,
that the abasement of the flesh was, nevertheless, like a veil, by which
His divine majesty was covered. This was why He did not want His
transfiguration to be made public until after His resurrection (Matt.
17.9); and when He perceives that the hour of His death is approaching,
He says, 'Father, glorify thy Son' (John 17.1). Hence, too, Paul
teaches elsewhere that He was declared to be the Son of God by His
resurrection (Rom. 1.4). And again, in another place (II Cor. 13.4),

that He suffered through the weakness of the flesh. In fine, the Image of God shone forth in Christ in such a manner that He was nevertheless abased in outward appearance and brought to nothing in the estimation of men; for He bore the form of a servant, and had assumed our nature, expressly that He might be the Servant of the Father, nay, even of men. For Paul calls Him the Minister of the circumcision (Rom. 15.8); and He Himself testifies of Himself, that He came to minister (Matt. 20.28); and the same thing had long before been foretold by Isaiah, 'Behold my servant, etc.' (42.1).

In the likeness of men. Γενόμενος is equivalent here to *constitutus* (having been made or appointed). For Paul means that He had been reduced to the level of mankind, so that in appearance He differed nothing from the common condition of mankind. The Marcionites perverted this declaration to prove the phantom of which they dreamed. They can, however, be refuted without much ado, inasmuch as Paul is treating here simply of the manner in which Christ manifested Himself, or the condition in which He lived when in the world. Even he who is truly man will nevertheless be reckoned unlike others if he conducts himself as if he were exempt from the conditions of others. Paul declares that it was not so with Christ; but that He lived in such a way that He seemed a man among the number of men, and yet He was very different from man, although He was truly man. The Marcionites therefore were completely childish, in drawing an argument from similarity of condition to deny reality of nature.

Found here means known or seen. For he treats, as has been said, of estimation. In other words, as he had affirmed previously that He was truly God, equal to the Father, so he here states that He was reckoned as abject and of the common rank. We must always keep in mind what I said a little ago, that such submission was voluntary.

8. *He became obedient.* Even this was immense humility, that from being Lord He became a servant; but he says that He went farther than this, because, while He was not only immortal but the Lord of life and death, He nevertheless became obedient to His Father, even so far as to undergo death. This was extreme abasement, especially when we consider the kind of death, which he immediately adds to emphasize it. For by dying in this way He was not only covered with ignominy in the sight of men, but also accursed in the sight of God. It is assuredly such an example of humility as ought to absorb the attention of all men; it is impossible to explain it in words suitable to its greatness.

9. *Wherefore God hath highly exalted.* By adding consolation, he shows that abasement, to which the human mind is averse, is in the highest degree desirable. There is no one, it is true, but will acknow-

ledge that it is a reasonable thing that is required from us, when we are exhorted to imitate Christ. This consideration, however, moves us to imitate Him the more cheerfully, when we hear that nothing is better for us than to be formed to His image. Now, that all are happy who, along with Christ, voluntarily humble themselves, he shows by His example; for from the most abject condition He was exalted to the sublimest height. Every one therefore that humbles himself will in like manner be exalted. Who will now refuse submission, by which he will ascend into the glory of the heavenly Kingdom?

This passage has given occasion to Sophists (or rather they have seized it) to allege that Christ merited first for Himself, and afterwards for others. First, even though they had said nothing false, we ought to avoid such profane speculations as obscure the grace of Christ, in imagining that He came for any other reason than for our salvation. Who does not see that it is a suggestion of Satan, that Christ suffered on the cross that He might acquire for Himself, by the merit of His work, what He did not possess? For the Holy Spirit wants us in the death of Christ, to see, taste, reckon, feel and acknowledge only God's unmixed goodness, and Christ's great and inestimable love towards us, that, regardless of Himself, He spent Himself and His life for our sakes. Whenever Scripture speaks of the death of Christ, it determines its advantage and price; that by it we are redeemed, reconciled to God, restored to righteousness, cleansed from our pollutions, life is procured for us, and the gate of life opened. Who, then, will deny that it is at the instigation of Satan that they maintain that the chief fruit is in Christ Himself, that He thought of Himself before us, that He merited glory for Himself before salvation for us?

More, I deny the truth of what they allege, and I say that they impiously pervert Paul's word to establish their falsehood. For that the inferential expression denotes here a consequence rather than a reason, appears from this, that it would otherwise follow that a man could merit divine honours and acquire the very throne of God; which is not merely absurd, but even dreadful to speak of. For what exaltation of Christ does the apostle here refer to? It is, that everything may be accomplished in Him that God claims for Himself alone in Isaiah. Hence the glory of God and the majesty so peculiar to Him that it cannot be transferred to another, will be the reward of human work.

Again, if they should press the language, without regard to the absurdity, the reply will be easy: that He has been given us by the Father in such a way that His whole life is a mirror that is set before us. As, then, a mirror is bright, yet not for itself, but so that it may be useful and profitable to others, so Christ did not seek or receive anything for Himself, but everything for us. For what need, I ask, had he, who was equal with the Father, of a new exaltation? Let godly readers, then, learn to detest the Sorbonnist Sophists with their twisted speculations.

Gave him the name. Name here is put for dignity; which is quite common in all languages: '*iacet sine nomine truncus*—he lies a headless corpse without a name.' The mode of expression, however, is especially common in Scripture. It means therefore that supreme power was given to Christ, and that He was placed in the highest rank of honour, so that there is no dignity found either in heaven or in earth equal to His. Hence it follows that this Name is divine. This, too, he explains by quoting the words of Isaiah, where the prophet, treating of the spreading of the worship of God throughout the whole world, introduces God as speaking thus: 'I live: every knee shall bow to me, and every tongue shall swear to me,' etc. (Isa. 45.23). Now it is certain that adoration is meant here, which belongs peculiarly to God alone. I am aware that some philosophize with subtlety on the name 'Jesus', as though it were derived from the ineffable name Jehovah. In the reasons, however, which they advance, I find no solidity. As for me, I have no pleasure in empty subtleties, and it is dangerous to trifle in such a great matter. Besides, who does not see that it is forced, and anything but a genuine exposition, when Paul speaks of Christ's whole majesty, to restrict his meaning to two syllables, as if any one were to investigate the basis of the word 'Alexander', in order to find there the greatness of the name that Alexander acquired for himself. Their subtlety, therefore, is insubstantial, and the contrivance is foreign to Paul's intention. But worse than ridiculous are the Sorbonnic Sophists, who infer from the present passage that we ought to bow the knee whenever the name Jesus is pronounced, as though it were a magic word which had complete power included in its sound. Paul, on the contrary, speaks of the honour that is to be rendered to the Son of God, not to syllables.

10. *Every knee should bow.* Though men also are venerated by this rite, there is nevertheless no doubt that what is here spoken of is that adoration which is proper to God, of which the sign is the bending of the knee. As to this, we ought to notice that God is to be worshipped, not only with the inward affection of the heart, but also by outward profession, if we would render Him what is His own. Hence, on the other hand, when He would describe His genuine worshippers, He says that they have not bowed the knee to the image of Baal (I Kings 19.18).

But here the question arises, whether this pertains to Christ's divinity or humanity. For either of the two is not without inconsistency, inasmuch as nothing new could be given to His divinity; and

His humanity in itself, viewed separately, by no means possesses such exaltation that it should be adored as God. I answer, that this, like many other things, is affirmed of Christ's entire Person, as He was God manifested in the flesh (I Tim. 3.16). For He did not abase Himself either as to His humanity alone, or as to His divinity alone, but inasmuch as, clothed in our flesh, He hid under its infirmity. So again, God exalted His Son in the same flesh in which He had lived in the world abject and obscure to the highest rank of honour, that He may sit at His right hand.

But Paul seems inconsistent; for in Rom. 14.11 he quotes this same passage, when he wants to prove that Christ will one day be the judge of the living and the dead. Now, it would not be apposite to that subject, if it were already accomplished, as he here declares. I answer, that the nature of the kingdom of Christ is that it every day grows and improves, but perfection is not yet attained, nor will be until the final day of judgment. Thus both are true, that all things are now subject to Christ, and yet that this subjection will not be complete until the day of the resurrection, because that which is now only begun will then be completed. Hence, it is not without reason that this prophecy is applied in different ways at different times, as also all other prophecies of the reign of Christ do not restrict it to one particular time, but describe it in its entire course. From this, however, we infer that Christ is that eternal God who spoke by Isaiah.

Things in heaven, things on earth, things of the world below. Since Paul subjects to Christ all things from heaven to hell, Papists trifle childishly when they infer purgatory from his words. Their reasoning, however, is this, that devils are so far from bowing the knee to Christ, that they are in every way rebellious against Him, and stir up others to rebellion. As if it were not written that they tremble at the mere mention of God (James 2.19). What, then, when they come before the judgment seat of Christ? I confess, indeed, that they are not, and never will be, subject of their own accord and by cheerful submission; but Paul is not speaking here of voluntary obedience. In fact, we can retort on them in ἀντιστρέφον,[1] like this: 'The fire of purgatory, according to them, is temporary, and will be done away at the day of judgment. Hence this passage cannot be understood of purgatory, because Paul elsewhere declares that this prophecy will not be fulfilled until Christ shall appear in judgment.' Who does not see that they are worse than children in these disgusting frivolities?

11. *To the glory of God the Father.* It could also be read, 'in the glory', because the particle εἰς is often used in place of ἐν. I prefer, however, to retain its proper signification, in this sense, that as the

---

[1] Rejoinder.

majesty of God has been manifested to men through Christ, so it shines forth in Christ, and the Father is glorified in the Son. See John chapters 5 and 17, and you will have an exposition of this passage.

So then, my beloved, as ye have always obeyed, not as in my presence only, but now much more in my absence, work out your own salvation with fear and trembling: for it is God which worketh in you, both to will and to work, for his good pleasure. Do all things without mur-murings and disputings; that ye may be such as none can complain of, and sons of God, sincere, unreprovable, in the midst of a crooked and perverse generation, among whom shine as luminaries in the world: upholding the word of life, to my glory in the day of Christ, that I did not run in vain, neither labour in vain. (12-16)

12. *So then, etc.* He concludes the whole of the preceding exhortation with a general statement, that they should humble themselves under the Lord's hand. For that will easily bring it to pass, that, laying aside all fierceness, they will be gentle and kind to each other. This is the only befitting way in which the human mind may learn gentleness, when instead of pleasing himself in his hiding-places, he examines himself in comparison with God.

As ye have always obeyed. He commends their previous obedience, that he may encourage them the more to persevere. As, however, it is the part of hypocrites to approve themselves before other eyes, but so soon as they are out of sight, to indulge themselves more freely, as if every reason for reverence and fear were removed, he admonishes them not to show themselves obedient only in his sight, but also, and even much more, in his absence. For if he were present, he could stimulate and urge them on by continued admonitions. Now, therefore, when their teacher is far from them, they need to urge themselves on.

With fear and trembling. He wants the Philippians to testify and approve their obedience by being submissive and humble. Now the source of humility is to know how wretched we are, and devoid of all good. To this he calls them in this statement. For whence comes pride, but from the assurance which blind confidence produces, when we are pleased with ourselves, and are more puffed up with confidence in our own strength, than resting upon the grace of God. In contrast to this vice is the fear to which he exhorts. Now, although exhortation comes before doctrine in the context, it is after it in arrangement, inasmuch as it is derived from it. I shall begin, accordingly, with doctrine.

13. *It is God which worketh.* This is the true artillery (*machina*) for destroying all haughtiness; this is the sword for killing all pride, when

we hear that we are utterly nothing, and can do nothing, except through the grace of God alone. I mean supernatural grace, which comes forth from the Spirit of regeneration. For, considered as men, we already 'are, and live and move in God' (Acts 17.28). But Paul reasons here of a movement different from that universal one. Let us now see how much he ascribes to God, and what he leaves to us.

There are, in any action, two principal parts, the will, and the effective power. Both of these he ascribes wholly to God; what more remains to us to glory in? Nor is there any doubt that this division has the same force as if Paul had expressed the whole in a single word. For the will is the foundation; the effecting of it is the top of the building completed. And he has expressed much more than if he had said that God is the author of the beginning and of the end. For in that case the Sophists would have quibbled that something between the two was left to men. But as it is, what will they find that is in any degree our own? They toil hard in their schools to reconcile free-will with the grace of God. Such a free-will, I mean, as they conceive of, which can turn by its own movement and have a peculiar and separate capacity, by which it can co-operate with the grace of God. I do not dispute as to the name, but as to the thing itself. In order, therefore, that free-will may harmonize with grace, they divide it in such a way that God restores in us a free choice, by which we can will aright. Thus they agree that we have received from God the power of willing aright, but assign to men a good will. Paul, however, declares this to be a work of God, without any exception. For he does not say that our hearts are simply turned or stirred up, or that the weakness of a good will is helped, but that a good will is wholly the work of God.

Now, when they slander us that we make men like stones when we teach that they have nothing good except from pure grace, they act shamelessly. For we acknowledge that we have a will from nature; but as it is evil through the corruption of sin, it begins to be good only when it has been reformed by God. Nor do we say that a man does anything good without willing it, but only when his inclination is ruled by the Spirit of God. Hence, in so far as concerns this part, we see that the whole is ascribed to God, and that what the Sophists teach us is frivolous, that grace is offered to us and placed, as it were, in our midst, that we may embrace it if we choose. For if God did not work in us efficaciously, He could not be said to effect in us a good will. The same must be said of the second part. 'God', he says, 'is ἐνεργῶν ἐνεργεῖν.' He brings, therefore, to perfection those godly affections which He has inspired in us, that they may not be ineffectual, as He promises by Ezekiel, 'I will cause them to walk in my commandments' (Ezek. 11.20). From this we infer that perseverance, also, is His pure gift.

For his good pleasure. Some interpret it 'the good intention of the mind'. I refer it rather to God, and understand by it His benevolent attitude, which is commonly called *beneplacitum*, good pleasure. For the Greek word is more frequently employed in this sense; and the context requires it. For Paul wants to ascribe everything to God and to take everything from us. Accordingly, not satisfied with having attributed to God the effect both of good will and of action, he ascribes both to His free mercy. By this means he shuts out the contrivance of the Sophists as to subsequent grace, which they imagine to be the reward of merit. Hence he teaches that the whole course of our life, if we live aright, is directed by God, and that, too, from His free goodness.

With fear and trembling. From this Paul deduces an exhortation, that they must with fear work out their own salvation. He conjoins, in his usual way, fear and trembling, for the sake of emphasis, to denote serious and anxious fear. He, accordingly, drives away drowsiness as well as security. By the term *work* he reproves our indolence, which is always ingenious in seeking success. Now it seems as if it had in the grace of God a pleasant encouragement; for if He works in us, why should we not rest at ease? The Holy Spirit, however, tells us that He wishes to work in living organs; but He immediately represses arrogance by commending fear and trembling.

The inference, also, is to be carefully noted: 'You have', he says, 'all things from God; therefore be careful and humble.' For there is nothing that should train us more to modesty and fear than when we hear that it is by the grace of God alone that we stand, and that we shall instantly collapse if He even in the slightest degree withdraws His hand. Self-confidence produces carelessness and wildness. We know from experience that all who confide in their own strength grow insolent through arrogance, and at the same time, sleep in carelessness. The remedy for both evils is, when, distrusting ourselves, we depend entirely on God alone. And assuredly, that man has made good progress in the knowledge both of the grace of God and of his own weakness, who is aroused from carelessness and diligently seeks God's help; while those that are puffed up with confidence in their own strength must necessarily be at the same time drunken in their security. Hence it is a shameless calumny that the Papists level against us, that in extolling the grace of God and putting down free-will, we make men lazy, shake off the fear of God and destroy all concern. But readers will see that Paul finds his matter of exhortation here, not in the doctrine of the Papists, but in ours. '*God*', says he, '*works all things*

in you; therefore submit to Him with fear.' I do not, indeed, deny
that there are many who, hearing that there is in us no good, indulge
themselves the more freely in their vices. But I deny that this is the
fault of the doctrine, which, when received as it ought to be, produces
carefulness in our hearts.

The Papists, however, pervert this passage so as to shake the assurance of faith, for the man that trembles is unsure. They, accordingly,
take Paul's words as if we ought, during our whole life, to waver as
to confidence of salvation. But unless we want Paul to contradict
himself, he does not by any means exhort us to hesitation here, inasmuch as he everywhere recommends confidence and πληροφορίαν.[1]
The solution, however, is easy, if anyone seeks the true meaning
without contention. There are two kinds of fear; the one produces
anxiety along with humility; the other hesitation. The former is
opposed to fleshly carelessness and laziness, as well as to arrogance;
the latter to assurance of faith. Further, we must observe, that, as
believers repose with assurance upon the grace of God, so, when they
turn their eyes to their own frailty, they do not by any means sleep
securely, but are stirred up to prayer by fear of dangers. Yet, so far
is this fear from disturbing tranquillity of conscience and shaking
confidence, that it rather confirms it. For distrust of ourselves leads us
to lean more boldly upon the mercy of God. And this is what Paul's
words import, for he requires nothing from the Philippians but that
they submit themselves to God with true self-renunciation.

Work out your own salvation. As Pelagians of old, so Papists today
arrogantly claim this passage, to extoll man's power. More, when
the preceding statement is objected to them, 'It is God that worketh
in us, etc.', they immediately ward it off with this shield (so to speak),
'Work out your own salvation.' Inasmuch, then, as the work is
ascribed to God and man in common, they assign half to each. In
short, from the word 'work' they derive free-will; from the term
'salvation' the merit of eternal life. I answer, that *salvation* is taken
to mean the entire course of our calling, and that this term includes
all things by which God accomplishes that perfection, to which He has
determined us by His free election. This no one will deny, that is not
obstinate and impudent. We are said to perfect it, when, governed
by the Holy Spirit, we aspire after the blessed life. It is God who calls
us and offers us salvation; it is our part to embrace by faith what He
gives, and by obedience to respond to His calling. But we have
neither from ourselves. Hence we act only when He has prepared us
for acting.

The word he uses properly signifies 'to carry through to the end'.

---

[1] Full assurance.

But we must keep in mind what I have said, that Paul does not reason here as to how far our ability extends, but simply teaches that God acts in us in such a manner, that He does not allow us to be inactive, but exercises us diligently, having moved us by His secret impulse.

14. *Without murmurings.* These are fruits of the humility to which he had exhorted them. For every man that has learned carefully to submit himself to God, ascribing nothing to himself, will also behave quietly among men. When everyone pleases himself, two faults prevail: they contradict one another; and this leads to open contentions. He adds, thirdly, that they must give no occasion to others of complaint, a thing which is wont to arise from excessive peevishness. It is true that hatred is not always to be feared; but care must be taken that we do not make ourselves odious through our own fault, so that the saying should be fulfilled in us, 'They hated me without a cause' (Ps. 35.19). If, however, anyone would extend it farther, I do not object. For murmurings and disputations spring up, whenever anyone, devoted to himself beyond measure, gives others cause for complaint. In fact, this expression may be taken actively, so as to mean 'not troublesome or querulous'. And this signification will not accord ill with the context, for μεμψιμοιρία[1] is the seed of nearly all quarrels and detractions. He adds *sincere*, because this refuse will never come forth from purified minds.

15. *The sons of God, unreprovable.* It ought to be rendered 'unreprovable, because ye are the sons of God'. For God's adoption of us ought to be a reason for a blameless life, that we may in some degree resemble our Father. Now, although there never has been such perfection in the world as to have nothing blameworthy in it, those are, nevertheless, called unreprovable who aim at this with the whole bent of their mind, as has been observed elsewhere.

In the midst of a perverse generation. Believers, it is true, live on earth, intermingled with the wicked; they breathe the same air, they enjoy the same soil; and at that time they were even more intermingled, inasmuch as there could scarcely be found a single godly family that was not surrounded on all sides by unbelievers. So much the more does Paul stir up the Philippians to guard carefully against all corruptions. The meaning therefore is this: 'You are, it is true, shut up among the wicked; but nevertheless, remember that you are, by God's adoption, separated from them. Let there be, therefore, in your life, conspicuous marks which distinguish you. Nay more, this consideration ought to stir you up the more to aim at a godly and holy life, that we may not also be a part of the crooked generation, involved in their vices and contagion.'

[1] The word Aristotle uses for 'faultfinding'.

As to his calling them *a perverse and crooked generation*, this corresponds with the context. For he tells us that we must the more carefully take heed because many offences are stirred up by unbelievers, which disturb their right course; and the whole life of unbelievers is, as it were, a labyrinth of various windings, that draw us off from the way. These epithets however, are perpetually relevant and descriptive of unbelievers of all nations and times. For if the heart of man is wicked and unsearchable, what will be the fruits springing from such a root? Hence we are taught in these words, that in the life of man there is nothing pure, nothing right, until he has been reformed by the Spirit of God.

Among whom shine as luminaries in the world. The termination of the Greek word is doubtful, for it might be read as indicative, 'ye shine'; but the imperative suits the exhortation better. He wants unbelievers to be like lamps, which shine in the darkness of the world; as though he had said, 'unbelievers, it is true, are children of the night, and there is in the world nothing but darkness. But God has enlightened you for this end, that the purity of your life may shine forth in that darkness, that His grace may appear the more brightly.' Thus, also, it is said by the prophet, 'The Lord will arise upon thee, and his glory will be seen in thee' (Isa. 60.2). There immediately follows, 'The Gentiles shall walk in thy light, and kings in the brightness of thy countenance.' Though Isaiah speaks there rather of doctrine, while Paul speaks here of a good life, yet, even in regard to doctrine, Christ elsewhere specially calls the apostles the light of the world (Matt. 5.14).

16. *Upholding the word of life.* The reason why they ought to be luminaries is that they carry the Word of life, by which they are enlightened, that they may give light also to others. And he alludes to lamps, in which wicks are placed to burn, and he makes us resemble the lamps. He compares the Word of God to the wick, from which the light comes. If you prefer another metaphor, we are candlesticks, the doctrine of the Gospel is the candle, which, being placed in us, gives light on all sides. Now he intimates that we do injustice to the Word of God, if it does not shine forth in us in purity of life. This is the import of Christ's saying, 'No man lighteth a lamp, and putteth it under a bushel,' etc. (Matt. 5.15). We are said, however, to bear the words of life in such a way as to be nevertheless borne by it, inasmuch as we are founded on it. But the manner of carrying it, of which Paul speaks, is that He has entrusted His doctrine to us on condition, not that we should keep its light suppressed and inactive, but that we should hold it forth to others. The sum is this: That all that are enlightened with heavenly doctrine carry about with them a light, which detects and discovers their sins if they do not walk in

holiness and purity; but that this light has been kindled not only that they may themselves be guided in the right way, but that they may also show it to others.

To my glory. That he may encourage them, he declares that it will turn out to his glory, if he has not laboured among them in vain. Not that those who labour faithfully, but unsuccessfully, lose their pains and their reward. Since, however, success in our ministry is a singular blessing from God, let us not be surprised if God, among His other gifts, makes this the crowning one. Hence, as the many churches won to Christ by him now bring honour to Paul's apostleship, so there is no doubt that these trophies will have a place in Christ's Kingdom, as he says a little later, 'You are my crown' (Phil. 4.1). Nor can it be doubted that the greater the exploits, the more splendid the triumph.

Should anyone inquire how it is that Paul now glories in his labours, when he elsewhere commands us to glory only in the Lord, the answer is easy: when we have prostrated ourselves and all that we have before God, and have placed in Christ all our glory, it is also allowable for us to glory through Christ in God's benefits, as we have seen in the First Epistle to the Corinthians.[1]

The expression, *in the day of the Lord,* is to stir up the Philippians to perseverance, when the judgment seat of Christ is set before them, from which the reward of faith is to be expected.

Yea, and if I am offered upon the sacrifice and worship of your faith, I joy, and rejoice with you all. For the same cause also do ye joy, and rejoice with me. But I hope in the Lord to send Timothy shortly unto you, that I also may be of good comfort when I know your state. For I have no man like-minded, who will genuinely care for your state. For all seek their own, not the things of Christ Jesus. But ye know the proof of him, that, as a son with the father, he hath served with me in the gospel. Him therefore I hope to send, so soon as I shall see how it will go with me. But I trust in the Lord that I myself also shall come shortly. (17-24)

17. *If I should be offered.* The Greek is σπένδομαι, and accordingly it seems to me to allude to those victims by whose slaughter agreements and treaties were confirmed among the ancients. For the Greeks strictly use σπονδαί for the victims by which treaties are confirmed. In this way, he calls his death the confirmation of their faith, which it certainly would be. But to make the whole passage clearer, he says that he sacrificed to God, when he consecrated them by the Gospel. There is a similar expression in Rom. 15.16, where he represents himself as a priest, who offers up the Gentiles to God by the Gospel.

[1] In his commentary on I Cor. 1.31.

Now, as the Gospel is a spiritual sword for slaying victims, so faith is, as it were, the oblation; for there is no faith without mortification, through which we are consecrated to God.

He says, θυσίαν καὶ λειτουργίαν, the former of which refers to the Philippians, who had been offered up to God; and the latter to Paul, for it is the very act of sacrificing. The term, it is true, is equivalent to 'administration', and thus it includes functions and offices of every kind; but here it relates properly to the worship of God, as they say in Latin, *operari sacris* (to be employed in sacred rites). Now Paul says that he will rejoice, if he shall be offered up upon such a sacrifice, that it may be the more ratified and confirmed. This is to teach the Gospel in earnest, when we are prepared to confirm with our own blood what we teach.

From this a useful lesson is to be gathered as to the nature of faith, that it is not an empty thing, but such as to consecrate man to God. The ministers of the Gospel, too, have here a singular consolation in being called priests of God, to present sacrifices to Him; for with what ardour ought that man to apply himself to preaching, who knows that this is an acceptable sacrifice to God? The unhappy Papists, knowing nothing of this kind of sacrifice, contrive another, which is utter sacrilege.

I rejoice with you, he says. So that if it should happen that he died, they would know that this took place for their profit, and they would receive advantage from his death.

18. *Rejoice ye*. He encourages the Philippians with this cheerfulness and inflames them to meet death boldly, inasmuch as believers suffer no harm from it. For he has formerly taught them that death would be gain to him; here, on the other hand, he takes special care that his death may not upset the Philippians. And so he declares that it is no cause for sorrow, rather of joy, inasmuch as they will find it profitable. For, although it was in itself a serious loss to be deprived of such a teacher, it was no light compensation that the Gospel was confirmed by his blood. Meanwhile, he tells them that to himself personally death would be joyful. The rendering of Erasmus in the present tense, 'Ye rejoice,' is quite wrong.

19. *But I hope*. He promises that Timothy will come, so that, by expecting him, they may bear up more courageously, and not give way to impostors. For as in war an expectation of reinforcements heartens soldiers and stops them from giving way, so this consideration, too, would encourage the Philippians greatly: 'Soon one will come, who will oppose the scheming of our enemies.' But if the mere expectation of him was of such avail, his presence would be much more effective. We must note the condition by which he submits

himself to the providence of God, deciding nothing but with His leading the way, as assuredly it is not allowable to determine anything as to the future, except, so to speak, under the Lord's hand.

When he adds, *that I may be of good comfort*, he declares his love for them, in that he was so concerned about their dangers that he was not at ease until he had learned that all was well with them.

20. *I have no man like-minded.* Although some draw another meaning from the passage, I interpret it thus: 'I have no one equally well-affected in attending to your interests.' For Paul, in my opinion, compares Timothy with others rather than with himself, and he pronounces this eulogy upon him, with the express design that he might be the more highly esteemed because he was unique.

21. *For all seek their own things.* He does not speak of those who had openly abandoned the pursuit of godliness, but of those very persons whom he reckoned brethren, even those whom he admitted to his own circle. These persons, he nevertheless says, were so warm in pursuing their own interests that they were cold in the work of the Lord. It may seem at first sight as if it were no great fault to seek one's own; but how insufferable it is in the servants of Christ appears from the fact that it renders those whom it possesses utterly useless. For it is impossible that he who is devoted to self, should spend himself for the Church. Then, you will say, did Paul cultivate men who were worthless and pretenders? I answer that it is not to be understood as if they had been intent only on their own interests, and had no care whatever for the Church, but that, involved in their own private affairs, they were the more negligent to promote the public advantage of the Church. For it must necessarily be, that one or other of two dispositions rules in us: either that, overlooking ourselves, we are devoted to Christ and the things that are Christ's, or that, too intent on our own advantage, we serve Christ perfunctorily.

From this it appears how great a hindrance it is to the ministers of the Church to seek their own interests. Nor is there any force in these excuses: 'I do harm to no one'; 'I must also have a regard to my own affairs'; 'I am not so hard as not to be prompted by a regard to my own advantage.' For you must give up your own right if you would discharge your duty: a regard for yourself must not be preferred to Christ's glory, or even put on a level with it. Whithersoever Christ calls you, you must go promptly, leaving all other things. Your calling ought to be regarded by you in such a way that you shall turn away all your senses from everything that would divert you. It might be in your power to be richer elsewhere, but God has bound you to a Church which affords you only a moderate sustenance. You might elsewhere have more honour, but God has assigned you a place in which you live humbly. You might elsewhere have a better climate, or more pleasant scenery, but it is here that your station is appointed. You might wish to have to do with a more cultured people; their ingratitude, or barbarity, or pride offends you; in short, you have no sympathy with the disposition or customs of the nation in which you are, but you must struggle with yourself, and do violence in a manner to opposing inclinations, that you may cherish the Sparta where you find yourself. For you are not free, or at your own disposal. In short, forget yourself, if you would serve God.

If, however, Paul reproves so severely those who were influenced by a greater concern for themselves than for the Church, what judgment may they expect who are completely given up to their own affairs and care nothing for the edification of the Church? However they may now flatter themselves, God will not pardon them. It must be conceded that ministers of the Church may seek their own interests, so long as they are not prevented from seeking the Kingdom of Christ. But in that case they will not be said to seek their own interests; for a man's life is estimated according to its chief aim.

When he says *all*, we are not to make the term universal, as implying that there could be no exception; for there were others also, like Epaphroditus, but they were few, and he ascribes to all what was generally prevalent.

When, however, we hear Paul complaining that even in that golden age, when all virtues flourished, so few were rightly affected, let us not be disheartened, if such is our condition today; only let everyone take heed to himself, that he be not justly reckoned in that catalogue. I should wish, however, that Papists would tell me where Peter was then; for he must have been at Rome, if what they say is true. O the sad and vile description that Paul gave of him! They utter, therefore, mere fables, when they pretend that he at that time presided over the Church of Rome. Observe, that the edification of the Church is termed τὰ Χριστοῦ because we are truly engaged in His work when we labour in the cultivation of His vineyard.

22. *But the proof.* It is literally, 'You know the proof of him,' unless you prefer the imperative 'know ye' (for there had scarcely been time to make trial); but this is not very important. What is chiefly to be noticed is that he bears witness of Timothy's fidelity and modesty. As to his fidelity, he declares that he had served with him in the Gospel, for such a connexion was a token of true sincerity. And for his modesty, he states that he had submitted to him as to a father. It is not surprising that this virtue is expressly praised by Paul, for it has in all ages been rare. Where today will you find a youth who will give way to his seniors, even in the smallest thing? To such an extent

does insolence triumph and riot in this age! In this passage, as in many others, we see how diligently Paul takes care to honour godly ministers, and that not so much for their own sakes as because it is for the good of the whole Church that such men should be loved and honoured, and possess the highest authority.

24. *I trust that I myself.* He adds this, too, lest they should imagine that something had happened to change his intentions as to the journey he had earlier mentioned. But he always speaks conditionally: 'If it shall please the Lord.' For although he expected deliverance from the Lord, yet because, as we have said, there had been no express promise, this expectation was by no means certain, but was, as it were, suspended upon the secret purpose of God.

> But I counted it necessary to send to you Epaphroditus, my brother and
> fellow-worker, and fellow-soldier, but your apostle, and minister to
> my wants. Since he longed after you all, and was sore troubled, because
> ye had heard that he had been sick. For indeed he was sick nigh unto
> death: but God had mercy on him; and not on him only, but on me also,
> that I might not have sorrow upon sorrow. I have sent him therefore
> the more diligently, that, when ye see him again, ye may rejoice, and
> that I may be the less sorrowful. Receive him therefore in the Lord
> with all joy; and hold such in honour: because for the work of Christ
> he came nigh unto death, hazarding his life to supply what was lacking
> in your service towards me. (25-30)

25. *Epaphroditus.* After encouraging them by the promise of the coming of himself and of Timothy, he fortifies them also for the present, because he had already sent Epaphroditus, that in the mean time, while he awaited the issue of his own affairs (for this was the cause of his delay), they might not lack a pastor who should take care that matters were properly managed. He recommends Epaphroditus by many titles; that he is his brother, and his helper in the affairs of the Gospel; that he is his fellow-soldier, by which word he expresses the condition of the ministers of the Gospel in that they are engaged in an incessant warfare, for Satan will not allow them to promote the Gospel without a conflict. Let those, then, who prepare themselves for edifying the Church, know that war is declared against them and already prepared. This, indeed, is common to all Christians, to serve in the camp of Christ; for Satan is the enemy of all. It is, however, more particularly applicable to the ministers of the Word, who lead the ranks and bear the standard. Paul, however, might especially boast of his military service, inasmuch as he was exercised to an incredible extent in every kind of contest. He praises Epaphroditus, because he had been the comrade of his conflicts.

The word *apostle* here, as in many other passages, is taken generally for any evangelist; unless any one prefers to understand it as an ambassador sent by the Philippians, so that these two things are read together; an ambassador to afford service to Paul. The former sense, however, is in my opinion more suitable. He mentions also, among other praises, that he had *ministered to him in prison*, a matter which will soon be treated of more fully.

26. *He longed after you.* It is a sign of a true pastor, that when he was far away and willingly detained by a religious duty, he was nevertheless concerned about his flock, and longed for them; and on learning that his sheep were distressed on his account, he was worried about their grief. On the other hand, the godly anxiety of the Philippians for their pastor is here indicated.

27. *But God had mercy on him.* He had expressed the severity of the disease (that Epaphroditus had been so ill that his life was despaired of), in order that the goodness of God might shine forth more clearly in his restored health. It is, however, surprising that the apostle should ascribe it to the mercy of God that Epaphroditus had had his life prolonged, when he had previously declared that he himself preferred death. And what would be better for us than to remove to the kingdom of God, delivered from the many miseries of this world, and more especially, rescued from that bondage of sin in which he elsewhere exclaims that he is wretched (Rom. 7.24), to enjoy more fully that liberty of the Spirit, by which we cleave to the Son of God? It would be tedious to enumerate all the things which make death better and more desirable than life to believers. Where, then, is the mercy of God, when it merely lengthens out our miseries? I answer, that all these things do not prevent this life from being, considered in itself, an excellent gift of God. More especially those who live to Christ are happily exercised here in hope of heavenly glory; and so, as we saw a little ago, life is gain to them. Besides, another thing must be considered, that it is no small honour when God glorifies Himself in us; for it becomes us to look not so much to life itself, as to the purpose of life.

But on me also, that I might not have sorrow. Paul acknowledges that the death of Epaphroditus would have been bitter to him, and he recognizes that God had spared him in restoring him to health. Therefore, he does not claim the ἀπάθειαν of the Stoics, as if he were a man of iron and exempt from human feelings. 'What then!' some one will say, 'where is that unconquerable stoutheartedness? where is that indefatigable constancy?' I answer, that Christian patience is very different from philosophical obstinacy, and still more from the stubborn and fierce sternness of the Stoics. For what virtue would

there be in patiently enduring the cross, if there were in it no feeling
of pain and bitterness? But when the consolation of God overcomes
that feeling, so that we do not resist, but rather willingly give our back
to the rod, we then offer God an acceptable sacrifice of obedience. Thus
Paul acknowledges that he felt some trouble and sorrow from his
bonds, but that he nevertheless cheerfully endured these same bonds
for the sake of Christ. He acknowledges that the death of Epaphroditus
would have been a heavy blow to him, but he would at length have
composed his mind to the will of God.

But the difficulty is not yet quite removed; for we give proof of
our obedience when we bridle our depraved affections, and do not
give way to the infirmity of the flesh. Two things, therefore, are to
be observed; first, that the affections which God originally implanted
in our nature are not evil in themselves, because they do not arise
from the fault of corrupt nature, but flow from God their Author;
such is the grief that is felt at the death of friends. Secondly, that
Paul had many other reasons for sadness in the death of Epaphroditus,
and that these were not merely excusable, but altogether necessary.
In the first place, it is the case for all believers, that, at the death of
any one, they are reminded of the anger of God against sin; but Paul
was the more moved by the Church's loss, which he saw would be
deprived of a good pastor when the good were so few. Those who
would have dispositions of this kind altogether subdued and extinguished, do not imagine merely men of stone, but men that are
wild and savage. In the depravity of our nature, however, everything
in us is so perverted, that in whatever direction our minds are bent,
they always go beyond measure. Hence it is that there is nothing
that is so pure or right in itself as not to bring with it some contagion.
In fact, I do not deny that Paul, as a man, would have experienced in
his grief something human, for he was subject to infirmity, and had to
be tried with temptations, in order to have occasion of victory by
striving and resisting.

28. *I have sent him the more diligently.* The presence of Epaphroditus
was no small comfort to him; yet to such a degree did he prefer the
welfare of the Philippians to his own advantage, that he says that he
rejoices at his departure, because it grieved him that, on his account,
he was taken away from the flock committed to him, and was reluctant
to avail himself of his services, however agreeable they were, at the
price of their loss. Hence he says that he will be happier at the joy of
the Philippians.

29. *Receive him with all joy.* He uses 'all' for sincere and abundant.
He also recommends him again to the Philippians; so insistent is he
in this, that all who approve themselves as good and faithful pastors

may be held in the highest estimation. For he does not speak merely
of one, but exhorts that all such should be held in estimation. They
are precious pearls from God's treasuries, and the rarer they are, the
more worthy of esteem are they. Nor can it be doubted that God
often punishes our ingratitude and proud disdain by depriving us of
good pastors, when He sees that the best that He gives are ordinarily
despised. Let every one, then, who desires the Church to be fortified
against the stratagems and assaults of wolves, make it his care, after
the example of Paul, that the authority of good pastors be established;
as, on the other hand, there is nothing upon which the instruments of
the devil are more intent, than on undermining it by every means in
their power.

30. *Because for the work of Christ.* I refer this to that infirmity which
he had brought upon himself by incessant work. Hence he reckons
the distemper of Epaphroditus among his virtues, as it certainly was
a signal token of his ardent zeal. Sickness, indeed, is not a good thing;
but it is a virtue not to spare yourself that you may serve Christ.
Epaphroditus felt that his health would be in danger if he applied
himself beyond measure; yet he would rather neglect his health than
fail in his duty. And that he may commend this conduct the more to
the Philippians, he says that it was a filling up of their deficiency,
because, living far away, they could not furnish aid to Paul at Rome.
Therefore Epaphroditus was sent for this purpose and acted in their
stead. He calls the services rendered to him 'the work of the Lord',
for assuredly there is nothing in which we can better serve God than
when we help His servants who labour for the truth of the Gospel.

CHAPTER THREE

For the rest, my brethren, rejoice in the Lord. To write the same things to you, to me indeed is not irksome, but for you it is safe. Beware of the dogs, beware of the evil workers, beware of the concision. For we are the circumcision, who worship God in the spirit, and glory in Christ Jesus, and have no confidence in the flesh. Though I myself might also have confidence even in the flesh. If any other man seemeth to trust in the flesh, I more: circumcised the eighth day, of the stock of Israel, of the tribe of Benjamin, an Hebrew of the Hebrews; as touching the law, a Pharisee; as touching zeal, persecuting the Church; as touching the righteousness which is in the law, blameless. (1-6)

1. *Rejoice in the Lord.* The conclusion of what goes before; for as Satan never ceased to dishearten them with daily rumours, Paul bids them be easy and of good courage. In this way he exhorts them to constancy, that they may not fall back from the doctrine they have once received. The phrase *for the rest* denotes a continued course, that, in the midst of many hindrances, they may not cease to exercise holy joy. It is a rare virtue that when Satan endeavours to irritate us by the bitterness of the cross, so as to make God's name unpleasant to us, we rest in the taste of God's grace alone, so that all annoyances, sorrows, anxieties and griefs are sweetened.

To write the same things to you. Here he begins to treat of the false apostles; yet he does not fight directly, as in the Epistle to the Galatians, but in a few words harshly refutes them, so far as was necessary. For as they had merely made an attempt on the Philippians and had not overcome them, it was not so necessary to enter into a full-scale disputation and refute errors to which they had never lent an ear. Hence he simply warns them to be diligent and attentive in detecting and guarding against impostors.

In the first place, however, he calls them *dogs*; the metaphor meaning that, for the sake of filling their belly, they assailed true doctrine with their foul barking. Accordingly, it is as though he had said, 'impure or profane persons'; for I do not agree with those who think that they are so called because they envy others, or bite them.

Secondly, he calls them *evil workers*, meaning that, under the pretext of building up the Church, they did nothing but ruin and destroy everything. For many are busy who would do better to remain idle. Like the public crier, who was mockingly asked by Gracchus what he was doing, because he was sitting idle. He had his answer ready, 'Nay, but what are you doing?' for Gracchus was the ringleader of a pernicious sedition. Hence Paul would have a distinction made among workers, that believers may beware of those that are evil.

In the third name, there is an elegant προσονομασία.[1] They boasted that they were the circumcision. He mocks this boasting by calling them the concision, for they tore asunder the unity of the Church. In this we have an example which shows that the Holy Spirit in His instruments has not always avoided wit and humour, although He has kept from scurrility, which is unworthy of His majesty. There are innumerable examples in the prophets, and especially in Isaiah, so that there is no profane author who abounds more in witty allusions and metaphors. We ought, however, more carefully still to observe the vehemence with which Paul attacks the false apostles, which will assuredly break forth wherever there is the ardour of godly zeal. But in the mean time we must beware lest any intemperance or excessive bitterness should creep in under the cloak of zeal.

When he says that to write the same things is not grievous to him, he seems to hint that he had already written to the Philippians. We could, however, just as well understand him as meaning that he now by his writings reminds them of the same things as they had frequently heard him speak when he was with them. For there is no doubt that he had often told them when he was with them, how much they ought to be on their guard against such pests. Yet he is not weary of repeating these things, for danger threatened Philippians if he were silent. And, unquestionably, it is the part of a good pastor, not only to supply the flock with pasture and to rule the sheep by his guidance, but to drive away the wolves when they threaten to attack the fold; and that not just once, but to be constantly on the watch, and to be indefatigable. For as thieves and robbers are always looking for opportunities to harm the Church, what excuse will the pastor have if, after courageously repelling them several times, he gives way at the ninth or tenth attack?

He says also, that a repetition like this is useful to the Philippians, lest they should be (as sometimes happens) over fastidious, and despise it as superfluous. For many are so touchy, that they cannot bear the same thing to be said to them a second time, and yet they do not consider that what is impressed on them daily hardly stays in their memory ten years later. But if it was profitable to the Philippians to listen to this exhortation of Paul, that they should recognize the wolves, what are the Papists aiming at, who will not allow any judgment on their doctrine? For to whom, I ask you, did Paul address himself when he said, *Beware*? Was it not to those whom they do not

[1] Appellation.

allow any right to judge? And of the same people Christ says similarly, 'My sheep hear my voice, and they follow me; they flee from a stranger, and they hear not his voice' (John 10.5, 27).

3. *For we are the circumcision.* That is, we are the true seed of Abraham and heirs of the testament which was confirmed by the sign of circumcision. For the true circumcision is of the spirit and not of the letter, inward, and situated in the heart, not visible according to the flesh (Rom. 2.29).

By *spiritual worship* he means that which is recommended to us in the Gospel and consists of trust in God and calling upon Him, self-renunciation and a pure conscience. We must supply an antithesis, for he censures, on the other hand, legal worship, which alone was urged by the false apostles. To paraphrase: 'They command that God should be worshipped with outward observances; and because they observe the ceremonies of the law, they boast on false grounds that they are the people of God. But we are the truly circumcised, who worship God in spirit and in truth.'

But here someone will ask whether truth excludes the sacraments, for the same thing might be said of Baptism and the Lord's Supper. I answer, that the principle must always be remembered that figures were abolished by the advent of Christ, and that circumcision gave way to baptism. It follows, also, from this principle, that the pure and genuine worship of God is now free from the legal ceremonies and that believers have the true circumcision apart from its figure.

And we glory in Christ. We must still continue the antithesis. 'We cleave to the reality; they to the symbols. We remain in the substance; they look to the shadows.' And this corresponds well with the opposing clause which he adds: 'We have no confidence in the flesh.' For in the term 'flesh' he includes everything external in man that he could glory in, as will appear from the context; or, to express it briefly, he calls 'flesh' everything that is outside Christ. He thus reproves severely the perverse zealots of the law, because, not satisfied with Christ, they flit away to other glorying. He has used 'glorying', and 'having confidence', for the same thing. For confidence uplifts a man, so that he ventures even to glory, and thus the two things are connected.

4. *Though I myself might also.* He does not speak of his attitude but points out that he has also ground of glorying, if he were inclined to imitate their folly. The meaning therefore is, 'My glorying, indeed, is placed in Christ, but, were it warrantable to glory in the flesh, I also have good reason to do so.' And from this we learn how to refute the arrogance of those who glory outside Christ. If we have ourselves the same things in which they glory, let us not allow them to triumph

over Christ with this absurd boasting, without retorting upon them also our grounds of glorying, that they may understand that it is not through envy that we reckon of no value, and even voluntarily renounce, those things which they put first. Let, however, the conclusion be always this, that all confidence in the flesh is vain and ridiculous.

If anyone has confidence in the flesh, I more. Not satisfied with putting himself on a level with any one of them, he even gives himself the preference. Hence he cannot on this account be suspected of being envious of their excellence, and extolling Christ to minimize his own deficiencies. He says, therefore, that, if they were to match their relative values, he would be superior to the rest. For they had nothing (as we shall see soon) that he did not possess equally with them, while in some things he greatly excelled them. He says, imprecisely, that he has confidence in the flesh, because, without placing confidence in them, he was furnished with those grounds of freshly glorying, by which the others were puffed up.

5. *Circumcised on the eighth day.* It is literally, 'the circumcision of the eighth day'. But it makes no difference to the sense, for he means that he was circumcised with the proper ceremony and according to the appointment of the law. Now this usual circumcision was reckoned superior; and, besides, it was a distinguishing mark of his race; a point he touches on immediately afterwards. For it was not the same for foreigners. After they had become proselytes they were circumcised in youth, or as men, and sometimes even in old age. He says, accordingly, that he is of *the race of Israel.* He names the tribe, not, in my opinion, because *the tribe of Benjamin* was superior to the others, but to confirm that he really was an Israelite, as it was the custom that every one was reckoned according to his tribe. With the same view he adds again, that he is an *Hebrew of the Hebrews.* For this name was the most ancient and that by which Abraham himself is designated by Moses (Gen. 14.13). The sum, therefore, is this, that in his remotest ancestry Paul was descended from the seed of Jacob, so that he could refer back to grandfathers and great-grandfathers, and right into the dim past.

As touching the law, a Pharisee. Having spoken of the nobility of his descent, he now proceeds to speak of special and so-called personal endowments. It is well known that the sect of the Pharisees was celebrated above the others for its reputation for sanctity and doctrine. He states that he was one of them. The common opinion is, that the Pharisees were so called from their separateness; but I approve rather of what I was once told by Capito, that man of sacred memory, that they were given the name because they boasted that they possessed

the gift of interpreting Scripture; for פָּרַשׁ in Hebrew means interpretation. While others declared themselves to be literalists, they
preferred to be regarded as 'Pharisees', who kept to the interpretations
of the ancients. And it is certain that, under the pretext of antiquity,
they corrupted the whole of Scripture by their inventions; but as, at
the same time they retained some sound interpretations, handed
down by the ancients, they were held in the highest esteem.

But what is meant by the clause *as touching the law*? For unquestionably nothing is more opposed to the law of God than sects; for in it
alone is communicated the truth of God, which is the bond of unity.
Moreover, Josephus tells us in the 13th book of his *Antiquities*, that all
the sects began during the high priesthood of Jonathan. Paul uses the
word 'law' loosely for the teaching of religion, however much corrupted it was at that time, as Christianity is today in the Papacy. As,
however, there were many among the teachers who were less skilful
and learned, he mentions also his zeal. It was, indeed, a terrible sin
that Paul persecuted the Church, but as he had to dispute with rascals,
who, by mixing up Christ with Moses, pretended zeal for the law,
he says in opposition that he was so keen a zealot of the law, that this
is why he persecuted the Church.

6. *As to the righteousness which is in the law.* There is no doubt he
means the entire righteousness of the law, for it would be too weak
to understand it merely of ceremonies. The meaning, therefore, is
more general, that he cultivated the integrity of life required of a man
who was devoted to the law. To this, again, it is objected that the
righteousness of the law is perfect in the sight of God. For the sum
of it is that men be fully devoted to God, and what more can be
desired for perfection? I answer, that Paul speaks here of the righteousness which would satisfy the common opinion of mankind. For he
separates the law from Christ. Now, what is the law without Christ
but a dead letter? To make the matter plainer, I say that there is a twofold righteousness of the law. The one is spiritual—perfect love to God
and our neighbours: it is contained in doctrine, and never existed in
the life of any man. The other is literal—such as appears in the view
of men, while nevertheless, hypocrisy reigns in the heart, and there is
in the sight of God nothing but iniquity. Thus, the law has two
references; the one to God, the other to men. Paul, then, was in the
judgment of men holy and free from all blame. A rare praise and
almost unique. But let us see how much he cared for it.

Howbeit what things were gain to me, those I counted loss for Christ.
Yea verily, and I count all things to be loss for the excellency of the
knowledge of Christ Jesus my Lord: for whom I have suffered the loss of

all things, and do count them but refuse, that I may gain Christ. And may find them in him, not having mine own righteousness, which is of the law, but that which is through the faith of Christ, the righteousness which is, I say, of God by faith: that I may know him, and the power of his resurrection, and the fellowship of his sufferings, being conformed unto his death; if by any means I might attain unto the resurrection of the dead. (7-11)

7. *What things were gain to me.* He says that those things were gain to him before he knew Christ. For ignorance of Christ is the sole reason why we are puffed up with vain confidence. Hence, where we see a false estimate of a man's own goodness, where we see arrogance, where we see pride, we may be sure that Christ is not known. On the other hand, so soon as Christ shines forth, all those things that formerly dazzled our eyes with a false splendour instantly vanish, or at least become paltry. Those things, then, which had been gain to Paul when he was yet blind, or rather had deceived him by their appearance of gain, he acknowledges to have been loss to him, when he had been enlightened. Why loss? Because they were hindrances against his coming to Christ. What is more hurtful than anything that keeps us from coming to Christ? Now, he speaks chiefly of his own righteousness, for we are not admitted to Christ, except as naked and emptied of our own righteousness. Paul recognizes that nothing was more harmful to him than his own righteousness, for he was shut out from Christ by it.

8. *Yea, verily, and I count.* He means that he continues to be of the same mind, because it often happens that, transported with delight at new things, we forget everything else, and afterwards regret it. Hence Paul, having said that he renounced all hindrances that he might possess Christ, now adds that he continues to be of this mind.

For the excellency of the knowledge. He extols the Gospel in opposition to all the notions that deceive us. For many things have an appearance of excellence, but the knowledge of Christ so far surpasses everything else by its sublimity that, compared with it, there is nothing that is not contemptible. Let us, therefore, learn from this, what value we ought to set upon the knowledge of Christ alone. He calls Him *his Lord*, to express the intensity of his feeling.

For whom I have suffered the loss of all things. He says more than he had done previously; at least he speaks more expressly. It is a similitude taken from seamen, who, when pressed by danger of shipwreck, throw everything overboard, that, the ship being lightened, they may reach the harbour safely. Paul, then, preferred to lose everything that he had, rather than be deprived of Christ only.

But it is asked whether it is necessary for us to renounce riches and honours and nobility of descent and even external righteousness, that we may become partakers of Christ. For all these things are gifts of God, and, in themselves, not to be despised. I answer that the apostle does not speak here so much of the things themselves, as of their property. It is, indeed, true that the Kingdom of Heaven is like a precious pearl, for the purchase of which no one should hesitate to sell everything that he has (Matt. 13.46). There is, however, a difference between the substance and the property of things. Paul did not reckon it necessary to abdicate from his tribe and from the race of Abraham, and make himself an alien, that he might become a Christian; but he had to renounce trust in his descent. It was not befitting that from being chaste he should become unchaste; that from being sober, he should become intemperate; and that from being respectable and honourable, he should become dissolute. But he had to divest himself of a false estimate of his own righteousness and treat it with contempt. We, too, when treating of the righteousness of faith, do not attack the substance of works but that property with which the Sophists invest them, inasmuch as they contend that men are justified by them. Paul, therefore, divested himself, not of works, but of that perverted confidence in works with which he had been puffed up.

As to riches and honours, when we have shaken off our attachment to them, we will also be prepared to renounce the things themselves whenever the Lord requires; and so it should be. It is not directly necessary that you be a poor man, to be a Christian; but if it please the Lord that it should be so, you ought to be prepared to endure poverty. In fine, it is not lawful for Christians to have anything outside Christ. I call 'outside Christ' everything that prevents Christ alone being our glory, and reigning over us completely.

And I count them but refuse. Here, not merely by words, but also in reality, he amplifies greatly what he had said before. For those who cast their merchandise and other things into the sea, that they may escape in safety, do not despise riches, but they prefer to live in misery and want, than to be drowned along with their riches. They part with them, indeed, but it is with regret and with a sigh; and when they have escaped, they bewail the loss of them. Paul, on the contrary, declares that he had not merely abandoned everything that he formerly reckoned precious, but that they stank like dung to him, or were disesteemed like things thrown away in contempt. Chrysostom renders it 'straws'. Grammarians, however, think that σκύβαλον is used as κυσίβαλον, of what is thrown to dogs. And certainly there is good reason why everything that is alien to Christ should be offensive to us, inasmuch as it is an abomination in the sight of God. It should

273

certainly be offensive to us also, since it is nothing but a false imagination.

That I may gain Christ. By this expression he intimates that we cannot gain Christ otherwise than by losing everything that we have. For he would have us rich in His grace alone; he would have Him alone to be our entire blessedness. Now, in what way we must suffer the loss of all things has been already stated, so that nothing will lead us away from trust in Christ alone. But if Paul, with his innocence and integrity of life, did not hesitate to reckon his own righteousness to be loss and dung, what mean these present-day Pharisees who, covered with every kind of wickedness, feel no shame in upholding their own merits against Christ?

9. *And may find them in him.* The verb is passive, and hence all others have rendered it, 'I may be found.' They pass over the context carelessly, however, as though it had no force. If you read it in the passive, an antithesis must be understood, that Paul was lost before he was found in Christ, as a rich merchant is like one lost, so long as he has his vessel laden with riches; but when they have been thrown overboard, he is found. For here that saying is very pertinent 'I had been lost, unless I had been lost.' But as the verb εὑρίσκομαι has an active meaning with its passive ending, and means to recover what you have voluntarily given up, as Budaeus shows by many examples, I have not hesitated to differ from the opinion of others. For, in this way, the meaning will be more complete, and the doctrine fuller, that Paul renounced everything that he had, that he might recover it in Christ; and this corresponds better with the word 'gain', for it means that it was no trivial or ordinary gain, since Christ contains all things in Himself. And, unquestionably, we lose nothing when we come to Christ naked and stripped, for those things which we once wrongly imagined that we possessed, we then begin really to obtain. He therefore shows more fully how great are the riches of Christ, because we obtain and find all things in Him.

Not having mine own righteousness. A remarkable passage, if anyone desires to have a good description of the righteousness of faith, and to understand its true nature. For Paul here compares two kinds of righteousness. The one he says belongs to man, and he calls it at the same time the righteousness of the law; the other, he teaches, is from God, is obtained through faith, and resides in faith in Christ. These he shows to be so directly opposed, that they cannot stand together. Hence there are two things to be observed here. The righteousness of the law must be given up and renounced, that you may be righteous through faith; and secondly, the righteousness of faith comes from God and does not belong to man. On both of these we have today a great controversy with the Papists; for they do not allow that the righteousness of faith is altogether from God, but ascribe a part to man; and, on the other hand, they mix them together, as if the one did not take away the other. Hence we must carefully examine each of Paul's words, for every one of them is full of meaning.

He says that believers have no righteousness of their own. But it cannot be denied that if there were any righteousness of works, it might very properly be called ours. Therefore he leaves no room whatever for the righteousness of works. Why he calls it the righteousness of the law, he shows in Rom. 10.5; because the sentence of the law is, 'He that doeth these things shall live in them.' The law, therefore, pronounces the man to be righteous through works. Nor is there any truth in the quibble of the Papists, that all this must be restricted to ceremonies. For first, it is contemptible nonsense to affirm that Paul was righteous only through ceremonies; and secondly, in this way he contrasts those two kinds of righteousness, the one being of man, the other from God. He indicates, accordingly, that the one is the reward of works, the other a free gift of God. He thus, in general, places man's merit in opposition to Christ's grace. For whereas the law employs works, faith presents man naked before God, that he may be clothed with the righteousness of Christ. When, therefore, he declares that the righteousness of faith is from God, it is not only because faith is the gift of God, but because God justifies us by His goodness, or because we receive by faith the righteousness which He has conferred upon us.

10. *That I may know him.* He describes the power and nature of faith, that it is the knowledge of Christ, and that, too, not bare or indistinct, but such that the power of His resurrection is felt. *Resurrection* he puts for the completion of redemption, so that it also involves within it the idea of death. But as it is a little thing to know Christ crucified and raised from the dead, unless you apprehend also the fruit of this, he speaks expressly of efficacy. Christ therefore is rightly known, when we feel how powerful His death and resurrection are, and how efficacious they are in us. Now all things are there furnished to us: expiation and destruction of sin, freedom from guilt, satisfaction, victory over death, the attainment of righteousness and the hope of a blessed immortality.

And the fellowship of his sufferings. Having spoken of that free righteousness which was procured by the resurrection of Christ and which we obtain through faith, he goes on to speak of the exercises of the godly, so that it might not seem as though he introduced an inactive faith, which produces no effects in the life. He also hints that these are the exercises in which the Lord would have His people employed; whereas the false apostles pressed for the useless elements of ceremonies. Let every one, therefore, who has become through faith a partaker of all Christ's benefits, acknowledge that a condition is presented to him—that his whole life be conformed to His death.

There is, however, a twofold fellowship and communication in the death of Christ. The one is inward, which the Scripture usually calls the mortification of the flesh, or the crucifixion of the old man, of which Paul treats in the sixth chapter of Romans. The other is outward, what is termed the mortification of the outward man. This is the bearing of the cross, of which he treats in the eighth chapter of the same epistle, and here too, if I am not mistaken. For after comprehending also the power of His resurrection, Christ crucified is set before us, that we may follow Him through tribulations and distresses; and hence the resurrection of the dead is expressly mentioned, that we may know that we must die before we live. This is the continual meditation of believers so long as they sojourn on the earth.

This, however, is a great consolation, that in all our miseries we are sharers in Christ's cross, if we are His members; so that through afflictions the way is opened up for us to everlasting blessedness, as we read elsewhere, 'If we die with him, we shall also live with him; if we suffer with him, we shall also reign with him' (II Tim. 2.11-12). We must all, therefore, be ready for our whole life to represent nothing but an image of death, until it produces death itself, even as the life of Christ is nothing but a prelude to death. We enjoy, nevertheless in the mean time, the consolation that the end is everlasting blessedness. For the death of Christ is joined to His resurrection. Hence Paul says that he is conformed to His death, that he may attain the glory of the resurrection.

The phrase, *if by any means*, does not indicate doubt, but expresses difficulty, to stimulate our earnest endeavour. For it is no light contest, inasmuch as we must struggle against so many and such serious hindrances.

Not that I have already attained, or am already made perfect; but I follow after, if that I may apprehend, seeing that I also am apprehended by Christ Jesus. Brethren, I count not myself yet to have apprehended: but this one thing I do, forgetting those things which are behind, and stretching forward unto those things which are before, I press toward the mark, unto the prize of the high calling of God in Christ Jesus. Let us therefore, as many as be perfect, be thus minded: and if in any thing ye are otherwise minded, God shall reveal even this unto you. Only, whereto we have already attained, that we may mind the same things, let us walk by the same rule. Brethren, be ye imitators together

of me, and mark them which so walk, as ye have us for an ensample.
(12-17)

12. *Not that I have already apprehended.* Paul dwells on this, that he may convince the Philippians that he thinks of nothing but Christ, knows nothing else, desires nothing else, is occupied with no other subject of meditation. And so there is much weight in what he now adds, that he himself, who had given up all hindrances, had nevertheless not yet attained that goal and therefore always aimed and strove after something further. How much more was this necessary for the Philippians, who were still far behind him?

It is asked, however, what it is that Paul says he has not yet attained. For unquestionably, so soon as we are by faith engrafted into the body of Christ, we have already entered the Kingdom of God; and, as it says in Eph. 2.6, we already, through hope, sit in heavenly places. I answer that our salvation is placed in hope; so that the inheritance indeed is secure, but we do not yet enjoy the possession of it. At the same time, Paul here is thinking of something else, the advancement of faith and of the mortification which he had mentioned. He had said that he aimed and eagerly strove for the resurrection of the dead through fellowship in the cross of Christ. He adds that he has not yet arrived at this. At what? At having entire fellowship in Christ's sufferings, so as to have a full taste of the power of His resurrection and know Him perfectly. He teaches, therefore, by his own example, that we must make progress, and that the knowledge of Christ is so difficult, that even those who strive after it alone are nevertheless not perfect, so long as they live. This, however, does not detract at all from Paul's doctrine, inasmuch as he had grasped as much as was sufficient for discharging the office committed to him. In the mean time, this wonderful (*divinus*) teacher of others had to make progress that he might be trained in humility.

As also I have been apprehended. This clause he has inserted as a correction, that he might ascribe all his virtues to the grace of God. It is not important whether you read 'as', or 'in so far as'; for the meaning remains the same: that Paul was apprehended by Christ that he might apprehend Christ; that is, that he did nothing save by Christ's influence and guidance. I have chosen, however, the clearer rendering, as it seemed to be an open choice.

13. *I count not myself yet to have apprehended.* He is not here calling in question the certainty of his salvation, as though he were still in suspense, but repeats what he had said before, that he still aimed at further progress, because he had not yet attained the end of his calling. He goes on to show this by saying that he was intent on this one

thing, leaving everything else. Now, he compares our life to a race-course, the limits of which God has marked out for us to run in. For as it would profit the runner nothing to have left the starting-point unless he went forward to the goal, so we must also pursue the course of our calling until death and not cease until we have obtained what we seek. Moreover, as the way is marked out for the runner, that he may not tire himself to no purpose by wandering in this direction and that instead of making for the goal, so there is also a mark set before us, by which we ought to direct our course undeviatingly; and God does not permit us to wander about aimlessly. Thirdly, as the runner requires to be unencumbered, and not stop running for any impedi-ment, but must continue his course, surmounting every obstacle, so we must take heed that we do not turn our thoughts or mind to any-thing irrelevant, but must, on the contrary, make it our endeavour to be free from every distraction and apply ourselves exclusively to God's calling. These three things Paul comprehends in one similitude. When he says that he does this one thing, and forgets all the former things, he expresses his assiduity, and excludes all diversions. When he says that he presses toward the mark, he means that he is not wander-ing from the way.

Forgetting those things which are behind. He alludes to runners, who do not turn their eyes aside lest they should slacken speed in their course, and more especially, do not look behind to see how much ground they have gone over, but hasten forward straight on to the goal. Thus Paul teaches us that he does not think of what he has been or of what he has done, but only presses forward towards the appointed goal, and that with such ardour, that he runs towards it, as it were, with outstretched arms. For a metaphor of this sort is implied in the participle that he uses.

Should anyone object that the remembrance of our past life is of use for rousing us, both because the graces already conferred upon us encourage us to hope, and because we are admonished by our sins to improve our life, I answer that thoughts like this do not turn away our view from what is before us to what is behind, but rather help our sight, so that we discern the goal more clearly. Paul, however, condemns here the looking back which either destroys or impairs zeal. Thus, should any one persuade himself that he has made enough progress, reckoning that he has done his duty, he will become lazy, and want to hand over the lamp to others; or, if anyone has regrets for the situation that he has abandoned, he cannot apply his mind entirely to what he is engaged in. Such were the thoughts from which Paul's mind required to be turned, if he would in good earnest pursue Christ's calling. As, however, there has been mention made here of endeavour, care, course, perseverance, and someone might imagine that salvation consists in these things, or even ascribe to human industry what comes from elsewhere, he points out the cause of all these things and adds, *in Christ Jesus.*

15. *As many as be perfect.* Lest anyone should understand this as spoken of mankind in general, as though he were prescribing the rudiments to children in Christ, he declares that it is a rule which all who are perfect ought to follow. Now, the rule is this: we must renounce trust in all things, that we may glory in Christ's righteousness alone, and, preferring it to everything else, aspire after a participation in His sufferings, which will lead us to the blessed resurrection. Where now will be that state of perfection which monks dream of? where the confused medley of so many contrivances? where the whole Papacy, which is nothing but an imaginary perfection that has nothing in common with this rule of Paul? Undoubtedly, whoever will understand this one word, will clearly perceive that everything that is taught in the Papacy, as to the attainment of righteousness and salvation, is stinking dung.

If in anything. By the same means he both humbles them and rouses them to good hope, for he admonishes them not to be proud of their ignorance and at the same time bids them be of good courage, when he says that we must wait for the revelation of God. For we know how great an obstacle to truth obstinacy is. This, therefore, is the best preparation for teachableness, when we do not take pleasure in error. Paul, therefore, teaches indirectly that we must make way for the revelation of God, if we have not yet attained what we seek. And when he says that we must advance by degrees, he encourages them not to fail in mid-course. At the same time, he maintains beyond all controversy what he has previously taught, when he says that others who differ from him will have revealed to them what they do not yet know. For it is as though he had said, 'The Lord will one day show you that the very thing which I have stated is a perfect rule of true knowledge and right living.' No one could speak like this, if he were not fully assured of the reasonableness and truth of his doctrine. Let us in the meantime learn also from this passage that we must bear for a time with ignorance in our weak brethren and pardon them if it is not given them immediately to be altogether of one mind with us. Paul was assured as to his doctrine, but he allows those who could not yet receive it time to make progress, and he does not cease on that account to regard them as brethren; only he cautions them against flattering themselves in their ignorance. The rendering of the Latin in the perfect tense, *revelavit*, I have no hesitation in rejecting as absurd and inappropriate.

16. *Only, whereto we have attained.* The Greek manuscripts also differ as to the division; for in some there are two complete sentences. If anyone prefers the division, the meaning will be as Erasmus has rendered it. I prefer a different reading, that Paul exhorts the Philippians to imitate him, that they may at last reach the same goal, that they may mind the same thing and walk by the same rule. For where sincere affection flourishes, such as reigned in Paul, the way is easy to a holy and godly concord. As, therefore, they had not yet learned what true perfection was, he wishes them to be imitators of him in order that they might attain it; that is, to seek God with a pure conscience, to arrogate nothing to themselves, and quietly to subject their understanding to Christ. For in the imitating of Paul all these virtues are included, pure zeal, fear of the Lord, modesty, self-renunciation, docility, love, and desire of concord. And he bids them to be imitators together of him; that is, all with one consent and one mind.

Observe, that the goal of perfection to which he invites the Philippians by his example is that they *think the same thing* and *walk by the same rule.* He has, however, put first the doctrine in which they ought to harmonize and the rule to which they should conform themselves.

17. *Mark them.* By this word he means that it is all one to him whom they choose for imitation, provided they conform themselves to that purity of which he was a pattern. By this means all suspicion of ambition is taken away, for the man that is devoted to himself avoids rivals. At the same time he warns them that all are not to be imitated indiscriminately, as he explains more plainly.

For many walk, of whom I have told you often, and now tell you even weeping, that they are the enemies of the cross of Christ: whose end is perdition, whose God is their belly, and whose glory is in their shame, who mind earthly things. For our conversation is in heaven; from whence also we wait for the Saviour, the Lord Jesus Christ: who shall transform our humble body, that it may be conformed to his glorious body, according to the working whereby he is able even to subject all things unto himself. (18-21)

18. *For many walk.* This is a simple statement, in my opinion: Many walk who mind earthly things; meaning, that there are many who grovel on the ground, not feeling the power of God's Kingdom. He adds the marks by which such persons may be distinguished. These we will examine in order. By 'earthly things' some understand ceremonies and the outward elements of the world, which cause true godliness to be forgotten. I prefer, however, to refer it to carnal affection, that those who are not regenerated by the Spirit of God care for nothing but the world. This will appear more clearly from what

follows; for he blames them on the ground that, desiring only their own honour, ease and gain, they neglected the edification of the Church.

Of whom I have told you often. He shows that it is not without good reason that he has often warned the Philippians, for he now strives to remind them by letter of the things he had formerly spoken to them. His tears also are evidence that he is not motivated by envy or hatred of men, or by any wish to revile, or by hastiness of temper, but by godly zeal, inasmuch as he sees that the Church is miserably destroyed by such pests. It becomes us to be so affected, that when we see the place of pastors occupied by wicked and worthless men, we shall sigh, and testify, at least by our tears, that we are deeply grieved for the calamity of the Church.

It is important, also, to note of whom Paul speaks; not of open enemies, who avowedly wanted the doctrine to be undermined, but of impostors and profligates, who trampled under foot the power of the Gospel for the sake of ambition or of their own belly. And unquestionably men like this, who weaken the strength of the ministry by seeking their own interests, sometimes do more harm than if they openly opposed Christ. We must, therefore, by no means spare them but must point them out with the finger as often as there is occasion. Let them complain of our severity afterwards as much as they choose, provided they do not allege anything against us that we cannot justify from Paul's example.

That they are the enemies of the cross of Christ. Some expound 'cross' as the whole mystery of redemption, and they explain that this is said because, by preaching the law, these men made void the benefit of Christ's death. Others, however, explain that they fled from the cross and were not prepared to expose themselves to dangers for the sake of Christ. I take it more generally that, while they pretended to be friends, they were nevertheless the worst enemies of the Gospel. For it is not unusual for Paul to mean the entire preaching of the Gospel by the word Cross. For as he says elsewhere, 'If any man is in Christ, let him be a new creature' (II Cor. 5.17).

19. *Whose end is perdition.* He adds this in order that the Philippians, frightened by the danger, may be the more on their guard and not involve themselves in the ruin of those men. As, however, worthless fellows of this sort, by means of show and various artifices, frequently so dazzle the eyes of the simple for a time that they are preferred even to the best servants of Christ, the apostle declares with great confidence that the glory with which they are now puffed up will be exchanged for ignominy.

Whose god is their belly. As they urged circumcision and other ceremonies, he says that they did not act from zeal for the law, but to win favour from men, so that they might live peacefully and free from annoyance. For they saw that the Jews burned with a fierce rage against Paul and those like him, and that Christ could not be purely proclaimed by them with any other result than of stirring up the same rage against themselves. Accordingly, consulting their own ease and advantage, they adulterated the Gospel with these corruptions so as to pacify the anger of others.

20. *But our conversation is in heaven.* This statement overturns all empty shows, in which pretended ministers of the Gospel are accustomed to glory; and he indirectly blames all their objects, because they only fly about above the earth and do not aspire towards heaven. For he teaches that nothing is to be reckoned of any value except God's spiritual Kingdom, since believers ought to lead a heavenly life in this world. As if he said, 'They mind earthly things: it is therefore befitting that we, whose associations are in heaven, should be separated from them.' We are, it is true, intermingled here with unbelievers and hypocrites; in fact, the chaff is more conspicuous in the granary of the Lord than wheat. Farther, we are exposed to the common troubles of this earthly life; we require also meat and drink and other necessaries, but we must, nevertheless, exist (*versari*) in heaven in mind and affection. For, on the one hand, we must pass swiftly through this life, and, on the other hand, we must be dead to the world that Christ may live in us, and that we, in our turn, may live to Him. This passage is a most abundant source of exhortations, and it is easy for anyone to deduce them.

Whence also. From the union that we have with Christ, he proves that our citizenship is in heaven, for it is not right that the members should be separated from their Head. Accordingly, as Christ is in heaven, it is necessary that we should in mind dwell outside this world if we are to cleave to Him. Besides, where our treasure is, there is our heart also (Matt. 6.21). Christ, our blessedness and glory, is in heaven: let our souls, therefore, dwell with Him on high. On this account he expressly calls Him 'Saviour'. Whence does salvation come to us? Christ will come to us from heaven as Saviour. Hence it is absurd for us to be taken up with this earth. This epithet, Saviour, is suited to the context; for we are said to be in heaven in our souls because it is from thence alone that the hope of salvation shines forth upon us. As the coming of Christ will be terrible to the wicked, so it rather turns away their minds from heaven than draws them thither. For they know that He will come to them as Judge, and they flee from Him so far as they can. From these words of Paul godly souls derive the sweetest consolation, for they hear that the coming of Christ is to be desired, since it will bring them salvation. On the other hand, it is a sure token of unbelief, when anyone trembles at the mention of it. See the eighth chapter of Romans. While, however, others are carried away by vain desires, Paul would have believers contented with Christ alone.

Farther, we learn from this passage that nothing mean or earthly is to be imagined of Christ; for Paul bids us look upward to heaven, that we may seek Him. Now, those that reason subtly that Christ is not shut up or hid in some corner of heaven, and prove from this that His body is everywhere and fills heaven and earth, say something, but not everything. For, as it would be rash and foolish to mount up beyond the heavens, and assign to Christ a station, or seat, or place of walking in this or that region, so also it is a foolish and destructive madness to drag Him down from heaven by any carnal consideration, so as to seek Him on earth. Therefore, lift up your hearts, that they may be with the Lord!

21. *Who shall change.* By this argument he stirs up the Philippians yet more to lift up their minds to heaven, and cleave wholly to Christ; because this body which we bear is not an everlasting abode but a frail tabernacle, which will soon be reduced to nothing. Besides, it is liable to so many miseries and so many shaming infirmities, that it may justly be called vile and full of ignominy. Whence, then, is its restoration to be hoped for? From heaven, at Christ's coming. Hence there is no part of us that ought not to aspire after heaven with whole-hearted desire. We see, even in life, but chiefly in death, the present meanness of our bodies; but the glory which they will have, conformably to Christ's Body, is incomprehensible. For if the disciples could not endure the slight taste which He gave in His transfiguration, which of us may comprehend its fulness? Let us now be contented with the testimony of our adoption, and we shall know the riches of our inheritance when we enjoy them.

According to the working. As nothing is more incredible, or more contrary to carnal perception than the resurrection, Paul places before our eyes the boundless power of God, that it may swallow up all doubt. For distrust arises from our measuring the thing itself by the narrowness of our own understanding. Nor does he simply mention *power*, but also *working*, which is the effect, or power showing itself in action, so to speak. Now, when we bear in mind that God, who created all things out of nothing, can command the earth and the sea and the other elements to render back what has been committed to them, our minds are immediately roused up to a firm hope, even to a spiritual sight of the resurrection.

But it is important to notice, also, that the right and power of raising the dead, in fact, of doing everything according to His own pleasure, is assigned to the person of Christ, a panegyric by which His divine majesty is lucently set forth. More, we gather from this that the world was created by Him, for to subject all things to Himself belongs to the Creator alone.

CHAPTER FOUR

Therefore, my brethren, beloved and longed for, my joy and crown, so stand fast in the Lord, my beloved. I exhort Euodias, and I exhort Syntyche, to be of the same mind in the Lord. Yea, I beseech thee also, true yokefellow, help those women which maintained the struggle alongside me in the gospel, with Clement also, and the rest of my fellow-workers, whose names are in the book of life. (1-3)

1. *Therefore, my brethren.* He concludes his doctrine with his usual very strong exhortations, that he may fix it the more firmly in their minds. He also wins their friendliness with endearing names, though they are not flattery, but sincere love. He calls them his *joy* and *crown*, because, delighted that those who had been won through his efforts were persevering in the faith, he hoped for that triumph of which we have spoken, when the Lord will crown those things which have been done under His guidance.

When he bids them *so stand fast in the Lord,* he means that he approves of their condition, although the particle 'so' could be referred to the foregoing doctrine. But the former exegesis is more suitable; so that, by praising their present condition, he exhorts them to perseverance. They had already, it is true, given some evidence of their constancy. Paul, however, knowing human weakness, reckons that they have need of confirmation for the future.

2. *I exhort Euodias and Syntyche.* It is an almost universally received opinion that Paul wanted to settle a quarrel of some sort between these two women. While I am not inclined to argue against this, Paul's words are not definite enough for such a conjecture to satisfy us that it really was so. It appears, from the testimony he gives them, that they were very excellent women; for he assigns them so much honour as to call them fellow-soldiers in the Gospel. Hence, as their agreement was a matter of great moment, and there was great danger in their disagreement, he stirs them up particularly to concord.

We must notice, however, that, whenever he speaks of agreement, he adds also its bond: *in the Lord.* For every union will inevitably be accursed, if it is outside the Lord; nor is anything so disjoined, but that it must be reunited in Christ.

3. *I beseech thee, also, true yokefellow.* I am not inclined to dispute about the gender, and therefore leave it undetermined whether he

addresses a man or a woman. Yet Erasmus' solution is very weak. He infers that it is a woman from the fact that women are mentioned here—as if Paul did not immediately subjoin the name of *Clement* in the same context. I refrain, however, from that dispute: but I do deny that it is Paul's wife that is designated by this term. Those who maintain this, cite Clement and Ignatius as their authorities. If they quoted correctly, I would certainly not despise such men. But as writings are put forward from Eusebius which are spurious, and were made up by ignorant monks, they do not deserve much credit among serious readers.

Let us therefore inquire as to the thing itself, without being influenced by men. When Paul wrote I Corinthians, he mentioned that he was then unmarried. 'To the unmarried,' he says, 'and widows, I say: it is good that they should continue even as I am' (I Cor. 7.8). He wrote that epistle at Ephesus, when he was preparing to leave. Not long after, he proceeded to Jerusalem, where he was put in prison, and then sent to Rome. Everyone must see how unsuitable a time (spent partly in prison) it would have been for marrying a wife. In addition to this, he was even at that time prepared to endure imprisonment and persecutions, as he himself testifies in Luke (Acts 21.13). I am, at the same time, aware of the objection usually brought against this, that Paul, though married, refrained from conjugal intercourse. The words, however, convey another meaning, for he is desirous that unmarried persons should be able to remain in the same condition as himself. Now, what is that condition but celibacy? As to their bringing forward the passage, 'Is it not lawful for me to lead about a wife?' (I Cor. 9.5) to prove he had a wife, it is too silly to require any refutation. But even granting that Paul was married, how came his wife to be at Philippi, a city which we do not read of his entering on more than two occasions, and in which it is probable he never remained so much as two whole months? In short, nothing is more unlikely than that he is speaking here of his wife. Nor does it seem probable to me that he is speaking of any woman. I leave it, however, to the judgment of the readers. The word which Paul uses here, συλλαμβάνεσθαι, means to grasp a thing and embrace it along with another person, so as to help him.

Whose names are in the book of life. The book of life is the roll of those who are fore-ordained to life, as in Moses, Exod. 32.32. God has this roll laid up with Himself. Hence the book is nothing but His eternal counsel, determined in His own breast. In place of this, Ezekiel speaks of the writing of the house of Israel. The same thought comes in Ps. 69.28, 'Let them be blotted out of the book of the living, and let them not be written among the righteous'; that is, let them not be numbered among the elect of God, whom He receives within the borders of His Church and Kingdom.

Should anyone object that Paul therefore acts rashly in usurping to himself the right of pronouncing on the secrets of God, I answer that we may in some measure judge from the signs by which God manifests His election, but only in so far as our capacity admits. All those, therefore, in whom we see the marks of adoption shine forth, let us reckon to be the sons of God until the books are opened which will thoroughly reveal all things. It belongs, it is true, to God alone now to know them that are His, and to separate the lambs from the kids; but it is our part to reckon from love all to be lambs who obediently submit to Christ their Shepherd, who gather together into His fold, and remain there constantly. It is our part to set so high a value upon the gifts of the Holy Spirit, which He confers peculiarly on His elect, that they shall be to us the seals, as it were, of His hidden election.

Rejoice in the Lord always: again I say, Rejoice. Let your moderation be known unto all men. The Lord is at hand. Be anxious for nothing: but in everything by prayer and supplication with thanksgiving, let your requests be made known unto God. And the peace of God, which passeth all understanding, shall guard your hearts and your thoughts in Christ Jesus. Finally, brethren, whatsoever things are true, whatsoever things are dignified, whatsoever things are just, whatsoever things are pure, whatsoever things are lovely, whatsoever things are of good report; if there be any virtue, and if there be any praise, think on these things. The things which ye have both learned and received and heard and seen in me, these things do: and the God of peace shall be with you. (4-9)

4. *Rejoice in the Lord.* It is an exhortation suited to the age; for, as the condition of the godly was exceedingly troubled, and dangers threatened them on every side, it was possible that they might give way, overcome by grief or impatience. Hence he enjoins them to rejoice in the Lord, even amidst hostility and disturbance. For assuredly these spiritual consolations, by which the Lord refreshes and gladdens us, ought most of all to show their strength when the whole world tempts us to despair. Let us, from the circumstances of that age, consider what efficacy there must have been in this word uttered by the mouth of Paul, who could have had special occasion of sorrow. For if they are frightened by persecutions, or imprisonments, or exile, or death, here is the apostle showing that, amidst imprisonments, in the very fire of persecution, and even in apprehension of death, he is not only joyful himself, but even cheers up others. The sum, then, is

that, come what may, believers, having the Lord standing on their side, have amply sufficient ground for joy.

The repetition serves to extend his exhortation, as if he said: 'Be steadfast and constant in this, to rejoice in the Lord; not for a moment merely, but so that your joy in Him may go on and on.' For unquestionably it differs from the joy of the world in that we know from experience that this joy is deceptive, frail and fading, and Christ even pronounces it to be accursed (Luke 6.25). Hence, that joy that is settled in God is one that is never taken away from us.

5. *Your moderation.* This can be explained in two ways. Either that he bids them give up their right sooner than that anyone should be able to complain of their sharpness or severity; as if he said, 'Let all that have to deal with you, experience your fairness and humanity.' In this way knowledge will mean experience. Or that he exhorts them to endure all things placidly. This latter meaning I prefer; for τὸ ἐπιεικές is what the Greeks use for moderation of spirit, when we are not easily moved by injuries, when we are not easily upset by adversity, but keep our equanimity. On this, Cicero says: 'My mind is tranquil, and takes everything in good part.' Such equanimity, which is as it were the mother of patience, he requires here from the Philippians, and, indeed, such as will be apparent to all, according as occasion will require, by producing its effects.

The term *modesty* does not seem appropriate here, because Paul is not in this passage forbidding haughty insolence, but directing them to conduct themselves calmly in everything, and to control themselves, even in the endurance of injuries or inconveniences.

The Lord is at hand. An anticipation, by which he forestalls any objection. For carnal sense cries out against the foregoing statement. For as the rage of the wicked is the more inflamed by our mildness, and the more they see us prepared for enduring, the more are they emboldened to lay on injuries, we are with difficulty induced to possess our souls in patience. Hence those proverbs: 'We must howl among the wolves'; 'Those who act like sheep will quickly be devoured by the wolves.' And so we conclude that the ferocity of the wicked must be repressed by corresponding violence, that they may not insult us with impunity. To such considerations Paul here opposes confidence in the Divine providence. He replies, I say, that 'the Lord is at hand', whose power can overcome their audacity, and whose goodness can conquer their malice. He promises that He will be with us, if we obey His commandment. Now, who would not rather be protected by the hand of God alone than have all the resources of the world at his command?

This is a most beautiful statement, from which we learn, in the first place, that ignorance of the providence of God is the cause of all impatience, and that this is the reason why we are so quickly, and for trivial reasons, thrown into confusion and often, too, become disheartened because we do not realize that the Lord cares for us. On the other hand, the only remedy for calming our minds is to repose unreservedly on His providence, as knowing that we are not exposed either to blind fortune, or to the caprice of the wicked, but are under the governance of God's fatherly care. In fine, the man who believes that God is present with him, has something to rest upon with security.

Now, there are two ways in which the Lord is said to be at hand: either because His judgment is at hand, or because He is prepared to give help to His people. It is used here in the latter sense, as also in Ps. 145.18, 'The Lord is near to all that call upon Him.' The meaning therefore is, the state of the godly would be wretched, if the Lord were far from them. But as He has received them under His protection and guardianship, and defends them by His hand, which is everywhere present, let them rest on the consideration that they may not be intimidated by the rage of the wicked. It is well known and common that the word *solicitudo* ('carefulness') is used for that anxiety which proceeds from distrust of Divine power or help.

6. *But in all things.* Paul uses the singular number but the neuter gender. So ἐν παντί, is equivalent to *in omni negotio* (in every matter), for προσευχή (prayer) καὶ δέησις (supplication) are feminine. In these words he exhorts the Philippians, as David does all the godly (in Ps. 55.22), and Peter also (in I Pet. 5.7), to cast all their care upon the Lord. For we are not made of iron, so as to be unshaken by temptations. But our consolation, our relief, is to deposit, or (to speak more correctly) to unload into the bosom of God everything that harasses us. Confidence, it is true, brings tranquillity to our minds, but only if we exercise ourselves in prayers. Whenever, therefore, we are assailed by any temptation, let us betake ourselves forthwith to prayer, as to a sacred refuge.

He uses *requests* here to denote desires or wishes. He would have us make them known to God by prayer and supplication, as though believers poured forth their hearts before God, when they commend themselves and all that they have to Him. Those, indeed, who look hither and thither to the vain solace of the world, may appear to be in some degree relieved; but there is only one safe haven, leaning upon the Lord.

With thanksgiving. Because many often pray to God amiss, with complaints or murmurings, as though they had just ground for accusing Him, while others cannot brook delay if He does not immediately obey their wishes, Paul joins thanksgiving with prayers. It is as though he had said, that those things which are necessary for us ought to be desired from the Lord in such a way that we nevertheless subject our affections to His will, and give thanks while asking. And, unquestionably, gratitude will have the effect upon us that the will of God will be the chief sum of our desires.

7. *And the peace of God.* Some, by turning the future tense into the optative mood, convert this statement into a prayer, but incorrectly. For it is a promise in which he shows the fruit of a firm confidence in God and of invocation. 'If you do that,' he says, '*the peace of God will guard your minds and hearts.*' Scripture is accustomed to divide the soul of man, as to its faculties, into two parts, the mind and the heart. The mind means the understanding, while the heart denotes all the dispositions or wills. These two terms, therefore, include the entire soul, in this sense: 'The peace of God will guard you, so that you shall not turn back from God in wicked thoughts or desires.'

He is right to call it *the peace of God*, inasmuch as it does not depend on the present aspect of things, and does not bend itself to the various shiftings of the world, but is founded on the firm and immutable word of God. He is right, also, to speak of it as surpassing all understanding or perception, for nothing is more foreign to the human mind, than to hope even in the depth of despair, in the depth of poverty to see riches, and in the depth of weakness not to give way, and, in fine, to promise ourselves that nothing will be wanting to us when we are destitute of all things; and all this in the grace of God alone, which is itself only known through the Word and the inward earnest of the Spirit.

8. *Finally.* There follow general exhortations relating to the whole of life. In the first place, he commends *truth*, which is simply the integrity of a good conscience, along with its fruits. Secondly, *dignity*, or sanctity, for τὸ σεμνόν denotes both—a virtue which consists in our walking worthy of our vocation, keeping away from all profane filthiness. Thirdly, *justice*, which has to do with the mutual intercourse of mankind; that we do not injure any one, that we do not defraud any one. Fourthly, *purity*, which denotes chastity in every part of life. Paul, however, does not reckon all these things to be sufficient, if we do not at the same time endeavour to be loving to all (so far as is lawful in the Lord), and have regard also to our good name. For so I interpret the words προσφιλῆ καὶ εὔφημα.

If any praise, that is, anything praiseworthy. For amidst such a corruption of morals there is so great a perversity of judgment that praise is often bestowed on what is blameworthy, and it is not allowable for Christians to desire even true praise among men, inasmuch as they are elsewhere forbidden to glory except in God alone (I Cor.

1.31). Paul, therefore, does not bid them try to gain applause or praise by good deeds, nor even to regulate their life according to the judgment of the people, but only that they should devote themselves to good works, which deserve praise, that the wicked, and the enemies of the Gospel, while they deride and reproach Christians, may yet be forced to praise their morals. Λογίζεσθαι, among the Greeks, is used, like *cogitare* in Latin, to mean 'meditate'. Meditation comes first, and then the deed follows.

9. *What things ye have learned, received, heard.* By this accumulation of words he shows that he was assiduous in these declarations; as if he said: 'This was my doctrine, my instruction, my discourse among you.' Hypocrites, on the other hand, insisted on nothing but ceremonies. Now, it was shameful to abandon the holy instruction which they had thoroughly accepted, and with which they had been imbued.

You have seen in me. The first thing in a preacher is that he should speak, not with his mouth only, but by his life, and procure authority for his doctrine by rectitude of life. Paul, accordingly, procures authority for his exhortation on the ground that he had, by his life no less than by his mouth, been their leader and master in virtues.

And the God of peace. He had spoken of the peace of God. He now more particularly confirms what he had said, by promising that God Himself, the Author of peace, would be with them. For the presence of God brings us every kind of blessing. As though he had said that they would be aware that God was present with them to make all things turn out well and prosperously, provided they applied themselves to godly and holy works.

But I rejoiced in the Lord greatly, that at length you have revived your thought for me; wherein ye did indeed take thought, but ye lacked opportunity. Not that I speak in respect of want: for I have learned, in whatsoever state I am, therewith to be content. I know both how to be abased, and I know how to abound: every where and in all things I have learned both to be full and to be hungry, both to abound and to suffer need. I can do all things in Christ which strengtheneth me. Howbeit ye did well that ye had fellowship with my affliction. (10-14)

10. *But I rejoiced.* He now declares the gratitude of his mind towards the Philippians, that they may not regret their beneficence, as usually happens when we think that our services are despised or reckoned of no account. They had sent him by Epaphroditus supplies for his necessity; he declares that their gift had acceptable to him, and says that he rejoiced that they had gained new vigour so as to exercise care for him. The metaphor is taken from trees, the strength of which is drawn inward, and lies concealed during winter, and

begins to flourish in spring. But at once he adds a correction and qualifies what he had said, that he may not seem to reprove their negligence in the past. He says, therefore, that they had formerly, too, been concerned for him, but that the circumstances of the times had not admitted of his being sooner relieved by their kindness. Thus he throws the blame on external circumstances. I refer the phrase ἐφ' ᾧ to the person of Paul; that is its strict meaning and in this way it is also more in accordance with Paul's context.

11. *Not that I speak in respect of want.* Here is a second correction, by which he forestalls any suspicion that his spirit was pusillanimous and broken down by adversities. For it was important that his constancy and moderation should be known by the Philippians, to whom he was a pattern of life. Accordingly he declares that he had been so cheered by their liberality that he could in the future endure want patiently. 'Want' refers here to disposition, for that man can never be poor in mind, who is satisfied with the lot assigned to him by God.

In what state I am, he says; that is, 'Whatever my condition may be, I am satisfied with it.' Why? because the saints know that this is pleasing to God. Hence they do not measure sufficiency by abundance, but by the will of God, which they judge of from the event, for they are persuaded that their affairs are governed by His providence and good pleasure.

12. *I know both how to be abased.* There follows a division; that he has a mind capable of bearing good luck or bad. Prosperity is wont to puff up the mind beyond measure; adversity, on the other hand, to depress. From both faults he declares himself free. 'I know', he says, 'how to be abased', that is, to bear abasement with patience. He puts περισσεύειν twice, but in the first place it is used for 'to excel'; and in the second for 'to abound', so as to correspond to their antithesis. He who knows how to use present abundance soberly and temperately with thanksgiving, prepared to part with everything whenever it may please the Lord, giving also a share to his brother according to his ability, and is also not puffed up, that man has learned to excel and to abound. This is an excellent and rare virtue, and much greater than the endurance of poverty. Let all who wish to be Christ's disciples exercise themselves in acquiring this knowledge of Paul's; but yet let them so accustom themselves to the endurance of poverty that it will not be grievous and burdensome to them when they come to be deprived of their riches.

13. *I can do all things in Christ.* Because he had boasted of very great things, and that this might not be attributed to pride or furnish others with occasions of foolish boasting, he adds that it is by Christ that he has been endowed with this fortitude. 'I can do all things,' says he,

'but it is in Christ, not by my own power, for it is Christ who supplies me with strength.' Hence we infer that Christ will not be less strong and invincible in us also if, conscious of our own weakness, we rely on His power alone. When he says 'all things', he means only those things that belong to his calling.

14. *Howbeit ye did well.* How prudently and cautiously he acts, looking carefully in both directions, that he may not lean too much to the one side or to the other! By proclaiming magnificently his steadfastness, he meant to provide against the Philippians supposing that he had given way under the pressure of want. He now takes care that it may not, from his speaking stoutly, seem that he despised their kindness—which would not merely show cruelty and obstinacy, but also pride. At the same time he provides for this, that if any other of the servants of Christ should stand in need of their help they may not be slow to assist him.

Now, ye Philippians also know, that in the beginning of the gospel, when I departed from Macedonia, no church communicated with me, in the matter of giving and receiving, but ye only. For even in Thessalonica, ye sent once and again unto my need. Not that I desire a gift; but I desire fruit that may abound to your account. But I have received all things and abound: I am full, having received from Epaphroditus the things which were sent from you, as an odour of a sweet smell, a sacrifice acceptable, well-pleasing to God. But my God shall supply all your need according to his riches in glory by Christ Jesus. Now unto God and our Father be glory for ever and ever. Amen. Salute every saint in Christ Jesus. The brethren which are with me greet you. All the saints salute you, especially they that are of Caesar's household. The grace of our Lord Jesus Christ be with you all. Amen.

Written from Rome by Epaphroditus. (15-23)

15. *And ye know.* I interpret this as having been added by way of excuse, inasmuch as he often received something from them. For if the other Churches had done their duty, it might have seemed as though he were too grasping. So in clearing himself, he praises them; and in praising them, he modestly spares others. We must also, after Paul's example, take heed lest the godly, on seeing us too much inclined to receive, should deservedly reckon us insatiable. 'You also know,' he says. In other words: 'I do not require to call other witnesses, for ye yourselves also know.' For it frequently happens, that when one thinks that others are deficient in duty, he is the more liberal in helping. Thus the liberality of some escapes the notice of others.

In the matter of giving and receiving. He alludes to money matters, in which there are two parts, the one receiving, the other expending. These have to be balanced by mutual compensation. There was an account of this nature between Paul and the churches. While Paul administered the Gospel to them, they had an obligation in return to supply him with the necessities of life; as he says elsewhere, *If we dispense to you spiritual things, is it a great matter if you give in return carnal things?* (I Cor. 10.11). Hence, if the other churches had relieved Paul's necessities, they would have been giving nothing gratuitously, but would have been simply paying their debt, for they ought to have acknowledged themselves indebted to him for the Gospel. This, however, he affirms, had not been the case, inasmuch as they had not laid out anything for his sake. What base ingratitude, and how unworthy, to neglect the apostle to whom they knew themselves to be under an obligation beyond their power to discharge! On the other hand, how great the meekness of this holy man, to bear with their inhumanity with so much gentleness and indulgence, as not to accuse them more sharply!

17. *Not that I desire a gift.* Again he refuses to accept the unfavourable opinion of immoderate cupidity, that they might not suppose that he was hinting that they ought alone to act for all, and as if he abused their kindness. He accordingly declares that he consulted not so much his own good as theirs. 'While I receive from you,' he says, 'you received just as much; for there is as much income as expenditure on this table of accounts.' The meaning of this word depends on the similitude of exchange or compensation in financial affairs.

18. *I have received all things and abound.* He declares more explicitly that he has sufficient, and honours their liberality with remarkable testimony, by saying that *he has been filled.* It was undoubtedly a moderate sum that they had sent; but he says that by means of that moderate sum he is filled to satiety. But he bestows an even more outstanding commendation on the gift in what follows, when he calls it a sacrifice acceptable to God and presented as an odour of a good fragrance. For what better thing can be desired than that our acts of kindness should be sacred offerings, which God receives from our hands and in whose sweet odour He takes pleasure? For the same reason Christ says, 'Whatsoever ye shall have done unto one of the least of these in my name, ye have done it unto me' (Matt. 25.40).

The similitude of sacrifices, however, adds much emphasis, by which we are taught that the exercise of love which God demands of us is not merely bestowed upon men, but is also a spiritual and sacred service performed to God, as we read in the Epistle to the Hebrews, that He is truly satisfied with such sacrifices (Heb. 13.16). Woe to our indolence, that when God invites us so kindly to the honour of priesthood, and even puts sacrifices in our hands, we nevertheless do not sacrifice to Him, and those things which were set apart for sacred oblations we not only lay out for profane uses, but squander them wickedly upon the most polluted corruptions. For the altars on which sacrifices from our resources ought to be presented, are the poor and the servants of Christ. To the neglect of these some waste their resources on every kind of luxury, others upon the palate, others upon ornaments, others upon fine houses.

19. *My God shall supply.* Some read *impleat*, in the optative, 'May he supply!' While I do not reject this reading, I approve more of the other. He expressly calls God 'his', because He owns and acknowledges as done to Himself whatever kindness is shown to His servants. They had therefore been truly sowing in the Lord's field, from which a sure and abundant harvest was to be expected. Nor does he promise them only a reward in the future life, but even in respect of the necessities of the present life; as if he said, 'Do not think that you have impoverished yourselves; God, whom I serve, will abundantly furnish you with everything necessary for you.'

The phrase, *in glory*, ought to be taken as the adverb 'gloriously', as meaning magnificently, or splendidly. He adds, however, *by Christ*, in whose name everything that we do is acceptable to God.

20. *Now unto God and our Father.* This can be taken as the general thanksgiving, with which he closes the epistle; or it may be referred particularly to the last clause on the liberality shown to Paul. For in respect of the help which the Philippians had given him, it became him to reckon himself indebted to them for it and to acknowledge that this aid had been afforded to them by the mercy of God.

22. *All the saints salute you.* In these salutations he names first his closest associates, afterwards all the saints in general, that is, the whole Church at Rome, but chiefly those of the household of Nero. This is worthy of notice; for it is no common evidence of divine mercy that the Gospel had penetrated that sink of all crimes and iniquities. It is also the more wonderful, because it is a rare thing for holiness to reign in courts. The conjecture of some, that Seneca is here referred to among others, has no basis; for he never gave any evidence, even the slightest, of being a Christian; nor did he belong to the household of Caesar but was a senator and praetor.

The Epistle to
THE COLOSSIANS

THE THEME OF THE EPISTLE
TO THE COLOSSIANS

THERE were three neighbouring cities in Phrygia, mentioned by Paul in this epistle, Laodicea, Hierapolis and Colosse, which, as Orosius testifies, were overthrown by an earthquake in the reign of Nero. Accordingly, not long after this epistle was written, three famous churches perished in a lamentable and horrible disaster. This is a remarkable mirror of divine judgment, if we had but eyes to see it. The Colossians had been, not indeed by Paul, but faithfully and purely by Epaphras and other ministers, instructed in the Gospel; but immediately afterwards, Satan had crept in with his tares, according to his usual and invariable manner, to pervert the true faith there.

Some think that there were two sorts of men who endeavoured to seduce the Colossians from the purity of the Gospel; that, on the one hand, the philosophers, by disputing about stars, fate, and similar trifles, and that the Jews, on the other hand, by urging their ceremonies, had enveloped everything in mists and hidden Christ. Those, however, who hold this opinion are influenced by the very flimsy conjecture that Paul mentions thrones, and powers and heavenly creatures. Their adding also the term 'elements' is worse than ridiculous. As, however, it is not my intention to refute the opinion of others, I shall simply state how things seem to me, and what may be inferred by sound reasoning.

In the first place, it is quite clear from Paul's words, that those rascals were intent on mixing up Christ with Moses and keeping the shadows of the law along with the Gospel. Hence it is probable that they were Jews. But because they painted over their fallacies with special disguises, Paul calls it a vain philosophy. At the same time, in my opinion, he inserts this word with an eye to the speculations with which they amused themselves. These were subtle, it is true, but useless and profane; for they invented an access to God through the angels, and put forth many speculations of that nature, such as are contained in the books of Dionysius on the *Celestial Hierarchy*, drawn

297

from the school of the Platonists. Therefore, the principal object at which he aims is to teach that all things are in Christ, and that He alone ought to be sufficient and more than sufficient for the Colossians.

The order he follows is this: after his customary inscription, he praises them, with a view to gaining their attention. Then, to bar the way against all new and foreign contrivances, he bears testimony to the doctrine which they had previously received from Epaphras. Afterwards, in praying that the Lord would increase their faith, he hints that something is still lacking to them, that he may pave the way for more solid instruction (*catechesin*). On the other hand, he extols with suitable commendations the divine grace towards them, that they may not make light of it. Then follows the instruction (*catechesis*), in which he teaches that all parts of our salvation are placed in Christ alone, that they may not seek anything elsewhere; and he reminds them that it was in Christ that they had obtained all their blessings, in order that they might the more carefully make it their aim to retain Him to the end. And, truly, even this one article is of itself perfectly sufficient to make us reckon this epistle, short as it is, an incomparable treasure; for what is greater in the whole of heavenly doctrine than to have Christ drawn to the life, that we may perceive His power, His office and all the fruits that come to us from Him?

For in this especially we differ from the Papists, that while we are both called Christians, and profess to believe in Christ, they invent for themselves one that is torn, disfigured, emptied of His power, denuded of His office, in fine, such as to be a spectre rather than Christ Himself. We, however, embrace Him as He is here described by Paul, living and efficacious. This epistle, therefore, to express it in one word, distinguishes the true Christ from a fictitious one. And nothing better or more excellent can be desired than this. Towards the end of the first chapter he again secures authority for himself from the role assigned him, and magnificently extols the dignity of the Gospel.

In the second chapter he opens up more clearly than he had done before the reason why he wrote, that he might forestall the danger which he saw to be impending over them. At the same time he touches, in passing, on his love for them, that they may know that their welfare is his concern. From this he proceeds to exhortation, by which he applies the foregoing doctrine, as it were, to present use; for he bids them rest in Christ alone, and condemns as vanity everything that is outside Christ. He speaks particularly of circumcision, abstinence from foods and other outward exercises—to which they mistakenly bind the service of God; and also of the absurd worship of angels, whom they put in Christ's place. Having made mention of circumcision, he takes occasion to notice also, in passing, what is the office and what is the nature of ceremonies, from which he determines that they have been abrogated by Christ. These things continue to the end of the second chapter.

In the third chapter, in opposition to those vain precepts, to the observance of which the false apostles wanted to bind believers, he mentions the true duties of godliness in which the Lord would have us occupied; and he begins from the very fountain head, that is, mortification of the flesh and newness of life. From this he derives the streams, that is, particular exhortations, some of which apply to all Christians alike, while others relate personally to particular individuals, according to the nature of their calling.

In the beginning of the fourth chapter he follows out the same subject. Afterwards, having commended himself to their prayers, he shows by many signs how much he loves them, and desires to promote their welfare.

CHAPTER ONE

Paul, an apostle of Jesus Christ through the will of God, and Timothy our brother. To the saints which are at Colosse and the faithful brethren in Christ: grace' to you and peace, from God and our Father and the Lord Jesus Christ. We give thanks to God and the Father of our Lord Jesus Christ, praying always for you, having heard of your faith which is in Christ Jesus, and of the love which ye have toward all the saints; because of the hope which is laid up for you in heaven, whereof ye heard before in the word of the truth, that is, of the Gospel, which is come unto you, even as it is also in all the world, bearing fruit and increasing as it doth in you also, since the day ye heard, and knew the grace of God in truth; even as ye learned of Epaphras our beloved comrade, who is a faithful minister of Christ to you; who also declared unto us your love in the Spirit. (1-8)

1. *Paul an apostle.* I have already often explained the point of these inscriptions. As, however, the Colossians had never seen him, and for that reason his authority was not yet so strong among them as to make his own personal name by itself sufficient, he begins by saying that he is an apostle of Christ set apart by the will of God. From this it followed that he did not act rashly in writing to unknown people, inasmuch as he was discharging the embassy with which God had entrusted him. For he was not restricted to one Church, but his apostleship extended to all.

The name *saints* which he applies to them is more noble, but in calling them *faithful brethren*, he attracts them more winningly to listen to him. The other things may be found explained in the foregoing epistles.

3. *We give thanks to God.* He praises the faith and love of the Colossians, that he may encourage them the more to persevere with alacrity and constancy. Moreover, by showing that he has this persuasion of them, he gains their friendship, that they may be the more ready and teachable for receiving his doctrine. We must always notice that he uses 'thanksgiving' for 'congratulation'; by which he teaches us that in all our joys we must quickly call to remembrance the goodness of God, inasmuch as everything that is pleasant and favourable to us is His benefit. Besides, he admonishes us by his example to acknowledge with gratitude those things which the Lord confers not only upon us, but also upon others.

But for what does he give thanks to the Lord? For the faith and love of the Colossians. He acknowledges, therefore, that both are given by God: otherwise the gratitude would be insincere. And what have we apart from His liberality? If, however, even the smallest favours come to us from that source, how much more ought this same acknowledgment to be made for those two gifts, in which the entire sum of our pre-eminence consists?

To the God and Father. Understand it thus: 'To God who is the Father of Christ.' For it is not lawful for us to know any other God than Him who has manifested Himself to us in His Son. And this is the only key that opens the door to us, if we want to come to the true God. For on this account, also, is He the Father to us, because He has embraced us in His only begotten Son and in Him sets forth His paternal favour for our contemplation.

Always for us. Some explain it thus: 'We give thanks to God for you always, that is, continually.' Others: 'Praying always for you.' It can also be expounded in this way, 'Whenever we pray for you we at the same time give thanks to God.' And this is the more simple meaning, 'We give thanks to God, and at the same time we pray.' By this he means that the condition of believers is never in this world so perfect, as not always to lack something. For even the man who has begun admirably may fail a hundred times a day; and we must ever be making progress while we are still on the way. Let us therefore bear in mind that we must rejoice in the graces that we have already received and give thanks to God for them in such a way as to seek from Him perseverance and increase.

4. *Having heard of your faith.* It aroused his love towards them and his concern for their salvation, when he heard that they excelled in faith and love. And unquestionably, such excellent gifts of God ought to have the effect on us of stirring us up to love them wherever they appear. He says, faith *in Christ,* that we may always bear in mind that Christ is the proper object of faith (*proprium fidei scopum*).

He uses *love towards the saints* not to exclude others, but because anyone who is joined to us in God we ought to embrace the more closely with a special love. True love, therefore, will extend to mankind universally, because all are our flesh, and created in the image of God, but in respect of degrees, it will begin with those who are of the household of faith.

5. *Because of the hope which is laid up for you in heaven.* For the hope of eternal life will never be inactive in us and fail to produce love in us. For it must needs be that the man who is fully persuaded that the treasure of life is laid up for him in heaven will aspire thither, despising this world. Meditation on the heavenly life ravishes our affections to

the worship of God and to exercises of love. The Sophists misuse this passage to extol the merits of works, as if the hope of salvation depended on works. Their reasoning, however, is futile. For it does not follow that, because it stimulates us to upright living, it is therefore founded upon works; for nothing is more effective for this than God's free goodness, which utterly annihilates all confidence in works.

Now, there is a metonymy in the word 'hope', as it is taken for the thing hoped for. For the hope that is in our minds is the glory which we hope for in heaven. But when he says that there is a hope laid up for us in heaven, he means that believers ought to be as assured of the promise of eternal felicity, as if they had already a treasure laid up in a safe place.

Whereof ye heard before. Because eternal salvation is something that surpasses the grasp of our mind, he adds that the assurance of it had been brought to the Colossians by the Gospel; and at the same time he says at once, that he is not bringing forward anything new, but only doing this to confirm them in the doctrine which they had previously received. Erasmus has rendered it, 'the true word of the Gospel'. I am also aware that, following the Hebrew idiom, the genitive is often used by Paul in place of an adjective. But Paul's words here are more emphatic. For he calls the Gospel, κατ' ἐξοχήν, *the word of truth*, to honour it, that they may more steadfastly and firmly adhere to the revelation which they have received. Thus the word *gospel* is introduced by way of apposition.

6. *Even as it is also in all the world bearing fruit.* It avails both to confirm and to comfort the godly to see the effect of the Gospel far and wide in gathering many to Christ. Its credit does not, it is true, depend on its success, as though we should believe because many believe. Though the whole world should fail and heaven itself fall, the conscience of a godly man should not waver, because God, on whom it is founded, remains true in spite of everything. This, however, does not hinder our faith from being helped, whenever it perceives God's power, which undoubtedly exerts itself more strongly the greater the number of people that are won to Christ.

In addition to this, in the multitude of the believers at that time there was seen the fulfilment of the many prophecies extending the reign of Christ from the east to the west. Is it a trivial or common aid to faith to see accomplished before our eyes what the prophets long before predicted as to the spreading of the kingdom of Christ through all countries of the world? There is no believer who does not experience in himself what I speak of. Paul accordingly wanted to encourage the Colossians the more by this statement, that, by seeing everywhere the fruit and progress of the Gospel, they might embrace it with more eager zeal.

Αὐξανόμενον, which I have rendered *propagatur* (is increased), is not read in some copies; but because it fits the context better, I did not want to omit it. It also appears from the commentaries of the old writers that this reading was always the more customary.

Since the day ye heard, and knew the grace. He praises their docility, in immediately embracing sound doctrine; and he praises their constancy, in that they persevered in it. And the faith of the Gospel is rightly called the knowledge of God's grace; for no one has ever tasted of the Gospel but the man who knew himself reconciled to God and took hold of the salvation held forth in Christ.

In truth means 'truly' and 'without pretence'. For as he had previously declared that the Gospel is undoubted truth, so he now adds that it had been sincerely delivered to them, and that by Epaphras. For because all claim to preach the Gospel and yet at the same time there are many evil workers, through whose ignorance, or ambition, or avarice, its purity is adulterated, it is most important that faithful ministers should be distinguished from the less upright. For it is not enough to keep to the name 'Gospel', unless we know that it is the true Gospel which was preached by Paul and Epaphras. Hence Paul confirms the teaching of Epaphras by giving it his approbation, that he may retain the Colossians in it, and may, by the same means, call them back from those scoundrels who endeavoured to introduce strange doctrines. At the same time, he gives Epaphras a special distinction, that he may have more authority among them. And lastly, he presents him as deserving the Colossians' love, by saying that he had borne testimony to him of their love. Paul everywhere labours, by his recommendation, to make those whom he knows to be faithful servants of Christ very dear to the churches; as, on the other hand, the ministers of Satan are wholly intent on alienating, by injurious reports, the minds of the simple from faithful pastors.

Love in the Spirit I take to mean 'spiritual love', with Chrysostom, with whom, however, I do not agree on the preceding words. Now spiritual love is that which is not concerned with the world, but is consecrated to the service of godliness, and has, as it were, an inward root, while carnal friendships depend on external causes.

For this cause we also, since the day we heard it, do not cease to pray for you, and to desire that ye might be filled with the knowledge of his will in all wisdom and spiritual prudence; that ye might walk worthy of God unto all pleasing, bearing fruit in every good work, and increasing in the knowledge of God; strengthened with all might, according to the power of his glory, unto all long-suffering and patience with joy. (9-11)

9. *For this cause we also.* As he has previously shown his affection for them in his thanksgivings, so he now shows it in the earnestness of his prayers. And, assuredly, the more the grace of God is conspicuous in anyone, we ought specially to love and care for them and be concerned as to their welfare. But what does he ask for them? That they may know God more fully. By this he suggests that something is still wanting in them, that he may prepare the way for teaching them, and may win a hearing for a fuller statement of doctrine. For those who think that they have already attained everything worth knowing, despise and disdain anything more advanced. He removes this idea from the Colossians, lest it should be a hindrance to their willing progress, and allowing what had been begun in them to be finished. But what knowledge does he desire for them? The knowledge of *the divine will*, by which expression he rejects all inventions of men and all speculations foreign to the Word of God. For His will is not to be sought anywhere else than in His Word.

He adds, *In all wisdom*; by which he means that the will of God, of which he had spoken, was the only rule of right knowledge. For he who desires in simplicity to know those things which it has pleased God to reveal, will know what it is to be truly wise. If we desire anything beyond that, we shall only become foolish, by not keeping within due bounds. By the word συνέσεως, which we render 'prudentiam' (prudence), I understand that discrimination which proceeds from understanding. Both are called spiritual by Paul, because they are not attained otherwise than by the guidance of the Spirit. For the animal man does not perceive the things that are of God (I Cor. 2.14). So long as men are regulated by their carnal perceptions, they have also their own wisdom, but it is mere vanity, however complacent they may be about it. We see what sort of theology there is under the Papacy, what is contained in the books of philosophers, and what wisdom secular men esteem. Let us, however, bear in mind that the wisdom which is alone commended by Paul is comprehended in the will of God.

10. *That ye may walk worthy of God.* First he teaches what is the aim of spiritual understanding, and for what purpose we must advance in God's school—that we may walk worthy of God, that is, that it may appear in our life that we have not been taught by God in vain. Those who do not direct their endeavours towards this object, may possibly toil and labour a great deal, but they are really only wandering about in endless circuits, without making any progress. Then he admonishes us that, if we would walk worthy of God, we must above all

things take heed to devote our whole course of life to the will of God, renouncing our own views, and bidding farewell to all the inclinations of our flesh.

This also he again confirms by adding 'unto all compliance' (*obsequium*), or, as they commonly say, well-pleasing. Hence, if it is asked what kind of life is worthy of God, let us always remember this definition of Paul, that it is one that, leaving what accords with men, and leaving, in short, all carnal inclination, is adjusted to obedience to God alone. From this follow good works, which are the fruits that God requires from us.

Increasing in the knowledge of God. He again repeats that they have not got so far that they do not need further increase; by which admonition he prepares them, and as it were leads them by the hand, to an eagerness for advancing, that they may show themselves ready to listen and teachable. What is here said to the Colossians, let all believers take as said to themselves, and draw from it a common exhortation: that we must always make progress in the doctrine of godliness until death.

11. *Strengthened with all might.* As he had previously prayed that they might have both a sound understanding and the right practice of it, so also now he prays that they may have courage and constancy. In this way he puts them in mind of their own weakness; for he says that they will be strong only by the Lord's help. And moreover, to magnify this grace the more, he adds, 'according to his glorious power'; as if he said: 'So far from anyone being able to stand by depending on his own strength, the power of God shows itself grandly in helping our infirmity.' Lastly, he shows in what it is that the strength of believers ought to display itself: 'in all patience and long-suffering'. For they are continually, while in this world, exercised with the cross, and a thousand temptations daily weigh on them and press them down and they see nothing of what God has promised. They must, therefore, arm themselves with a wonderful patience, that what Isaiah says may be accomplished. 'In hope and in silence shall be your strength' (Isa. 30.15).

It is preferable to connect with this sentence the clause *with joy.* For although the other reading is more common in the Latin versions, this one is more in accordance with the Greek manuscripts. And unquestionably, patience is only sustained by cheerfulness, and none will ever have a steadfast and brave heart unless he is pleased with his lot.

Giving thanks unto God and the Father, who made us meet to be partakers of the inheritance of the saints in light: who delivered us from the power of darkness, and translated us into the kingdom of his dear Son;

in whom we have redemption through his blood, the forgiveness of sins:
who is the image of the invisible God, the first-born of every creature:
for in him were all things created, that are in heaven, and that are upon
the earth, visible and invisible, whether thrones or dominions or princi-
palities or powers; all things were created by him, and unto him: and
he is before all things, and in him all things consist. (12-17)

12. *Giving thanks.* Again he returns to thanksgiving, as an opportunity for enumerating the blessings given them through Christ, and
thus he enters upon a full description of Christ. For the only remedy
for the Colossians against all the snares by which the false apostles
endeavoured to trap them was to grasp thoroughly what Christ was.
For how comes it that we are carried about with so many doctrines,
but because the power of Christ is not perceived by us? For Christ
alone makes all other things suddenly disappear. Hence there is
nothing that Satan tries so hard to do as to raise up mists to obscure
Christ; for he knows that by this means the way is opened up for
every kind of falsehood. Therefore, the sole means of retaining as
well as restoring pure doctrine is to set Christ before our eyes, just as
He is with all His blessings, that His power may be truly perceived.

We are not concerned here merely with a name. Papists in common
with us confess the one Christ; yet how great a difference there is
between us and them! For they, after confessing Christ to be the Son
of God, transfer His power to others and scatter it hither and thither,
and thus leave Him next to empty, or at least rob Him of a great part
of His glory, so that although He is called the Son of God, He is not
such as the Father wished Him to be towards us. If, however, Papists
would cordially embrace what is contained in this chapter, we would
soon be in agreement, but the whole Papacy would collapse, for it
can stand only by ignorance of Christ. This will undoubtedly be
acknowledged by everyone that will but consider the main article of
this first chapter; for his only object here is that we may know that
Christ is the beginning, middle and end; that it is from Him that all
things must be sought; that nothing is, or can be found outside Him.
Now, therefore, let readers carefully and attentively observe in what
colours Paul depicts Christ to us.

Who made us meet. He is still speaking of the Father, because He is
the beginning and efficient cause (as they say) of our salvation. As
the name 'God' expresses majesty more strongly, so the name 'Father'
conveys clemency and benevolence. It becomes us to contemplate
both in God, that His majesty may inspire us with fear and reverence
and that His fatherly love may win our confidence. Hence it is not
without reason that Paul has joined these two things, if you prefer the

reading which the Vulgate has followed, and which some very ancient Greek manuscripts agree with. Yet, there will be no inconsistency in saying that he contents himself with the single word, 'Father'. And as it is necessary that His incomparable grace should be expressed by 'Father', it is no less necessary that we should, by the name 'God', be carried away with wonder at such great goodness, that He who is God has so lowered Himself.

But for what kindness does he give thanks to God? For having made him and others meet to be partakers of the inheritance of the saints. For we are born children of wrath, exiles from God's Kingdom. It is God's adoption alone that makes us meet. Now, adoption depends on free election. The Spirit of regeneration is the seal of adoption. He adds, *in light*, that there might be a contrast, as opposed to the darkness of Satan's kingdom.

13. *Who delivered us.* Note that here is the beginning of our salvation, when God delivers us from the depth of ruin in which we were plunged. For wherever His grace is not, there is darkness, as it is said in Isa. 60.2, 'Behold, darkness shall cover the earth, and gross darkness the peoples; but the Lord shall arise upon thee, and his glory shall be seen upon thee.' First we ourselves are called darkness, and then afterwards the whole world and Satan the prince of darkness, under whose tyranny we are held captive until we are set free by Christ's hand. From this you may gather that the whole world, with all its pretended wisdom and righteousness, is regarded as nothing but darkness in the sight of God, because, outside the Kingdom of Christ there is no light.

And translated us into the kingdom. It is the beginning of our blessedness when we are translated into the Kingdom of Christ, for we pass from death into life. Paul ascribes this also to the grace of God, that no one may imagine that he can attain such a blessing by his own efforts. As, then, our deliverance from the slavery of sin and death is the work of God, so also is our transition into the Kingdom of Christ. He calls Christ *the Son of his love*, or beloved by God the Father, because it is in Him alone that His soul is satisfied (as we read in Matt. 17.5), and through whom all others are loved. For we must hold it as a settled point that we are not acceptable to God otherwise than through Christ. Nor can it be doubted that Paul wanted to point out indirectly the enmity that exists between men and God until love shines forth in the Mediator.

14. *In whom we have redemption.* He now follows this up with a list of how all the parts of our salvation are contained in Christ and how He alone ought to shine forth and be seen conspicuous above all creatures, inasmuch as He is the beginning and end of all things.

First, he says that we have redemption, and immediately explains it as *the remission of sins*; for these two things belong together by apposition. For, without doubt, when God remits our sins, He exempts us from condemnation to eternal death. This is our liberty, this our glorying against death, that our sins are not imputed to us. He says that this redemption was procured by *the blood of Christ*, for by the sacrifice of His death all the sins of the world have been expiated. Let us, therefore, remember that this is the sole price of reconciliation, and that all the trifling of Papists about satisfactions is blasphemy.

15. *Who is the image of the invisible God.* He mounts higher in discoursing on the glory of Christ. He calls Him the image of the invisible God, meaning by this, that it is through Him alone that God, who is otherwise invisible, is manifested to us, as it is said: 'No man hath even seen God: the only begotten, who is in the bosom of the Father, hath manifested him to us' (John 1.18). I am aware how the old writers used to explain this. For, having a controversy with the Arians, they emphasize the equality of the Son with the Father, and the ὁμοουσίαν; yet they are silent on the chief point as to how the Father reveals to us the knowledge of Himself in Christ. Chrysostom lays the whole stress of his defence on the word 'image', by contending that the creature cannot be said to be the image of the Creator; but this is very weak; in fact, it is refuted by Paul, whose words are, 'The man is the image and glory of God' (I Cor. 11.7).

Therefore, that we may not receive anything but what is sound, let us note that the word 'image' is not used of His essence, but has a reference to us. For Christ is the image of God because He makes God in a manner visible to us. At the same time, we gather also from this His ὁμοουσία, for Christ would not truly represent God if He were not the essential Word of God. For Paul is not concerned here with those things which by communication belong also to creatures, but with the perfect wisdom, goodness, righteousness and power of God, for the representing of which no creature would suffice. We shall have, therefore, in this term a powerful weapon against the Arians; but nevertheless we must begin with the reference I have mentioned and not insist on the essence alone. The sum is, that God in Himself, that is, in His naked majesty, is invisible; and that not only to the physical eyes, but also to human understanding; and that He is revealed to us in Christ alone, where we may behold Him as in a mirror. For in Christ He shows us His righteousness, goodness, wisdom, power, in short, His entire self. We must, therefore, take care not to seek Him elsewhere; for outside Christ, everything that claims to represent God will be an idol.

The first-born of every creature. The reason for this name immediately follows: *For in him all things are created.* In the same way He is, three verses later, called 'the first-begotten from the dead', because through Him we all rise again. Hence, He is not called the firstborn because He preceded all creatures in time, but because He was begotten by the Father, that they might be created through Him, and that He might be, as it were, the substance or foundation of all things. It was, then, foolish of the Arians to argue from this that He was consequently a creature. For what is here treated of is, not what He is in Himself, but what He accomplishes in others.

16. *Visible and invisible.* Both these kinds were included in the foregoing distinction of heavenly and earthly things. But as Paul meant chiefly to refer to the angels, he now mentions things invisible. Not only, therefore, the heavenly creatures which are visible to us, but spiritual creatures also have been created by the Son of God. What immediately follows, *whether thrones, etc.,* is as though he had said: 'By whatever name they are called.'

By 'thrones' some understand the angels. I think, however, that the heavenly palace of God's majesty is meant. Yet we must not imagine it to be such as our mind can conceive of, but such as belongs to God Himself. We see the sun and the moon and the whole world of heaven, but the glory of God's Kingdom is hidden from our perception, because it is spiritual and above the heavens. In short, let us understand by 'thrones' that seat of blessed immortality which is free from all change.

By the other words he undoubtedly describes the angels. He calls them powers, principalities and dominions, not as if they exercised some dominion of their own, or were endued with their own power, but because they are the ministers of the divine power and dominion. It is customary, however, for God's names to be transferred to creatures in so far as He exerts His power in them. Thus He Himself is alone Lord and Father, but they are also called fathers and lords whom He dignifies with this honour. Hence it is that angels, and judges too, are called gods. This is also why in this passage angels are denoted by magnificent titles, which declare, not what they can do of themselves or apart from God, but what God does by them, and what functions He has assigned to them. We must understand these things in such a way as to detract nothing from God's unique glory. For He does not so communicate His power to angels as to lessen His own; He does not work by them in such a way as to resign His power to them; He does not want His glory to shine forth in them, and be obscured in Himself. Paul, however, purposely extols the dignity of angels magnificently, yet in such a way that no one may think that it prevents Christ alone having the pre-eminence over them. He makes use, therefore, of these names, as it were by way of concession; as if he had said that all their excellence detracts nothing from Christ, however lofty the titles with which they are adorned. As for those who philosophize on these words so subtly and draw from them different orders of angels, let them enjoy themselves; but they are assuredly very far from Paul's mind.

17. *All things were created by him and unto him*. He subjects the angels to Christ, that they may not obscure His glory, for four reasons: Because they were created by Him. Secondly, because their creation ought to be referred to Him, as their legitimate end. Thirdly, because He himself existed always, before they were created. Fourthly, because He sustains them by His power, and upholds them in their state. Yet, he does not affirm this of angels alone, but also of the whole world. Thus he places the Son of God in the highest seat of honour, that He may preside over angels as well as men, and may bring into order all creatures in heaven and on earth.

And he is the head of the body, the church; who is the beginning, the first-born from the dead; that in all things he might have the pre-eminence: for it was the good pleasure, that in him should all fulness dwell: and through him to reconcile all things unto himself having made peace through the blood of his cross; through him, whether things upon earth, or things in heaven. (18-20)

18. *The head of the body*. Having discoursed generally on Christ's excellence and on His sovereign dominion over all creatures, he returns to those things which relate peculiarly to the Church. Some consider that many things are included under the word 'head'. And certainly he later uses the same metaphor in the sense that, as in the human body it serves as the root from which vital energy flows to all the members, so the life of the Church flows out from Christ, etc. Here, however, in my opinion, he speaks chiefly of government. He shows, therefore, that it is Christ who alone has authority to govern the Church, that it is He to whom alone believers should look and on whom alone the unity of the body depends.

When the Papists want to support the tyranny of their idol, they allege that the Church would be ἀκέφαλον, if the Pope did not rule in it as a head.

Paul, however, does not allow this honour even to angels. And yet he does not behead the Church; for as Christ claims for Himself this title, so He truly exercises the office. I am also aware of the quibble by which they try to escape, that the Pope is a ministerial head. But the name of head is too noble to be transferred to any mortal man under any pretext, especially without the command of Christ. Gregory is more modest, when he writes in Epistle 92, Book 4 that Peter was indeed the chief member of the Church, but that he and the other apostles were members under one Head.

He is the beginning. As ἀρχή sometimes means in Greek the end to which all things are referred, we might understand that Christ is ἀρχή in this sense. I prefer, however, to explain Paul's words thus: That He is the Beginning, because He is the Firstborn from the dead. For in the resurrection there is the restoration of all things, and thus it is the beginning of the second and new creation, for the former had fallen in the ruin of the first man. As, then, Christ in rising again had inaugurated the kingdom of God, He is rightly called the beginning. For we truly begin to exist in the sight of God, when we are renewed and become new creatures.

He is called *the first-begotten from the dead,* not only because He was the first to rise again, but because He has also restored life to others, as He is elsewhere called the firstfruits of them that rise (I Cor. 15.20).

That he may in all things. From this he concludes that supremacy belongs to Him in all things. For if He is the Author and Restorer of all things, it is certain that this honour is justly due to Him. But the phrase 'in all things', may be taken in two ways, either over all creatures, or, in everything. This, however, does not matter much, for the simple meaning is, that all things are subjected to His rule.

19. *Because it hath been the good pleasure.* To confirm what he has declared about Christ, he now adds that it was so settled by the providence of God. And, indeed, in order to adore this mystery with reverence, we must be led back to that fountain. 'This', he says, 'was done by the counsel of God, that all fulness may dwell in Him.' Now he means a fulness of righteousness, wisdom, power and every blessing. For whatever God has He has conferred upon His Son, that He may be glorified in Him, as it is said in John 5.20.[1] He shows us, however, at the same time, that we must draw from the fulness of Christ all the good that we desire for our salvation, because it is the determination of God not to communicate Himself or His gifts to men otherwise than by His Son. Therefore it is as if he had said, 'Christ is all things to us: apart from Him we have nothing.' Hence it follows that all that detract from Christ or minimize His power, or rob Him of His offices, or, in fine, take away one drop from His fulness, weaken, so far as they can, God's eternal counsel.

20. *And by him to reconcile all things to himself.* This also is a magnificent commendation of Christ, that we cannot be joined to God otherwise than through Him. First, let us consider that our happiness consists in our cleaving to God, and that, on the other hand, there is

[1] This should probably be John 3.35.

nothing more miserable than to be alienated from Him. He declares, accordingly, that we are blessed through Christ alone, inasmuch as He is the bond of our union with God (*vinculum nostrae cum Deo coniunctionis*), and, on the other hand, that, apart from Him, we are most miserable, because we are shut out from God. Let us bear in mind, however, that what he ascribes to Christ belongs to Him peculiarly, that no portion of this praise may be transferred to any other. Hence the antithesis must be supplied, that if this is Christ's prerogative, it does not belong at all to others. For he is expressly arguing against those who imagined that the angels were peace-makers, through whom access to God could be opened up.

Making peace through the blood of his cross. He says of the Father, that He is propitious to His creatures through the blood of Christ. Now he calls it 'the blood of the cross', because the pledge and price of our reconciliation with God was the blood of Christ, which was poured out on the cross. For the Son of God had to become an expiatory victim and endure the punishment of sin, that we might be the righteousness of God in Him. *The blood of the cross*, therefore, means the blood of the sacrifice which was offered upon the cross for appeasing the anger of God.

In adding 'by him', he did not mean to say anything new, but to express more distinctly what he had previously stated, and to impress it still more deeply on our minds, that Christ alone is the Author of reconciliation, and therefore excludes all other means. For no one else has been crucified for us. Hence it is He alone by whom and for whose sake we have God propitious to us.

Both upon earth and in heaven. If you are inclined to understand this only of rational creatures, it will mean, men and angels. But there would be no absurdity in extending it to all without exception. But that I may not have to philosophize too subtly, I prefer to understand it of angels and men. As to the latter, there is no difficulty about their needing a peace-maker in the sight of God. As to angels, however, there is a question not easy of solution. For how can there be reconciliation where there is no discord or enmity? Many, motivated by this consideration, have explained the present passage like this: that angels have been brought into concord with men, and that by this means the heavenly has been restored to favour with the earthly. But Paul's words say something different, *that God hath reconciled to himself.* That explanation, therefore, is forced.

It remains to see what is the reconciliation of angels and men. I say that men have been reconciled to God because they were previously alienated from Him by sin, and because they would have experienced Him as the Judge to their ruin, had not the grace of the Mediator interposed to appease His anger. Hence the nature of the peace-maker between God and men is that enmities have been abolished through Christ, and thus God from a Judge becomes a Father.

Between God and angels the relationship is very different, for there was there no revolt, no sin and consequently no separation. It was, however, necessary for two reasons for angels also to be set at peace with God; for, being creatures, they were not beyond the risk of falling, had they not been confirmed by the grace of Christ. It is of no small importance for the perpetuity of peace with God to have a fixed standing in righteousness, so as no longer to fear fall or revolt. Further, in that very obedience which they render to God, there is not such absolute perfection as to satisfy God in every respect and without pardon. And this, without doubt, is the sense of that statement in the Book of Job, 'He will find iniquity in his angels' (4.18). For if it is expounded of the devil, what would be the point of it? But the Spirit declares there that the greatest purity is soiled, if measured by the righteousness of God. We must, therefore, lay it down that there is not in the angels so much righteousness as would suffice for full union with God. They have, therefore, need of a peace-maker, through whose grace they may wholly cleave to God. Hence Paul rightly declares that the grace of Christ does not reside in men alone but is common also to the angels. Nor is any injustice done to angels in sending them to the Mediator, that they may through His benefit have complete peace with God.

Should anyone, on the plea of the universality of the expression, ask in reference to devils, whether Christ is their Peace-maker also, I answer, 'No; not even of the ungodly.' Though I confess that there is a difference, inasmuch as the benefit of redemption is offered to the ungodly, but not to the devils. This, however, has nothing to do with Paul's words, which only say that it is through Christ alone that all creatures who have any connexion at all with God cleave to Him.

And you, being in time past alienated, and enemies in your mind in evil works, yet now hath he reconciled in the body of his flesh through death, to present you holy and unreproveable in his sight; if ye continue in the faith grounded and steadfast, and be not moved away from the hope of the gospel which ye heard, which was preached to every creature which is under heaven; whereof I Paul was made a minister. (21-23)

21. *And you, being in time past.* He now applies the general doctrine particularly to them, that they may feel guilty of great ingratitude, if they allow themselves to be drawn away from Christ to new in-

ventions. And this arrangement must be carefully observed, because the particular application, so to say, of a doctrine is more affecting. Then, he recalls them to experience, that they may recognize in themselves the benefit of that redemption which he had mentioned. As if he said, 'You are yourselves a sample of that grace which I declare to have been offered to men through Christ. For ye were *alienated*; that is, from God. Ye were *enemies*; now ye are received into favour. Whence comes this? It is because God, appeased by the death of Christ, has become reconciled to you.' At the same time, there is in this statement a change of person, for what he has hitherto declared of the Father, he now affirms about Christ. For we must necessarily expound it as, 'in the body of His flesh'.

The term διανοίας I explain as used for amplification, as if he had said that they were altogether and in the whole of their thinking alienated from God; so that no one may imagine philosophically that the alienation is in one particular part, in the way that the Papal theologians restrict it to the lower appetites. 'In fact,' says Paul, 'what made you hateful to God had taken possession of your whole mind.' In short, he wanted to say that man, whatever he may be, is wholly at variance with God, and is an enemy to Him. The Vulgate renders it *sensum* ('sense'), and Erasmus *mentem* ('mind'). I have used the term *cogitationis*, to denote what the French call *intention*. For such is the force of the Greek word, and Paul's meaning requires it.

Moreover, while the word 'enemies' has a passive as well as active signification, it is well suited to us in both respects, so long as we are outside Christ. For we are born children of wrath, and every thought of the flesh is enmity against God.

In evil works. He shows from its effects the inward hatred which lies hidden in the heart. For as men endeavour to shift from themselves all blame, until they have been openly convicted, God shows their impiety by outward works, as is more fully treated in Rom. 1.19. Farther, what is told us here about the Colossians is applicable to us also, for we are no different by nature. There is only the difference that God calls some from their mother's womb, and forestalls their malice so as to prevent them from breaking forth into open fruits, while others, after wandering for a great part of their life, are brought back to the fold. We all, however, need Christ as our Peace-maker, because we are the slaves of sin, and where sin is, there is enmity between God and men.

22. *In the body of his flesh.* The expression seems absurd; but the 'body of his flesh' means that human body which the Son of God had in common with us. He meant, therefore, to express that the Son of God had put on the same nature with us, that He took upon Him this

COLOSSIANS 1 [v. 22-23]

lowly and earthly body, subject to many infirmities, that He might be our Mediator.

When he adds *through death*, he again recalls us to sacrifice. For the Son of God had to become man and be partaker of our flesh, that He might be our Brother; He had to become a sacrifice by dying, that He might reconcile His Father to us.

That he might present us holy. The second principal part of our salvation is newness of life. For the entire blessing of redemption consists mainly in these two things: remission of sins and spiritual regeneration (Jer. 31.33). What he has already said was great, that righteousness has been procured for us by the death of Christ, so that, our sins being abolished, we are acceptable to God. Now, however, he teaches us that there is in addition to this another benefit equally great, the gift of the Holy Spirit, by which we are reformed to the image of God. And this is a passage worthy of note, that free righteousness is not conferred upon us in Christ without our being at the same time regenerated by the Spirit to the obedience of righteousness; as he teaches us elsewhere that Christ is made to us righteousness and sanctification (I Cor. 1.30). The former we obtain by free acceptance, and the latter by the gift of the Holy Spirit, when we are made new men. And there is an inseparable connexion between these two graces.

Let us, however, note that this holiness is only begun in us, and is every day progressing, but will not be perfected until Christ shall appear for the restoration of all things. For the Coelestinians and Pelagians in ancient times wickedly abused this passage, to exclude the grace of the remission of sins. For they imagined a perfection in this world which could satisfy the judgment of God, so that mercy was superfluous. Paul, however, does not by any means show us here what is accomplished in this world, but what is the end of our calling, and what blessings are brought to us by Christ.

23. *If ye continue.* This is an exhortation to perseverance, by which he admonishes them that all the grace bestowed upon them hitherto would be vain, unless they remained in the purity of the Gospel. And thus he intimates that they are still only *en route* and have not yet reached the goal. For the stability of their faith was at that time endangered through the stratagems of the false apostles. And he depicts assurance of faith graphically when he bids the Colossians to be grounded and settled in it. For faith is not like a mere opinion, which is shaken by various movements, but has a firm steadfastness, able to withstand all the machinations of hell. Hence the whole Papist theology will never afford even the slightest taste of true faith, for it holds it as an axiom that we must always be in doubt about the present state of grace and about final perseverance.

He afterwards notices the relationship between faith and the Gospel, when he says that the Colossians will be settled in the faith only if they do not fall away from the hope of the Gospel, that is, the hope which shines forth upon us through the Gospel; for where the Gospel is, there is the hope of everlasting salvation. Let us, however, bear in mind that the sum of all things is contained in Christ. Hence he enjoins them here to shun all doctrines which lead away from Christ, and make men's minds occupied elsewhere.

Which ye heard. Because even the false apostles, who tear and rend Christ in pieces, are accustomed proudly to claim the support of the Gospel (a common trick of Satan to trouble men's consciences under a false pretence of the Gospel, so as to confuse the truth of the Gospel), Paul expressly declares that that was the genuine, the undoubted Gospel, which the Colossians had heard from Epaphras. And he says this lest they should lend an ear to contrary teaching. He adds the confirmation that it is the very same as was preached over the whole world. It is, I say, no ordinary confirmation when they hear that they have the whole Church agreeing with them, and that they follow no other sort of doctrine than what the apostles had alike taught and was everywhere received.

It is, however, a ridiculous boasting of Papists, when they attack our doctrine with the argument that it is not preached everywhere with approbation and applause, inasmuch as we have few that assent to it. For though they should burst with trying, they will never deprive us of the fact that we today teach nothing but what was preached of old by the prophets and apostles, and is obediently received by the whole band of saints. For Paul did not mean that the Gospel should be approved by the consent of all ages in such a way that, if it were rejected, its authority would be shaken. But rather, he was concerned with that commandment of Christ, 'Go, preach the gospel to every creature' (Mark 16.15), which depends on so many predictions of the prophets, proclaiming that the Kingdom of Christ would be spread over the whole world. What else then does Paul mean by these words than that the Colossians had also been watered by those living waters, which, springing forth from Jerusalem, were to flow out through the whole world?

We also do not glory in vain, or without wonderful fruit and consolation, that we have the same Gospel which is preached among all nations by the commandment of the Lord, which is received by all the churches, and in the profession of which all the godly have lived and died. It is also no common help for fortifying us against so many assaults, that we have the consent of the whole Church—such, I mean, as is worthy of so sublime a title. We also freely subscribe to

Augustine, who refutes the Donatists by this argument, particularly that they bring forward a Gospel unheard of and unknown in any of the churches. And this is very good; for if it is the true Gospel that is brought forward, and yet it is not ratified by the approbation of any church, it follows that the many promises are vain and false in which it is predicted that the preaching of the Gospel will be carried to the whole world, and which declare that the sons of God shall be gathered from all peoples and countries, etc. But what do Papists do? Having bidden farewell to the prophets and apostles, and neglecting the ancient Church, they want their revolt from the Gospel to be regarded as the consent of the catholic Church. Where is the resemblance? Hence, when there is a dispute on the consent of the Church, let us return to the apostles and their preaching, as Paul does here. Moreover, lest any one should explain too rigidly the mark of universality, Paul means simply that it had been preached everywhere far and wide.

Of which I was made. He deals also with his own person; and this was very necessary. For we must always take care not to intrude ourselves rashly into the office of teaching. Therefore, that he might secure for himself right and authority, he declares that this office was laid upon him. And, indeed, he so connects his apostleship with their faith, that they cannot reject his doctrine without abandoning the Gospel which they had embraced.

Now I rejoice in my sufferings for you, and fill up that which is lacking of the afflictions of Christ in my flesh for his body's sake, which is the Church; whereof I am made a minister, according to the dispensation of God which was given me to you-ward, to fulfil the word of God; even the mystery which hath been hid from ages and generations, but now hath been manifested to his saints: to whom God willed to make known what is the riches of the glory of this mystery among the Gentiles; which is Christ in you, the hope of glory: whom we proclaim, admonishing every man and teaching every man in all wisdom; that we may present every man perfect in Christ Jesus: whereunto I also labour, striving according to his power, which worketh in me mightily. (24-29)

24. *Now I rejoice.* He has previously declared his authority on the basis of his calling. Now, however, he takes steps to prevent the dignity of his apostleship being lowered by the bonds and persecution which he endured for the sake of the Gospel. For Satan perverts these things, too, into occasions of making the servants of God more contemptible. However, he encourages them by his example not to be intimidated by persecutions, and he commends his own zeal, that his

317

words may have greater weight. More, he gives proof of his affection towards them by no common pledge when he declares that he willingly bears for their sake the afflictions he endures. 'But whence', someone may ask, 'arises his joy?' From seeing the fruit that sprang from it. As if he had said, 'Affliction for your sake is sweet to me, because I do not suffer it in vain.' Just as in I Thessalonians he says that he rejoiced in all necessities and afflictions, because of what he had heard of their faith (I Thess. 3.6, 7).

And fill up what is lacking. I understand the conjunction as causative. He assigns a reason why he is joyful in his sufferings, that he is in this matter a partner with Christ, and nothing happier can be desired than this partnership. He also brings forward a consolation common to all the godly, that in all tribulations, especially in so far as they suffer anything for the sake of the Gospel, they are partakers of the cross of Christ, so that they may enjoy fellowship with Him in the blessed resurrection.

More, he declares that there is thus filled up what is lacking in the afflictions of Christ. As he says in Rom. 8.29, 'Whom God elected, them he also predestinated to be conformed to the image of Christ, that he might be the first-born among the brethren.' Moreover, we know that there is so great a unity between the Head and the members that the name of Christ sometimes includes the whole body, as in I Cor. 12.12. For while discoursing there on the Church, he concludes at length that in Christ the same thing holds as in the human body. As, therefore, Christ has suffered once in His own Person, so He suffers daily in His members, and in this way there are filled up those sufferings which the Father has by this decree appointed for His Body. There is a second consideration which ought to bear up and comfort our minds in afflictions, that it is fixed and determined by the providence of God that we shall be conformed to Christ by bearing the cross, and that the fellowship that we have with Him extends to this also. He adds also a third reason, that his sufferings are fruitful, and that not only to a few, but to the whole Church. He had previously stated that he suffered for the sake of the Colossians, and he now declares further that the fruit extends to the whole Church. This fruit was spoken of in Phil. 1.12. What could be clearer, less forced, or more simple, than the explanation that Paul is joyful in persecution because he considers, as he writes elsewhere, that we must carry about in our body the mortification of Christ, so that His life may be manifested in us? (II Cor. 4.10). And again, to Timothy, 'If we suffer with Him, we shall also reign with him: if we die with him, we shall also live with him' (II Tim. 2.11, 12), and thus the issue will be blessed and glorious. Moreover, he says that we must not refuse the condition which God has laid down for His Church, that the members of Christ may have a suitable correspondence with the Head. And, thirdly, that afflictions must be cheerfully endured, since they are profitable to all the godly, and promote the welfare of the whole Church, by adorning the doctrine of the Gospel.

Papists, however, disregarding and setting aside all these things, have struck out a new invention to make their indulgences acceptable. They give the name of indulgences to the remission of punishments obtained by us through the merits of martyrs. For, as they deny the free remission of sins, and imagine that they are redeemed by works of satisfaction, when the satisfactions do not fill up the right measure they call to their help the blood of the martyrs, that it may, along with the blood of Christ, avail as expiation at the judgment of God. And this mixture they call the 'Treasury of the Church', the keys of which they afterwards entrust to whom they think fit. Nor are they ashamed to twist this passage, to support so execrable a blasphemy, as if Paul here affirmed that his sufferings availed for expiating the sins of men.

They emphasize the word ὑστερήματα, as if Paul denied that the sufferings of Christ were sufficient for the redemption of men. No one, however, can fail to see that Paul speaks like this because it is necessary that the Body of the Church should be brought to its perfection by the afflictions of the godly, when the members are conformed to their Head. I should also be afraid of being suspected of slander in repeating things so monstrous, if their books did not bear witness that I impute nothing to them falsely.

They emphasize also that Paul says that he suffers for the Church. It is surprising that this clever interpretation never occurred to any of the ancients, for they all interpret it as we do—that the saints suffer on behalf of the Church in that they confirm the faith of the Church. Papists, however, gather from this that the saints are redeemers and shed their blood for the expiation of sins. That my readers, however, may perceive more clearly their impudence, I grant that the martyrs, as well as Christ, suffered for the Church, but in a different way, which I prefer to express in Augustine's words rather than in my own. He writes in his 84th homily on John, 'Though we brethren die for the brethren, yet no blood of any martyr is poured out for the remission of sins. This Christ did for us. Nor has he in this conferred upon us something to imitate, but to give thanks for.' Also, in the fourth book of Bonifacius, 'As the only Son of God became the Son of man that he might make us sons of God, so he alone, without guilt, endured the punishment for us, that without merit we may through him obtain undeserved grace.' Similar to these is the statement of Leo, Bishop of Rome, 'The righteous received crowns, they did not give them; and from the fortitude of believers there have come forth examples of patience, not gifts of righteousness. For their deaths were private, and no one by his end paid the debt of another.'

Now, that this is the meaning of Paul's words is very clear from the context. For he adds that he suffers according to the dispensation that was committed to him. And we know that there was committed to him the ministry, not of redeeming the Church, but of building it; and he himself immediately afterwards expressly acknowledges this. This is also what he writes to Timothy, that he endures all things for the sake of the elect, that they may obtain the salvation which is in Christ Jesus (II Tim. 2.10). Also, in II Cor. 1.6, that he willingly endures all things for their consolation and salvation. Let godly readers learn, therefore, to hate and detest those profane sophists, who deliberately corrupt and adulterate the Scriptures to give some colour to their inventions.

25. *Of which I am made a minister.* Mark under what character he suffers for the Church—as a minister; not to pay the price of redemption (as Augustine nicely and properly expresses it), but to proclaim it. He now calls himself a minister of the Church in a different sense from when he said elsewhere 'a minister of God', and a little ago 'of the Gospel'. For the apostles serve God and Christ to promote Their glory: they serve the Church and administer the Gospel for men's salvation. There is, therefore, a different reason for the ministry in these expressions, but the one cannot subsist without the other. He says, however, *towards you*, that they may know that his office concerned them also.

To fulfil the word. He states the end of his ministry: that the Word of God may be effectual. And this happens when it is obediently received. For the strength of the Gospel is that it is 'the power of God unto salvation to every one that believeth' (Rom. 1.16). God, therefore, gives efficacy and effect to His Word through the apostles. For although preaching itself is the fulfilling of the Word, whatever may be its issue, yet it is the fruit that shows at length that the seed has not been sown in vain.

26. *The mystery which hath been hid.* Here we have a commendation of the Gospel; that it is the wonderful secret of God. It is not without good reason that Paul so frequently extols the Gospel with the highest praises in his power; for he saw that it was a stumbling-block to the Jews and foolishness to the Greeks (I Cor. 1.23). We see also in what hatred it is held today by hypocrites, and how haughtily it is despised by the world. Paul, therefore, to revoke judgments so unfair and perverse, extols magnificently the dignity of the Gospel as often as opportunity presents itself, and for that purpose he uses various

arguments, according to the circumstances of the passages. Here he calls it a sublime secret which was hid from ages and generations, that is, from the beginning of the world, through so many revolving ages. Now, that it is of the Gospel that he speaks, is evident from Rom. 16.25, Eph. 3.9, and similar passages.

The reason, however, why it is so called, may be demanded. Because Paul expressly mentioned the calling of the Gentiles, some think that the sole reason for this term is that the Lord had, in a manner, contrary to all expectation, poured out His grace upon the Gentiles whom He had seemed to have shut out for ever from participation in eternal life. Anyone, however, who will examine the whole passage more closely, will perceive that this is the third reason, not the only one, in so far as relates to the present passage and that other in Romans which I have cited. For the first is, that whereas God had, before the advent of Christ, governed His Church under dark coverings, both of words and of ceremonies, He has suddenly shone forth in full brightness by the teaching of the Gospel. The second is that, whereas nothing was previously seen but external figures, Christ has been exhibited, bringing with Him the full truth, which had been concealed. The third is what I have mentioned, that the whole world, which had hitherto been estranged from God, is called to the hope of salvation, and the same inheritance of eternal life is offered to all. The attentive consideration of these things constrains us to revere and adore this mystery which Paul proclaims, however it may be held in contempt by the world, or even ridiculed.

Which is now revealed. Lest anyone should misinterpret the word 'mystery', as though he were speaking of something still secret and unknown, he adds that it has now at length been published, that it might be made known to men. What, therefore, was in its own nature secret, has been revealed by the Will of God. Thus there is no reason why its obscurity should put us off, now that God has revealed it. He adds, *to the saints,* for God's arm has not been revealed to all, for them to understand His purpose.

27. *To whom God willed.* Here he puts a bridle on the boldness of men, that they may not let themselves be wiser or more inquisitive than they should, but may learn to be satisfied with this one thing, that it has so pleased God. For the Will of God ought to be perfectly sufficient for us as a reason. This, however, is said principally to commend the grace of God. For Paul suggests that men by no means provided any cause for God's making them participants of this secret, when he teaches that He was led to this of His own accord, and because *he willed* so. For it is customary for Paul to oppose the good pleasure of God to all human merits and external causes.

What are the riches. We must always notice how highly he speaks of the dignity of the Gospel. For he was aware that the ingratitude of men is such, that although this treasure is inestimable, and the grace of God in it is so wonderful, they nevertheless carelessly despise it, or at least think lightly of it.

Hence, not satisfied with the term *mystery*, he adds *glory*, and that, too, not trivial or common. For 'riches' to Paul means 'amplitude', as is well known. He states particularly that those riches have been manifested among the Gentiles; for what is more wonderful than that the Gentiles, who for so many ages had been sunk in death, so as to seem utterly beyond hope, are suddenly reckoned among the sons of God, and receive the inheritance of salvation?

Which is Christ in you. What he said of the Gentiles generally he applies to the Colossians in particular, that they may more effectually recognize in themselves the grace of God, and may embrace it with greater reverence. He says, therefore, 'which is Christ', meaning by this, that all that secret is contained in Christ, and that all the riches of heavenly wisdom are obtained by them when they have Christ, as he states more plainly a little afterwards. He adds, 'in you', because they now possess Christ, from whom they were before completely estranged.

Lastly, he calls Christ *the hope of glory*, that they may know that nothing is lacking in their complete blessedness when they have obtained Christ. This, however, is the wonderful work of God, that in earthen and frail vessels the hope of heavenly glory resides.

28. *Whom we preach.* Here he applies to his own preaching everything that he has previously declared about the wonderful and adorable secret of God; and thus he explains what he had already touched upon as to the dispensation committed to him. For his aim is to adorn his apostleship, and to claim authority for his teaching. For after extolling the Gospel so highly, he now adds that it is that divine secret which he preaches. It was not, however, without good reason that he had said a little before that Christ is the sum of that secret, that they might know that nothing more perfect can be taught than Christ.

The expressions that follow have also great weight. He represents himself as the teacher of all men; meaning by this, that no one is so outstanding in wisdom as to be entitled to exempt himself from tuition. As if he said, 'God has placed me in a lofty position, as a public herald of His secret, that the whole world without exception might learn from me.'

In all wisdom is equivalent to his affirming that his doctrine is such as to conduct a man to perfect and complete wisdom. And this is what he immediately adds—that all that show themselves to be true disciples will be made perfect. See I Cor. 2. Now, what better thing can be desired than what confers on us the highest perfection?

He again repeats *in Christ*, that they may not desire to know anything beyond Christ alone. From this passage, also, we may gather a definition of true wisdom: that by which we are presented perfect in the presence of God, and this is in Christ and nowhere else.

29. *Whereunto.* He amplifies the glory of his apostleship and of his doctrine by two circumstances. In the first place, he mentions his care, which is a sign of his difficulty; for those things are generally the most excellent that are difficult. The second is stronger, when he says that the power of God shines forth in his ministry. He does not speak, however, only of the outcome of his preaching (though in that too the blessing of God appears), but also of the efficacy of the Spirit, in which God manifestly showed Himself. For he rightly ascribes his super-human efforts to the power of God, which, he declares, is seen working powerfully in this matter.

CHAPTER TWO

For I would have you know what great conflict I have for you, and for them at Laodicea, and for as many as have not seen my face in the flesh; that their hearts might receive comfort, they being knit together in love, and unto all riches of the assurance of understanding, that they may know the mystery of God, and of the Father, and of Christ; in whom are all the treasures of wisdom and knowledge hidden. And this I say, that no one may delude you with persuasive words. For though I am absent in the flesh, yet am I with you in the spirit, joying and beholding your order, and the steadfastness of your faith in Christ. (1-5)

1. *I would have you know.* He declares his love towards them, that he may have more credit and authority. For we readily believe those whom we know to be thinking of our welfare. It is also a sign of no ordinary love that he was concerned about them in the midst of death, that is, when he was in danger of his life. And that he may express the more emphatically his affection and concern, he calls it *a conflict.* I do not find fault with the rendering of Erasmus, 'anxiety'; but the force of the Greek word must be kept, for ἀγών is used where there is strife. By the same argument he confirms that his ministry is directed to them. For whence springs such anxious concern for their welfare, but because the apostle of the Gentiles had the duty of embracing in his affection and concern even those who were unknown to him? As, however, there is commonly no love between those who are unknown to each other, he minimizes first-hand acquaintance, when he says, *as many as have not seen my face in the flesh.* For there is among the servants of God an aspect different from that of the flesh which wins love. Because it is almost universally agreed that I Timothy was written from Laodicea, some place in Galatia the Laodicea which Paul mentions here, whereas the other was the metropolis of Phrygia Pacatiana. It seems to me, however, more probable that that inscription is incorrect, as will be noticed in its proper place.

2. *That their hearts may receive consolation.* He now indicates what he desires for them, and shows that his affection is truly apostolic. For he declares that nothing else is in his heart than that they may be bound together in faith and love. He shows, accordingly, that it was by no unreasonable anxiety (as happens in the case of some) that he had been led to take upon himself so great a concern for the Colossians and others, but because the duty of his office required it.

'Consolation' is taken here for that true quietness in which they may repose. This he declares they will at length possess if they are joined in love and faith. From this it appears where the chief good is situated, and in what it consists: when, mutually agreed in one faith, we are also joined together in mutual love. This, I say, is the solid joy of the godly mind, this is the blessed life. Just as love is here commended from its effect, because it fills the mind of the godly with true joy, so its cause is indicated when he says, 'In all fulness of understanding.' The bond also of holy unity is the truth of God, when we embrace it with one consent. For peace and agreement with men flow from that fountain.

Riches of the assurance of understanding. Since many, content with a slight taste, have nothing but a confused and fitful knowledge, he mentions expressly 'the riches of understanding'. By this phrase he means full and clear perception. And at the same time he admonishes them that, according to the measure of understanding, they must make progress also in love.

In the word 'assurance' he distinguishes faith from opinion. For that man truly knows God who does not vacillate or waver in doubt, but stands fast in a firm and constant persuasion. This constancy and stability Paul frequently calls πληροφορίαν (he uses it here also), and always connects it with faith, for undoubtedly it can no more be separated from faith than heat or light from the sun. The dogma of the Schoolmen is devilish, therefore, for it takes away assurance, and substitutes in its place moral conjecture, as they call it.

That they may know the mystery. This clause must be read in apposition; for he explains what that knowledge is which he has mentioned; that it is nothing but the knowledge of the Gospel. For the false apostles try to sell their fakes under the trade name of wisdom. But Paul keeps the sons of God in the Gospel alone, that they may desire to know nothing else. Why he uses the word 'mystery' for the Gospel, has been already explained. Let us, however, learn from this that the Gospel can be understood by faith alone, not by reason, nor by the perspicacity of the human understanding; because otherwise it is a thing that is hidden from us.

'The mystery of God' I understand passively, as that in which God is revealed. For he goes on to add, *And of the Father, and of Christ,* by which phrase he means that God cannot be known otherwise than in Christ; as, on the other hand, the Father must necessarily be known where Christ is known. For John affirms both: 'He that hath the Son, hath the Father also: he that hath not the Son, neither hath he the Father' (I John 2.23 and 5.12). Hence all who think they know anything of God apart from Christ, invent for themselves an idol in the place of God. Just as, on the other hand, that man is ignorant of Christ who is not led by Him to the Father and who does not in Him embrace God wholly. Now this is a memorable passage for proving Christ's deity and the unity of His essence with the Father. For having spoken previously of the knowledge of God, he immediately applies it to the Son as well as to the Father. From this it follows that the Son is the same God with the Father.

3. *In whom.* The phrase 'in whom', may either refer to everything he had said about knowing the mystery, or it may relate simply to what came immediately before, namely, Christ. While there is little difference between them, I prefer the latter, and it is the more generally received. The meaning, therefore is that all the treasures of wisdom and knowledge are hidden in Christ. By this he means that we are perfect in wisdom if we truly know Christ, so that it is madness to wish to know anything besides Him. For, since the Father has manifested Himself wholly in Him, that man wishes to be wise apart from God who is not contented with Christ alone. Should anyone choose to explain it of the mystery, the meaning will be that all the wisdom of the godly is included in the Gospel, by which God is revealed to us in His Son.

He says, however, that the *treasures are hidden*, because they are not seen shining brightly, but rather, as it were lie hidden under the contemptible humility and simplicity of the cross. For the preaching of the cross is always foolishness to the world (as we heard in Corinthians[1]). I do not put any great difference between *wisdom* and *understanding* in this passage, for the duplication is only to strengthen it; as if he had said that no knowledge, erudition, learning, wisdom, can be found elsewhere.

4. *This I say, that no one.* Because the inventions of men have (as we shall afterwards see) an appearance of wisdom, the minds of the godly ought to be pre-occupied with the conviction that the knowledge of Christ is of itself amply sufficient. And certainly, this is the key that can lock the door against all wicked errors. For why have men involved themselves in so many ungodly opinions, in so many idolatries, in so many foolish speculations, but that, despising the simplicity of the Gospel, they have dared to aspire higher? All the errors that are in the Papacy, therefore, must be reckoned as proceeding from the ingratitude that, not resting in Christ alone, they have given themselves up to alien teaching.

And so the apostle speaks well in Hebrews, when, wishing to exhort believers not to allow themselves to be led astray by strange or new doctrines, he first of all lays this foundation: 'Christ yesterday, and

[1] I Cor. 1.18.

today, and for ever' (Heb. 13.8). By this he means that those are out of danger who remain in Christ, but that those who are not satisfied with Christ are exposed to all fallacies and deceptions. So Paul here would have everyone that does not want to be deceived, fortified by this principle, that it is not lawful for a Christian man to know anything beyond Christ. Everything that is brought forward afterwards, however imposing its appearance, will nevertheless be nothing. In short, there will be no *pithanologia*[1] that can turn aside a finger's breadth the minds of those that have devoted their understanding to Christ. It is a passage, certainly, that ought to be singularly esteemed. For as he who has taught men to know nothing but Christ, has provided against all ungodly dogmas, so there is the same reason why we should at this day destroy the whole of Papacy, which, it is manifest, is constructed of ignorance of Christ.

5. *For though I am absent in body.* Lest anyone should object that an admonition from so far away was out of place, he says that his love for them made him present with them in spirit, and judge of what was expedient for them, as though he were present. By praising their present condition, he admonishes them not to fall back from it, or turn aside.

Rejoicing, says he, *and seeing*; that is, 'because I see'. For the conjunction is equivalent to the causative, as is customary in Latin and Greek. To paraphrase: 'Go on as you have begun, for I know that hitherto you have pursued the right course; distance does not prevent me from beholding you with the eyes of my mind.'

Order and steadfastness. He mentions two things in which the perfection of the Church consists: order among themselves and faith in Christ. By 'order', he means agreement and properly regulated customs and all discipline. He praises their faith for its constancy and steadfastness, meaning that it is an empty shadow of faith when the mind wavers and vacillates between various opinions.

As therefore ye received Christ Jesus the Lord, so walk in him; rooted and built in him, and stablished in the faith, as ye were taught, abounding in it with thanksgiving. (6-7)

6. *As therefore.* To praise he adds exhortation, in which he teaches them that their having once received Christ will be of no advantage to them unless they remain in Him. Moreover, as the false apostles proclaimed Christ's name in order to deceive, he twice forestalls this danger by exhorting them to go on as they had been taught and as they had received Christ. For in these words he admonishes them to adhere steadfastly to the doctrine which they had embraced, as de-

[1] Persuasive argument.

livered to them by Epaphras, and to be on their guard against every other doctrine and belief. As Isaiah said, 'This is the way, walk ye in it' (Isa. 30.21). And, indeed, we must act in such a manner that the truth of the Gospel, when it has been manifested to us, may be to us a brazen wall to repulse all impostures.

Now he expresses by three metaphors what steadfastness of faith he requires from them. The first is in the word *walk*. For he compares the pure doctrine of the Gospel, as they had learned it, to a sure way, so that if anyone will keep it he will be in no danger of error. He exhorts them, accordingly, if they would not go astray, not to turn aside from the course on which they have set out.

The second is taken from trees. For as a tree that has struck its roots deep has enough support for withstanding all the assaults of winds and storms, so, if anyone is deeply and thoroughly fixed in Christ, as in a firm root, he cannot be thrown down from his upright position by any machinations of Satan. On the other hand, if anyone has not fixed his roots in Christ, he will easily be carried about with every wind of doctrine, as a tree without the support of a root is blown down at the first blast.

The third metaphor is that of a foundation; for a house that is not supported by a foundation quickly falls to ruins. So also with those who lean on any other support than Christ, or at least are not solidly founded on Him, but have the building of their faith in suspense, as it were, because of their weakness and levity.

Two things are to be observed in the apostle's words: that the stability of those who rely upon Christ is immovable, and their course is not at all hesitant or liable to error; and this is a great praise of faith from its effect. Secondly, that we must make progress in Christ until we have taken deep root in Him. From this we may readily gather that those who do not hold to Christ, only wander in bypaths and are tossed about in disquietude.

7. *And confirmed in the faith.* He now repeats without a figure what he had said in metaphors, that the following of the way, the support of the root and of the foundation, is the firmness and steadfastness of faith. And observe that this argument is set before them because they have been well taught in the past, in order that they may securely and confidently plant their steps in the faith which had been made known to them.

Abounding. He did not want them merely to stand immovable, but to grow every day more and more. When he adds, *with thanksgiving*, he would have them always remember from what source faith itself proceeds, that they may not be puffed up with arrogance, but may rather with fear rest in the gift of God. And certainly, ingratitude is most often the reason why we are deprived of the light of the Gospel, as well as of other gifts of God.

Take heed lest anyone make spoil of you through philosophy and vain deceit, after the tradition of men, after the rudiments of the world, and not after Christ: for in him dwelleth all the fulness of the Godhead bodily. And ye are complete in him, who is the head of all principality and power: in whom also ye are circumcised with the circumcision not made with hands, in the putting off the body of the sins of the flesh, by the circumcision, I say, of Christ; having been buried with him in baptism, wherein also ye are risen with him through faith in the working of God, who raised him from the dead. (8-12)

8. *Take heed lest anyone.* He again warns them about the poison, which the antidote he gave them would counteract. For although this, as we have stated, is the universal remedy against all the impostures of the devil, it had nevertheless at that time a special use among the Colossians, to which it had to be applied. 'Beware,' he says, 'lest anyone make spoil of you.' He uses a very appropriate word, for he alludes to plunderers, who, when they cannot carry off the flock by violence, drive them away by stealth. Thus he makes Christ's Church a sheep-fold, and the pure teaching of the Gospel the wall of the fold. He means, then, that we who are the sheep of Christ repose in a safe place when we hold the unity of faith; and, he likens the false apostles to plunderers who carry us away from the fold. Would you be reckoned as belonging to Christ's flock? Would you remain in His fold? Do not deviate a nail's breadth from the purity of the Gospel (*doctrinae*). For unquestionably Christ will fulfil His office as the good Shepherd by protecting us if we will only hear His voice and reject the voices of strangers. In short, the tenth chapter of John will explain the present passage.

Through philosophy. As many have mistakenly imagined that Paul here condemns philosophy, we must define what he means by the word. In my opinion, he means everything that men contrive of themselves when wishing to be wise in their own understanding—and that not without the specious pretext of reason and apparent probability. For the difficulty is, not in rejecting those inventions of men which have nothing to commend them, but in rejecting those that captivate men's minds by a false idea of wisdom. Or if anyone wants it in a nutshell, philosophy is nothing but persuasive speech, which insinuates itself into men's minds by fine and plausible arguments. Of such a nature, I acknowledge, will all the subtleties of philosophers be, if they try to add anything of their own to the pure word of God. Hence philosophy will be only a corruption of spiritual doctrine if it is mixed up with Christ. Let us, therefore, bear in mind that under the term philosophy Paul has only condemned all spurious doctrines which spring from man's head, whatever appearance of reason they may have.

What immediately follows, as to *vain deceit*, I explain thus: 'Beware of philosophy, which is nothing but vain deceit.' So that this is added in apposition.

According to the tradition of men. He shows more precisely what kind of philosophy he disapproves of, and at the same time convicts it of vanity on two accounts: because it is not according to Christ, but according to the inclinations of men; and because it is placed in the elements of the world. Observe, however, that he opposes Christ both to the elements of the world, and to the tradition of men; by which he means that whatever is hatched in man's brain is not in agreement with Christ, who has been appointed by the Father as our sole Teacher, that He might retain us in the simplicity of His Gospel. But that is corrupted by even a small leavening of human traditions. He means also, that all doctrines are foreign to Christ which place the worship of God (which we know to be spiritual, according to Christ's rule) in the elements of the world, and also which hinder men's minds by these trifles and frivolities, whereas Christ calls us directly to Himself.

But what does he call *the elements of the world*? Without doubt, ceremonies. For he immediately afterwards cites an example, circumcision. The reason why he calls them by such a name is usually explained in two ways. Some think that it is a metaphor, so that the elements are childish rudiments, which do not lead forward to mature doctrine. Others take it in its proper signification, as external things which are liable to corruption and avail nothing for the Kingdom of God. I prefer the former exposition, as also in Gal. 4.3.

9. *For in him dwelleth.* Here is the reason why those elements of the world, which are taught by men, do not accord with Christ. They are additions to supply a deficiency, as they say. But in Christ is a perfection to which nothing can be added. Hence everything that men add of themselves, attacks Christ's nature, because it charges Him with imperfection. This argument alone will suffice for refuting all the inventions of the Papists. For what is their real purpose, but to perfect what was commenced by Christ? Now this insult to Christ is by no means to be endured. They plead, it is true, that they add nothing to Christ, inasmuch as what they have woven into the Gospel is, as it were, a part of Christianity; but they cannot escape by such a quibble. For Paul does not speak of an imaginary Christ, but of a Christ preached, who has revealed Himself by sure doctrine.

Further, when he says that *the fulness of the Godhead dwells in Christ*, he means simply that the whole God is found in Him, so that he who is not satisfied with Christ alone, desires something better and more excellent than God. The sum is that God has manifested Himself to us fully and perfectly in Christ.

Interpreters explain variously the adverb *bodily*. I do not doubt that it is employed imprecisely for 'substantially'. For he places the manifestation of God which we have in Christ over against all others that have ever been made. For God has often exhibited Himself to men, but only in part. In Christ, however, He communicates Himself to us wholly. He has also manifested Himself otherwise, but in figures, or by power and grace. In Christ, however, He has appeared to us essentially. Thus the statement of John holds good: 'He that hath the Son, hath the Father also' (I John 2.23). For those who possess Christ have God truly present, and enjoy Him wholly.

10. *And ye are complete in him.* He adds that this perfect essence of Deity which is in Christ is profitable to us, in that we are also perfected in Him. To paraphrase: 'As to God's dwelling wholly in Christ, it is in order that we, having obtained Him, may possess in Him an entire perfection.' Those, therefore, who do not rest in Christ alone, injure God in two ways; for besides detracting from the glory of God, by desiring something above His perfection, they are also ungrateful, inasmuch as they seek elsewhere what they already have in Christ. Paul, however, does not mean that the perfection of Christ is transfused into us, but that there are in Him the resources from which we may be filled, that nothing may be wanting to us.

Who is the head. He has introduced this clause again on account of the angels, meaning that the angels also will be ours, if we have Christ. But more of this later. In the mean time, we must observe that we are surrounded above and below by bars, that our faith may not deviate even to the slightest extent from Christ.

11. *In whom also ye are circumcised.* From this it appears that he has a controversy with the false apostles, who mixed the law with the Gospel, and in that way constructed, so to say, a bi-form Christ. And he specifies one instance as an example. He proves that the Mosaic circumcision is not merely superfluous, but even alien to Christ, because it destroys the spiritual circumcision of Christ. For circumcision was given to the Fathers to be the figure of something absent. Those, therefore, who retain that figure after Christ's advent, deny the accomplishment of what it figures. Let us, therefore, bear in mind that outward circumcision is here compared with spiritual, just as a figure with the reality. The figure is of something absent; hence it destroys the presence of the reality. What Paul contends for is that,

because what was shadowed forth by a circumcision made with hands
has been fulfilled in Christ, it now has no fruit or practice. Hence he
declares that the circumcision which is made in the heart is *the circum-*
cision of Christ, and that therefore what is outward is not now required;
for where the reality exists, that shadowy sign vanishes, since it has
no place except in the absence of the reality.

By the putting off of the body. He calls 'body', by an elegant metaphor,
the mass made up of all vices. For as we are encompassed by our
bodies, so we are surrounded on all sides by an accumulation of vices.
And as the body is composed of various members, each of which has
its own action and offices, so from that accumulation of corruption
all sins take their rise as members of the whole. There is a similar
expression in Rom. 6.13.

He takes *flesh*, as he usually does, to denote corrupt nature. 'The
body of the sins of the flesh', therefore, is the old man with his deeds.
Only there is a difference in the manner of expression, for here he
expresses strictly the mass of vices which proceed from corrupt nature.
He says that we obtain this divesting through Christ, so that unquestionably an entire regeneration is His benefit. It is He who circumcises the foreskin of our heart, that is, mortifies all the lusts of the
flesh, not with the hand, but by His Spirit. Hence there is in Him
the reality of the figure.

12. *Buried with him through baptism.* He explains still more clearly
the manner of spiritual circumcision in that, buried with Christ, we
are partakers of His death. He expressly declares that we obtain this
through baptism, so that it may be more clear that there is no practice
of circumcision under the reign of Christ. For someone might otherwise object: 'Why do you abolish circumcision on the pretext that
its effect is in Christ? Was not Abraham, also, circumcised spiritually,
and yet this did not prevent the sign being added to the reality? Outward circumcision, therefore, is not superfluous, even though that
which is inward is conferred by Christ.' Paul anticipates such an
objection by mentioning baptism. Christ, he says, accomplishes in
us spiritual circumcision, not through means of that ancient sign,
which was in force under Moses, but by baptism. Baptism, therefore,
is a sign of the thing exhibited, which when it was absent was figured
by circumcision. The argument is taken from the economy which
God appointed; for those who retain circumcision invent a mode of
dispensation different from that which God instituted.

When he says 'We are buried with Christ,' it means more than that
we are crucified with Him. For burial expresses a continued process
of mortification. When he says that this is done through baptism (as
also in Rom. 6.4), he speaks in his usual manner, ascribing efficacy to

the sacrament, that it may not fruitlessly signify what does not exist. By baptism, therefore, we are buried with Christ, because the mortification which Christ there figures, He at the same time effectively executes, that the reality may be conjoined with the sign.

In which also ye are risen. He magnifies the grace which we obtain in Christ, as being far superior to circumcision. 'We are not only engrafted into Christ's death,' he says, 'but we also rise to newness of life.' Hence the greater the injury done to Christ by those who endeavour to bring us back to circumcision. He adds, *by faith*; for unquestionably it is by this that we receive what is offered to us in baptism. But what faith? That in His efficacy or operation; by which he means that faith is founded upon the power of God. As, however, faith does not wander in a confused and undefined (as they say) contemplation of the divine power, he declares what efficacy it ought to consider—that by which He raised Christ from the dead. He takes this, however, for granted, that, because it is impossible for believers to be severed from their head, the same power of God which showed itself in Christ is diffused to them all in common.

And you, when ye were dead through your sins and the uncircumcision of your flesh, did he quicken together with him, by forgiving you all trespasses; blotting out the hand-writing of ordinances that was against us, which was contrary to us, and took it out of the way, nailing it to the cross; spoiling principalities and powers, he made a show of them openly, triumphing over them in it.[1] (13-15)

13. *And you, when ye were dead.* He admonishes the Colossians to apply to themselves what he had treated of generally, which is by far the most effectual way of teaching. Moreover, they were Gentiles when they were converted to Christ, and from this he shows them how absurd it is to pass over from Christ to the Mosaic ceremonies. 'Ye were', he says, 'dead in uncircumcision.' This term, however, may be understood either in its proper signification, or figuratively. If you take it in its strict sense, the meaning will be, 'Uncircumcision is the sign of alienation from God; for where the covenant of grace is not, there is pollution, and, consequently, curse and ruin. But God has called you to Himself from uncircumcision, and, therefore, from death.' Thus he is not making uncircumcision the cause of death, but a testimony that they were estranged from God. We know, however, that men cannot live otherwise than by cleaving to their God, who alone is their life. Hence it follows, that all the ungodly, however they may seem to themselves to be in the highest degree living and flourishing, are, nevertheless, spiritually dead. In this manner the

[1] *Margin: or in himself.*

333

passage will correspond with Ephesians, where it is said, 'Remember that in time past when ye were Gentiles, and called uncircumcision by that circumcision which is made with hands in the flesh, ye were at that time without Christ, alienated from the commonwealth of Israel, and strangers to the promises' (2.11). Taking it metaphorically, there would, indeed, be an allusion to natural uncircumcision, but Paul would here be speaking of the obstinacy of the human heart against God and of a nature defiled by corrupt affections. I prefer the former exposition, because it corresponds better with the context. For Paul declares that uncircumcision was no hindrance to their becoming partakers of Christ's life. Hence it follows that circumcision derogated from the grace of God, which they had already obtained.

As to his ascribing death to uncircumcision, this is not as its cause, but as a symbol, similar to that other passage in Ephesians, which we have quoted. It is also customary in Scripture to denote deprivations of the reality by deprivation of the sign, as in Gen. 3.22, 'Lest peradventure Adam eat of the fruit of life, and live.' For the tree did not confer life, but its removal was a sign of death. Paul has here briefly expressed both. He says that they were dead in sins. This is the cause, for sins alienate us from God. He adds, *in the uncircumcision of your flesh*. This was outward pollution, the testimony of spiritual death.

By forgiving you. God does not quicken us by the remission of sins alone; but he makes mention here of this particularly, because free reconciliation with God, which overthrows the righteousness of works, belongs especially to the point in hand, where he treats of abrogated ceremonies (as he declares more fully in the Epistle to the Galatians). For the false apostles, by establishing ceremonies, bound their consciences with a halter, from which Christ has set them free.

14. *Having blotted out the hand-writing*. He now attacks the false apostles at close quarters. For the point at issue was whether the observance of ceremonies was necessary under the reign of Christ. Now Paul contends that ceremonies have been abolished; and to prove this he compares them to a 'hand-writing', by which God holds us as it were bound, that we may not be able to deny our guilt. He now says that we have been freed from guilt in such a way that even the hand-writing is blotted out, and no remembrance of it remains. For we know that in debts the obligation is still in force so long as the hand-writing remains; and that, on the other hand, by the erasing, or tearing up of the hand-writing the debtor is free. Hence it follows, that all those who still press for ceremonies diminish the benefit of Christ, as though absolution were not procured for us through Him. For they restore its freshness to the hand-writing, and hold us still under obligation.

This is a truly theological reason for proving the abrogation of ceremonies, because, if Christ has fully redeemed us from guilt, He must also have effaced the remembrance of the obligation, that consciences might be pacified and tranquil in the sight of God; for these two things are joined together. Although interpreters explain this passage in various ways, none of them satisfies me. Some think that Paul speaks simply of the moral law, but they are mistaken. For Paul is accustomed to give the name of ordinances to that part which consists in ceremonies, as in the Epistle to the Ephesians (2.15) and soon afterwards here. More especially, the passage in Ephesians convinces me that Paul is here speaking of ceremonies.

Others, therefore, do better in restricting it to ceremonies; but they, too, err, for they do not add the reason why it is called handwriting, or rather they assign a reason different from the true one, and they do not apply this similitude properly to the context. Now, the reason is, that all the Mosaic ceremonies had in them some acknowledgment of guilt, which bound those that observed them more firmly, as it were, to God's judgment. For example, what else were washings but a testimony of pollution? Whenever any victim was sacrificed, did not the people that stood by behold in it a representation of their death? For when men substituted in their place an innocent animal, they confessed that they were themselves deserving of that death. In short, all these ceremonies were exhibitions of human guilt and hand-writings of obligation.

Should anyone object that they were sacraments of the grace of God, as Baptism and the Eucharist are to us today, the answer is easy. For there are two things to be considered in the ancient ceremonies: that they were suited to the time, and that they led men to the Kingdom of Christ. Whatever was done at that time displayed mere obligation. Grace was in a manner suspended until the advent of Christ; not that the Fathers were excluded from it, but they had not a present manifestation of it in their ceremonies. For they saw nothing in the sacrifices but the blood of beasts, and in their washings nothing but water. Hence, as to present view, the guilt remained; in fact, the ceremonies themselves sealed the condemnation. The apostle speaks in this manner in the whole of the Epistle to the Hebrews, because he places Christ in direct opposition to ceremonies. But how do things stand now? The Son of God has not only by His death delivered us from the condemnation of death, but in order that absolution might be made more certain, he abrogated those ceremonies, that no monument of obligation might remain. This is full liberty, that Christ has by His blood blotted out not only our sins, but every hand-writing which might declare us to be exposed to the judgment of God. Erasmus in his version has confused Paul's argument, by rendering it thus: 'which was contrary to us by ordinances'. Retain, therefore, the reading which I have given, as true and genuine.

Took it out of the way, fastening it to his cross. He shows how Christ effaced the hand-writing. For as He fastened to the cross our curse, our sins and also the punishment due to us, so also that bondage of the law and everything that tends to bind consciences. For when He was fastened to the cross, He took all things to Himself and tied them to Him, that they might have no more power over us.

15. *Spoiling principalities.* No doubt he means devils, to whom Scripture ascribes the function of accusing us before God. Paul, however, says that they are disarmed, so that they cannot bring forward anything against us, the attestation of our guilt being itself destroyed. He expressly adds this to show that the victory of Christ, which He has won for Himself and us over Satan, is marred by the false apostles, and that we are deprived of its fruit when they restore the ancient ceremonies. For if our liberty is the spoil that Christ snatched from the devil, what are these others doing, who would bring us back into bondage, but restoring to Satan the spoils of which he had been stripped?

Triumphing over them in it. The Greek word permits the reading, 'in himself'. In fact, most of the manuscripts have ἐν αὐτῷ, with an aspirate. The connexion of the passage, however, definitely requires that we read it otherwise; for what would be weak as applied to Christ, fits in well with the cross. For as he has previously compared the cross to a signal trophy or triumphal march, in which Christ paraded His enemies, so he now also compares it to a triumphal car, in which He appeared illustriously. For although in the cross there is nothing but curse, this was nevertheless so swallowed up by the power of the Son of God, that it has put on, as it were, a new nature. For there is no tribunal so magnificent, no kingly throne so stately, no show of triumph so distinguished, no chariot so lofty, as the gibbet on which Christ subdued death and the devil, the prince of death; more, has utterly trodden them under His feet.

Let no man therefore judge you in meat, or in drink, or in respect of a feast day, or a new moon, or a sabbath day; which are a shadow of the things to come; but the body is Christ's. Let no man rob you of your palm in desiring humility and the worshipping of angels (to do it), intruding into those things which he hath not seen, vainly puffed up by his fleshly mind; and not holding fast the head, from whom all the body being supplied and knit together by joints and bands, increaseth with the increase of God. (16-19)

16. *Let no one therefore.* What he had previously said of circum-cision, he now extends to the discrimination of meats and days. For circumcision was the initiation into the observance of the law; the other things then followed. *To judge* means here, to hold guilty of a crime, or to impose a scruple, so that we are no longer free. He denies, therefore, that it is in the power of men to subject us to the observance of rites which Christ has abolished by His death, and exempts us from their yoke, that we may not allow ourselves to be fettered by the laws which they impose. And he tacitly contrasts Christ to all mankind, lest anyone should be so bold as to try to take away what He has given.

In respect of a feast-day. Some understand τὸ μέρος to mean partici-pation. Chrysostom, accordingly, thinks he said 'part', because they did not observe all festival-days, nor did they even keep holy days strictly, in accordance with the appointment of the law. This is weak. Consider whether it may not be taken to mean 'separation'; for those who make a distinction of days, separate, as it were, one from another. Such a partition was suitable for the Jews, that they might celebrate religiously the days appointed, by separating them from others. Among Christians such a division has ceased.

But someone will say, 'We still keep some observance of days.' I answer, that we do not by any means observe days, as though there were any sacredness in holy days, or as though it were not lawful to work on them, but this is done for government and order, not for the days. And this is what he immediately adds.

17. *Which are a shadow of the things to come.* He frees Christians from the observances of them because they were shadows at a time when Christ was still in a sense absent. For he contrasts shadows with revelation, and absence with manifestation. Those, therefore, who still adhere to those shadows act like one judging of a man's appear-ance from his shadow, while he has the man himself before his eyes to look at. For Christ is now manifested to us, and hence we enjoy Him as being present.

The body, he says, *is of Christ,* that is, 'in Christ'. For the substance of those things which the ceremonies once figured is now presented before our eyes in Christ, in that He contains in Himself everything that they pointed to as future. Hence, anyone who calls back the ceremonies into use either buries the manifestation of Christ, or robs Christ of His power, and makes Him as it were empty. Accordingly, should any mortal assume to himself in this matter the office of judge, let us not submit to him, for Christ, the only competent judge, sets us free. For when he says, 'Let no man judge you,' he does not address the false apostles, but prohibits the Colossians from bowing their neck to a wrong yoke. Thus to abstain from swine's flesh is in itself harmless, but the obligation is pernicious, because it annuls the grace of Christ.

Should anyone ask, 'What, then, are we to think of our sacraments? Do they not also figure the absent Christ to us?' I answer, that they differ widely from the ancient ceremonies. For as painters do not in the first draft bring out a likeness (*imaginem*) in life-like colours and εἰκονικῶς, but first sketch rough and obscure lines with charcoal, so the representation of Christ under the law was unpolished, and was, as it were, a first sketch, but in our sacraments a true likeness (*ad vivam expressam*) is seen. Paul, however, had something more in view, for he contrasts the bare aspect of the shadow with the solidity of the body, and admonishes them that men are mad to take hold of empty shadows, when they can handle the solid body. Moreover, our sacraments figure Christ absent as to sight and place, but testify that He has been once manifested, and they now also present Him to be enjoyed. They are not, therefore, bare shadows, but rather symbols of Christ's presence, for they contain that Yea and Amen of all the promises of God which has been once manifested in Christ.

18. *Let no one take from you the palm.* He alludes to runners or wrestlers, to whom the palm was given, on condition that they did not give up in mid course, or after the fight had just begun. He warns them, therefore, that the false apostles aimed only at snatching from them the palm, inasmuch as they draw them aside from the straight course. Hence it follows that they must be shunned as most injurious pests. The passage is also carefully to be marked, in that all those who draw us away from the simplicity of Christ cheat us out of the prize of our high calling.

Desiring in humility. Something must be supplied; hence I have inserted in the text *to do it.* For he points out the kind of danger which they had to guard against. To paraphrase: all want to defraud you of the palm who, under pretence of humility, commend to you the worship of angels. For they make you wander out of the way, leaving the one object. I read *humility and worship of angels* conjointly, for the one follows the other. Just as today the Papists make the same pretence when philosophizing about the worship of saints. For they reason from man's abasement that we must seek for mediators to help us. But Christ has humbled Himself for the very reason that we might betake ourselves directly to Him, however miserable sinners we may be.

I am aware that the worship of angels is by many interpreted differently, as what they think has been delivered to men by angels; for the devil has always sold his quackery under this name. The Pope today boasts that all the trifles with which he has adulterated the pure worship of God are revelations. Likewise the Theurgians[1] of old alleged that all the superstitions that they contrived were delivered over to them directly by angels. These commentators accordingly think that Paul here condemns all fictitious worship that is falsely set forth under the authority of angels. But, in my opinion, he rather condemns the invention of the worshipping of angels. This is why he has so carefully applied himself at the very commencement of the epistle to bring angels into their true rank, lest they should obscure the brightness of Christ. In short, as he had in the first chapter prepared the way for abolishing the ceremonies, so he had also for removing all other hindrances which draw us away from Christ alone. In this class is the worship of angels.

Superstitious men have from the beginning worshipped angels, to make a way to God through them. The Platonists infected even the Christian Church with this error. For although Augustine sharply attacks them in the tenth book of *The City of God* and strongly condemns all their disputations on the worship of angels, we can see what has happened. Should anyone compare the writings of Plato with the Papist theology, he will find that they have drawn completely from Plato their prattling about the worship of angels. The sum of what he says is, that we must honour angels (whom Plato calls demons) χάριν τῆς εὐφήμου διαπορείας.[2] He puts this statement in Epinomis, and he confirms it in Cratylus, and many other places. In what respect do the Papists differ at all from this? 'But they do not deny that the Son of God is Mediator.' Neither did those with whom Paul contends. But as they imagined that God is approached by the assistance of the angels, and that, consequently, some worship must be shown to them, so they placed angels in the seat of Christ, and adorned them with Christ's office. Let us know, then, that Paul here condemns all invented kinds of worship rendered either to angels or to the dead, as though they were subsidiary mediators, after Christ, or alongside Christ. For just so far do we recede from Christ, when we transfer the smallest part of what belongs to Him to any others, whether they be angels or men.

Intruding into those things which he hath not seen. The verb ἐμβατεύειν, the participle which Paul here uses, has various significations. The rendering which Erasmus, following Jerome, has given it, 'advancing proudly', would not suit ill, were there an example of this meaning in any good author. For we see every day with how much confidence and pride rash men pronounce on things unknown. Nay, even in the

---

[1] See Hastings' *Encyclopaedia of Religion and Ethics*, 12, pp. 319ff. Presumably Calvin says 'of old' to distinguish them from the contemporary esoteric movement.   [2] For the sake of their auspicious intercession.

present subject of which Paul treats, there is a remarkable example. For when the Sorbonnic divines trifle about the intercession of saints or angels, they declare, as if from the Delphic oracle,[1] that the dead know and behold our needs, inasmuch as they see all things in the reflected light of God. And yet, what is less certain? Nay, what is more obscure and doubtful? But such, truly, is their magisterial freedom, that they fearlessly and boldly assert what is not only unknown to them, but cannot be known by men at all.

This meaning, therefore, would be suitable if that signification of the term were usual. But, among the Greeks it is taken simply for 'to advance'. It also sometimes means 'to inquire'. Should anyone choose to understand it thus in this passage, Paul will then be reproving a foolish curiosity in the investigation of things that are obscure, and even hidden from and transcending our mind. It appears to me, however, that I have followed Paul's thought and rendered it faithfully in this way: 'intruding into those things which he hath not seen'. For the common signification of the word ἐμβατεύειν is 'to enter upon an inheritance', or 'to take possession', or 'to set foot anywhere'. Accordingly, Budaeus renders the passage thus: 'Setting foot upon, or entering on the possession of those things which he has not seen.' I have followed his authority, but have chosen a better word. For such people in reality break through and intrude into secrets which God does not wish to reveal to us yet. The passage ought to be noted, for the purpose of reproving the rashness of those who inquire farther than is allowable.

Puffed up in vain by a fleshly mind. He calls 'fleshly mind' the perspicacity of the human intellect, however great. For he opposes it to that spiritual wisdom which is revealed to us from heaven; according to the saying: 'Flesh and blood hath not revealed it unto thee' (Matt. 16.17). Paul therefore declares that anyone who leans on his own understanding and who is activated wholly by the acumen of the flesh *is puffed up in vain.* And truly all the wisdom that men have of themselves is mere wind; hence there is nothing solid except in the Word of God and the illumination of the Spirit. And observe, that those are said to be puffed up who creep in under a show of humility. For it happens (as Augustine elegantly writes to Paulinus) in incredible ways that the soul of man is more puffed up from a false humility than if it were openly proud.

19. *Not holding fast the head.* He condemns in one word whatever is not referred to Christ. He also confirms his statement on the ground that all things flow from Him and depend on Him. Hence, should

[1] Latin: *ex tripode*, literally 'from the tripod', the tripod over the chasm, on which the priestess at Delphi sat when she consulted the oracle.

anyone call us elsewhere than to Christ, though in other respects he were full of heaven and earth, he is empty and windy. Let us, therefore, without concern, bid him farewell. Observe of whom he is speaking; namely, those who did not openly reject or deny Christ, but, not really understanding His office and power, sought out other helps and means (as they commonly say) of salvation, and were not firmly fixed in Him.

From whom all the body by joints. He simply means that the Church only stands if all things are supplied to her by Christ her Head and, consequently, that her entire safety lies in Him. The body, it is true, has its own nerves, joints, and ligaments, but all these things derive their force solely from the head, so that the whole binding of them together is from there. What, then, must be done? The constitution of the body will be in a right state if the Head alone which furnishes the several members with everything that they have, without hindrance has the pre-eminence. This Paul calls *the increase of God,* by which he means that it is not every increase that is approved by God, but only that which is directed to the Head. For we see that the kingdom of the Pope is not merely tall and large, but swells out to a monstrous size. But because we do not see there what Paul requires in the Church, what shall we say but that it is a humpbacked body and a confused mass that will fall to pieces of itself.

Therefore, if ye died with Christ from the rudiments of the world, why, as though living in the world, are ye subject to ordinances, eat not, taste not, handle not; all which things are to perish with the abuse of them, after the precepts and doctrines of men? Which things have indeed a show of wisdom in superstition, and humility of the mind and neglecting of the body; not in any honour to the satisfying of the flesh. (20-23)

20. *If ye died.* He had previously said that the ordinances were fastened to the cross of Christ. He now employs another figure of speech—that we are dead to them. Just as he teaches elsewhere that we are dead to the law, and the law also to us (Gal. 2.19). The word death signifies abrogation, but is more expressive καὶ ἐμφατικώτερον. He says, therefore, that the Colossians have nothing to do with ordinances. Why? Because they have died with Christ to ordinances; that is, after they died with Christ by regeneration, they were, through His benefit, set free from ordinances, that they might not belong to them any more. Hence he concludes that they are by no means bound by the ordinances which the false apostles tried to impose upon them.

21. *Eat not, taste not.* Hitherto they translated this 'handle not', but as another word immediately follows, which means the same thing,

anyone can see how cold and absurd is such a repetition. Moreover, the verb ἅπτεσθαι is used by the Greeks for eating (among other things), as I have translated it. Plutarch uses it in Caesar, when he relates that his soldiers, for lack of other things, ate the sort of animals that they had not eaten before. And this arrangement is both natural in other respects and is also most accordant with the context. For Paul expresses μιμητικῶς how far the puritans who trap consciences in their laws will go. From the beginning they are unduly rigorous. Hence he takes his beginning from their prohibition, not simply against eating, but even against slightly partaking. After they have obtained what they wish, they go beyond that command and then declare it unlawful to taste what they do not want to be eaten. At length they make it wicked even to touch. In short, when men have once taken upon them to tyrannize over souls, there is no end of the new laws daily added to old ones and of new regulations always springing up. How bright a mirror of this there is in the Papacy! Hence Paul acts admirably in warning us that human traditions are a labyrinth, in which consciences are more and more entangled; nay, are snares, which from the beginning bind in such a way that at length they strangle.

22. *All which things tend to corruption.* He sets aside by a twofold argument the decree which he has mentioned: that they make religion consist in things outward and frail, which have nothing to do with the spiritual kingdom of God; and secondly, that they are from men, not from God. He combats the first argument also in the Epistle to the Romans: 'The kingdom of God is not in meat and drink' (14.17). Likewise in Corinthians, 'Meat for the belly and the belly for meats: God will destroy both' (I Cor. 6.13). Christ also Himself: 'Whatever entereth into the mouth defileth not the man, because it goes down into the belly, and is cast forth' (Matt. 15.11). The sum is that the worship of God, true godliness, and the holiness of Christians, do not consist in drink and food and clothing, which are transient and liable to corruption and perish by abuse. For abuse is applied strictly to those things which are corrupted by the use of them. Hence tenets are of no value in things which tend to excite scruples of conscience. But in the Papacy you scarcely find any other holiness than what consists in little observances of corruptible things.

A second refutation follows, that they originated with men, and have not God as their Author. And by this thunderbolt he prostrates and overwhelms all the traditions of men. For what cause? This is Paul's reasoning: 'Those who bring consciences into bondage do injury to Christ, and make void his death. For whatever is of human invention does not bind the conscience.'

23. *Which have indeed a show.* This is an anticipation. He concedes to his adversaries what they allege, but at the same time reckons it wholly worthless. For it is as though he had said that he cares nothing for their having a show of wisdom. But 'show' is opposed to 'reality', for it is an appearance (as they commonly say) which deceives by resemblance.

Observe, however, of what colours this show consists, according to Paul. He mentions three: self-invented worship, humility and neglect of the body. Superstition in Greek is called ἐθελοθρησκεία, the term which Paul here uses. He is, however, thinking of the etymology, for ἐθελοθρησκεία literally denotes a voluntary worship which men choose of their own will, without a command from God. Human traditions, therefore, please us because they accord with our own mind, for anyone will find in his own brain the first outlines (*idea*) of them. This is the first pretext.

The second is humility, for obedience both to God and men is put forward, so that men do not refuse even unfair burdens. And for the most part traditions of this kind are such as to seem admirable exercises of humility.

They please, also, for a third reason, inasmuch as they seem to be of the greatest avail for the mortification of the flesh, and there is no sparing of the body. Paul, however, bids these disguises depart; for what is high among men is often an abomination in the sight of God. Moreover, it is a treacherous obedience, and a perverse and sacrilegious humility, that transfers to men the authority of God. Nor is neglect of the body not of so great importance, as to deserve to be set forth as the service of God. But some will be surprised, that Paul does not take more pains to pull off those masks. I answer, that he is right to be satisfied with the one word 'show'. For the principles which he had taken up in opposition are incontrovertible: the body is in Christ; therefore, those who set shadows before wretched men are merely imposing upon them. Secondly, the spiritual Kingdom of Christ is by no means taken up with frail and corruptible rudiments. Thirdly, by the death of Christ such observances were ended, so that they have nothing more to do with us. And, fourthly, God is our only lawgiver. Whatever may be put forward on the other side, however splendid it may be, is fleeting show.

Secondly, he reckoned it enough to admonish the Colossians not to be deceived by these empty things. There was no necessity for harping on reproving them. For it should be an axiom among all the godly, that the worship of God ought not to be measured according to our understanding; and that, consequently, the mere fact that it pleases us does not make a service lawful. It also ought to be an axiom that we owe God the humility of yielding obedience simply to His commands, so as 'not to lean to our own understanding, etc.' (Prov. 3.5), and that the object of humility towards men is that each one should submit himself to others by love. Now, when they contend that the wantonness of the flesh is repressed by abstinence from meats, the answer is easy. We must not for that reason abstain from any particular food as being unclean, but must eat sparingly of what we do eat, both in order that we may soberly and temperately make use of the gifts of God, and that we may not, involved too much in food and drink, forget the things that are God's. Hence it was enough to say that these were masks; so that the Colossians might be warned and be on their guard against false pretexts.

Thus, today, Papists do not lack specious pretexts by which to commend their own laws, however either impious and tyrannical or silly and trifling. When, however, we have granted them every-thing, there still remains this refutation by Paul, which is of itself more than sufficient for dispelling all their mists—not to say how far they are from such an honest appearance as Paul describes. The principal holiness of the Papacy today consists in monasticism, and of what nature that is, I am ashamed and grieved to mention, lest I should stir up so foul a stench. Moreover, it is important to consider here, how prone, nay, how forward, the mind of man is to invented worship. For the apostle here graphically depicts the state of early monasticism, which came into being a hundred years after his death as if he had never spoken a word. The zeal of men for superstition is incredibly mad; it could not be restrained by so plain a declaration of God from breaking forth, as the histories testify.

Not in any honour. 'Honour' means 'care', according to the Hebrew use. 'Honour widows' (I Tim. 5.3), that is, take care of them. Now Paul censures them for teaching neglect of the body. For as God forbids us to indulge the body unduly, so He commands that it shall be given as much as is necessary for it. Hence Paul, in Rom. 13.14, does not expressly condemn care for the flesh as such, but that which indulges lusts. 'Have no care', he says, 'for the flesh, to the gratifying of its lusts.' What, then, does Paul point out as faulty in those traditions of which he treats? It is that they gave no honour to the body for satisfying the flesh, that is, according to the measure of necessity. For satisfying here means a mean, which restricts itself to the simple use of nature, and thus is opposed to luxury and all superfluous delicacies; for nature is content with little. Hence, to refuse what it requires for sustaining the necessity of life, is no less alien to godliness, than in-human.

CHAPTER THREE

If then ye were raised with Christ, seek the things that are above, where Christ is, seated on the right hand of God. Set your mind on things above, not on things on the earth. For ye are dead, and our life is hid with Christ in God. When Christ, our life, shall appear, then shall ye also appear with him in glory. (1-4)

To those fruitless exercises which the false apostles urged, as though perfection consisted in them, he opposes the true ones, in which it becomes Christians to employ themselves. And this is very much to the point. For when we see what God wants us to do, we easily despise the inventions of men. And when it appears that what God commends to us is far more lofty and excellent than what men insist on, our alacrity of mind in following God increases, and we disregard men. Paul here exhorts the Colossians to meditation on the heavenly life. And what of his opponents? They wanted to keep them in childish rudiments. This doctrine, therefore, leads them to despise ceremonies the more. Hence it is manifest that in this passage Paul exhorts them in order to confirm the foregoing doctrine. For, in describing genuine godliness and holiness of life, his aim is the disappearance of those vain shows of human traditions. At the same time, he anticipates an objection with which the false apostles might attack him. 'What then? Would you rather have men idle than occupied with some sort of exercises?' When, therefore, he bids Christians apply themselves to far better exercises, he removes any occasion for this slander; in fact, he loads them with no small odium, on the ground that they hinder the straight course of the godly with worthless diversions.

1. *If ye were raised.* Ascension goes along with resurrection. Therefore, if we are members of Christ, we must ascend into heaven, because when He had been raised from the dead, He was received up into heaven, that He might draw us up with Him. Now, we seek those things which are above when in our minds we are truly sojourners in this world, and are not bound to it. The word *Cogitate* ('set your mind on') expresses rather assiduity and intensity; as if he said, 'Let your whole meditation be on this; to this apply your abilities and mind.' But if we ought to think of nothing but what is heavenly, because Christ is in heaven, how much less right would it be to seek Christ

on earth! Let us therefore remember that that is the true and holy thinking about Christ which takes us straight up into heaven, that we may there adore Him and our minds dwell with Him.

As to the right hand of God, it is not confined to heaven, but fills the whole world. Paul has mentioned it here to indicate that Christ encompasses us by His power, lest we should think that distance is a cause of separation between us and Him, and that at the same time His majesty may move us wholly to reverence Him.

2. *Not on things that are on the earth.* He does not mean, as a little after, vicious lusts which reign in earthly men, or even riches, or fields, or houses, or any other things of the present life, which we must use as though we did not use them. But he is still pursuing his argument on ceremonies, which he likens to entanglements that force us to grovel on the ground. 'Christ', he says, 'calls us upwards to Himself; but these drag us down.' For this is the conclusion and exposition of what he had just considered on the abolition of ceremonies through the death of Christ. To paraphrase: 'The ceremonies are dead to you through the death of Christ, and you to them, that, raised to heaven with Christ, you may think only of the things that are above. Therefore leave off earthly things.' I shall not contend against others who think differently; but certainly the apostle appears to me to proceed step by step, so that, in the first instance, he opposes traditions about trivial matters to meditation on the heavenly life, and afterwards, as we shall see, goes a step farther.

3. *For ye are dead.* No one can rise again with Christ, if he has not first died with Him. Hence he draws the argument from resurrection to death, as from a consequent to an antecedent, meaning that we must be dead to the world that we may live to Christ. Why did he teach that we must seek those things that are above? Because the life of the godly is above. Why does he now teach that the things that are on earth are to be set aside? Because they have died to the world. As if he said: 'Death precedes that resurrection of which I have spoken. Hence both of them must be seen in you.'

It is worthy noticing that our life is said to be hid, so that we may not murmur or complain if our life, buried under the ignominy of the cross and various distresses, differs nothing from death, but may patiently wait for the day of revelation. And in order that our waiting may not be anxious, let us observe the particles, *in God,* and *with Christ,* which show that our life is out of danger, although this does not appear. For God is faithful, and therefore will not deny what has been committed to Him, nor disappoint us in the guardianship which He has undertaken. And the fellowship of Christ brings still greater security. For what is to be more desired than that our life dwell with

the very fountain of life? Hence there is no reason why we should
be alarmed if, wherever we look, we nowhere see life. For we are
saved by hope. But those things which are already before our eyes
are not hoped for. Nor does he teach that our life is hid merely in
the opinion of the world, but even as to our own senses; because
this is the true and necessary trial of our hope, that being encompassed, as it were, with death, we may seek life elsewhere than in the
world.

4. *But when Christ shall appear.* A beautiful consolation, that the
coming of Christ will be the manifestation of our life. And, at the
same time, he tells what a perverted passion for the future it would
be that refused to wait patiently till that day. For if our life is shut up
in Christ, it must be hid until He appears.

*Mortify therefore your members which are upon the earth: fornication,
uncleanness, passion, evil concupiscence, and covetousness, which is
idolatry: for which things' sake cometh the wrath of God on the sons of
disobedience. In the which ye also walked aforetime, when ye lived in
them. But now put ye also away all these; anger, wrath, malice, railing,
shameful speaking out of your mouth.* (5-8)

5. *Mortify therefore.* Hitherto he has been speaking of contempt of
the world. He now proceeds further, and enters upon a higher
philosophy, on the mortification of the flesh. That this may be clearer,
let us note that there is a twofold mortification. The former relates
to those things that are around us, of which he has hitherto treated.
The other is inward: that of the faculties and will, and of the whole
of our corrupt nature. He enumerates certain vices which he calls,
imprecisely but elegantly, members. For he imagines our nature as
being, as it were, a mass composed of various vices. They are, therefore, our members, inasmuch as they are, in a manner, fastened to us
and cleave to us. He calls them also earthly, alluding to what he had
said, 'Not the things that are on earth,' though in a different sense.
These words are equivalent to his saying, 'I have admonished you
that earthly things are to be disregarded: you must, however, strive
to mortify those vices which detain you on the earth.' He means that
we are earthly so long as the vices of our flesh flourish in us, and that
we are made heavenly by the renewing of the Spirit.

After *fornication* he adds *uncleanness*, by which term he expresses all
the kinds of licentiousness with which lustful people pollute themselves. To these is added πάθος, that is, *passion*, which comprehends
all passionate allurements. This word, it is true, denotes mental
perturbations of other kinds, and disorderly motions contrary to

reason; but passion fits the context quite well. Why covetousness is here called the worshipping of images, consult the Epistle to the Ephesians,[1] that I may not say the same thing twice.

6. *On account of which things.* I do not find fault with Erasmus' rendering, 'is wont to come'; but as the present tense is often taken in Scripture instead of the future, according to the Hebrew idiom, I have preferred to leave the rendering undecided, so that it might be adapted to either meaning. He warns the Colossians, then, either of the ordinary judgments of God which are seen daily, or of the vengeance which He has once denounced upon the wicked, and which hangs over them, but will not be manifested until the last day. But I willingly accept the former meaning, that God, the perpetual Judge of the world, is accustomed to punish the crimes in question.

He says expressly that the wrath of God will come, or is wont to come, upon the unbelieving or disobedient, instead of threatening them personally with anything of this sort. For God would rather that we should see His wrath on the reprobate, than feel it in ourselves. It is true that when the promises of grace are set before us, every one of the godly ought to embrace them as destined for himself particularly. But let us dread the threatenings of wrath and destruction in such a way that those things which belong to the reprobate may be a warning to us. Although God is often said to be angry even with His children, and sometimes chastens their sins severely, Paul speaks here of eternal destruction, of which a mirror is seen only in the reprobate. In short, whenever God threatens, He shows the punishment indirectly, as it were, that, beholding it in the reprobate, we may be deterred from sinning.

7. *In which ye walked.* Erasmus mistakenly refers this to men, translating it, 'among whom'. For there is no doubt that Paul meant the vices in which he says the Colossians had walked, during the time that they lived in them. For 'living' and 'walking' differ from each other, as ability (*potentia*) does from action. Living comes first: walking follows, as in Gal. 5.25, 'If ye live by the Spirit, walk by the Spirit.' By these words he means that it would be unworthy to give themselves up any more to the vices to which they had died through Christ. See the sixth chapter of Romans. It is an argument from the removal of the cause to the removal of the effect.

8. *But now etc.* That is, after having ceased to live in the flesh. For the power and nature of mortification are such, that all corrupt affections are extinguished in us, so that sin may not afterwards produce in us its usual fruits. What I have translated 'indignation' is in Greek θυμός, which denotes a more impetuous wrath than ὀργή.

[1] see p. 198.

Here, however, as may easily be perceived, he enumerates forms of vice different from those previously mentioned.

Lie not in opposition to one another, seeing that ye have put off the old man with his deeds; and have put on the new man, which is renewed unto knowledge after the image of him that created him: where there is neither Greek nor Jew, circumcision nor uncircumcision, Barbarian, Scythian, bond nor free: but Christ is all, and in all. Put on therefore, as God's elect, holy and beloved, bowels of mercies, kindness, humility, meekness, long-suffering; forbearing one another, and forgiving each other, if any man have a complaint against any: even as Christ forgave you, so also do ye. (9-11)

9. *Lie not.* When he forbids lying, he condemns every sort of cunning, and all wicked tricks of deception. For I do not take it only as calumnies, but I contrast it generally to sincerity. Hence it might be allowable to render it more briefly, and I am not sure but that it might not also be better: 'Lie not one to another.' He follows his argument on the fellowship which believers have in the death and resurrection of Christ, but uses other forms of expression.

The 'old man' means whatever we bring from our mother's womb, and whatever we are by nature. It is put off by all that are renewed through Christ. The new man, on the other hand, is he who is reformed by the Spirit of Christ to the obedience of righteousness; or it is nature restored to its true integrity by the same Spirit. The 'old man' comes first, because we are first born from Adam and afterwards born again through Christ. And as what we have from Adam grows old and tends towards ruin, so what we obtain through Christ remains for ever, and is not perishable, but tends towards immortality. This passage is noteworthy, in that a definition of regeneration may be gathered from it. For it contains two parts: the putting off of the old man, and the putting on of the new; and these Paul here mentions. It is also to be noticed that the old man is distinguished by his works, as a tree by its fruits. Hence it follows that the depravity that is innate in us is denoted by the term 'old man'.

10. *Which is renewed unto knowledge.* He shows first that newness of life consists in knowledge; not that a simple and bare knowledge is sufficient, but he speaks of the illumination of the Holy Spirit, which is lively and effectual, so as not only to enlighten by kindling the light of truth, but also to transform the whole man. And this is what he immediately adds, that we are renewed after the image of God. Now, the image of God resides in the whole of the soul, since it is not only the reason that is upright, but also the will. Hence, too, we learn both what is the end of our regeneration (that is, that we may be made like

God and that His glory may shine forth in us) and also what is the image of God which Moses speaks of[1]; that is, the rectitude and integrity of the whole soul, so that man represents as in a mirror the wisdom, righteousness and goodness of God. He speaks somewhat differently in Ephesians, but the meaning is the same. (Eph. 4.24). Paul at the same time says that there is nothing better for the Colossians to aspire to, for our highest perfection and blessedness is to bear the image of God.

11. *Where there is neither Jew.* He added this deliberately, to draw the Colossians away from ceremonies. For the words mean that Christian perfection does not need those outward observances; in fact, they are altogether alien to it. For under the distinction of circumcision and uncircumcision, Jew and Greek, he includes, by synecdoche, all externals. The terms that follow, *barbarian, Scythian, bond, free,* are added by way of amplification.

Christ is all, and in all. That is, Christ alone holds, as they say, the prow and the stern—the beginning and the end. Moreover, by Christ he means the spiritual righteousness of Christ, which abolishes ceremonies, as we have already seen. They are, therefore, superfluous in true perfection; they ought not even to have a place, inasmuch as injustice would otherwise be done to Christ, as though it were necessary to call in those helps to supply His deficiencies.

13. *Put on therefore.* As he has enumerated some parts of the old man, so now of the new. 'It will', he says, 'be clear that you are renewed by Christ if you are merciful and kind etc. For these are the effects and evidence of renewal.' Hence the exhortation depends on the second clause, and, accordingly, he keeps up the metaphor in the words 'put on'.

He puts, first, *bowels of mercy*; by which expression he means an earnest affection, with yearnings, as it were, of the inward parts. Secondly, *kindness*; for so have I chosen to render χρηστότητα, by which we make ourselves beloved. To this he adds *humility*; because no one will be kind and gentle but the man who, laying aside haughtiness and high-mindedness, subjects himself to modesty, claiming nothing for himself.

Gentleness, which follows, is wider than kindness, which is chiefly in look and speech, whereas this is also in inward disposition. As, however, it frequently happens that we fall in with wicked and ungrateful men, there is need of patience, to increase our mildness. He at length explains what he meant by *long-suffering*: that we treat each other leniently, and forgive also where there is any injury. As, however, this is hard and difficult, he confirms his teaching by the example of

[1] Gen. 1.26; 9.6.

Christ, and says that the same thing is required from us; that as we, who have so frequently and grievously offended, have nevertheless been received into favour by Christ, we should manifest the same kindness to our neighbours by forgiving whatever injuries they have done to us. Hence he says, *If anyone have a quarrel against another*. By this he means that even what men think are just quarrels ought not to be followed up.

As God's elect. Elect I take here for 'set apart'. To paraphrase: 'God has chosen you to Himself, has sanctified you, and received you into His love on condition that you shall be merciful, etc. In vain does the man that has not these virtues boast that he is holy and beloved of God; in vain does he reckon himself among the number of believers.

On account of all these things put on love, which is the bond of perfect-ness. And let the peace of God gain the palm in your hearts, to the which also ye are called in one body; and be ye thankful. Let the word of Christ dwell in you richly in all wisdom; teaching and admonishing one another with psalms and hymns and spiritual songs with grace, singing in your hearts to the Lord. And whatsoever ye do in word or deed, do all in the name of the Lord Jesus, giving thanks to God and the Father through him. (14-17)

14. *On account of all these things*. That some translate it 'above all these things', for 'over and above', or 'besides' is, in my opinion, weak. It would be more suitable to say, 'before all these things'. I have chosen, however, the more ordinary sense of the word ἐπί. For as all the things that he has hitherto enumerated flow from love, he now on good grounds exhorts the Colossians to cherish *love* among themselves, for the sake of these things; that is, that they may be merciful, gentle, ready to forgive; as if he had said that they would be such only if they had love. For where love is wanting, all these things are sought for in vain.

That he may commend it the more, he calls it *the bond of perfection*; meaning by this that the multitude of all the virtues is contained in it. For this truly is the rule of our whole life and all our actions, so that everything that is not regulated according to it is wrong, however beautiful it may otherwise be. This is the reason why it is called here the bond of perfection; for there is nothing in our life that is well regulated unless it is directed towards it, but everything that we attempt is mere waste.

The Papists, however, are ridiculous to misuse this declaration, so as to construct a justification by works. 'Love', they say, 'is the bond of perfection. But perfection is righteousness. Therefore we are justified by love.' The answer is twofold; for Paul here is not discussing how men are made perfect in the sight of God, but how they may live perfectly among themselves. For the genuine exposition of the passage is that other things will be in a good state in our life, if love is strong among us. When, however, we grant that love is righteousness, their maintaining from this that we are justified by love is in vain and childish, for where will perfect love be found? But we do not say that men are justified by faith alone, in that the observance of the law is not righteousness, but because, since we are all transgressors of the law, we are destitute of any righteousness of our own and therefore forced to borrow righteousness from Christ. There remains, therefore, only the righteousness of faith, because nowhere is there perfect love.

15. *And the peace of God.* He calls the peace of God that which God has established among us, as will appear from what follows. He would have it reign in our hearts. He employs, however, a very good metaphor. For as among wrestlers he who has vanquished all the others carries off the palm, so he means that the peace of God is superior to all carnal affections, which often carry us away to contentions, disagreements, quarrels, secret grudges. He accordingly forbids us to loose the reins to corrupt affections of this kind. As, however, it is difficult to restrain them, he also shows the remedy, that the peace of God may win the victory, because it must be a bridle, by which carnal affections may be restrained. Therefore he says, *in your hearts*; because we constantly feel there great conflicts, while the flesh lusts against the Spirit.

The clause, *to which ye are called*, declares what sort of peace this is: the unity which Christ has consecrated among us under His own rule. For God has reconciled us to Himself in Christ, so that we may live in harmony. He adds, *in one body*; meaning by this, that we cannot be in accord with God except by being united among ourselves as members of one body. When he bids us *be thankful*, I do not refer this so much to the remembrance of benefits, as to sweetness of manners. Hence, to remove ambiguity, I prefer, 'be lovable'. Yet I admit that, if gratitude fills our minds, we shall without fail be inclined to cherish mutual love among ourselves.

16. *Let the word of Christ dwell.* He wants the teaching of the Gospel to be familiar to them. Hence we may infer by what spirit they are actuated today, who cruelly forbid it to Christian people, and furiously vociferate that no pestilence is more to be dreaded than the reading of the Scriptures by the common people. For, unquestionably, Paul here addresses men and women of all ranks. Nor would he only have them take a slight taste of the Word of Christ, but he says that it should dwell in them; that is, that it should have a settled abode, and that

largely, that they may aim to advance and increase more and more
every day. As, however, the desire of learning is perverted in many,
and they misuse the Word of the Lord for their own ambition, or for
vain curiosity, or in some way corrupt it, he therefore adds, *in all
wisdom*, that we may be instructed by it and be wise as we ought to be.

Moreover, he briefly defines this wisdom: that the Colossians
teach one another. *Teaching* is taken here as useful instruction, which is
able to edify, as in Rom. 12.7: 'He that teacheth, on teaching'; also
in Timothy: 'All Scripture is profitable for teaching' (II Tim. 3.16).
This is the true use of Christ's word. As, however, doctrine is sometimes in itself cold, and, as someone says, when it is simply shown
what is right, virtue is praised and starves, he adds at the same time
admonition, which is, as it were, a confirmation of the doctrine and
a spur. Nor does he mean that the Word of Christ ought to be of
benefit only to individuals, that they may teach themselves, but he
requires mutual teaching and admonition.

Psalms, hymns. He does not restrict the Word of Christ to these
particulars, but means that all our words should be disposed to edification, that even those which serve cheerfulness may not be pointless.
To paraphrase: 'Leave to unbelievers that foolish delight which they
get from ludicrous and frivolous jests and witticisms. Let your words,
not merely those that are serious, but those also that are joyful and
cheerful, contain something profitable. In place of their obscene, or
at least barely modest and decent, songs, it becomes you to sing
hymns and songs that sound forth God's praise.' Moreover, under
these three terms he includes all kinds of songs. They are commonly
distinguished in this way: a psalm is sung to the accompaniment of
some musical instrument; a hymn is properly a song of praise, whether
it be sung simply with the voice or otherwise; an ode contains not
merely praises, but exhortations and other matters. He wants the
songs of Christians to be spiritual, and not made up of frivolities and
worthless trifles. For this relates to his argument.

The clause, *in grace*, Chrysostom explains in various ways. I, however, take it simply, as also afterwards in chapter 4.6, where he says,
'Let your speech be seasoned with salt, in grace,' that is, by an acceptable aptness, and pleasing the hearers with its usefulness, so that it may
be opposed to buffoonery and similar nonsense.

Singing in your hearts. This relates to feeling; for as we ought to stir
up others, so also we ought to sing from the heart, that there may
not be merely an outward sound with the mouth. Yet we must not
understand it as though he is telling everyone to sing inwardly to
himself, but he wants both to be conjoined, provided the heart precedes the tongue.

17. *And whatsoever ye do.* We have already explained this and what goes before, in the Epistle to the Ephesians, where the same things are said almost word for word.[1] As he had already begun to speak of the parts of the Christian life and had only touched on a few precepts, it would have been too lengthy to follow out the rest one by one; he therefore concludes by way of summary, that our life must be so regulated that whatever we say or do may be wholly governed by the authority of Christ, and may look to His Glory as its aim. For we shall fitly comprehend under this term two things: that all our endeavours shall start out from the invocation of Christ and serve His glory. From invocation follows the blessing of God, which gives us cause for thanksgiving. It is also to be observed, that he teaches that we must give thanks to the Father through Christ, as we obtain through Him every good thing that God confers upon us.

Wives, be in subjection to your own husbands, as is fitting in the Lord. Husbands, love your wives, and be not bitter against them. Children, obey your parents in all things, for this is pleasing unto the Lord. Fathers, provoke not your children, lest they be discouraged. Servants, obey in all things them that are your masters according to the flesh; not with eye-service, as men-pleasers; but in singleness of heart, as those who fear God: and whatsoever ye do, do it heartily, as unto the Lord, and not unto men; knowing that from the Lord ye shall receive the reward of the inheritance: for ye serve the Lord Christ. But he that doeth wrong shall receive again the reward for his iniquity: and there is no respect of persons. (18-25)

18. *Wives.* Now follow what are called particular duties, which depend on the calling of individuals. In handling these it would be superfluous to employ many words, for I have already said in the Epistle to the Ephesians[2] almost everything that was necessary. Here I shall only add briefly what relates strictly to an exposition of the present passage.

He commands wives to be subject. This is clear, but what follows is ambiguous: *as it is fit in the Lord.* For some connect it thus: 'Be subject in the Lord, as is fitting.' I, however, view it differently: 'As it is fitting in the Lord'; that is, according to the appointment of the Lord, so that he confirms the subjection of wives by the authority of God. He requires love from husbands, and that they be not bitter, because there is a danger lest they should abuse their rule by tyranny.

20. *Children, obey your parents.* He enjoins it upon *children* to obey their parents, without exception. But what if parents try to force them to do something unlawful; will they in that case, too, obey

---

[1] See pp. 202ff.   [2] See pp. 204-216.

without discriminating? Now it would be most unworthy for the authority of men to prevail at the expense of neglecting God. I answer, that here too we must supply what he expresses elsewhere (Eph. 6.1): 'in the Lord'. But why the universal phrase? I answer again, that it is to show that obedience must be given, not only to just, but also to unfair, commands. For many show themselves agreeable to the wishes of their parents only when it is not difficult or inconvenient. But children ought to consider this one thing—that whatever their parents may be, they have been allotted to them by the providence of God, who by His appointment subjects children to their parents.

In all things, therefore, that they may not refuse anything, however hard or disagreeable; 'in all things', that in things indifferent, they may defer to them as parents; 'in all things', that they may not make themselves equal with them by questioning and arguing, or wrangling— yet always the conscience must be free. He prohibits parents from an immoderate harshness, lest their children should be so cowed as to be incapable of receiving any training (*disciplinae liberalis*); for we see, from daily experience, the advantage of a liberal education (*ingenua educatio*).

22. *Servants, be obedient.* Nothing here about servants requires any explanation, as it has all been already expounded in Eph. 6.1,[1] except for these two expressions: 'For we serve the Lord Christ'; and, 'He that will act unjustly will receive the reward of his iniquity.'

By the former statement he means that service is so rendered to men that Christ nevertheless holds supremacy of dominion, and is the supreme Master. Here, truly, is real consolation for all that are under subjection, when they hear that, while they willingly serve their masters, their obedience is as acceptable to Christ as if it had been rendered to Him. From this Paul also gathers that they will receive from Him a reward, but it is the reward of inheritance; by which he means that the very thing that is paid to works is freely given to us by God, for inheritance comes from adoption.

In the second clause he again comforts servants, by saying that, if they are oppressed by the unjust cruelty of their masters, God Himself will take vengeance, and will not, because they are servants, overlook the injuries inflicted on them; for there is no respect of persons with Him. For this consideration might discourage them if they imagined that God had no regard for them, or no great regard, nor concern for their miseries. Besides, it often happens that servants themselves endeavour to avenge bad and cruel treatment. He forestalls this evil, therefore, by admonishing them to wait patiently for the judgment of God.

[1] I.e. 6.5ff. See pp. 214ff.

CHAPTER FOUR

Masters, render unto your servants that which is just and mutually fair; knowing that ye also have a Master in heaven. Continue in prayer, watching therein with thanksgiving; withal praying also for us, that God may open unto us a door of utterance, to speak the mystery of Christ, for which I am also in bonds; that I may make it manifest, as I ought to speak. (1-4)

1. *Masters, what is just.* He mentions first, 'what is just'; by which term he expresses that humanity on which he had instructed them in the Epistle to the Ephesians. But because masters, as if on high, despise the condition of servants, so that they think that they are bound by no law, Paul puts them in their proper place, because both are equally under subjection to the authority of God. Hence that equity which he mentions.

And mutual equity. Some explain it otherwise, but I have no doubt that Paul here employed ἰσότητα to mean analogical or distributive right, as in Eph. 6.8, τὰ αὐτά. For masters do not have their servants bound to them in such a way as not to owe them something in their turn, for analogical right should be in force among all estates.

2. *Continue in prayer.* He returns to general exhortations, in which we must not expect an exact order, for in that case he would have begun with prayer. But Paul was not thinking like that. Moreover, he commends here two things in prayer; first, assiduity; secondly, alacrity, or earnest intentness. For when he says, 'Continue,' he exhorts them to perseverance; and he opposes 'watching' to coldness, and listlessness.

He adds, *thanksgiving*, because we must ask God for our present necessity in such a way that we do not forget benefits already received. And also we ought not to be so importunate as to murmur and be resentful if God does not immediately meet our wishes, but we must accept contentedly whatever He gives. Thus a twofold giving of thanks is necessary. On this something has also been said in Phil. 4.6.[1]

3. *Pray also for us.* He does not say this insincerely, but because, conscious of his own necessity, he earnestly desired to be helped by their prayers, and was convinced that they would be of advantage to him. Who now will dare to despise the intercessions of brethren, when Paul declares that he needs them? And, certainly, it is not in

[1] See pp. 289f.

356

vain that the Lord has appointed this exercise of love between us, that we pray for each other. Not only, therefore, ought each of us to pray for his brethren, but we ought also, on our side, diligently to seek help from the prayers of others, as often as occasion requires. But the argument of the Papists is childish, when they infer from this that the dead must be implored to pray for us. For what has this got to do with it? Paul commends himself to the prayers of the brethren, with whom he knows that he has mutual fellowship according to the commandment of God. Who will deny that this reason is no longer true in regard to the dead? Leaving such trifles, therefore, let us return to Paul.

As we have a remarkable example of modesty in Paul calling others to his assistance, so are we also told that it is a most difficult thing to persevere steadfastly in the defence of the Gospel, especially when danger presses. For it is not without cause that he desires the churches to stand by him in this matter. Consider, too, his amazing zeal. He is not worried about his own safety; he does not ask that prayers may be poured forth by the churches on his behalf, that he may be delivered from danger of death. He is content with this one thing, that he may, unconquered and undaunted, persevere in the confession of the Gospel; nay, he fearlessly makes his own life secondary to the glory of Christ and the spread of the Gospel.

By *a door of utterance*, however, he simply means what, in Eph. (6.19) he calls 'the opening of the mouth', and what Christ calls 'a mouth and wisdom' (Luke 21.15). For this expression is no different from the other in meaning, but only in form. For he here declares, by an elegant metaphor, that it is no whit easier for us to speak confidently about the Gospel than to break through a door that is barred and bolted. For this is truly a divine work, as Christ Himself said, 'It is not ye that speak, but the Spirit of your Father that speaketh in you' (Matt. 10.20). Having, therefore, set forward the difficulty, he stirs up the Colossians the more to prayer, by declaring that he cannot speak aright unless his tongue is directed by the Lord. Secondly, he argues from the dignity of the matter, when he calls the Gospel *the mystery of Christ*. For we cannot labour carelessly in a matter of such importance. Thirdly, he mentions also his danger.

4. *As I ought.* This clause emphasizes the difficulty, for he hints that it is no ordinary matter. In Eph. (6.20) he adds, ἵνα παρρησιάσωμαι from which it appears that he desired for himself an undaunted confidence, such as befits the majesty of the Gospel. Moreover, as Paul here only desires grace for the discharge of his office, let us bear in mind that a like rule is prescribed to us, that we may not give way to the fury of our adversaries but strive even to death in proclaiming the

Gospel. As this, however, is beyond our power, it is necessary that we should continue in prayer, that the Lord may not leave us destitute of the spirit of confidence.

Walk in wisdom towards them that are without, redeeming the time. Let your speech be always with grace, seasoned with salt, that ye may know how ye ought to answer each one. All my affairs shall Tychicus make known unto you, the beloved brother and faithful minister and fellow-servant in the Lord: whom I have sent unto you for this very purpose, that ye may know my estate, and your hearts may be comforted. Together with Onesimus, the faithful and beloved brother, who is one of you: they shall make known unto you all things that are done here. (5-9)

5. *Walk wisely.* He contrasts those that are without to those that are of the household of faith. For the Church is like a city of which all believers are the inhabitants, joined with each other by a mutual kinship; but unbelievers are foreigners. But why does he want them to be considered, rather than believers? There are three reasons: first, lest any stumbling-block be put in the way of the blind; for nothing is more likely to happen, than that unbelievers are driven from bad to worse through our imprudence, and their minds are wounded, so that they shrink from religion more and more. Secondly, lest any occasion be given for disparaging the Gospel, and thus exposing the name of Christ to derision, men are made more hostile and disturbances and persecutions stirred up. Lastly, lest, while we are mingled together in social intercourse and general affairs, we are defiled by their pollutions and gradually become profane.

To the same effect, also, is what follows, *redeeming the time*; that is, because intercourse with them is dangerous. For in Eph. 5.16 he assigns the reason, 'because the days are evil'. As if he said, 'Amidst so great a corruption of the world we must seize opportunities of doing good and struggle against hindrances.' The more, therefore, that our path is blocked by offences, so much the more carefully must we take heed lest our feet should stumble, or we should fail through laziness.

6. *Your speech.* He requires pleasantness of speech, which will attract the hearers by its usefulness, for he does not merely condemn openly wicked or ungodly speech, but also what is worthless and idle. Hence he says they must be 'seasoned with salt'. Profane men have their saltiness, but he is not speaking of them; in fact, because witticisms are pleasant, and for the most part win favour, he indirectly prohibits believers from the use and practice of them. For he reckons as tasteless everything that does not edify. The word *grace* is used in the same

sense, as the opposite of talkativeness, taunts, and all sorts of trifles which are either injurious or vain.

That ye may know how. The man who has accustomed himself to discreet speech will not fall into many absurdities, into which talkative and prating men fall from time to time, but, by constant practice, will acquire for himself expertise in correct and apt replies. On the other hand, silly people will necessarily expose themselves to derision whenever they are asked about something; and in this they pay the just punishment of their silly talkativeness. Nor does he only say 'what', but also *how*, and not to all indiscriminately, but to *each one*. For it is not the least part of prudence to have regard to individuals.

7. *My things.* That the Colossians may know what concern he has for them, he confirms them, by giving them, so to say, a pledge. For although he was in prison and in danger of his life, he neglects care for himself and consults their interests by sending Tychicus to them. In this, both the singular zeal and the prudence of the holy apostle shine forth. For it is no small matter that, while he is held prisoner, and is in extreme danger for the sake of the Gospel, he nevertheless does not cease to employ himself in advancing the Gospel and caring for all the churches. Thus, the body is imprisoned, but the mind, anxious to be busy, roams far and wide. His prudence shows itself in sending a fit and sensible man to confirm them, so far as was necessary, and to withstand the craftiness of the false apostles. And it shows, moreover, in his keeping Epaphras by him, until they should see what and how great an agreement there was in doctrine among all true teachers, and might hear from Tychicus the same thing that they had previously learned from Epaphras. Let us carefully meditate on these examples, that they may stir us up to an imitation of the like carefulness.

He adds, *Onesimus*, that the embassy may have the more weight. It is, however, uncertain who this Onesimus was. For it is scarcely credible that this is the slave of Philemon, for the name of a thief and a fugitive would have been liable to reproach. He distinguishes them both by honourable titles, that they may do the more good, and especially Tychicus, who was to exercise the office of teaching.

Aristarchus my fellow-prisoner saluteth you, and Marcus, the kinsman of Barnabas; (touching whom ye received commandments, if he come unto you, to receive him;) and Jesus, which is called Justus, who are of the circumcision, these only are my fellow-workers unto the kingdom of God, which have been a comfort unto me. Epaphras, who is one of you, a servant of Christ, saluteth you, always striving for you in his prayers, that ye may stand perfect and complete in all the will of God.

For I bear him witness, that he hath a great zeal for you, and for them in Laodicea, and for them in Hierapolis. (10-13)

10. *Fellow-prisoner.* From this it appears that there were others associated with Paul, after he was taken to Rome. It is also probable that his enemies exerted themselves at the outset to deter any of the godly from giving him help, by threatening them with the like danger, and that this was effective for a time; but that afterwards some plucked up courage and despised everything that was put forward to terrify them.

That ye receive him. Some manuscripts have 'receive' in the imperative; but it is a mistake, for he expresses the nature of the command which the Colossians had received, that it was a commendation of either Barnabas or Mark. The latter is the more probable. In the Greek it is in the infinitive, but it should be rendered in the way I have done. Let us observe that they were careful in giving testimonies, so as to distinguish good men from false brethren, pretenders, impostors and multitudes of vagrants. The same care is more than necessary today, both because good teachers are coldly received, and because credulous and foolish men are too exposed to impostors.

11. *These only are fellow-workers.* That is, of the circumcision; for he afterwards names others, but they were of the uncircumcision. He means, therefore, that there were few Jews at Rome who showed themselves to be helpers to the Gospel; rather the whole nation was opposed to Christ. By 'workers' he means those only who were endowed with gifts necessary for promoting the Gospel. But where was Peter at that time? Unquestionably, he has either been shamefully passed over here, and quite unjustly, or else those who maintain that he was then at Rome are romancing. Moreover, he calls the Gospel *the kingdom of God*, for it is the sceptre by which God reigns over us, and by which we are adopted to life eternal. But of this form of expression we shall treat more fully elsewhere.

12. *Always striving.* This is an example of a good pastor, whom distance cannot induce to forget the Church or prevent him from carrying the care of it with him beyond the sea. We must notice, also, the force of entreaty expressed in the word 'striving'. For although the apostle here wanted to express intensity of affection, he at the same time admonishes the Colossians not to reckon the prayers of their pastor useless, but, on the contrary, to know that they would be a great help. Lastly, let us infer from Paul's words, that the perfection of Christians is when they stand complete in the will of God, that they may not base their plan of life on anything else.

Luke, the beloved physician, and Demas, salute you. Salute the

*brethren that are in Laodicea, and Nymphas, and the church which is
in his house. And when this epistle hath been read among you, cause
that it be read also in the church of the Laodiceans; and that ye likewise
read the epistle from Laodicea. And say to Archippus, Take heed to
the ministry, which thou hast received in the Lord, that thou fulfil it.
The salutation by the hand of me Paul. Remember my bonds. Grace
be with you. Amen.*

Sent from Rome by Tychicus and Onesimus. (14–18)

14. *Luke saluteth you.* I do not agree with those who understand
this as Luke the Evangelist. For I think that he was too well known
to need such a designation, and he would have been given a more
splendid title. He would undoubtedly have called him his fellow-
helper, or at least his faithful companion and participant in his conflicts.
I rather conjecture that he was absent at that time, and that this is
another who is called a physician, to distinguish him from the Evangelist. But I do not argue as if this were certain. It is only a conjecture.
Demas, whom he mentions, is undoubtedly the man he complains of
afterwards as deserting him (II Tim. 4.10).

When he speaks of the Church which was in the house of Nymphas,
let us remember that in one family he prescribes what all Christian
families ought to be—so many little churches. Let everyone, therefore,
know that the charge is laid on him to train up his house in the fear
of the Lord, to keep it under a holy discipline, and, in short, to form
in it the likeness of the Church.

16. *Let it be read in the church of the Laodiceans.* Therefore, although
it was addressed to the Colossians, it would nevertheless be profitable
to others. We should think the same of all the Epistles. They were
indeed written once to particular churches, but, as they contain
doctrine that is always in force and is common to all ages, it is un-
important what title they bear. For the subject-matter belongs to us.
It has been wrongly supposed that the other epistle he mentions was
written by Paul. They were quite wrong who thought Paul wrote
to the Laodiceans. I have no doubt that it was an epistle sent to Paul,
the reading of which might be profitable to the Colossians, as neighbouring towns have usually many things in common. There was,
however, an exceedingly gross imposture when some worthless fellow,
I know not who, had the audacity to forge, on this pretext, an epistle[1]
that is so weak, that nothing can be conceived more foreign to Paul's
spirit.

17. *Say to Archippus.* So far as one may conjecture, this Archippus
was discharging the office of pastor during the absence of Epaphras.

[1] I.e. the apocryphal Epistle to the Laodiceans.

But perhaps he was not sufficiently diligent of himself without being stirred up. Paul, accordingly, wants him to be heartened and improved by the exhortation of the whole Church. He could have admonished him in his own name individually; but he gives this charge to the Colossians, that they may know that they must themselves apply the spur, if they see their pastor cold, and the pastor himself does not refuse to be admonished by the Church. For the ministers of the Word are endowed with great power, but it is not exempt from laws. Hence, it is necessary that they should show themselves teachable if they would duly teach others. As to Paul's commending again his bonds, he hints by this that his was no light affliction. For he was mindful of human infirmity and without doubt felt some twinges of it in himself, inasmuch as he was so very urgent that all the godly should be mindful of his distresses. It is, however, no evidence of distrust that he calls in from all sides the helps appointed him by the Lord.

The subscription, by his own hand, means, as we have seen elsewhere, that there were even then spurious epistles in circulation, so that it was necessary to provide against fraud.

INDEX OF SCRIPTURE REFERENCES

INDEX OF SCRIPTURE REFERENCES

INDEX OF NAMES

GENERAL INDEX

adoption, 74f, 105, 257, 307
allegory, *see* Scripture
anakephalaiōsis, 129, 162f
angels, 15, 129f, 137, 309, 310, 312, 313, 331, 338f
apostle, 8f, 25, 30ff, 34f, 123, 154f, 161f, 178, 264, 300, 315, 323
assurance, 183, 229, 256, 325
atheism, 90, 148f

Baptism, 68f, 95, 173, 206, 332f
blessing, 124

calling, 8ff, 19ff, 229
ceremonies, 36, 37f, 66f, 72f, 77, 92, 151, 269, 333ff, 337, 342f
children, 212f, 354f
Church
 Body of Christ, 181, 341
 care for ministry, 112f, 293f
 government, 33, 34, 99, 118, 178ff
 household of God, 154
 ministry, 80, 83, 227f, 261f
 mother of believers, 87f
 purity, 10f, 207
 temple of God, 156
 unity, 10, 26, 98, 172f, 174f, 182, 185, 241, 244f, 280, 285, 352
circumcision, 26f, 93, 94, 95, 99, 118, 147f, 268f, 270, 331f, 333f
conscience, 111, 290
covenenant, 56f, 58, 63, 70ff, 76, 147

death, 238ff, 264ff

election, 20, 70, 122, 124-127, 128f, 146f, 286f
eternal life, 124, 187, 282f
ethical demands, 191ff, 290f, 349f
Eucharist, *see* Lord's Supper

faith, 14, 38ff, 48, 49f, 54f, 64, 65, 67, 95, 96, 131, 133, 164, 167f, 301, 315, 333
flesh, 48, 102f, 103, 106, 147f, 270, 304, 314, 332
free-will, 145f, 186, 253f

Gentiles, *see* Jews and Gentiles
God
 Fatherhood, 51, 76, 134, 173, 199, 301, 306
 grace, 20f, 44, 76f, 119, 121, 123, 128, 130, 133, 142-145, 228f, 243, 255
 glory, 99, 133, 253, 306, 309
 judgment, 188
 mercy, 50, 142
 power, 135, 136, 254f, 283f, 305
 providence, 288f, 311
 wisdom, 162ff, 304
 wrath, 141f, 198f, 348
Gospel, 13, 14ff, 25, 28, 46, 47, 48, 98f, 115, 128, 131, 152f, 159, 178, 181, 206, 231, 234ff, 258f, 281, 302ff, 315f, 322f, 326, 352f, 356ff, 360

Holy Spirit, 47f, 49, 75, 87, 102f, 105ff, 131f, 134, 154, 166, 177, 194f 237
hope, 170, 237f, 301f, 322
humility, 171, 245ff, 253, 257
hypocrisy, 90, 224

images, 47
idolatry, 198

Jesus Christ
 ascension, 174-7, 345f
 atonement, 11, 44, 55, 128f, 147, 149ff, 153f, 164f, 311f, 334
 crucifixion, 42, 44, 47, 55, 117, 152, 196, 312, 314, 336

368